LITERATURE

OF THE

LOW COUNTRIES

For Edith

LITERATURE

OF THE

LOW COUNTRIES

A SHORT HISTORY OF DUTCH LITERATURE
IN THE NETHERLANDS AND BELGIUM

BY

REINDER P. MEIJER

**PROFESSOR OF DUTCH LANGUAGE AND LITERATURE
IN THE UNIVERSITY OF LONDON**

First published in 1971 by Van Gorcum & Comp. N.V., Assen

New edition with corrections and additional material 1978, Stanley Thornes
(Publishers) Ltd.

© Reinder P. Meijer, 1978.

Published by Stanley Thornes (Publishers) Ltd.,
Educa House, 32 Malmesbury Road, Kingsditch Estate,
CHELTENHAM GL51 9PL

ISBN 0 85950 094 2

Reproduced and printed by photolithography and bound in
Great Britain at The Pitman Press, Bath

CONTENTS

PREFACE

In any definition of terms, Dutch literature must be taken to mean all literature written in Dutch, thus excluding literature in Frisian, even though Friesland is part of the Kingdom of the Netherlands, in the same way as literature in Welsh would be excluded from a history of English literature. Similarly, literature in Afrikaans (South African Dutch) falls outside the scope of this book, as Afrikaans from the moment of its birth out of seventeenth-century Dutch grew up independently and must be regarded as a language in its own right.

Dutch literature, then, is the literature written in Dutch as spoken in the Kingdom of the Netherlands and the so-called Flemish part of the Kingdom of Belgium, that is the area north of the linguistic frontier which runs east-west through Belgium passing slightly south of Brussels. For the modern period this definition is clear anough, but for former times it needs some explanation. What do we mean, for example, when we use the term 'Dutch' for the medieval period? In the Middle Ages there was no standard Dutch language, and when the term 'Dutch' is used in a medieval context it is a kind of collective word indicating a number of different but closely related Frankish dialects. The most important of those were the dialects of the duchies of Limburg and Brabant, and of the counties of Flanders and Holland. The term 'Holland' itself can be confusing as it may refer to the present-day Kingdom of the Netherlands but also to the medieval county or the later province of Holland. In this book the term 'Holland' will be used to refer to the county or province, the term 'the Netherlands' when referring to what is now the Kingdom of the Netherlands. The term 'Low Countries' will be used when reference is made to the combined territories of the Kingdom of the Netherlands and the Kingdom of Belgium.

The plan of the book is the simplest possible: a chronological narrative divided into periods of a century. For a first introduction to a literature this arrangement, however crude, has advantages over a subtler division into short periods and over arrangements according to genres or generations of writers.

The book is presented as a history of literature, and a short one at that. This starting-point placed limitations on its scope and led to treatment of only the most important writers. Although the selection is a fairly conventional one, it has been made in full awareness of the fact that no-one can escape his own preferences. Also, since history is normally understood to deal with the past, the temptation to include a running commentary on what is being written in the Netherlands and Belgium at the present time, has been resisted. Time, the much maligned anthologist, will have to do its work first.

The absence of footnotes does not imply a claim to originality. My indebtedness to Dutch literary scholarship in general can best be expressed by stating that if acknowledgment had been made wherever it was due, the notes would have become unwieldy.

Special thanks are due to Professor Jacob Smit, Dorothea R. Coverlid and Elizabeth Meijer-Mollison who read the manuscript and who are responsible for many improvements.

It remains to thank the Minister for Culture, Recreation and Social Work of the Netherlands for commissioning the book, and the Australian Humanities Research Council, now the Australian Academy of the Humanities, for awarding a Myer Foundation Research Grant for short-term study leave in the Netherlands.

PREFACE TO THE SECOND EDITION

In this new edition the text has been thoroughly revised and brought up to date. Writers who should have been discussed in the first edition, but were not, have been included. Jacob Geel now has, I hope, his rightful place, as have Piet Paaltjens, Herman Heijermans, Nescio and others.

I express my sincere thanks to Professor Peter King of the University of Hull for his helpful criticism of the first edition. I am particularly grateful to Mr. Paul Vincent, Lecturer in Dutch at Bedford College, University of London, for many valuable suggestions.

London, February 1978

I

THE EARLY STAGES
TWELFTH AND THIRTEENTH CENTURIES

When does a literature begin? With the first text, one would say, and the answer seems neat and simple. But the literary historian, more often than not, is not satisfied with a first text and asks for more. The first text, he argues, is only the first text that has been preserved, and he is prepared to spend a great deal of time and energy in trying to find out whether there were any texts before this first one, and if so, what these lost texts were like. So he milks the available evidence down to the last drop of information, with results that are often spectacular, but at the same time highly speculative.

In Dutch literature, too, a great deal of speculation has been going on about the question of whether there was a literature in the vernacular before the first texts appear in the twelfth century. It seems beyond doubt now that there was. The comparatively high standard of literary technique of the oldest preserved works suggests this very strongly, and, moreover, we do have some references to works that did exist once. We know the name of Bernlef, a Frisian bard, who is mentioned in Altfridus's biography of Liudger. Bernlef lived in the Carlovingian period (he died in 809), and Altfridus says of him that he sang the heroic deeds of the Frisians and the wars of their kings, accompanying himself on the harp. So the pre-twelfth-century silence was not completely unbroken, but we do not know whether Bernlef was a lone figure or one of many, nor what his work was like. A notorious apodictic statement 'Frisia non cantat'— the origin of which has not yet been traced—seems to

1

suggest that there were not very many Bernlefs, but it is a statement that allows of many interpretations: it may have been an overstatement, a wild generalization, an angry outburst by an embittered poet, or a home-truth. We do know, on the other hand, that in that same period there were Frankish songs, because Charlemagne showed great interest in them and made an effort to have them collected and recorded. Unfortunately, not a single song of this collection has been preserved; they were destroyed, it is said, by order of Charlemagne's son.

The political disintegration of the post-Carlovingian period was on the whole not very conducive to literary production. Western Europe was in constant turmoil, and the internal unrest and uncertainty were aggravated by frequent invasions of the Norsemen. Much of what was written must have been destroyed under these circumstances. The only text we have left of this period is extremely short, little more than one full sentence. It is to be found on the last page of a manuscript in the Bodleian Library at Oxford and was discovered in 1932. On that page someone must have been trying out a new pen by writing 'probatio pennae si bona sit' ('test to see whether the pen is good', an early version of 'the quick brown fox'). To this he added a Latin sentence with a version of the same sentence in what the philologists call Old West Lower Frankish, the oldest known stage of Dutch. This sentence reads: hebban olla vogala nestas hagunnan hinase hic enda thu wat unbidan we nu (all birds have begun their nests except me and you; what are we waiting for now). It dates probably from the middle of the eleventh century and stands therefore at the beginning of Dutch literature. Some read it as an expression of home-sickness of a Flemish monk who lived in England, others interpret it as the desire for the spiritual peace of monastic life, but it looks most like a love poem, or at any rate the beginning of one.

The first complete work of literature in Dutch comes from the southern part of the Low Countries. In fact, most medieval Dutch literature originates from the south, that is from Limburg, Flanders and Brabant. Holland remained a backwater for a long time and did not come out of its cultural isolation until the fourteenth century. The southern regions had the advantage of their geographical position, close to the cultural centres of Western Europe and at the cross-roads of several trade-routes. The county of Flanders, with the port of Bruges, grew rapidly to great prosperity through its wool trade and cloth industry (Ypres, Ghent), establishing in this way a firm basis for cultural development. Moreover, Flanders was a fief of the king of France, so that French culture had easy access and provided a strong stimulus for the development of local cultural life. Limburg, which lay open to the Rhineland, was at first more orientated towards Germany: it belonged to the diocese of Liege, which in its turn was part of the archdiocese of Cologne. In the later Middle Ages, however, Limburg gravitated more towards France, and when the first literary work appeared in Limburg, it showed a closer relationship with French literature than with German. Much the same can be said of Brabant: its original ties with the German Rhineland were gradually resolved in favour of an orientation towards France. In addition to this, the nobility at the courts of Flanders and Brabant was to a large extent gallicized, so that their authority in cultural matters became an instrument for the spreading of French culture rather than for the development of something really Dutch.

It is not surprising then that the first phase of literary life in the Low Countries was dominated by French literature. Most works of the twelfth and thirteenth centuries were translated or adapted from the French. Even the odd original among them, such as *Karel ende Elegast*, is part and parcel of the French literary tradition. But although medieval Dutch literature is on the whole derivative, there are some notable exceptions, the most outstanding of which is the animal epic *Vanden Vos Reinaerde*, the first literary product of that typically individualistic culture that was growing up in the Dutch cities and that was to exert such a strong

influence on the shaping of intellectual life in the Low
Countries later on.

The earliest work of literature in Dutch dates from the
years between 1160 and 1170 (which are also the years in
which the first works in English appear again after the great
silence following the Norman Conquest). It is the biography
of a saint, *Het leven van Sint Servaes* (The Life of St.
Servatius), written by Hendrik van Veldeke, a Limburg
nobleman. Veldeke has always been a puzzle to literary
historians, as the biography of St. Servatius is the only work
of his that we have left in Middle Dutch. His other works,
the *Eneid* and his love poems, are only extant in Middle
High German. A discussion has long been going on about
the question of which is the original language of these works
and whether they may have been translated from Middle
Dutch into Middle High German. It now seems likely that
Veldeke began his *Eneid* in Dutch. Before he had finished it,
however, he lent the manuscript to a friend, the Countess of
Cleve, who lost it. It turned up again in Thuringia, where
Veldeke completed it and where it was presumably translated
into Middle High German. From then onwards Veldeke
exercised a strong influence on Middle High German
literature and became the man who really established the
tradition of the love lyric in Germany. He was regarded as
the master by German poets such as Wolfram von
Eschenbach and Gottfried von Strassburg, and was mentioned
and praised by several of his German successors as an
innovater of poetic technique. The strange fact that none of
his Dutch contemporaries or successors makes any mention
of his technical innovations might perhaps be explained by
the view, held by Van Mierlo, that in Dutch literature he was
not an innovator at all, but one of a group of poets who
were already using the same technique, i.e. lines of more or
less equal length and pure rhymes.

Het Leven van Sint Servaes is not an original poem, but
an adaptation from a Latin source, *Vita et Miracula,* a
collection of stories about saints and miracles, dating back to

the end of the eleventh century. It is a poem of about 6000 lines, written in rhyming couplets as most Middle Dutch literature was. As a work of art it is not very remarkable and it certainly does not come up to the level of the *Eneid*. It tells rather drily the life and death of Servatius, a fourth-century bishop of Maastricht, and the miracles performed by him after his death. The most interesting passage is probably the one in which Servatius—with typical medieval lack of historical perspective—comes into contact with King Attila of the Huns (fifth century) and converts him to Christianity, for a short while at any rate.

This hagiographic genre—biographies of saints and accounts of miracles—was an important and much-practised genre in the Middle Ages, but also one which rarely produced literature of any great merit. More interesting from a literary point of view are the romances of chivalry, the first of which appear in the Low Countries in the second half of the twelfth century and which continue right through into the fourteenth century. In Dutch literature they are usually divided into four groups: Frankish, British, Eastern and Classical romances. This division is made only on the basis of their subject-matter; the originals were all written in France and came to the Low Countries from French literature. The vexed question of the genesis and development of the French originals is therefore a problem that strictly speaking does not concern Dutch literary history: the genre originated and developed in France and reached the Low Countries as a finished product. So far as Dutch literature is concerned, their development is pre-history. It is interesting to note, however, that scholars are more and more inclined to accept Germanic epic songs as the basis of the French *chansons de geste*.

With one exception (*Flovent*), the Frankish romances deal with the Carlovingians and usually centre on Charles the Great (Charlemagne), his friends and his enemies. Their main theme is the contrast between loyalty and treachery, the main events are the rebellions of the feudal tenants and vassals against their overlords, and in particular against

Charles. It is significant that Charles does not usually appear
in these poems as the great strong king, but rather as a weak
old man who is all the time pressed hard by his opponents: a
theme that does not really surprise when one recalls that the
feudal world was in ferment. One finds this clearly shown in
one of the best-known Frankish romances, *Renout van Montalbaen*. There is not much left of the Dutch version, no more
than about 2000 lines, but we can fill in the gaps from a
fifteenth-century prose adaptation. Judging by what we have
left, it must have been a very good poem indeed, written in a
concise, terse, matter-of-fact style, a little like a chronicle
perhaps, but with an economy of words that is rare in a
medieval poet. It describes the rebellion of Haymijn against
Charles. Actually, the poem begins with an attempted
reconciliation between the two on the occasion of Haymijn's
marriage to Charles's sister Aye. Charles, however, refuses to
come to the wedding, which infuriates Haymijn to such an
extent that he swears to kill all children to be born from his
marriage to Aye. In the course of years, Aye bears him four
sons, but she manages to conceal the events and to keep the
boys away from their father, in which she is greatly helped
by Haymijn's always being away waging war at the crucial
times. When Charles is growing old and his son Louis about
to succeed him, Haymijn is also invited to the coronation.
But he refuses from a sense of humiliation because he has no
son himself. Aye then triumphantly produces the four sons,
the famous 'Heemskinderen'. Haymijn, elated, gives them the
horse Beyaert, which seats four, and they set off for the court.
The four sons behave rather brashly, they kill the cook, and
defeat Louis in a stone-throwing game and later on also at
chess. Louis loses his temper, strikes one of the brothers, is
killed by another, and it is war again. Haymijn, his four
sons, the invincible horse Beyaert and a guerilla band of
knights fight the king for many years. When the two parties
finally decide to make peace, the king's first condition is that
they kill the horse. Reinout, the brother who had killed
Louis, does this and then makes a pilgrimage to the Holy

Land. On his return he helps to build St. Peter's at Cologne, but is killed by the workmen who resent his working so hard.

This *Renout van Montalbaen* was a very popular poem and was still known as a folk story in certain parts of France, Germany and Italy at the end of the last century. Just as popular, or perhaps even more so, was another Frankish romance, *Karel ende Elegast*. It was one of the first books printed in the Low Countries, and the fact that no less than six copies of these early prints are extant, is indicative of its high degree of popularity. In comparison with other Frankish romances, it is a very short poem, consisting of only 1414 lines. These are not fragments, as in the case of *Renout van Montalbaen*, but they constitute the whole poem. It is the only Frankish romance that has been preserved in its entirety. No French original has been found, and as the poem itself gives no indication of being a translation, we may assume it to be an original Dutch poem, though wholly bound up in the tradition of the French epic romance.

The theme of *Karel ende Elegast* is the usual one: loyalty versus treason, but the approach is rather different. In this poem Charles the Great is neither weak and bungling nor cruel and unforgiving. He is the great Christian king, with a clear ethical code, who is capable of forgiving and who is not above setting right an injustice which he has once committed. Elegast, who is really the central character, is also quite different from the usual heroes of a Frankish romance. His name, meaning King of the Elves, suggests strongly that he is a fairy-tale figure and his actions in the poem also place him in a fairy-tale atmosphere rather than in the grimly realistic world of the Frankish romance: he can put people to sleep with a magic code, he opens locks without a key, and he possesses a herb which, when he puts it in his mouth, makes him understand the language of animals. He is an old friend of Charles, but has fallen into disgrace and is now roaming the forest as a kind of gentleman-thief, robbing the rich and protecting the poor. Charles, who is obeying a heavenly command to go stealing, meets him in the forest at night and

defeats him in a duel. Elegast makes himself known to
Charles, but Charles hides his own identity and pretends to
be a thief too. Charles proposes to burgle the king's castle,
but Elegast rejects this indignantly: though Charles has
treated him unjustly, he remains loyal to him. They decide to
go to Eggeric van Eggermonde's (a Germanic name, by the
way, just like Elegast). On the way, there is an amusing
scene when Charles, badly equipped for a robbery, picks up
a ploughshare to break in with, thereby neatly demonstrating
his amateur status. He gives another demonstration of this
when Elegast lets him try out the magic herb and then
abstracts it from the mouth of the king without him noticing
it. They break into Eggeric's castle and Elegast overhears a
conversation between Eggeric and his wife about a plot that
Eggeric is hatching to murder the king. When Charles hears
this, his thieving expedition begins to make sense to him.
The next day Eggeric and his cronies arrive at Charles's
court. They are searched, their weapons found, but they deny
everything. Their guilt is proved by a duel between Eggeric
and Elegast, and Eggeric is duly killed. As Eggeric's wife
had remained loyal to Charles, she is given in marriage to
Elegast who is fully rehabilitated.

Karel ende Elegast is undoubtedly the best of the Frankish
romances. It is very well written, with a great sense of
humour, it wastes no words and contains no dull spots.
There is more attempt at characterization than is usually
found in this type of literature, and above all it has a very
tight dramatic structure which, without getting side-tracked
at all, logically leads up to the answer to the puzzling
question: why should Charles go out stealing?

The author is unknown and one cannot be absolutely sure
about the date of origin either. Some scholars are positive
that it was written at the end of the twelfth century, others
place it in the thirteenth century. Arguments in favour of the
earlier date are the shortness of the poem and the fact that in
some instances it still shows the old construction of three-
beat lines.

Still in the twelfth century, but outside the tradition of the epic romance, we find a curious poem known as *De Reis van Sint Brandaen* (The Voyage of St. Brandan). It is a kind of Christian Odyssey and describes the voyage around the world made by Brandaen, a monk of Galway. Brandaen reads a book that deals with the miracles of creation. He refuses to believe what he reads and throws the book angrily into the fire. An angel then tells him that the truth has now been destroyed and that he has to sail around the world for nine years in order to discover again what is true and what is not. Brandaen does this and finds a great deal worth recording: a man on a rock in the middle of the sea who claims to have been king of Pamphilia and Cappadocia and who is now doing penance for having married his sister; a number of people with wolves' teeth, swine's heads and dogs' legs, carrying bow and arrow and being very hostile; an enormous fish that takes its tail in its mouth and in this way encircles the ship for a fortnight; Judas frozen on one side and burning on the other; a particularly small man who sails the sea in a leaf and is busy measuring its water content by letting drops of water run off a stick into a small cup, and so on and so forth. It is a lively poem, quite humorous at times because of Brandaen's laconic comments on all these wonders and horrors. When the erstwhile king of Pamphilia, for example, tells his tale of woe, Brandaen's only reaction is to ask him what he is going to do when it turns cold. The Dutch poem seems to go back to a Middle High German text that has not been preserved and is a combination of Celtic elements from Ireland with fairy tales and Christian motifs. It belongs to the tradition of the *Imrama*, stories of voyages, which as a genre date from the seventh century. The English *Life of Saint Brandan* is a much later poem, belonging to the fourteenth century, and translated from the French.

In the thirteenth century we find a much greater variety of genres than in the twelfth century. The tradition of the Frankish epic romances was continued in the large and sombre poem *De Lorreinen* (The Lorrains), which deals with a never-ending feud between the lords of Lorraine and their numerous enemies. But after that the Frankish romance disappears and its place is taken by the British romance.

The British romances also originate from France, but instead of dealing with Charlemagne and his entourage, they are concerned with King Arthur and his knights. Just as important as the change of subject-matter is the change of atmosphere of these poems. The Frankish romances were poems of battle, into which women fitted badly. The British romances on the other hand breathe the atmosphere of the court with its refinement, its strict code of honour and its high regard for women. Particularly in the attitude to women the difference between the two kinds of romances is striking. In the Frankish romances women were given short shrift and were supposed to be meek, docile and ever-loving. When they dared to express an opinion which displeased the Frankish hero, no words were wasted and no half-measures taken. When Aye in *Renout van Montalbaen* very rightly berated her husband for his bad manners, she was silenced by terrible blows, but her only reaction was to go up to him and kiss him; when Eggeric's wife in *Karel ende Elegast* disapproved of her husband's murder scheme, she was struck hard on the nose and mouth, while later on she was given to Elegast without having any say in the matter whatsoever. In the British romances one does not find anything of this kind. When in *Ferguut*, for example, Arthur expresses his admiration for the fair Galiene, he says that he would not mind marrying her, but only if she were willing to have him.

The British romances are full of adventures and often contain fairy-tale elements. The adventures are usually set within the framework of a quest, the object of which may be a mysterious veil, a shield with an interesting history, a particularly beautiful horn or a hovering chessboard. On these quests the knights enter enchanted castles, drink from rejuvenating springs, sleep on beds that heal their wounds, walk over bridges as narrow as the edge of a sword, fight winged and fire-breathing dragons, dwarfs, giants and other abominations.

The best example of a British romance in Dutch is *Walewein,* which has the additional interest of being an original, although the two authors, Penninc and Vostaert, drew upon several sources for the subject-material of their poem. It was written in the early years of the thirteenth century, probably between 1200 and 1214. The main theme is a quest, or rather a series of quests which Walewein undertakes and which give the poems its characteristic chain-like structure. The various quests are the links of the chain, all firmly connected to one another, but a few links more or less would not have affected the organization of the poem. From a structural point of view *Walewein* consists of a number of co-ordinating episodes, all of about equal intensity, and leading up to a dénouement rather than to a dramatic climax. In this respect *Walewein* forms a clear contrast to *Karel ende Elegast,* with its sub-ordinating structure in which each new element heightens the tension.

The series of quests through which Walewein, one of King Arthur's knights, has to work his way, is as follows. Walewein promises Arthur to find the chessboard that had come floating into the castle but which had disappeared again. He finds it at King Wonder's. The king is willing to give it to Walewein, but on condition that in return Walewein will find the sword with the two rings, which is in the possession of King Amoraen. When King Amoraen is approached, he is willing to part with the sword, but only if Walewein will bring him the beautiful Isabel, more beautiful than Venus, who is being kept prisoner by her father, King Assentijn, in a castle fortified by twelve walls, each with four times twenty towers and deep rivers in between. Walewein manages to enter this castle, he finds Isabel who falls in love with him, he is discovered by Assentijn and locked up, but he succeeds in escaping and sets out with Isabel on his way back to Amoraen (who in this part of the poem is called Amorijs, still retaining *amor* as the main part of his name).

Isabel does not know that she is to be traded for a sword, but fortunately Amoraen has died and she can stay with Walewein. From Amoraen's castle they move back to King Wonder's, where the sword is exchanged for the chessboard, and then further back to King Arthur who collects the original object of the quest. Whether Walewein married Isabel is uncertain, according to the poet.

In *Ferguut,* an adaptation of the French *Fergus* by Guillaume le Clerc, we find the life story of a peasant who wants to become a knight. It is a tale of two worlds: the world of the court and the world of the country, set in sharp contrast. Ferguut does the seemingly impossible and makes the leap from his lowly peasant background into the courtly world of the knights. At the very beginning of the poem it is made clear that Ferguut can only do this because on his mother's side there were some knights in his ancestry: without this he would not have had any chance at all. But his education is long and arduous and he has to put up with a great deal of contempt and scorn. When he first arrives at Arthur's court, he behaves clumsily and is ridiculed by Keye, the man with the sharpest tongue among Arthur's companions. Ferguut has offered to give advice to the knights, and then Keye delivers a cuttingly ironical speech in which he says that Ferguut has come at the right time as they are badly in need of some good advice. Also, he says, he has never seen a better-looking knight, nor any prince who held his lance and shield better. But Ferguut's worst moment comes when he meets Galiene. She falls in love with him, so violently that she has to tell him so. She hesitates, but comforts herself with the thought that her love is so strong that the lowliest peasant would have pity on her. She goes to his bedroom at night and tells him that she has lost her heart. Would he know where it is? Ferguut is unable to deal with the situation in a courtly fashion and laughs at her. He does not have her heart, he has not seen it, and he has no idea where it could be. He asks her to go away as he has more important things to do. His boorishness shames Galiene and she retires sadly. Later on Ferguut realizes that he has not behaved in the best tradition of a nobleman, and through his remorse and shame and his attempts to win Galiene back, he matures into a real knight. Although several other romances touch upon the distance between the world of the nobleman and that of the common man, no other romance demonstrates it as clearly as *Ferguut* does.

There are several other British romances, but they are mostly translations and adaptations from the French. The largest one is the *Lancelot* compilation, a manuscript of about 90,000 verses, containing the book of *Lancelot,* a short *Perceval,* the *Graal queeste* (Quest of the Grail), *Arthurs Dood* (Arthur's Death) and some others.

The eastern and classical romances are not very strongly represented in Dutch literature. In the first place one cannot point to any originals. What has been preserved are translations, and even those are few and far between. Apart from some fragments of *Parthenopeus van Bloys,* the only eastern romance that has been preserved is a version of *Floris ende Blancefloer,* a story with a Byzantine background which became one of the great medieval lovestories.

The two main classical romances were both written by the same man, Jacob van Maerlant, and they are really more important for the insight they give into the working method of this poet than for their intrinsic value. *Alexanders Geesten* (The Heroic Deeds of Alexander) seems to have been Maerlant's first poem and it is typical of his approach. Maerlant considered himself a historian, a man in search of facts, and not simply a narrator of interesting and more or less probable stories. He realized that the story of Alexander, in the course of the fifteen centuries that lay between Alexander's time and his own day, had become a tangle of history, myth and legend, and when he wrote his account of Alexander, he tried to scrape off the coat of myth to show only unadorned history. He deliberately chose a Latin source to work from, because he questioned the reliability of the French sources. His intentions, however, were better than his achievements, for his Latin source—Gauthier de Chastillon's *Alexandreis*—was not impeccable either. It was also characteristic of Maerlant that he did not translate the text literally or without discrimination, but that he left out some passages and on the other hand extended the poem by putting in a great deal of didactic material such as biblical history and geography. It is, however, ironical that he sometimes drew this material from the very sources that Gauthier rejected as being too fantastic. When Maerlant sensed later on that Gauthier was not as reliable as he had thought him to be, he dissociated himself from his own poem, but he was an economical enough poet to save some of the historical and geographical passages and to use them again in other works, for example in his second classical romance, *Historie van Troyen* (History of Troy). In this poem he also incorporated the only other classical romance in Dutch, a poem by an older contemporary, Segher Dengotgaf, who had begun to write the story of the Trojan war but had not finished it.

Jacob van Maerlant is the first poet we know a little more about, though it is still not a great deal. He was a West Fleming, who lived in the neighbourhood of Bruges, probably between 1235 and 1291. He is also the first poet whose entire *oeuvre* has been preserved, or very nearly, for we still lack a few poems. He made his debut with *Alexanders Geesten,* followed a few years later by *Historie van Troyen,* the poem with which he made his name. In between these two classical romances he tried his hand at some British romances: *Merlijn* (Merlin), a book about the great magician, and *Torec,* a story of the quest for a gold diadem. *Torec* contains a curious didactic digression about a Room of Wisdom in which for days on end a number of wise men and women are discussing the shocking morals of the higher circles, the predominant position of money and the evils thereof, and love. Maerlant never wrote purely for entertainment as the other poets of romances did; whenever he could he inserted didactic material or launched diatribes against the deplorable state the world was in.

After these works Maerlant took his leave of the epic romance and switched over to entirely didactic poetry. And when Maerlant turned away from the epic romance, this was also the turning-point for the genre as such. It was still practised in the late thirteenth century and also in the fourteenth century, but it no longer produced works of the calibre of *Karel ende Elegast* or *Walewein*. With the changes which took place in society in the thirteenth century giving the burghers a far more prominent position than they had had before, the interest in literature also changed. The glamour of the nobleman faded, and with it faded the genre of the epic romance. The burghers turned towards a literature that was closer to reality and offered more practical knowledge. And that was precisely what Maerlant offered them in his didactic poems. He began with a poem about dreams and one about stones, neither of which has been preserved. They were followed by *Der Naturen Bloeme* (The Best of Nature), a natural history, *Spieghel Historiael* (Mirror of History), a world history from creation up to 1250, *Hemelechede der Hemelijcheit* (Secret of the Mystery), a poem about statecraft, hygiene and morals, and *Rijmbijbel* (Verse Bible). None of these poems was original, all of them were adaptations of medieval Latin works. They do not contain very great poetry either, they are often dull and clumsy, more important as social phenomena than as works of art. But they were extremely popular, as can be measured by the number of manuscripts extant: of the *Rijmbijbel* there are no less than seventeen still in existence, of *Der Naturen Bloeme* eleven; it is thought that of this later work about one hundred copies were made, which is a great many indeed.

Maerlant shows himself a better poet in his *Strofische Gedichten* (Strophic Poems). They are so called because they were not written in the rhyming couplets of his other work, but in stanzas, each consisting of thirteen lines with two rhymes: 4 x *aab* and the last line *b*. Three of these poems were written in dialogue form: the poet and his friend

Martyn dicuss all sorts of problems concerning class, social
order, love and theology. They are full of social criticism,
very caustic at times, but also strongly coloured by
Franciscan humility and by the Franciscan views on wealth
and poverty: Maerlant was not for nothing also the translator
of Bonaventura's biography of St. Francis. This comes out
clearly in the first dialogue *Wapene Martyn* (Alas, Martin),
in which Maerlant states that all the troubles of the world
can be reduced to the words 'mine' and 'thine': if these two
words did not exist, there would be peace and freedom
everywhere. They are very incisive poems and far more
personal than his long didactic works, but in all Maerlant's
poetry there remains an inner dryness that is never quite
compensated by his emotions, however sincerely he must
have felt them and however forcefully he tried to express
them. This also applies to his last poems, his most personal
perhaps: *Der Kercken Claghe* (The Complaint of the
Church), a courageous and passionate attack on abuses in
the Church, and *Vanden Lande van Oversee* (Of the
Overseas Country), an exhortation, with all guns out, to a
new crusade. Although Maerlant's popularity was enormous
and his influence long-lasting, one must admit that he was
only occasionally a real poet. It is not in Maerlant's work
then that one finds the masterpieces of Dutch medieval
literature. They are to be found, after *Karel ende Elegast,* in
two very different genres: the literature of mysticism and the
animal epic.

The first representative of mystic literature was Beatrijs
van Nazareth, a nun who lived in the first half of the
thirteenth century. She must have written a great deal, but
the only work we have left in Dutch is a prose dissertation
Seven Manieren van Minnen (Seven Ways of Love). The
book describes the seven stages through which love is
purified and transformed before it can return to God.
Beatrijs, who was the earliest Dutch prose writer we know
of, wrote a simple and clear style, quiet and well-balanced,
but sometimes seasoned with a vehemence of expression that

foreshadows the later mystics. Her work reads as a kind of introduction to that of Hadewych, the great mystical poet. This may, of course, be an optical illusion, as most of Beatrijs's work has not been preserved, whereas the greater part of Hadewych's has. Moreover, it is not at all certain that Beatrijs was older than Hadewych.

About Hadewych's life we know next to nothing. The only certain facts are that she lived in the southern part of the Low Countries during the first half of the thirteenth century. As she was obviously well acquainted with things concerning nobility, it is not unlikely that she came from a noble family. The lack of information about her personal life is not a tragedy, however, for we have her work from which we get to know her personality very thoroughly.

Her work falls into three categories: poetry in stanzas and rhyming couplets, visions in prose, and letters in prose. In the *Brieven* (Letters), addressed to one or more friends whom she gave spiritual guidance, she developed her theology. The core of it is similar to Beatrijs's: the soul, created by God after his own image, strives to be re-united with God, through ascetic concentration and complete surrender to divine love. This love *(minne* is the word she uses), and the desire with which it is sought, take up a central position in her work. *Minne* escapes sharp definition: sometimes it seems to mean love of God, in other cases God himself, or the Holy Ghost, or even the soul. The fact that *minne* has so many connotations is not a symptom of unclear thinking, but evidence that to Hadewych these connotations were all aspects of the same thing: the relation between God and man. At the same time Hadewych wrote with the mentality of a knight. The qualities which she praised and aspired to —courage, loyalty, honour, and also cheerfulness, generosity, self-control—fit into the pattern of the courtly chivalric atmosphere. Although they were transplanted by her into a mystic-religious context, they are still recognizable as the old worldly ideals. The description of the effect *minne* has on her are often couched in remarkably sensual terms. A good

illustration of this is to be found in the seventh of the
fourteen prose pieces known as *Visioenen* (Visions):

At Whitsun something was shown to me at dawn and they were singing matins in the church, and I was there; and my heart and my
veins and all my limbs shook and trembled with desire; and I felt as I
often did before, so violent and so terrible, that I thought if I could
not satisfy my beloved, and my beloved could not satisfy my desire, I
would die, and would die insane. Then this covetous love had such a
terrible and woeful effect on me that all my limbs, one by one, were
breaking, and all my veins, one by one, were labouring. The desire in
which I was then was unspeakable, and what I could say about it
would be unheard of to all those who never practised love with the
works of desire and who were themselves never used by love.

Even if the concept of *minne* remains vague, the important
thing is the intensity and the passion with which she speaks
about it, and it is this intensity that makes her work so
outstanding in medieval literature. One of the remarkable
things in Hadewych's work is also that she tried to restrain
herself from a premature surrender to *minne* by letting
herself be guided by reason. Reason must lead the soul on its
way to God. This realization brings a strong intellectual and
analytical element into her work and makes it stand apart
from the work of many other mystics. Her language on the
whole is simple, images and metaphors are rare, but every
now and then her attempts to put her sensations into words,
to speak the unspeakable, lead her to particularly striking
images that would make any modern poet envious. In the
ninth vision, for example, she describes three young women
who walk in front of Queen Reason:

And the other young woman wore a green robe, and she held two
palmtrees in her hand; and with those she kept the dust of the day and
the night, of the moon and the sun, away from her lady, for she would
not be touched by any of these. The third young woman wore a black
robe, and in her hand she held something like a lantern full of days,
by which her lady examined the depth of the ground and the height
of the supreme ascent.

These cosmic images—the dust of the day and night, a
lantern full of days—give her work a surprisingly modern
flavour. One finds them mainly in the *Visioenen,* the work in
which she let herself go most. Her poetry is more sober and
more intellectual. Many of her poems begin with a short
scene describing a landscape, a few lines about spring or the
weather, which set the topic or the mood and from which the
poem is then developed (the *Natureingang* of the courtly love
lyric):

> Biden nuwen iare
> hoept men der nuwer tide
> die nuwe bloemen sal bringen.
> Ay waer es nuwe minne
> met haren nuwen goede?
> Want mi doet minen ellende
> te menech nuwe wee.
> Mi smelten mine sinnen
> in minnen oerewoede,
> die afgront daer si mi in sende,
> die es dieper dan die see.[1]

The first three lines stand outside the rhyming pattern (*abc
defg defg*), and in this way are clearly marked as
introductory. The word *new* which occurs six times in this
poem, is one of the key words of her poetry and often has
the additional meaning of true, real. From a formal point of
view, Hadewych's poetry owes much to the Provençal
troubadors whose stanza patterns she often uses in her own
poetry.
She also has ties with twelfth-century French mysticism and
with Hildegard van Bingen, a German mystic whom she
mentions in her own work. Conversely, Hadewych may have
exercised some influence on the German mystic movement,
as abstracts of some of her letters have been found in Bava-

[1] At the new year one hopes for a new season which will bring new
flowers. O, where is new love with its new good? For my misery causes me to much new woe. My senses are melting in the ecstasy of
love; the abyss into which they are driving me is deeper than the sea.

ria, where she was known as Adelwip. She was in every respect a better poet than Maerlant, because she had more to say, because she could express herself more intensely, because of her great sense of form and her economical use of the language, and last but not least, because of her unique imagery. All this combined makes her work a peak in medieval literature, not only of the Low Countries, but of Western Europe as a whole.

Mysticism was not the only aspect of the religious literature of this period. We find in the thirteenth century also some more hagiographies and two biographies of Jesus, the *Levens van Jezus*, one in verse and one in prose. The latter is of great interest as it goes back to the Latin adaptation of Tatianus's famous *Diatesseron* which also served as a model for Otfried's *Evangelienharmonie* and the Low Saxon *Heliand*. Another facet was added to religious literature by two narrative poems dealing with miracles. *Theophilus* is the story of a bishop who makes a pact with the devil but in the end obtains mercy from Mary. The other one, *Beatrijs*, a later poem, dates from the last quarter of the thirteenth century and was possibly written by Diederic van Assenede who was also the translator of the Middle Dutch *Floris ende Blancefloer*.

Beatrijs is an original poem, not a translation, although the story was a well-known one. Beatrijs is a nun who leaves the convent because of her love for a young man. They live together for seven years, but when poverty overtakes them, he deserts her. Beatrijs then has two children to look after, and not knowing how else to provide for them, she resorts to prostitution. After another seven years, she finds herself near her old convent again, and when she cautiously inquires what has become of a certain nun Beatrijs who used to live in this convent, she learns that she has never left it. During the night a voice urges her to go back to the convent. She obeys and finds that Mary had taken her place after she left and had fulfilled her duties during the years of her absence.

The basic material of *Beatrijs* can be found in Caesarius

von Heisterbach's *Dialogus Miraculorum,* a collection of miracle stories of 1223, and also in his *Libri octo miraculorum* of 1237. It is possible that the subject-matter of the story is originally Dutch and that Caesarius heard it when he travelled through the Low Countries, but we have no certainty about this. So much is certain that it became known in Western Europe through the collections of Caesarius and that there are versions of it in French, German, Spanish, Old Norse and even Arabic. The Dutch version is undoubtedly a very good poem, written in a simple and unadorned style, and it is claimed by Robert Guiette to be superior to any of the other versions. Apart from its intrinsic literary value, the poem is also an important document for the cultural history of the period as a meeting-place of secular courtliness, which places the veneration of woman in a central position, and the worship of Mary, which became such an important part of religious life during the twelfth and thirteenth centuries.

In the twentieth century the poem of Beatrijs has attracted the attention of several writers: the poet P.C. Boutens gave a modern adaptation of it in his *Beatrijs,* Herman Teirlinck made it into a play *Ik dien* (I Serve), Felix Rutten into an opera libretto *(Beatrijs).*

The seriousness of *Beatrijs* contrasts sharply with the cynicism of the poem *Vanden Vos Reinaerde* (Reynard the Fox), the work in which medieval literature of the Low Countries reached its pinnacle. Of the author we only know the name, Willem, and the fact that he also wrote another poem, *Madoc,* probably a British romance of chivalry, which has never been traced. *Vanden Vos Reinaerde* is an animal epic, or a mock-epic, and as such it is the only one of its kind in Dutch. One automatically asks the question: where does it come from, was there nothing of this kind before, were there no predecessors? The answer is that there were no predecessors in the strict sense of the word and that Willem's poem stands by itself. There were building materials of which he made good use but which he arranged in such a way that we are fully justified in regarding it as an entirely original piece of work.

The line of ancestry of the animal epic is long and goes back to the fable collection of Aesop which became known in Western Europe through the Latin versions of Phaedrus and Avianus, and possibly also through oral transmission. The fables became very popular and were the common property of several generations as they were often used in the schools, probably because of their useful combination of entertainment value and moral purpose. In the tenth century we find an allegorical poem in Latin, *Ecbasis cuiusdam captivi* (Escape of a Certain Captive), which uses some material contained in the fables and describes under the veil of an animal story the flight of a monk from his monastery and his subsequent return. The rivalry between the fox and the wolf is mentioned more or less in passing in this poem, but it became the main theme of another Latin poem, *Isengrimus,* attributed to Nivardus of Ghent and dating back to the middle of the twelfth century. The wolf is the principal character here, Reynard is only the instrument through which his destruction is brought about. *Isengrimus* is also the first poem in which the animals are given proper names instead of being called wolf, fox, bear etc.: they have become individuals rather than the types they were before. Poems such as these, in combination with the fables proper, must have been the sources from which the authors of the French *Roman de Renart* drew their material. One of the episodes, or *branches,* of the *Roman de Renart,* a poem known as *Le Plaid* (The Court Session), in its turn became the source of the Dutch *Vanden Vos Reinaerde.* But the Dutch author, the cryptic Willem, used his source so freely and independently, and gave the story such a personal twist and purpose, that it became a completely new poem, and a masterpiece at that.

Vanden Vos Reinaerde describes the attempts of Bruun the bear, Tibeert the tom-cat and Grimbeert the badger to bring Reynard to the court of King Nobel. The efforts of

Bruun and Tibeert are defeated by their own greed, but Grimbeert seems successful. Reynard follows him to the court and is sentenced to be hanged. While the gallows are being erected, he embarks on a long story of treason and conspiracy, introducing a hidden treasure, and accusing bear, cat and wolf of plotting against the king. By speculating on Nobel's cupidity and stupidity, Reynard gets away with it and is set free. Crime pays off handsomely, injustice triumphs, the stupid are left to pay the piper. It is a poem that attacks one and all: royalty, nobility, clergy, peasants, with the sole exception of the burgher, the city-dweller, for whom the poem was probably intended. It is not a wild or emotional attack, it does not seethe with indignation as some of Maerlant's poems do, nor is it written with the quiet earnestness of a man who wants to reform society. It rather has the tone of the light-hearted cynic, who cool and detached, but with a razor-sharp sense of humour and deep psychological insight, laughs at the stupidities of the world. *Vanden Vos Reinaerde* is an accomplished masterpiece, without any flaws or lapses, and Willem, whoever he was, must be regarded as one of the major poets of the Middle Ages. His sole authorship has not remained undisputed; one of the manuscripts also mentions a certain Aernout as the man who began the poem. Much has been written on the question of double or single authorship. What seems most likely is that Aernout wrote a first version of the Reynard poem, and that Willem rewrote it and incorporated it in a new work of his own.The poem as it stands now certainly shows no traces of a double authorship: in fact, it is so well-balanced, so harmonious, so much a unity, that it is difficult to believe that it could be the work of more than one poet. The date of the poem has also been the subject of much discussion. Some place it in the early years of the thirteenth century, others think that it was written before 1200. In the fourteenth century someone, also unknown, rewrote it, adding a great many details and changing the whole tenor of the poem. This version, known as *Reinaert II,* is a didactic and moralizing poem, in every respect inferior to the earlier version. It shows clearly how cleverly Willem had avoided the obvious trap, i.e. to make the animals too anthropomorphic. In Willem's poem the animals behave like humans, but retain at the same time their animal characteristics; in *Reinaert II*, on the other hand, the animals are simply humans who walk on all fours and sport a tail but in whose behaviour there is nothing left of the animal. This *Reinaert II*—unfortunately, one might say—became the basis of the Reynard stories in English and German. The prose version of *Reinaert II*, the so-called Gouda edition, was translated into English by William Caxton and published by him in 1481. The Low German *Reinke Vos* (1498), adapted into High German by Goethe, also goes back to *Reinaert II*. In later centuries the Middle Dutch text was often used for modern adaptations. There is a German version by A.F.H. Geyder (1844), a French prose version by O. Delepierre (1837) and an adaptation into French poetry by Charles Potvin (1891). Translations into modern Dutch are numerous: the best known ones are those of Jan Frans Willems, Julius de Geyter, Prudens van Duyse, Stijn Streuvels and Achilles Mussche. The modern Flemish author Louis Paul Boon used *Reinaert* as a kind of counter-point in his novel *De Kapellekensbaan* (Little Chapel Road, 1953), and also combined *Vanden Vos Reinaerde,* the *Roman de Renart* and *Isengrimus* into a new novel *Wapenbroeders* (Brothers in Arms, 1955).

II

INSTRUCTORS AND ENTERTAINERS
FOURTEENTH CENTURY

The fourteenth century opened with a bang in 1302 when an army of Flemish townspeople defeated an army of French noblemen. In the history of the Low Countries, this battle—known as the Battle of the Golden Spurs—has become a celebrated event, as it was the first successful feat of resistance against the French predominance. It was, however, more important as a symptom than for any lasting results: it did not make Flanders independent of France, but it showed impressively how strong the resistance had grown. There were more revolts against France and also against the French-orientated Count of Flanders, but the Flemish towns still lacked the unity that would be necessary to consolidate their position. The Flemish leader, Jacob van Artevelde, realized this and tried to create some political unity by bringing Flanders and Brabant together in an alliance clearly directed against France. Another attempt towards political unity was made in the middle of the fourteenth century by Jan III, Duke of Brabant, who came to terms with France and then tried to forge Brabant and Limburg into a unit.

Holland was still outside these miniature power blocs; it was torn by internal strife in which family feuds combined with social and economic factors to produce a long drawn-out and destructive civil war. The most dramatic incident in those years of fighting took place in 1296 when the Count of Holland, Floris V, was killed by a number of noblemen who opposed his policies which among other things were pro-French. The circumstances surrounding and following his death were echoed widely in literature, not only in a well-known poem of the fourteenth century, but also in seventeenth-century dramatizations by the poets Vondel and Hooft, and even at the beginning of the nineteenth century in a play by Willem Bilderdijk.

Economically too, the southern parts held a substantial advantage over Holland, thanks to the cloth industry of Bruges, Ypres and Ghent. Holland's industry was insignificant compared to that of the South, but when its sea-trade began to expand around the middle of the fourteenth century, Holland rapidly became a considerable economic power. At the same time Holland began to catch up on its cultural arrears.

In the literature of the fourteenth century one finds several reflections of what was going on in the political and economic life and on the battlefield. They are found particularly in what might be called the fringe of literature, the chronicles. One of the earliest works to be written in Holland was such a chronicle, *Rijmkroniek van Holland* (Rhyme Chronicle of Holland) by Melis Stoke, completed in 1305. The first part of it was written in 1283 and was dedicated to Count Floris V, of whom Stoke was a great admirer. Stoke's intention was to write the history of the Dutch Counts, not as an objective historian, but rather with the specific purpose of showing these Counts that they were high-born and had a legitimate claim to Friesland (a moot point indeed). The book had great appeal, and not only to the Counts of Holland. In particular Stoke's touching admiration for Floris V and the graphic details of his arrest, killing and funeral stirred the imagination, so much so that several popular notions about this Count can be traced back to Stoke's chronicle.

There are more of these rhyme chronicles, e.g. a Flemish one, *Rijmkroniek van Vlaanderen,* written by several authors, and Jan van Boendale's *Die Brabantsche Yeeste* (History of Brabant), but they are more interesting as early specimens of historiography than as works of literature.

They represent one facet of the didactic tradition which
carried on from Maerlant and became very strong during the
fourteenth century. Boendale must be regarded as the champion of fourteenth-century didacticism and as Maerlant's
successor in his intention and attitude, but without Maerlant's
cutting satire and his occasional flashes of poetry.

Boendale's principal work is *Der Leken Spieghel* (Lay-
men's Mirror), written between 1325 and 1333. It is a long
poem of more than 20,000 lines, divided into four parts and
dealing with ethics, biblical history, the history of Christianity
up to the reign of Charlemagne, and concluding with an
apocalyptic view of the end of the world, the whole supported
by moral stories and anecdotes. In the third part Boendale included a kind of *ars poetica* ('how poets ought to write')
in which he laid down his requirements for the poet: he must
be a grammarian, i.e. he must know the technique of writing,
he must be truthful, and he must be worthy of respect
('eerwaardig' is the word he uses). Boendale is very elaborate
about the poet's obligation to deal only with facts; he
polemizes against the author of *Karel ende Elegast* and
assures us that Charlemagne never went out stealing and that
he was not begotten on a cart as his name might suggest. As
it is the earliest specimen of a medieval *ars poetica* in the
vernacular, Boendale's poem is an important document in
the history of medieval literary theory, not only so far as
Dutch literature is concerned, but also with regard to the
other literatures of Western Europe. At the same time one
should not forget that Boendale represented only one strain
of medieval literature, the moralistic-didactic strain, and that
his ideas about what a poet should be and how he should
write were determined by his moralistic and didactic
preoccupation.His view of poetry was necessarily a very one-
sided one, although it may have been the majority view at
his time and place. If Maerlant had lived to read Boendale,
he would undoubtedly have subscribed to the theory. In fact,
one gets the impression that Boendale's theory was to a
large extent distilled from the work of Maerlant whom he

held in high regard and whom he called in his poem 'the father of all Dutch poets'. But there were also other views, and the author of *Vanden Vos Reinaerde* would have laughed at Boendale's prescriptions. Boendale's little *ars poetica* is a very interesting document, but one cannot help feeling that it would have been more so if it had come from a greater poet.

There are didactic poems in this century that are more convincing as works of literature than Boendale's poetry. *Vander Feesten* (The Feast) is one of those. It tells how a man meets a woman at a banquet and engages her in conversation. She appears to him to be in love, but he also notices that she looks sad. He asks her why, and she asks in return: what is love? The conversation then develops into a dialogue in which several aspects of love (courtly love) are discussed and analysed: how love is born, how do you win someone's love, how do you lose it, who is more steadfast in love, man or woman?

The most poetic didactic poem of this time is *Spieghel der Wijsheit* (Mirror of Wisdom) by Jan Praet, a Fleming of whom we know next to nothing. Within the framework of an allegory, the poem deals with man's life and death, heaven and hell, sin and salvation. But it is not so much for its content as for its form that the poem is noteworthy. Praet was a man who showed great interest in poetic form and who was one of the first to experiment with it. He did not write in the customary rhyming couplets but tried his hand at various kinds of form: stanzas with crossed rhymes, quatrains, poems in the form of motets with the rhymes *aab ccb dde ffe*. He also experimented with metrical schemes and every now and then came close to the modern iambic metre. From the point of view of form his work stands out from the other didactic poems of the time and represents a big step forward from poets like Boendale who coasted along comfortably on their never-changing rhyming couplets.

In the moralistic-didactic literature of the fourteenth century, a special place was taken by the literature of mysticism. Its great representative, Jan van Ruusbroec, continued to a certain extent the tradition of Hadewych, although the differences between the two are probably more striking than their similarities. In the first place, Ruusbroec wrote no poetry, but only prose. Secondly, Ruusbroec was far more systematic and didactic in setting out his religious ideas than Hadewych ever was. Hadewych was essentially lyrical in all her work, whereas Ruusbroec was a thinker and a writer of treatises rather than a man of literature.

Ruusbroec was born in 1293 in the village from which he derives his name, near Brussels. He became a priest and spent most of his life in an abbey which he and his followers established at Groenendaal, also close to Brussels. How highly his work was regarded can be seen from the fact that during his lifetime important parts of it were translated into Latin by several authors, among whom were Willem Jordaens and also Geert Groote, the leader of the Devotio Moderna. In this way Ruusbroec's work overcame the linguistic barriers, gained fame in Europe, and exercised a strong influence on the German mystics Suso and Tauler (who came to visit him several times at Groenendaal) and on the mystic movements in France, Spain and Italy.

His best-known work is *Die Chierheit der Gheesteliker Brulocht* (The Adornment of the Spiritual Wedding). It is a book on the theory of mystical aspiration, presented as an analysis of the text 'Behold, the bridegroom cometh; go ye out to meet him'. The four component parts of the text are analysed three times in their relation to the three levels of spiritual life, the highest of which is the 'god-seeing' life, attainable for only a few. A full description of Ruusbroec's mystical theory is a matter of theology rather than of literature; what we are concerned with here are his achievements as a prose writer. In a period when prose was still lagging a long way behind poetry as a means of literary expression, Ruusbroec's achievements were considerable. He wrote in a lucid, though not particularly fluent style and interspersed his work with many comparisons and parable-like passages of undoubted literary value. This applies not only to *Die Chierheit,* but also to other works such as *Vanden Blinckenden Steen* (The Sparkling Stone)) and *Vanden Rike der Gheliven* (The Kingdom of the Beloved).

Ruusbroec's influence also extended to the religious movement of the Devotio Moderna which sprang up in the second half of the century in the eastern part of the Netherlands. Its centres were the towns in the valley of the river IJssel, another indication, that the towns were gradually replacing the monasteries as the centres of cultural life. Although it cannot be called a really mystical movement, there were several points of contact between the Devotio Moderna and mysticism proper, particularly in their reaction against formalism in religion and their emphasis on asceticism. There were also some personal contacts between the two, as we know that Geert Groote, the founder and the leader of the movement, paid some visits to Ruusbroec at Groenendaal and translated part of his work into Latin. But the Devotio Moderna was far more directed towards practical purposes, far more concerned with the ethics and religion of every-day life than Ruusbroec was : its followers tried to improve the world from which Ruusbroec was escaping. It also lacked the atmosphere of ecstasy and exaltation which characterizes mysticism in its pure form, and it contained a greater element of rationalism. The Devotio in general was pragmatic, critical, sober-minded and free from theological hair-splitting. It was a movement which in a short time spread very widely: after some years its institutions were to be found not only in Holland and Brabant (Antwerp), but also in the Rhineland and Westphalia, and even in Prussia.

Geert Groote was born in 1340. This means that he grew up during the years when the Pope was exiled at Avignon and the authority of the Church was at a low ebb. There was a great deal of opposition to the secular power of the Church, particularly in towns which lay within Church territory.

Groote was born in such a town, Deventer, one of the
Hanseatic towns on the IJssel. His father was a well-to-do
magistrate who could afford to give his son a good
education. Groote studied in Holland and abroad, including
three years at the University of Paris. His interests must have
been almost universal, as he took courses in philosophy,
medicine, logic, law, and even studied magic for some time
(a lapse of which he was much ashamed in later years). After
having lived the life of a worldly scholar for some fourteen
years, enjoying a stipend, and sinning profusely according to
his own testimony, he suddenly put his past behind him,
entered a Carthusian monastery near Arnhem and was
ordained a deacon there. Then he started travelling around
as a kind of revivalist preacher of penitence, attacking
immorality where he saw it, inside or outside the Church, and
passionately calling for repentance. Judging by reports from
his contemporaries, he must have been a brilliant orator,
who gained his effects by blending his scholarly background
with a common touch. Also, the combination of his
personality and the predisposition of the environment in
which he worked, goes a long way to explain the rapid and
wide spread of his ideas. The reverse side of the popularity
medal shows a strong opposition from within the Church,
resulting in a ban on his activities as a preacher, imposed by
the Bishop of Utrecht in 1383, a year before his death. After
he had been silenced, he devoted much of the time that was
left to him to translating parts of the Latin church service
into Dutch, an almost heretical occupation as many
considered this as an attack on the sacredness of the liturgy.
Apart from these translations we do not have much literature
in Dutch by Groote, or by the other members of his
movement. They usually expressed themselves in Latin,
which of course helped to spread their ideas so quickly and
so widely. Groote's work in Dutch consists only of some
rather dry treatises which are without any great consequence
as works of literature: he was clearly first and foremost an
orator. Only Hendrik Mande, a lay brother, wrote exclusively

in Dutch, strongly under the influence of Ruusbroec.

It is clear, therefore, that Groote's importance lies not so much in what he contributed directly to Dutch literature, but rather in his indirect contributions: in the climate that he created. The religious communities which grew out of his movement, known as the Brethren of the Common Life, concerned themselves with education, establishing schools and student homes, and also with book production, copying manuscripts at first, and later on printing them. Their practical and critical attitude prepared the way for the Dutch Humanists: Rudolf Huisman, better known as Agricola, Wessel Gansfort, whom Luther called one of his predecessors, and Erasmus, all of whom were brought up in the atmosphere of the Brethren. When Erasmus, the cosmopolitan who had seen a great deal of Europe and who had little time for his native country, in later years sang the praise of the high standard of general education in the Low Countries, a large share of this honour must be credited to the Brethren of the Common Life.

In the purely religious field, the Devotio Moderna resulted in the Congregation of Windesheim, established by Groote's followers a few years after his death. The Congregation derived its name from the first monastery at Windesheim, near Zwolle. Like the association of the Brethren, the Congregation developed rapidly and comprised at its peak about one hundred monasteries and convents. The most famous personality to emerge from the Windesheim congregation was Thomas à Kempis, a monk in the Agnietenberg monastery near Zwolle, whose *Imitatio Christi*, written entirely in the spirit of Geert Groote's teachings, became one of the best-known books of all time.

The mystic writers of the fourteenth century whom we know by name were all prose writers; there was not a single poet among them. This is surprising when one considers the high standard of poetry reached in the work of Hadewych. One would expect that her example would have been followed and that some of the later mystics would have continued her work. If that was done at all, most of this poetry has been lost. There are only a small number of anonymous mystic poems, which resemble Hadewych's work so closely that they could have been written by her and which, in fact, were attributed to her until fairly recently:

> Alle dinghe
> Sijn mi te inghe:
> Ic ben so wijdt.
> Om een onghescepen
> Hebbic ghegrepen
> In ewighen tijt.
>
> Ic hebt ghevaen.
> Het heeft mi ontdaen
> Widere dan wijt;
> Mi es te inghe al el;
> Dat wette wel
> Ghi dies oec daer sijt.[1]

On the whole it is hard to say whether the fourteenth century was rich or poor in religious lyrical poetry. So much is certain that little has been preserved. Apart from that small group of mystic poems, only a few songs have come to us. One of these is an early Christmas song ('In dulci jubilo singet en weset vro'—sing and be merry) which is still very close to the Latin church hymns.

We have been more fortunate with regard to the secular lyric. Two important manuscripts have been preserved, the Gruythuyse manuscript and the Hulthem manuscript, which contain many songs and lyrical poems of the fourteenth century. Some of them are courtly love lyrics, continuing the tradition of Hendrik van Veldeke and Jan, Duke of Brabant, Others are laments about a dead lover or friend, such as the famous *Egidius* song. Among them is also a remarkably

---

[1] All things are too narrow for me: I am so wide. I have aspired to one un-created in eternal time. I have captured it. It has opened me wider than wide; all else is too narrow for me; you who are this too, know it well.

modern-looking poem in which the poet fights against his
own thoughts:

Vaer wech ghepeins, God gheve dir leit
Dattu ye quaems in mijn ghedacht.[2]

This poem, like the *Egidius* song and several others, was
written in the *rondeau* form—two rhymes and lines
recurring with subtle variation—which was very popular in
France at that time. Others were written in the French
ballade form, others again in forms that are reminiscent of
the German love lyric. Several also show in their language a
slight German colouring. It is not always easy to say whether
this means that the poems were of German origin or whether
they were made to look slightly German because that was
fashionable at the time when Holland was ruled by the dukes
of Bavaria who had married into the House of the counts of
Holland. That this latter possibility should not be dismissed
too lightly is suggested by the work of Dirc Potter, a Dutch
civil servant attached to the court of the Bavarians in
Holland, who very consciously gave his poetry a faintly
German look to keep up with the fashion.

In some of these poems we find echoes of what was going
on in political and social life. There is for instance a song of
lament for Count Willem IV of Holland who was killed in
1345 on an expedition against the Frisians. Another one
describes the death of Count Floris V; it is a curious poem,
as it completely ignores the political factors involved and
simply blames Floris's tragic ending on the fact that he
seduced the wife of Gerard van Velzen, one of the rebellious
noblemen. Most notable of all these poems is the *Kerelslied*
(The Song of the Churls), which reflects the hatred that the
nobleman must have felt for the peasants who were
challenging his power. It probably dates back to the 1320s
when there were several peasants' revolts against the Count

[2] Go away, thoughts, may God punish you for having entered my
mind.

of Flanders. It is one of the angriest poems of the Middle Ages; the author spits out his contemptuous hatred (and perhaps also his fear) of these uncouth peasants and tries to hurt them where it hurts most, by ridiculing their inane behaviour, sloppy dress and unsavoury manners. As is the case with all poems contained in the Gruythuyse manuscript, the melody is given with it, so that we know for certain that the poem was meant to be sung.

Apart from these songs and poems which were written down comparatively soon after they were composed, there is also a group of songs known as popular songs or folk songs, sometimes also called ballads, or romances. Some of these were written down during the Middle Ages, others as late as the nineteenth century, which makes it difficult to indicate with any degree of accuracy to which period they actually belong. The subject-matter of several of these poems is very old indeed and often goes back to legends and fairy-tales. Judging by its very simple form and the repetitiveness of the narration, the ballad of *Heer Halewijn* must be one of the oldest. It is the story of a kind of Bluebeard who lures young girls with a song that they cannot resist and who then kills them; finally, however, he is outwitted and decapitated by a cunning maid. The poem contains several elements of Germanic legend, for instance in Halewijn's magic song, which is reminiscent of the song of the Swedish water-sprite 'strömkarl'; the poem is also related to a number of German songs and to the English ballad of *May Colvin, or False Sir John* (known in a modernized version as *The Outlandish Knight*). In all its simplicity of form and language, it is a magnificent poem which in ninety matter-of-fact lines suggests a world of mysteriousness and drama. The twentieth-century Dutch composer Willem Pijper used it as the basis for his opera *Heer Halewijn,* for which the poet Martinus Nijhoff wrote the libretto.

Although many of the songs and poems of this time deal with subjects from the world of chivalry, it is clear that the knights no longer occupied the central position in literature.

A considerable amount of chivalresque literature was still written, but none of the epic romances of the fourteenth century can be compared with the best of the preceding centuries, with *Karel ende Elegast,* or with *Walewein.* They no longer brought anything new, they no longer contributed to the development of literature, and they give the impression of being reflections of a past age. It also seems that the genre of the romance of chivalry no longer attracted the best poets, as the writing of most of the fourteenth-century specimens is very much flatter and slacker than that of the earlier romances. As a genre the romance of chivalry was clearly in decline.

Most of the epic romances of this period, too, were adaptations from the French, e.g. *De Borchgravinne van Vergi* (The Viscountess of Vergi) and *De Borchgrave van Couchi* (The Viscount of Couchi). Some are originals, such as *Flandrijs,* of which only parts have been preserved, and the long *Roman van Heinric en Margriete van Limborch,* which must have been a popular poem as it was translated into German by Johannes von Soest as late as 1480. Holland made its debut in the literary world just after 1300 with a Lancelot romance, *Lantsloot van der Haghedochte,* written by un unknown author.

More important than these epic romances is the work of Hein van Aken, who was born in Brussels and who was a priest in a village near Louvain. He introduced something new to Dutch literature with his poem *Hughe van Tabariën.* It is an adaptation of the French *De l'Ordene de Chevalier* and can best be described as a cross between chivalresque and didactic literature. Didacticism as a feature of chivalresque literature was in itself nothing new. There had never really been a significant gap between the literature of entertainment and the literature of instruction in the Low Countries. Maerlant, after all, had used his epic romances to a certain extent as vehicles for instruction. But in the fourteenth century, didacticism began to weigh more heavily and began to turn the scales. The interest was shifting away from the heroic deeds and gallant adventures of the knight and the attention of the reader or listener was drawn towards the knight as a model of moral behaviour. Hein van Aken's poem—a strophic poem of 37 stanzas—is primarily didactic, intended to show what the virtues of chivalry are and what a good knight should be like. In certain respects it might be compared with a much later German poem, *Der Ritterspiegel* (Mirror of Chivalry), written at the beginning of the fifteenth century by Johannes Rothe, who had a similar admiration for the knight as Hein van Aken had (although Rothe was far more interested in the military aspects of chivalry than Van Aken was).

Hein van Aken is also known as the translator of the French *Roman de la Rose,* the monumental allegory begun by Guillaume de Lorris and finished about 1280 by Jean de Meung. Because of the different approaches and ideas of the two authors, the *Roman de la Rose* was a curious example of the marriage between courtly literature and didacticism. Its first part is a description of courtly love, presented in the form of a dream in which the author wanders through a mysterious garden seeking for the rose, symbol of the beloved. The second part, although continuing the allegory, is of a totally different nature: it is a didactic poem, full of learning, and also full of satire and attacks on the evils of society of the time. The poem became tremendously popular in medieval Europe, in spite of fierce resistance from the clergy, and it remained popular and influential for a very long time.

Hein van Aken made his translation shortly after 1300, which was early, certainly much earlier than the English translation made by Chaucer in the 1360s. Van Aken translated the first part quite faithfully, but he threw up a barrier against the heretical thoughts of Jean de Meun by making many changes in the second part: he left out or toned down several passages which to his mind were too daring, too indelicate, too cynical or too satirical (this in contrast to Chaucer who seems to have been very taken by the ideas of Jean de Meung). It is hard to decide whether Van Aken did this only to suit his own taste or because he was afraid of offending his Dutch public, or perhaps because he did not want to get into trouble. In any case, through his translation the poem became a great success in the Low Countries and we can follow its influence in the several allegorical poems about love that were written shortly after this translation, just as we can see the impact of the *Rose* in Chaucer's own allegories written after he had made his translation.

When the epic romance began to lose its appeal, a new genre emerged known as the *sproke*, which might be translated as 'metrical tale', and which was closely related to the French *dit* as written by Guillaume de Machaut. They were relatively short poems, usually of no more than a few hundred lines, written by professional poets who travelled around with them from town to town and from court to court. The material for these poems came from internationally known collections of stories, such as the *Gesta Romanorum*, produced in England during the last years of the thirteenth century. It contained a variety of stories, some of them of Roman origin, whereas others originated in the East. The story of Pyramus and Thisbe was a great favourite among them: we meet it in several literatures — Shakespeare used it later on for his *Midsummernights's Dream* — and it also became the basis of one of those *sproken* in Dutch under the title of *Van Tween Kinderen Die Droeghen ene Starke Minnen een Ontfermelijc Dinc* (A Moving Story of Two Children Who Bore a Strong Love). Again, most of these poems were essentially didactic, and a number of them show the combination of chivalresque subject-matter and moral purpose that was so typical of this period.

The best-known writer and reciter of this kind of poetry in the Low Countries was Willem van Hildegaersberch, one of the first authors to come from Holland. He lived in the second half of the century and came from the village of Hillegersberg, now a suburb of Rotterdam. He was the typical professional poet, a kind of didactic troubadour, who was hired regularly by the Count of Holland to perform at his court in The Hague, as the ducal account books show. His livelihood depended entirely on his poetry, and as he was not a very strong personality, he gave clear evidence that he knew on which side his bread was buttered. No dangerous or heretical thoughts are to be found in his work; on the contrary, he constantly gives the impression of being right behind the authorities on whom he depended. When he became satirical, he attacked only things that it was safe to attack, usually abstractions such as hypocrisy, flattery, immorality, corruption and parsimony (an unforgivable sin from the point of view of the professional poet). From what we know about him, we may assume that he wrote only what he could expect to be in demand, so that through his work we also get a good idea of what kind of poetry was popular in those days and in those circles.

He left about 120 poems on a variety of subjects. Some have a religious theme, others criticize the social evils mentioned above, others again discuss politics or history; some are lyrical, others could almost be described as mystical, several are in the form of an allegory, or use fables to drive their points home. But the common denominator of all his poetry is didacticism. Even when he let himself go most, as in his comic poems, the moralistic purpose is always there. He said so himself:

> Een dichter die te dichten pliet,
> Die pijnt hem gaerne te vinden yet
> Dat den luden in den oren
> Wat ghenoechte brenct te voren,
> Ende int verstaen oeck wijsheit mede;
> Want gherechte dichters zeede
> Dat is, die waerheit bringhen voert.[3]

[3] A poet at work likes to take pains to find something that gives pleasure to the ears of the people, and also wisdom; for the task of the real poet is to bring to light the truth.

This, of course, is still very much the theory of Boendale, although Hildegaersberch's verse had moved a long way from his. Willem van Hildegaersberch may not have been a great poet or a strong personality, but he did possess a certain amount of originality, a good command of poetic technique with an adroitness in handling different types of form, and every now and then a surprisingly acute sense of imagery.

The *sproken* and their author-performers, the *sprooksprekers,*may have played a significant part in the development of Dutch literature, as it is not impossible that from them the first plays originated. The Hulthem manuscript contains a remarkable set of four serious plays, the *abele spelen* (noble or beautiful plays), together with six farces, all dating back to the middle of the fourteenth century. These plays give the Low Countries an important 'first' in the history of medieval literature, as no earlier plays of this kind are known in Europe. Neither in Germany nor in England do we find secular plays at this time. In French literature one could point to the two plays of Adam de la Halle, written in the second half of the thirteenth century, but they are comedies and cannot be regarded as serious drama. The conclusion must be that the *abele spelen* are the very first specimens of serious secular drama in European literature.

The lack of predecessors is a puzzling aspect of these plays. It immediately poses the question of the origin of secular drama in the Middle Ages. It has often been argued that secular drama developed from religious drama, but as there is no positive evidence for the existence of religious drama in Dutch prior to the *abele spelen* this development seems unlikely for the Low Countries. There were, however, dramatic elements in the poetry of the *sprooksprekers.* Some of their poems were written as dialogues, for instance *Twee Coninghen, Deen Levende ende Dander Doot* (Two Kings, One Living and One Dead) or *Disputacie Tusschen den Sone ende den Vadere* (Dispute Between the Son and the Father). Poems such as these were

probably recited as dialogues, either by two performers, or by
one who acted out both parts. From these dramatized
dialogues the early secular plays may have grown.

The lack of certainty about the origin of the genre as such
is not the only puzzling aspect of the *abele spelen*. It is not
too much to say that they are surrounded by mystery. We
have no idea who wrote them, nor do we know whether they
are the work of one author or of several. On the basis of
style and language a case can be made out for single
authorship, at least for three of the four. It is also possible
that these plays formed the repertoire of a travelling
company of actors. This possibility is strenghened by the
presence in the manuscript of the six farces which were
performed after the serious plays. The language of the plays
suggests that they were written by someone from Brabant
about the middle of the fourteenth century, but it is
impossible to give any more precise information about date
or place.

Three of these plays, *Esmoreit, Gloriant* and *Lanseloet van
Denemarken,* are romantic plays, dealing with love and
showing it as an irresistible force in life. The main characters
in these three plays are princes and princesses, the setting is
foreign and exotic, the subject-matter is closely related to
that of the romances of chivalry, in particular the courtly
eastern romances. One might say that the outmoded
chivalresque literature was given a new lease of life in the
form of the stage play, which at that time was probably a
novelty.

The main theme of *Esmoreit* is that of the royal foundling,
a much used theme in medieval literature. Esmoreit, son of
the king of Sicily, is sold into captivity by his evil cousin
who wants to clear his own way to the throne. The Sicilian
prince is brought up at the Saracen court of Damascus by
Damiët, the daughter of the king. The two fall in love, but
when Esmoreit hears that he is a foundling, he feels that he
cannot marry Damiët until he has solved the mystery of his
origin. This attitude provides the dramatic conflict of the

play, as his origin is of no interest at all to Damiët: she only wants him and is afraid of losing him. The motif of religious difference, which the modern reader might expect to lead to dramatic developments, is only of secondary importance. When Esmoreit returns to Sicily, he is quickly converted back to Christianity: his father simply tells him that he now ought to honour Mary and God. Esmoreit does not even reply, but shows that he has been converted by invoking 'holy mother and maid' and 'the lord that made me' instead of Mahomet and Apollo. To the medieval audience it must have been self-evident that Esmoreit became a Christian after he had been told the truth, so unthinkable that he should do anything else but accept it, that there was no need for words to be wasted on it. His conversion, if that is the word, was for the audience only an anticipated satisfaction, for the playwright only a matter of dotting his i's; it could not be material for dramatic conflict.

The play of *Gloriant* portrays the passionate love between the Christian prince Gloriant and Florentijn, a Saracen princess from Abelant. Both had said that they would never find a partner worthy of them. When Gloriant said this, he was warned that the Lady Venus would not like his rejection of love and would take revenge on him. The revenge comes when he is given a portrait of Florentijn: he falls wildly in love with her in spite of the hopelessness of the situation, as Florentijn is the daughter of his father's arch-enemy. His love, however, is so powerful that it overcomes all difficulties and after a dangerous expedition Gloriant takes Florentijn home. Her conversion takes place even more as a matter of course than Esmoreit's as she is never directly told or asked to become a Christian. At one stage Gloriant prays that Florentijn may escape death and may receive Christianity, and a little later, without any more information, we hear Florentijn pray to 'God who was born of the virgin'.

From a modern critical point of view, plays such as *Gloriant* and *Esmoreit* represent dramatic art in its infancy. There is little attempt at characterization, the characters are worked out only so far as is absolutely necessary for an understanding of the plot, psychological motivation is completely absent, the heroes are white, the villains an unrelieved black. The plays simply make statements, they do not search for what goes on behind the actions.

Lanseloet van Denemarken strikes us as more modern than *Gloriant* and *Esmoreit*. The reason for this is that there is more 'psychology' and development in it than in the other two, and that there is more gradation between good and evil in the main character. Lanseloet, the prince of Denmark, is in love with one of his mother's servants, Sanderijn. The mother wants a princess for her son and tries to destroy Lanseloet's love. She makes him a proposition: she will send Sanderijn to him once to satisfy his desire, but afterwards he shall send her away, saying: 'I am as sick of you as if I had eaten seven sides of bacon'. Lanseloet is torn between his desire and the cruel vulgarity with which he will have to pay for it, but he soothes his conscience by telling himself that he does not mean what he is going to say. Sanderijn goes to Lanseloet in good faith, thinking that he is ill, but comes out of his room in utter despair. She leaves the court, goes away to another country where she meets a knight with whom she becomes very happy. Lanseloet in the meantime is consumed by remorse and sends one of his servants to find her. Sanderijn is found but she prefers to stay with her knight. The servant realizes that she will never go back to Lanseloet and decides to tell him that she is dead. Lanseloet then dies of a broken heart.

For a medieval play the character of Lanseloet is quite subtly drawn. He is neither wholly good nor wholly bad. His love for Sanderijn is sincere enough, and certainly not only sensual, as has sometimes been suggested, but his moral weakness causes him to treat her in such a contemptible way. His main fault is this weakness, this lack of moral courage to resist the miserable scheme that his mother has thought up. It is the flaw in his personality that leads to his destruction, not any influence from outside. But even this weakness is not presented as incapable of remedy, for through his grief after Sanderijn has gone he grows strong enough to say to his servant: 'I will marry her spite my kindred all'.[4]

Not only its psychological approach but also its poetry makes *Lanseloet van Denemarken* superior to the other two. One of the highlights occurs in a speech of Sanderijn's. After she has met the knight, he asks her to marry him, but she feels she has to tell him first what has happened to her:

> Look at this tree shapely and tall,
> How gloriously it blossoms out.
> Its noble smell goes all about
> The orchard and the lovely dell.
> So sweet it is, and grown so well,
> That all this orchard it doth adorn.
> If now a falcon nobly born
> From high upon this tree flew down,
> And picked one flower, only one,
> And after that never one more,
> Nor ever took but that one flower,
> Now pray you tell me faithfully,
> Would you therefore hate the tree? [5]

After this the knight can only reply: 'One single flower, that is nought'. The image of the falcon must have pleased the poet himself, for he used it again, in a slightly different version, when Sanderijn rejects Lanseloet's plea to come back to him.

Lanseloet van Denemarken is also the only play of the three that contains some humour. *Gloriant* and *Esmoreit* are both very serious, without any humorous or comic relief, but in *Lanseloet* we find the part of the gamekeeper who is so impressed by his master finding a beautiful woman in the forest that he goes to that same spot every day for a full

---

[4] *A beautiful play of Lancelot of Denmark*. Translated by Dr. P. Geyl, The Hague, Nijhoff (1924), p. 29.
[5] Geyl, p. 25.

year, hiding behind a bush, hoping that he may meet with
the same kind of good fortune. All he finds, though, is
Lanseloet's servant. Through his long and fruitless wait he
has become so tense and so fierce-looking that the servant
takes fright when he sees him:

> Deus God! How shall I know
> What the man wants who there appears!
> Methinks he has a mien so fierce,
> And so heavy a club to bear,
> He is a murderer, I swear. [6]

The understated dry humour that we find in *Lanseloet*
becomes very 'wet' in the farces that were played after each
abel spel. The Hulthem manuscript contains six of them,
which might indicate that two serious plays have been lost.
The farces provide a contrast in almost every respect: they
are not set in the refined, courtly and noble atmosphere of
the serious plays, but in a kind of lower middle-class
environment. They are coarse, hardly humorous but broadly
comical and slapstick. The tenor of most of them is the
same: to show the stupidity of man and the superior
cleverness of woman.

The fourth serious play, *Een Abel Spel vanden Winter ende
vanden Somer* (A Beautiful Play of the Winter and the
Summer) is in a different category from the other three. It is
an allegory which presents in a light-hearted way a dispute
between the summer and the winter about their respective
importance. When the dispute threatens to degenerate into a
duel, Venus arbitrates by pronouncing them eternal brothers.
Although it is well-written and not as lifeless as some of the
later allegories, it does not measure up to the standard of the
romantic plays, certainly not to that of *Lanseloet*. It also
seems that our modern preference for *Lanseloet* was shared
by medieval man, for it was the only one of the four to be
printed as a chapbook (about 1486) and also the only one

[6] Geyl, p. 32.

that crossed the border, in a German translation made at the
end of the fifteenth century and printed in Cologne.

III

RULERS AND RHETORICIANS
FIFTEENTH CENTURY

During the fifteenth century radical changes took place in the
political situation of the Low Countries. The foundation for
these changes was laid in the second half of the fourteenth
century when the daughter of the Count of Flanders married
a French prince, Philip, Duke of Burgundy. This marriage
brought the House of Burgundy into the Low Countries and
with it a force of such energy that one might be justified in
calling the fifteenth century after them. By means of a
cleverly worked-out marital policy, and helped considerably
by deaths occurring at the right times and places, the
Burgundians in an incredibly short time brought the whole of
the Low Countries under their rule. In 1383 the Duke of
Burgundy succeeded to the county of Flanders, and in 1430,
less than two generations later, Holland, Zealand, Brabant,
Limburg and Hainault were Burgundian, while the dioceses
of Utrecht and Liege were also governed by members of the
Burgundian clan.

The acquisition of territories was only the first stage of the
Burgundian grand design. The main object was to forge these
territories into a new state, a new Burgundy outside France.
The Dukes visualized this state as a kind of 'third force' on
the continent of Europe, in between France and Germany,
and they hoped in due course to have it recognized as a
kingdom. Charles the Bold came close to the royal crown,
and even negotiated to be nominated successor to the
Emperor of Germany, but both plans misfired. The
Burgundian creation remained a kind of federal state,

47

without royal status, even without a name: the Burgundians simply referred to it as 'the lands over here'.

In their endeavours to mould the various provinces into one single unit, the Burgundians were guided by the concept of a central administration such as existed in France. Several institutions were set up to bring about this centralization: a Grand Council as a central advisory body, audit-offices for the implementation of financial policy, a central Court of Justice. These measures which made the fourteenth-century efforts at unification look very puny, clashed in many cases with local privileges and prerogatives, and were therefore not always accepted without resistance.Several peasant rebellions occurred in Holland in the 1420s, and a serious revolt took place in Flanders in the 1450s when the cities of Bruges and Ghent made a firm stand against the Burgundian policies. The rebellions were forcibly put down by the Duke, Philip the Good, and Ghent was humiliated in the same way as Calais had been a hundred years earlier. The reason for these uprisings was primarily economic (the regular taxes which the Burgundians introduced were highly unpopular), but dissatisfaction with the language situation often played a part too. For the Burgundians were French, very consciously so, whereas the federation over which they ruled was predominantly Dutch-speaking. The language of the administration was French, and this led to clashes, particularly where juridical matters were concerned. In much of the resistance that was put up against the Burgundian rule one can detect an undertone of resentment of the discrimination against the Dutch language. In 1477, when the last of the strong Dukes died and an organized reaction set in, one of the first concessions made was the introduction of Dutch as the language of the administration in all Dutch-speaking provinces.

During the fifteenth century Dutch civilization was steadily developing its own characteristics and was no longer largely a derivative of French civilization. A clear example of this is to be found in the fifteenth century Flemish school of painting: Jan van Eyck, Rogier van der Weyden, Hugo van der Goes, Dirc Bouts, Hans Memlinc who for the first time developed a really national style. In architecture one could point to Dutch Gothic, which although based on French Gothic, acquired in a short while a character all its own. In music it was the polyphonic school of Johannes Ockeghem, Jacob Obrecht and Josquin des Prez which for almost a century dominated musical life in Europe. In literature the growing autonomy of Dutch civilization was illustrated by the emergence of secular drama without any foreign models or predecessors. On the whole one can say, contradictory as it may seem, that when the French Burgundians came to power in the Low Countries, the French influence on their culture had passed its peak.

The Burgundians took a great interest in the arts, far more so than the former rulers of the various provinces had done (with the possible exception of the thirteenth-century Duke Jan I of Brabant, who was a poet himself). Jan van Eyck was made official painter of the court of Philip the Good and received several commissions from him, among which was an assignment to go to Portugal to paint Philip's future wife. The sculptor Claus Sluter, originally from Haarlem, worked at the Burgundian court at Dijon as head of the ducal studios. It goes without saying that the French-speaking Burgundians took a greater interest in the painting, sculpture and music of the Low Countries than in the literature which was foreign to them (although Philip the Good had learned to read and speak Dutch reasonably well). Their library, famous for its size, contained very few manuscripts of Dutch works; almost everything was in French and Latin. They did show some interest in the literary organizations known as Chambers of Rhetoric by allowing themselves to be appointed honorary members and by attending their festivals. But there is no doubt that the organization of literature in the Low Countries was closer to their hearts than the literature itself. Interested in unification as they were, they realized that these Chambers of Rhetoric could play a part in their policies. They therefore approved wholeheartedly of the literary festivals which the Chambers organized and which, in days of little inter-provincial traffic, drew large crowds from various parts of the country. They recognized the value these meetings had for intensification of contact between the provinces, the levelling out of dissimilarities and the increase of homogeneity. Philip the Fair even concerned himself with the organization of the Chambers: in 1493, guided by the Burgundian ideal of centralization, he appointed the Chamber of Ghent as the central and sovereign Chamber. But the other Chambers resented and opposed his interference, and nothing much came of this.

The development of these Chambers of Rhetoric—the organization of literature in an age of organization—is the most curious aspect of fifteenth-century literature. It is no exaggeration to say that the literature of that period was entirely dominated by the Chambers. The *Rederijkers,* as the members of the Chambers called themselves, also put their stamp on a great deal of the literature of the sixteenth century, and even in the seventeenth century several of the prominent writers were still influenced by and connected with the Chambers of Rhetoric. The origin of the Chambers was not Dutch, but French. Associations of *Rhétoriqueurs* existed in the north of France as early as the twelfth century, and in the fifteenth century we also find them centred on the court of Burgundy. Their theorist was Jean Molinet, a Walloon who worked at the Burgundian court in Brussels, and whose *L'art de rhétorique* had some influence on the aesthetic ideas of the Dutch writers.

The oldest Chambers of Rhetoric in the Low Countries date back to the first years of the fifteenth century, although they were not known by that name yet. The name *Camer van Rhetorica* appeared for the first time in 1441 at Oudenaarde in Flanders. The Chambers may have originated from the Church, as associations which added lustre to processions and celebrations, and which performed religious plays. At all events, there was a close relationship between the Chambers and the Church, particularly in the South. But the *Rederijkers* were also in demand by the secular authorities. They were called upon by the local governments to organize pageants, to entertain at receptions, to put on plays or mimes on festive occasions. In exchange for these services they often received financial subsidies and privileges such as exemption from certain taxes. Membership of a Chamber was regarded as an honour and gave considerable standing in society.

The Chambers were organized very much like trade-guilds. Their membership varied a great deal, some Chambers had only ten or a dozen members, others well over a hundred. The head of the Chamber, called the Prince, was usually a prominent and well-to-do citizen who was chosen for his administrative rather than for his poetic capacities. The most important man from the point of view of literature was the Factor. He was the man in charge of all literary activities: he wrote the plays or the poems for performances and contests, and he was the producer of the plays. Apart from these functionaries, the Chambers also had a standard bearer and a fool. Every Chamber had a standard with a blazon (often a flower) and a motto: the Amsterdam Chamber, for instance, was called *De Eglantier* (The Eglantine) and had as motto *'In Liefde bloeiende'* which meant both 'flowering in love' and 'bleeding in love'; the pun was continued in its blazon which showed Christ crucified on an eglantine tree.

A characteristic aspect of the *Rederijkers* was their competitiveness. From the beginning of the fifteenth century the Chambers organized drama contests in which plays were performed that had been written for the occasion on a set subject. Sometimes the contest was between two Chambers only, but in the bigger contests many Chambers took part, as in Antwerp in 1498 when twenty-eight Chambers participated. Contests such as these developed into popular festivals lasting for days, sometimes for weeks. After the performances of the serious plays, there was the light relief of comedies and farces, there were pageants and banquets. The popularity of these contests shows that the *Rederijkers* played a very important part in the social life of the time. Belonging to a Chamber and taking part in its proceedings was a respected social activity. In this way writing poetry and plays, acting and reciting became a widespread, almost popular occupation, without anything esoteric about it. When the number of Chambers increased greatly during the sixteenth century, this meant that for several generations a considerable part of the population was actively engaged in literary activities. Much of what was written was understandably of little literary value, but the main thing was that the *Rederijkers* created a climate in which writing poetry became a regular, recognized and respected occupation. And although quantity is not a precondition for quality, the existence of a training ground such as they provided increased the possibility for works of superior quality to develop. It certainly helped to improve the standard of technique.

The *Rederijkers* were very interested in technique, unhealthily so, it has been said. Experimentation with form became one of their main concerns. Their favourite form was the *refrein* (refrain), a poem which developed from the fourteenth-century French *ballade,* and which consisted of an irregular number of stanzas, between eight and twenty-four lines long. Each stanza had the same last line, which stated the subject of the poem. The last stanza was as a rule dedicated to the head of the Chamber and began with the word *Prince.* In later years this basically simple form was decked out with all kinds of technical refinements and complexities. Not only in the refrain, but in their lyrical poetry in general, the *Rederijkers* exhausted themselves in showing what could be done with form. They wrote poems in which a date was concealed, acrostics of several kinds which gave names or mottoes when one deciphered them, poems that could be read backwards, and combinations of all this. Another popular form was the palindrome, a line that was identical whether one read it from left to right or from right to left: 'ons leven sy een snee ijs nevel sno' (our life is snow, ice, mist of little value), and a form which they called 'aldicht' (all-poem) in which the lines rhymed word for word. The most complicated *tour de force* was the chess-board: each of the 64 squares contained a line and if one made the right moves, 38 different poems could be produced. Add to this their experiments with rhyme: rich rhymes, double rhymes, or long stanzas with only two rhymes, expansion of rhyming possibilities by using intricate circumlocutions instead of a simple word, and one has some idea of what these poets did to form.

One can laugh, of course, at the technical games of the *Rederijkers,* and write off their poetry as artificial and gimmicky, but that would be ignoring the real importance they had for the development of form. The great advances in literary techniques made during the fifteenth and sixteenth centuries cannot be understood without taking into account these technical experiments, even the most outrageous ones. In many cases the *Rederijkers* were completely carried away by their verbal ingenuity, to the loss of poetry. But later generations, while ignoring the extremist forms, could start on the basis of the *Rederijker* discoveries and experiments; they could develop them into meaningful forms by handling them naturally, in the same way as Bach could handle the complicated form of the fugue in a natural manner.

The preoccupation with form and technique was not peculiar to literature only. On the contrary, one must regard it as one of the main characteristics of fifteenth-century cultural development. In several other fields we find the same dissatisfaction with traditional medieval form and similar attempts to expand the range of expression. We find it in the work of Jan van Eyck who constantly experimented with form, who broke with the traditional way of painting a flat background and who introduced a new element of realism into his portraits. Van Eyck also experimented with the composition of paint, in a persistent search to achieve the greatest possible richness of colour. In music, too, we meet this interest in technique, particularly in the second Flemish polyphonic school of Johannes Ockeghem († 1495) and Jacob Obrecht († 1505). The advances in the technique of composition made by this school were as striking as those of the *Rederijkers* and some of their experiments in form were amazingly similar to the extravagances of the poets, especially with regard to the canon: they wrote retrograde canons, inverted canons, augmented and diminished canons, canons containing a riddle etc. On another level the general interest in technique expressed itself in the often extremely complicated machinery designed to make the festivities of the Burgundians into great spectacles: a self-propelling pie on wheels containing a fourteen piece orchestra, wine-spouting fountains erected along the route the duke travelled, angels coming down from the ceiling during a banquet, and most spectacular of them all, Charles the Bold's floating palace with its mechanical monkeys, wolves and bears that danced and sang. Seen in this light, the *Rederijker* activities no longer look like unfortunate aberrations of eccentric poets, but become very much part and parcel of the general interest of the time.

Although the main function of the *Rederijkers* may seem in retrospect to have been that of pioneers whose work was brought to fruition by those who came after them, that does not mean that they left no literature of intrinsic value. Plays such as *Elckerlyc* and *Mariken van Nimweghen* show that they were capable of better things than just the verbal fireworks for which they are notorious. They were very active in the field of religious drama and practised the same three types of religious plays as their French and English contemporaries: mystery plays, miracle plays and morality plays.

The morality plays were often written in the form of an allegory, they were strongly didactic, often dull, and on the whole little literary value. But there is one great exception to the rule: the play of *Elckerlyc,* known in English as *Everyman. Elckerlyc* was written about 1470, gained first prize at a *Rederijker* contest held at Antwerp about 1485, and was first printed in 1495. There has been a sixty years' war between English and Dutch literary historians about the question of originality and translation, and although occasional shots are still fired by snipers on either side, the decisive blow has been struck. It is to the credit of the participants that nationalist prejudices played no part in the arguments: the staunchest defender of *Everyman's* priority was a Fleming, H. de Vocht, while it was an Englishman, E.R. Tigg, who finally proved that *Elckerlyc* must have been the original play. Tigg[1] closely examined the rhymes of both plays and found that in many cases the rhymes of *Elckerlyc* are present within the lines of the English play, followed by a more or less meaningless tag. In other words, the English poet translated quite literally and then had to add a few words in order to rhyme:

Wilt mi vergheven mijn *mesdade,*
Want ic begheer aen u *ghenade.*

Forgyve me my grevous *offence*
Here I crye the *mercy* in this presence.

Hier in desen aertschen *leven*
Die heylighe sacramenten *seven.*

Here in this transitory *lyfe* for the and me
The blessed sacraments *seven* there be

In the morality plays the didactic usually dominated the theatrical: they appealed to the intellect rather than to the eye.In this respect *Elckerlyc* is no exception. Right through the play the emphasis is on the text, on the spoken word rather than on the action. In its allegorical form, its choice of words and occasional complexity—as in the double rondeau towards the end—*Elckerlyc* is clearly the work of a *Rederijker,* but of a moderate who preferred a simple and

[1] 'Is *Elckerlyc* prior to *Everyman?' Journal of English and Germanic Philology* 1939, pp 568-96.

sober style to superficial brilliance. We know his name as
Pieter van Diest, who must have been an inhabitant of the
province of Brabant but about whom we know nothing
further. The *Rederijker* literature of the fifteenth century was
still largely anonymous: when a work was awarded a prize,
as in the case of *Elckerlyc*, the prize went to the Chamber,
not to the author.

The success of *Elckerlyc* was great, not only in the Low
Countries, but also abroad, as can be seen from the many
translations and adaptations that were made of it. The
English translation was the first, and must have been made
shortly after the play was written, in any case before the end
of the fifteenth century. It remained popular in England up to
the Reformation. In 1536 it was translated into Latin as
Homulus, and this translation served as the basis for a freer
adaptation, also in Latin, made by Macropedius in 1539
under the title of *Hecastus,* which in its turn was translated
into German by Hans Sachs about ten years later. In
Macropedius's adaptation Everyman is no longer saved by
Virtue as in the original version, but by Faith and
Repentance, so that the character of the play began to
change and Protestant tendencies were becoming obvious.
These tendencies did not pass unnoticed and in the preface
to a later edition of *Hecastus,* Macropedius had to defend
himself against accusations of heresy. At the same time the
play began to lose its allegorical aspect. The main character
in Macropedius's version is not so much 'everyman' as 'a
rich citizen'. The transformation of the allegorical figure into
a realist character was completed by Hugo von Hofmannsthal with his play *Jedermann* (1911) based on the English
Everyman and the version of Hans Sachs.

The miracle plays were more theatrical than the moralities; there was more action in them, more scene-shifting and
more pageantry. The best example of the miracle play in
Dutch is *Mariken van Nimweghen* (Mary of Nimeguen),
commonly regarded as the masterpiece of medieval drama in
the Low Countries. The central figure in this play is a young

girl who lives in a village three miles out of Nimeguen with her uncle, the village priest. She goes shopping in Nimeguen, but when she is about to return, she finds that it is late and she decides to spend the night with an aunt who lives in the town. When she asks for shelter for the night, the aunt brutally insults and abuses her. In utter despair Mariken walks out of the town, sits down by the road side, crying for help from 'God or Devil, it is all the same to me'. Out of nowhere appears a one-eyed man who promises to make her rich and famous and to teach her the seven liberal arts if she will come along with him. Although Mariken realizes who he is, she agrees: even Lucifer himself would not frighten her in her present frame of mind, she says. So she becomes the devil's pupil and mistress, and together they travel through the country. They settle down in Antwerp where the devil reaps a rich harvest of souls from the many unfortunates who are killed in brawls about Mariken. After some years Mariken insists that they go back to Nimeguen. There they witness a wagon-play in which it is shown that even the most wicked sinner may be saved if he is sincerely repentant. This proves the turning point for Mariken and she rejects the devil. But he, fearing that her soul will escape him, tries to kill her: he takes her high up into the air and flings her down to the ground. Mariken lives, however, and is found by her uncle. He takes her to the Pope as the only man who could absolve her sins. The Pope gives her three iron rings, to be forged around her neck and arms: if the rings fall off, her sins will be forgiven. After many years of penance in a convent, the miracle happens.

Although *Mariken van Nimweghen* is a religious play it has much of the raciness of realist drama, as for instance in the scene in which Mariken is chased away by her aunt, or in the dialogue between the aunt and the uncle, or in the elaborate inn-scene in Antwerp in which we are shown the kind of life Mariken and the devil are leading. Moreover, the play is not written in the elevated style of *Elckerlyc*, but in a much faster moving, far more colloquial and very uninhibited idiom. The *Rederijkers* touch is clearly recognizable in the frequent double and internal rhymes, and in some intricate stanza forms. But the author was not suffering from any obsession with form for form's sake as some of his contemporaries were. On the contrary, he must have been one of the first *Rederijkers* to use form in a significant manner. He saved his most complicated piece of prosody— a richly dressed up refrain—for a moment when such a form was really necessary: in the inn-scene, when Mariken, accomplished in the liberal arts, recites a eulogy of rhetoric. Another example of his ability to use form in a meaningful way is to be found in his use of the rondeau. He used it twice, both times in dialogue, and in both cases the form adds to the expressiveness of the scene: in the first instance the recurring lines underscore the incredulity of the uncle when the aunt tells him that Mariken had been drunk when she came to her house, in the second rondeau they bring out the hypocrisy of the devil. Apart from this sophisticated use of form, the author of *Mariken* was also a first-rate dramatist with a keen sense of how to keep his play moving and how to obtain optimal effects. Memorable in this connection is the wagon-play scene. At the very moment of a dramatic climax—Mariken's rejection of the devil—the author compels the audience to identify themselves with Mariken through the mirror-effect of the play within a play. His psychological motivation was also far more elaborate than that of his predecessors in the field of drama. For his subject-material he probably drew upon the many devil-and-witch stories that were current at that time. The end of the fifteenth century was a period in which the fear of witches was beginning to become epidemic. The Low Countries were mercifully free from witch-hunting on a large scale but not unaware of what was going on: in 1460 several witches were burned in Atrecht, in 1484 Pope Innocentius VIII issued his bull against witches and appointed two Dominicans as special inquisitors who two years later published their gruesome findings and recommendations in *Malleus Malifi-*

carum (The Witch Hammer), the most notorious anti-witch book ever written. In this atmosphere the play of Mariken must have been topical. Mariken, after all, is a kind of witch, a girl who gives herself to the devil in exchange for wealth and knowledge. Several details in the play help to create the atmosphere of witch and witchcraft: the devil refuses to teach Mariken necromancy as she would then become his equal, he forbids her to cross herself and orders her to drop her name since the name of Mary would make it impossible for him to exercise full power over her (she is allowed to keep the first letter, M, and calls herself Emmeken). It speaks highly for the author that he made no concession to the witch-hysteria and simply presented his character as an innocent girl who in a moment of weakness and great vulnerability enters into an agreement with the devil and extricates herself from it through her faith and repentance. Right through the play, his sympathy, and that of his audience, remains with Mariken.

One of the most remarkable aspects of *Mariken van Nimweghen* is its realism, in a period when plays were often completely allegorical or at least contained some allegorical features. From the first page to the last, the author binds his play to time and place. In the prologue he tells that Mariken lived at the time when Duke Arend of Guelders was imprisoned by his son Duke Adolf. What is more, he uses this not simply as an indication of time, but presents the imprisonment as the incident that sparks off the action of the play: when Mariken knocks at her aunt's door, the aunt has just had a violent argument about these two dukes with some of her neighbours, and in her excitement she bursts out against Mariken, causing her to fall for the devil. Later on in the play the motif of the misery of political passions is taken up again when the aunt commits suicide after hearing that the old duke has escaped from prison. Realism pervades the whole play and all its characters. It is present in small details, as in the opening scene when Mariken's uncle gives her eightpence to buy candles, oil, vinegar, salt, onions, and sulphur-matches; it is also present in the representation of the devil, who on the one hand combines several features of the devil as we know him from medieval literature, but who at the same time must have been recognizable to the audience as one of the numerous clever-but-seedy wandering students and scholars. The realism is so marked that although the play is basically a dramatized account of a miracle, it has also been called the first realist drama.

This realism, always one of the strong suits of Dutch literature, is also found in other miracle plays, but never to the same extent. *Het Spel vanden Heilighen Sacramente vander Nyeuwervaert* (The Play of the Holy Sacrament of Nieuwervaart) is also bound to a specific time and place, and also contains some realistic scenes, but it does not give the same picture of every-day life as *Mariken van Nimweghen* does, nor does it give a representation of predominantly 'round' characters. Significant in this respect are the two devils who keep up a lively enough dialogue and who every now and then take part in the action, but who are allegorical figures, presented under the allegorical names of 'Sinful Temptation' and 'Prevention of Virtue' and who to the modern observer are far removed from the realism of Mariken's devil. The main function of the devils in this and other plays was to provide comic relief, as the author of the play of *Nyeuwervaert* says himself in the prologue: 'We have put in devilry on purpose in order to prevent any heavy seriousness'. Medieval plays, however religious they may have been, very often mixed the serious content with broad comedy. The English mystery plays of the same period, the Towneley plays for instance, do exactly the same. In the English plays, as in the Dutch ones, the comedy part has the greatest appeal to the modern reader, probably because the author could let himself go more and was not bound to his source, whether it was the Bible or a chronicle, as in the case of the play of *Nyeuwervaert*.

Comic pairs such as the devils in *Nyeuwervaert* became an integral part of the later plays, and developed gradually from quarrelling and squabbling minor characters into important symbolical figures, personifying human qualities, usually defects of character, vices, passions, stupidities. The fact that they never appear by themselves in a play, but always at least in pairs, sets them aside from the allegorical figures in the French and English plays of the same period and gives the Dutch plays a character of their own. In the later plays their function was not only to provide comic relief, but there they often determine the action of the play, and by expressing approval or disapproval, comment on the action, not unlike the chorus in the classical play. This development, too, is typical of the Dutch plays.

Allegorical figures are also present in the mystery plays, which on the whole are older than the moralities and miracle plays, and which dramatize scenes from the Bible. They are not very fully represented in Dutch, but we know that there used to be more than we have now. There must have existed a cycle of seven plays celebrating the Joys of Mary, but only the first and the last have been preserved. When exactly they were written is uncertain, but we do know that they were performed, one every year, in Brussels in the years between 1448 and 1455. The *Eerste Bliscap van Maria* (First Joy of Mary) describes Mary's life up to the Annunciation, the Seventh Joy begins after the Ascension and deals with Mary's last days and her death. The two plays may have been written by the same author, but if this is so, his technique, particularly his sense of composition, must have developed considerably between the first and the last play.

There is still much uncertainty about the way in which these plays were performed. As a rule performances took place in the open air, on a stage which grew in the course of time from a simple platform into the complicated structures that were used in the sixteenth century. Stage directions are very rare in medieval plays; the four *abele spelen* together contain only one, the laconic 'here they hang Robert'. One of the mystery plays is a little more generous with stage directions and from those we can form some idea of how plays of this kind were staged. The play is called *Spel van de V Vroede ende van de V Dwaeze Maegden* (Play of the Five Wise and the Five Foolish Virgins) and deals with a subject from the Bible that was also dramatized in France and Germany. The conception of the play is allegorical: the virgins bear names such as Hope, Fear, Vain Glory and are simply personifications of human characteristics. In this respect the play is not of any special importance although it has distinct dramatic qualities. But it is unique because of its stage directions from which we may conclude that the days of the simple stage were over. It seems that a heaven was built in the middle of the stage, with a hell behind it; both could be opened and closed, probably with curtains. In between the two there may have been water, as mention is made of crossing over by boat. On either side of the stage were five cubicles ('little houses' they are called in the text) for the virgins. We also learn from the stage directions that music was played during the intervals and that songs were sung as part of the performance.

All these plays were still largely anonymous. We do not know the author of the play of the Virgins, nor do we know who wrote the Joys of Mary. We know the name of the author of *Elckerlyc* but our knowledge of the man ends with his name. Even the author of *Mariken van Nimweghen* is not known by name; all we know about him is that he probably was an Antwerp *Rederijker*. The play of *Nyeuwervaert* may have been written by a certain Jan Smeken, but there is no certainty about this and some scholars regard Smeken merely as the copyist of the manuscript. Even when we know the name of an author, we never come to know him in his entire literary production, but only in the one or two works that were more or less accidentally preserved. Anonymity prevailed throughout the fifteenth century, and the *Rederijkers* of that period had no ambition beyond it. They did not strive for any personal fame, but only for that of the Chamber of Rhetoric to which they belonged. Their art was collective, not yet individual. Not only the plays were anonymous, but also the many secular and religious songs which were written in this century and of which a great variety has been preserved: love songs, drinking songs, ballads and romances, some historical songs, songs for Christmas and Easter, many hymns of praise for Mary and Jesus. They have been handed down in manuscripts and also in some sixteenth-century prints, the most important of which are *Een Devoot ende Profitelijck Boecxken* (A Devout and Useful Book) of 1539, for the religious songs, and the so-called *Antwerpse Liedboek* (Antwerp Song Book) of 1544, for secular songs. There were, however, some exceptions to the general rule of anonymity. One of them was Anthonis de Roovere, a *Rederijker* from Bruges, another was Dirc Potter, a non-*Rederijker* and civil servant from The Hague.

Anthonis de Roovere was born between 1430 and 1435, and died in 1482. He must have been a precocious poet, for when he was seventeen years old the Chamber at Bruges conferred on him the title of Prince of Rhetoric. He became famous, at least locally, and the city of Bruges honoured him with a small annuity, which he probably needed for it seems that he was not well off. In the city records he is mentioned as a bricklayer, and although some scholars have tried to elevate him to the rank of builder or architect, the indications are that his social circumstances were humble. From his poetry one forms the impression that he was an embittered and thoroughly disillusioned man. It has been suggested that he had expected more recognition than was actually given, and one is tempted to draw the conclusion that he was one of the first poets who were no longer content to write for the honour of the Chamber but who wanted a larger measure of individual fame. De Roovere did not state this explicitly in his poetry; on the contrary, he assailed all power and glory, and wrote many satires in which he elaborated on the transitoriness of all worldly vanities. But his satire had such an unusually personal undertone of bitterness that some kind of personal disappointment must be at the bottom of it. 'He who in these days wants to succeed in the world', he wrote in one rondeau, 'must know the tricks'. And in another: 'He who wants to make his way in the world will have to run with the hare and hunt with the hounds'. In one of his satires—one that looks very much like being the immediate reflection of a particularly cruel disillusionment—he wrote: 'Now I no longer believe anyone'. This personal tone makes his work stand apart from the rank and file of medieval poetry, even more so if the interpretation of his bitterness as due to lack of recognition is correct.

On the whole his work is undeniably medieval, but there are some elements of newness in it which seem to foreshadow the Renaissance. One of his most remarkable, though not one of his best poems, describes a dream, *The Dream of De Roovere about the Death of Duke Charles of Burgundy of Blessed Memory*. The fact that he put his name in the title instead of masking it in an acrostic at the end, as was customary, almost proclaims the growing sense of individuality. The poet dreams that he walks through a cemetery in which the heroes of the past are buried. In addition to names from Biblical history, he also mentions classical and mythological names: Nestor, Aeneas, Alexander, Troilus, Caesar, Hector, Paris. The poet is then taken away from the cemetery by Compassion and is conducted to St. Salvator's at Bruges to watch Charles's funeral. Three allegorical figures, Clergy, Nobility and Commonalty, lament Charles's death. They evoke him as the protector of the Church, as the splendid hero, and the upholder of law and order. Compassion tries to console the poet and to reconcile him with his loss, not with the traditional notion of *sub specie aeternitatis*, as one would have expected, but by pointing out that Charles will gain immortality through his fame—a typical Renaissance notion. One cannot say that the Dutch Renaissance begins with De Roovere, but one can see that it will begin soon.

De Roovere's work has come to us in an edition put together in 1562, that is eighty years after his death, by Eduard de Dene, also a *Rederijker* from Bruges and a great admirer of De Roovere. De Dene's edition was a selection, not a complete edition, which means that the contents may reflect the preferences of the editor rather than those of the author. This may explain why there are so many religious poems, and, considering the popularity of the genre, so few erotic ones. We know that De Roovere made his name with a religious poem, *Lof van den Heylighen Sacramente* (Praise of the Holy Sacrament) which was accorded the high honour of being framed and hung in the cathedral of Bruges. Much of his religious poetry strikes us as contrived and arid, as if it were written without any inspiration or even enthusiasm at all. This applies in particular to his many Praises of Mary in which he employed all the tricks of the *Rederijker* trade: ABC poems of various kinds, retrogrades, and even a chessboard. To the modern reader he seems far more successful in his secular poetry, his satires and the few specimens of erotic poetry that have been preserved. His most impressive poem is *Vanden Mollenfeeste* (The Feast of the Moles), a poem that is related to the *dance macabre* which was so popular in the Burgundian period. All classes of people, each and everyone, are bidden underground to the King of the Moles. The satirical tone is subdued in this poem, yet one cannot help hearing a note of satisfaction in his description of how the noblemen, the clergy and the rich citizens, leaving behind their attics full of corn and their boxes full of money, will have to present themselves to the Mole, as well as in his advice to women to leave their finery at home, as the moles happen to be blind.

Although there were some Chambers of Rhetoric in the northern provinces at this time, the centre of *Rederijker* activity was in the South. All writings mentioned so far in this chapter were the works of southern poets, and all new ideas, all literary experiments and innovations originated from the South. The literature of the North was more conservative and closer to the fourteenth-century tradition than that of the southern provinces. There was no De Roovere in Holland, no one who experimented with language and form as he did, no one who admitted such a personal tone to his poetry. The best-known poet in Holland was Dirc Potter, who, it is true, was about sixty years older than De Roovere, but whose work, even when allowances are made for those sixty years, appears to be that of a straggler, not that of an innovator. In his approach to literature, Potter was closer to Willem van Hildegaersberch than to De Roovere. Yet, in contrast to De Roovere, Potter did not lack the opportunity to discover what was new in European literature, for he went on various missions abroad as an envoy of the Counts of Holland and even spent more than a year in Rome. In spite of this the Italian Renaissance completely by-passed him. There is no indication in his work that he followed Italian literature, he does not seem to have read anything by Dante, Petrarch or Boccaccio, nor is there any suggestion that he noticed any other aspect of Renaissance art. All he had to say about Italians was that they were 'dirty dogs' who lived in sin, beat their wives and were only capable of savagery, treason, lies and robbery. It is curious that a man like De Roovere, who so far as we know had no links with Italy, was closer to the Renaissance than Dirc Potter who for some time lived in the midst of it.

Potter's main work was a long poem in four parts, *Der Minnen Loep* (The Course of Love). It is a poem that belongs to the same family as John Gower's *Confessio Amantis,* written about thirty years earlier. It is also related, but more distantly, to the *Decameron* and the *Canterbury Tales,* although Potter had probably never heard of any of these books. Like Gower's poem, *Der Minnen Loep* is a compilation of stories illustrating various aspects of love. The first part deals with what he calls 'silly love', passionate love unchecked by reason, demonstrated by the case-histories of Jason and Medea, Paris and Helen, and others. Potter condemns this kind of love and shows that it always ends badly. In the second part he is concerned with 'good, pure love', by which he means courtly love free from the bonds of marriage, as found in the stories of Pyramis and

Thisbe, Tristan and Isolde. The third part is devoted to 'illicit love', illustrated by the exploits of wretches such as Pasiphae and Semiramis. This is the shortest book, not for lack of material, but because he feels that he should not be too generous with unsavoury detail. The fourth part finally brings him to married love — 'lawful love' he calls it — of which Penelope is the paragon. Potter's intention was obviously moralistic, but one hesitates to call him a didactic poet: he was really too much of an entertainer to be classified as such. He moralizes, of course, he quotes shattering examples of people who became involved in the wrong kind of love, but at the same time he relates their stories with great relish, and although there are certain things that he says are 'unspeakable', he rarely misses the opportunity to tell a good story. He is not free of a certain measure of hypocrisy and his moral yardstick is not always of the same length, but he deserves the credit of being a very entertaining story-teller. It seems that in later years Potter became aware of his ambivalent motives, for he gives the impression of being a little embarrassed, even ashamed, about *Der Minnen Loep*. In a prose book, *Blome der Doechden* (Flowers of Virtue), adapted from Gozzadini's *Fiore di virtu,* he apologized for the earlier poem and regretted the many untruths it contained, his excuse being that he was young when he wrote it.

Potter's prose—he also wrote a second prose book called *Mellibeus*—is entirely moralistic and didactic, as one would expect from a prose book at that time. Whoever wanted to entertain, to write fiction, or to give his work an artistic form, wrote poetry; prose was almost exclusively reserved for didactic purposes. Several prose writers of this period were associated with the *Devotio Moderna*. Hendrik Mande, 'the Ruusbroec of the North', was one of them, Gerlach Peters, author of the *Devote Epistele* (Devout Epistle) was another. The most famous among his contemporaries was the Franciscan Johannes Brugman (born about 1400) whose life in several respects ran parallel to that of Geert Groote: after years of study and a certain amount of high living, he suddenly turned over a new leaf and became an extremely successful popular preacher. His fame was so great that his name still lives on in the expression 'praten als Brugman': to talk very eloquently and persuasively. As an author he is known for his prose book *Leven van Jezus,* and two songs. In the first half of the fifteenth century Dirc van Delft, the first doctor of theology in Holland, wrote a long treatise *Tafel van den Kersten Ghelove* (Table of the Christian Faith), a book that was widely read at the time. Secular didactic prose was represented by an adaptation of the medieval classic *Ludus Scaccorum,* an allegory in which chess-men symbolize the various layers of society. It inspired a certain Jan van den Bergh to write a book in the same vein, *Dat Kaetsspel Ghemoralizeert* (Moralized Hand-ball) in which a hand-ball game is used to describe the rights and wrongs of juridical procedure.

All these authors were competent prose writers who were able to set out clearly what they wanted to say and who helped to shape prose in its infancy. Yet for none of them could a claim of exceptional literary talent be made. The honour of being the most genuine literary talent among the prose writers of this period should go to Sister Bertken, whose work has imaginative touches that make it stand out from the average prose of the time. She was the daughter of an Utrecht priest and she lived for several years as a nun in one of the convents of the Windesheim chapter. Then she decided to withdraw even further from the world and asked for permission to be locked in a cell attached to one of the churches of Utrecht. This happened in 1456 or 1457, and Sister Bertken stayed in her cell until her death, fifty-seven years later, submitting herself to a rigorous regime which forbade meat, butter, and cheese as well as shoes and heating, while the keys to her cell were kept in safe custody by the prior of a nearby monastery. Her literary output was not very large: all that literature gained from those fifty-seven years of seclusion were two short prose books and a few songs. It is a great pity that she did not write more, for the literary value of this small quantity of writing is greater than that of many large prose books. One should not expect from her any very profound or original thought; Bertken was not an original thinker as Ruusbroec was, nor was she a poet of the calibre of Hadewych. Her religious world was simple and so was her representation of it; the cliché of 'charming medieval simplicity' might have been coined to describe her work. In a way her work is didactic, written in the form of treatises, but it may never have been intended for an audience larger than herself: it was quite customary for nuns and monks to write this kind of book only for their own edification, as an aid to contemplation. Bertken's first book describes and discusses the most important events in the life of Christ, the second book contains prayers, a description of the birth of Christ, a dialogue between Bridegroom Jesus and the Loving Soul, and eight songs. What gives her work its special literary value is her eye for vivid detail and her ability to think herself into a situation and to enter into the feelings of the persons whom she writes about. This approach made her account of the birth of Christ almost that of an eye-witness and certainly one of the best pieces of prose writing of the fifteenth century. Little though she wrote, she was undoubtedly a born writer.

Bertken's poetry is characterized by the same simplicity as her prose, but it is more clearly mystical in its symbolism and imagery. Her feeling for form was obviously not very developed, but what her poetry lacks in art, it gains through artlessness:

> I went to pick herbs in my garden
> But I found only thistles and thorns.
>
> The thistles and thorns I threw out,
> I should like to grow other plants.
>
> Now I have found a good gardener:
> He will like to take over my cares.

A tree grew tall in very short time;
I could not take it out of the earth.

He was aware of this troublesome tree:
He pulled it out with root and branch.

Now I must be his servant,
Or he will not care for my garden.

In the last quarter of the fifteenth century prose writing was greatly boosted by the invention of the printing press which revolutionized book production. The price of books came down and the demand increased rapidly, particularly the demand for literature of entertainment. And, curiously enough, the demand then seems to have been for prose in preference to poetry. Admittedly, there were some poems among the early printed editions—the very popular *Karel ende Elegast* was one of them—but they were completely outnumbered by prose books. This was an important development, for although none of these prose books was an original work of fiction, and although it would be a long time before anything comparable to our modern novel appeared, these books were the first indications that prose was swinging away from its exclusively didactic tradition. The majority of these books were prose versions of the romances of chivalry, sometimes adapted from the Dutch poems, in other cases from French or German prose books. Before the middle of the sixteenth century the greater part of the epic romances had been treated and published in this way. The Frankish romances were represented by *De Historie van de Vier Heemskinderen* (The History of Haymijn's Four Children), an adaptation of *Renout van Montalbaen* printed about 1490; the classical ones were represented by a history of Alexander and one of the Trojan war, and the eastern ones by the Parthenopeus story and *De Historie van Floris ende Blancefloer*. A curious omission in this series are the British romances for which there seems to have been no demand, in contrast to the situation in France and England where they are well represented among the early printed prose books. One of the earliest printed books in Dutch was *De Historie van Reinaert de Vos*, printed in the 1470s, and translated into English by William Caxton as *The Historye of Reynart the Foxe*. The most successful of them all was *De Reis van Jan van Mandeville*, printed before 1470, as a translation of Jean de Bourgogne's famous mystification which became also a spectacular success in England under the title of *The Travels of Sir John Mandeville*. In the Low Countries the book went through more than twenty editions and was still in print in the eighteenth century.

IV

REFORMERS AND HUMANISTS

SIXTEENTH CENTURY

In the history of Dutch literature the sixteenth century is usually regarded as a period of transition in which the medieval conceptions gradually receded into the background and made way for those of the modern era. The term 'period of transition' is, of course, a facile one: from any given vantage point in time one can look down on a preceding period and regard it as a period of transition, pointing to the first appearance of certain phenomena of which one already knows the fully mature stage. But certain periods are characterized by particularly rapid and radical changes, and the sixteenth century in Dutch literature is undoubtedly one of those. The changes that took place are usually accounted for by that trinity of terms: Humanism, Renaissance and Reformation. These three factors, whether one regards them as an indivisible unity or as three separate movements, brought about a series of changes in the literature so far-reaching that the term period of transition is fully justified. These changes were on the whole international, and the change of direction which Dutch literature took was due to influence from outside. But apart from this, the direction of Dutch literature was also affected by an internal development: as a result of the war against Spain the centre of gravity of Dutch literature shifted from the southern to the northern provinces, and then stayed there. The province of Holland became the cultural as well as the economic and political centre of the Low Countries, and from the end of the sixteenth century onwards the most important writers lived in Holland. In view of all this one cannot object to a characterization of the sixteenth century as an age of transition, but the proviso must be added that no value-judgment is implied. It is true, the sixteenth century did not produce writers of the calibre of Vondel, Hooft, Bredero and Huygens, but it would be wrong to demote the sixteenth-century writers automatically to the status of fore-runners of the great writers of the seventeenth century. Their achievements are more satisfactorily, and more justly, assessed in terms of what they themselves accomplished than in terms of what the later writers made of their achievements.

Generalizing and dramatizing a little, one can say that medieval literature in the Low Countries came to an end with the development of the printing press. The works that reached print were multiplied in more copies than had been possible for any previous work, so that the preservation rate rose tremendously and the literature that has come to us no longer seems a collection of works that by some good chance have been preserved, but presents itself under the new aspect of a collection of *oeuvres* of individual writers. We begin to know more names in literature and the names are no longer just labels stuck on to one or two works, but behind the names we begin to see the writers. This did not happen overnight, the emergence of the writer from behind his work was a slow process. The early sixteenth-century *Rederijkers* certainly did not rush into print any more than Anthonis de Roovere did. The first printed volume of *Rederijker* poetry, a collection made by the Antwerp printer and publisher Jan van Doesborch, appeared between 1528 and 1530. Another large collection, put together by Jan van Stijevoort in 1524, remained in manuscript until the twentieth century. A good example of delayed publication is also the play *Spiegel der Minnen* (Mirror of Love) by Colijn van Rijssele, a *Rederijker* from Brussels. We know that this play, which has the distinction of being one of the earliest bourgeois dramas in European literature, had gained considerable fame before 1530, but it was published as late as 1561, and not by its

author but by Dirck Coornhert. The situation was characterized by the publisher of the book that was perhaps the most
famous *Rederijker* work of the sixteenth century, Matthijs de
Castelein's *De Const van Rhetoriken* (The Art of Rhetoric).
The book was finished in 1548 and published in 1555, that is
five years after the death of its author. In his preface the
publisher lamented the fact that so many poets did not
publish their work but left it in manuscript because they
regarded publication as a show of too much personal
ambition. Not all writers suffered from the same inhibition:
we know that Erasmus—who was about twenty years older
than Matthijs de Castelein—sent his manuscripts to the
printer as soon as the ink was dry. But Erasmus was the
exception rather than the rule; in his dealings with
publishers, with whom he negotiated fees and royalties, he
was about two hundred years ahead of his time. The rank
and file of the sixteenth-century writers published only hesi-
tantly, as they did in England, where neither Thomas Wyatt,
nor Philip Sidney, nor Surrey published anything in their
lifetimes.

The remarks made in the preface to *De Const van
Rhetoriken* are particularly telling as they were not prompted
by the work of a run-of-the-mill author, but by that of one
of the most prominent poets of his time, a poet whose work
was widely known and praised sky-high by his contemporaries. The book in question was the first full-blown *ars
poetica* in Dutch, written at about the same time as the first
rhetorics in English appeared, such as Richard Sherry's *A
Treatise of Schemes and Tropes* of 1550 and Thomas
Wilson's *The Arte of Rhetorique* of 1553. De Castelein's
book is different from Wilson's as it is mainly concerned
with poetic form whereas Wilson gives a systematic and
Ciceronian treatise on oratory[1], yet there are points of
contact between the two works as for instance in Wilson's

[1] When the *Rederijkers* use the word rhetoric they usually mean
poetry rather oratory.

sally against 'ynkepot termes' and De Castelein's call for a
pure and simple language. De Castelein would not have
approved of Wilson's book, had he known it, because it was
written in prose. That was also his main objection to *L'Art
de Rhétorique* by the Walloon Jean Molinet: by writing in
prose, he says, Molinet had degraded his noble art, and he
even advances Molinet's aberration as one of the reasons
why he wrote his own book. And then in verse. Deficiency in
the work of De Roovere was put forward as another reason,
although he did not specify in what respect De Roovere had
failed. Thirdly, he wrote his book as a protest against the
deterioration in the standards of poetry, against 'the idiots
who with unwashed hands tear the clothes of Rhetoric'.

In spite of this criticism, De Castelein leant heavily on
both De Roovere and Molinet whom he regarded after all as
the masters. Writers of *artes poeticae* are naturally inclined
to be conservative, to be more concerned with the *status quo*
in poetry than with the advancement of new ideas, and De
Castelein was no exception. He discussed the various forms
in use at the time, in poetry and in drama, and from this
discussion we come to know him as a middle-of-the-road
Rederijker who had no love for excessively intricate ballads
and refrains or for an over-ornate language. So far as the
new developments in rhyme and metre were concerned he
was sitting on the fence. Rhymes have to be pure, he does
not accept assonance as rhyme, but on the other hand he is
not in favour of extending rhyme into syllable rhyme, nor
does he approve of a regular alternation of masculine and
feminine rhymes as the French *rhétoriqueurs* advocated: 'I
do not anticipate that the Flemings will observe this; each
country should keep to its own style'. As to the question of
isosyllabism, De Castelein's opinion was that rhyming lines
should have the same number of feet, but he had no
objection to the varying length of non-rhyming lines,
provided that no line should ever be longer than fifteen
syllables which he regarded as the maximum that could be
recited in one breath (implying that one should never pause

to take breath within the one line).

Although De Castelein's approach was predominantly traditional, there are certain aspects of his work which show him to have been strongly influenced by Humanist ideas. All our knowledge, he wrote, has come to us through the pens of the classical writers, particularly the Greeks, who have explored the sciences and who have taught us how to write comedies, tragedies and epics. To the Latin writers, especially Martial, Horace and Virgil, we are indebted for the construction of the line and the stanza. He even made an attempt, though rather a weak one, to link up the poetic forms of the *Rederijkers* with those of the Greek and Latin writers. The thread running through his argument is that for the writers of his own day the study of classical literature is imperative. All this was largely theory, for although it is clear that he was well acquainted with the many classical authors whom he discussed, it is hard to see what positive contribution they made to his own poetry, apart from a greater than usual number of references to classical history and mythology. As a creative writer he stayed close to tradition, the themes of his poetry and the forms he used were the traditional *Rederijker* ones, very similar to the poetry contained e.g. in the Antwerp Song Book of 1544. Whatever the praise of his contemporaries, he does not strike us now as an exceptional poet, merely as a competent one, who in spite of his being a priest seemed more at ease in his love poetry than in his religious work which is often wooden and artificial. But he must be given the credit for having been the first *Rederijker* to state the Humanist view which expected great things from a return to the classics and made classical antiquity the norm for the new phase of western European literature. This does not mean, of course, that this was the first time that these ideas were expressed in the Low Countries, it only means that they were expressed for the first time in the vernacular literature. Erasmus had shown the way many years earlier in his own works and in his editions of the classics. But Erasmus wrote in Latin and had no great faith in the vernacular. In his *Ecclesiastes,* published towards the end of his life in 1535, he said that he accepted the word of his friends that there were works of literature in the vernacular which were not inferior to works in Latin, but that was as far as he was prepared to go. His attitude to the vernacular as a vehicle for literature was perhaps not one of contempt, rather one of tolerance, but decidedly not one of enthusiasm. He never contemplated stopping writing in the international language, for that would have severely restricted his audience and at the same time would have laid him further open to criticism from the Church, which always considered new ideas more dangerous when they were expressed in the vernacular. Most other Dutch Humanists shared Erasmus's view and wrote in Latin, with the result that it was some time before the Humanist ideas began to put their mark on the literature in Dutch.

Latin Humanist literature, on the other hand, flourished in the Low Countries in the first half of the sixteenth century. Erasmus quickly became the most authoritative voice of Humanism and the tremendous influence which his scholarship and his ideas had on the Humanists all over Europe is so well-known that it hardly needs to be discussed here. Writers of the Low Countries also played an important part in the development of Latin school drama. Willem de Volder of The Hague, who wrote under the name of Gnapheus, was one of the founders of this genre and gained an international reputation with *Acolastus* (1529), a dramatization of the parable of the prodigal son, a favourite theme in the sixteenth century. *Acolastus* was translated into English in 1540 and gave rise to a whole series of 'Prodigal Son' plays, including George Gascoigne's *Glass of Government* of 1575. A German translation of *Acolastus* by George Binder appeared in 1535, and an imitation by Jörg Wickram in 1540. George van Langveldt, a headmaster at Utrecht, who latinized his name to Macropedius, became known through his Latin *Elckerlijc* adaptation *(Hecastus)* and through a considerable number of satirical and Biblical plays in Latin

(Aluta, Andrisca, Adamus, Josephus) which also found response in Germany and England.

Latin Humanist poetry, which began in the second half of the fifteenth century with Petrus Burrus of Bruges, reached a peak in the sixteenth century with the work of Janus Secundus, born in The Hague in 1511. As a poet Janus Secundus was one of the child prodigies of which the Renaissance period seems to have had the secret. He began to write when he was fourteen years old and celebrated the Ladies' Peace of Cambrai with a *Hymnus* before he had turned eighteen.

Between this year and the year of his death at the age of twenty-five he wrote a great deal, including three volumes of elegies, a volume of epigrams, a volume of odes, verse epistles, diaries of his travels, and the magnificent volume of amatory poetry *Basia* (published after his death in 1539) on which rests his fame of being far and away the best of the Neo-Latin poets. What distinguished Secundus from the other Neo-Latinists was the personal tone of his poetry. He was not just an imitator who borrowed both the form and the feelings of the classical writers, but a poet who really gave himself in his work and who expressed emotions that were entirely his own. This was one of the reasons why his poetry made such an impact on the group of Pléiade poets in France who in the 1550s and 1560s were very consciously striving to create a truly personal lyrical verse. They recognized Secundus as the great innovator of poetry and at least five of the original Pléiade group—Ronsard, Belleau, de Baïf, du Bellay and Dorat—translated from his work. He was also followed and imitated by several Neo-Latinists: Muret in France, Buchanan in Scotland, Douza and Daniël Heinsius in Holland, to mention only a few. His influence on Dutch literature was not immediately apparent. In the early sixteenth century the gap separating the vernacular literature from the poetry in Latin was probably too wide to allow of much interplay. For some time these literatures existed side by side, or perhaps on top of one another, with very little influence from the Neo-Latinists on those who wrote in Dutch, and even less in the other direction, for there is little doubt that the sixteenth-century intelligentsia had a higher regard for the Neo-Latinists than for the vernacular poets. Yet the poetry of Secundus did contribute to the development of Dutch poetry, as it did to the development of poetry in German, French and English, but in a roundabout way. After the middle of the sixteenth century, when the poets of the Pléiade, and notably Ronsard, began to exercise a strong influence, several features which were originally part of Secundus's innovations found their way back to the Low Countries.

In general, the *Rederijker* poetry published before the middle of the sixteenth century showed no awareness of the achievements of the Neo-Latin poets. The *Rederijkers* of that period were traditionalists whose aesthetic ideas did not go beyond the conceptions of De Roovere and De Castelein. Only the influence of Erasmus was ubiquitous. His work was well-known in *Rederijker* circles and from 1523 onwards much of it was translated into Dutch by *Rederijker* writers. The playwright Cornelis Everaert of Bruges showed distinct affinities with the ideas of Erasmus in his views on war and peace, his criticism of the Church, his antipathy to Luther, in his satirical and critical attitude which stopped short of forcing a break. Another playwright and poet, Cornelis Crul, translated some of Erasmus's *Colloquia*. It was through Erasmus that the ideas of church reformation became known in *Rederijker* circles and several poets, like Crul and Everaert, wrote in the Erasmian spirit of reformation within the Church. But others went further and opted for Luther. In the 1520s and 1530s Lutheranism in the Chambers of Rhetoric had become so strong that the authorities, who up to that time had always morally and financially supported the Chambers, began to take measures against them. In Leiden a ban on stage performances was imposed, in Amsterdam several *Rederijkers* were ordered on a pilgrimage to Rome, in several places censorship of plays was

established, and in Antwerp a regulation was brought in
prohibiting non-Roman Catholics from being members of the
Chamber. Antwerp, with its many publishers and printers,
was one of the strongest centres of Humanism and
Reformation, and it was in Antwerp that some of the first
heavy blows fell: in 1523 two monks from the Antwerp
Augustin monastery were burnt at the stake in Brussels, a
few years later another monk was burnt alive, three printers
of heretical material were beheaded, the Humanist town-
clerk Grapheus—a friend of Albrecht Dürer's—was arrested and could only save his life by publicly recanting his
heresies. Another of the early victims was the English Bible
translator William Tyndale, who actually enjoyed a measure
of protection in Antwerp but who was arrested when he left
the city and was executed in Brussels in 1536. With the
Reformation represented so strongly in Antwerp, it is
perhaps not surprising that the loudest anti-Lutheran voice
in literature was raised in the same city. It was the voice of
Anna Bijns, a poet and school-teacher, and one of the last of
the traditional *Rederijkers*.

The poetry of Anna Bijns is almost entirely innocent of
the ideas of Humanism. She does refer to classical writers,
but she does it in such a stereotyped way and her references
read so much like echoes from medieval literature—
especially when she confounds Biblical history with mythology and classical history—that it does not seem likely that
she had studied them herself. She made her attitude to
Humanist study clear enough:

> What is the use of studying many books?
> What is the use of acquiring many goods
> Or of following in the skies
> The course of the stars and planets?
> What is the use of measuring the earth
> Or of learning many hidden secrets
> Through astronomy?

What she saw of the Renaissance she did not like either. She
berated the artists for painting nude portraits of Cupid,

Venus and Lucrece, and against the Renaissance glorification of the human body she placed her own view of it: 'Human figure, chalice of earth, mudlike bag of worms, created weakest of all'. Her whole attitude can be summed up in her own words: 'The old songs are the best'. And these she followed, violently rejecting anything that was new. Her poetry, published in three volumes between 1528 and 1567, encompasses the normal range of *Rederijker* verse: amatory, religious and comic refrains, and like so many of her colleagues she was at her most convincing in her love poems. Some of them celebrate almost ecstatically the joys of love, but most are in a minor key and lament a lost love, either real or fictitious. She extended the conventional range with her special brand of polemic verse, directed at Luther and his followers. Here her passionate temperament found an outlet and her attacks on Luther are so bitter, so personal, and so invariably below the belt that one has to restrain oneself from concluding that she was taking a frustrated love out on him. 'If sin is virtue, the Lutherans are saints' is one of her themes and she expands it through a whole spectrum of abuse. Luther is the devil incarnate, Lucifer's own pupil, who will finally receive the crown from his master as a reward for his destructiveness; he allows monks to marry nuns; he encourages people to live like dogs, nuns to become whores, monks pimps; the Lutherans talk big about the spirit, but the only thing they are interested in is the flesh; the Lutherans don't like sleeping alone and they borrow each other's wives even when they have one themselves: it is all a matter of common property; Luther's sect cannot bear virgins; there are rumours that Luther himself has a girl with whom he likes to play behind the curtains, and so on. No holds are barred when she sets upon Luther. Her fury makes her inventive and one cannot deny that several of her poems, in spite of the meagre content, acquire a certain stature through the very concentration of her fury. It would be too much to describe her as a great poet, but she occupies a special place in the history of literature, as it was her voice that sang the swan-song of medieval literature, for the most part eloquently, often melodiously, and at times strained to the point of breaking.

If Anna Bijns may be called the representative of the reactionary wing of the *Rederijkers,* Lucas de Heere represented the progressives. It was through his work that the poetic forms of the Renaissance were introduced into Dutch literature. Lucas de Heere was a painter as well as a poet. He was born in 1534, served his artist's apprenticeship with Frans Floris at Antwerp, then went to France where he stayed for some years. He was there in the 1550s, not too late to undergo the influence of Clément Marot, and in time to witness the clash between Marot's school and the new movement of Ronsard. There are several parallels between the work of Marot and that of De Heere, and with caution one might even call him the Dutch Marot. Like Marot, De Heere was a transitional figure, standing between the *Rederijkers* and the Renaissance poets. Both were rooted in tradition, experts in the old forms, yet both were closer to the new poetry than any of their predecessors. Neither was a great lyrical poet, yet both hold the distinction of having written the first sonnets in their own language. Lucas de Heere was the prototype of the trail-blazer. He was not a strong enough poet to put the stamp of his personality on the poetry that was coming, but he was intelligent and sentitive enough to see what was coming and enthusiastic enough to help it take shape.

In 1565 De Heere published his *Den Hof en Boomgaerd der Poesiën* (The Garden and Orchard of Poetry), a curiously hybrid volume containing poetry in the old *Rederijker* forms side by side with Renaissance forms such as sonnets, odes and epigrams. A large part of his work was modelled on Marot, whose social satire appealed to him and with whose Protestantism he was in sympathy (De Heere broke with the Roman Catholic Church in 1566). His love poetry, on the other hand, tended more towards Ronsard. He was well aware of his lack of originality and made no

attempt to mask it. In the dedication of his book he wrote
unequivocally that he was content to be 'a good imitator of
the other excellent poets', basing himself on the principle of
imitatio, which had also been warmly recommended by
Marot and du Bellay. De Heere only believed in imitating
the classics and the French poets, and firmly dissociated
himself from the older Dutch poetry 'which (to tell the truth
and with your permission) in many respects was too rough,
too clumsy and too undisciplined'. At the same time he was
as patriotically proud of his own language as befitted a
Renaissance poet, and, like du Bellay again, was critical of
the Neo-Latinists who had no regard for their mother
tongue. In a laudatory poem to Jan van der Noot's *Het
Theatre* he explicitly praised the author for having shown
that Dutch was in no way inferior to French, German,
Greek, Latin or Italian. The dedication of *Den Hof en
Boomgaerd der Poesiën* is also of interest for the technical
recommendations which De Heere makes there. He states
that he was careful to give each line of a poem a fixed
number of syllables, following the practice of the French
poets. This innovation, foreshadowed but not prescribed by
Matthijs de Castelein, and in fact not strictly adhered to by
De Heere himself, now became a permanent feature of
Dutch poetry, and would remain so until the end of the
nineteenth century. De Heere's favourite metre was the
alexandrine, which shortened the sometimes very long lines
of *Rederijker* poetry to twelve or thirteen syllables, but the
decasyllabic line also occurs frequently in his work. There is
no strict organization of his verse into the iambic metre yet,
and in many cases one finds the ten-syllable line, or even the
twelve-syllable line, combined with the old principle of the
four-beat line. In his rhymes De Heere used a much larger
number of masculine rhymes than the older *Rederijkers,* but
he no more committed himself to a regular alternation of
masculine and feminine rhymes than Marot or Ronsard had
done.

When De Heere went over to the Protestant Church, he

left the country and went to England. There he wrote a short prose book, *Corte Beschrijvinghe van Enghelant, Schotland en Irland* (Short Description of England, Scotland and Ireland), followed by a short history of England. It is a very readable account, written for the purpose of acquainting the Dutch with the English, with whom they had so many commercial contacts. The book never fulfilled its purpose, however, for it was not published and remained in manuscript until 1937! De Heere seems to have been unlucky with his manuscripts, for another book of his, a history of Flemish painting (which would have made him the first art-historian in the Low Countries), was also lost, and was never recovered in spite of a very extensive search. In England De Heere made the acquaintance of another exiled Dutch poet, Jan van der Noot, five or six years younger than he was, just as interested in the new poetry, but with a much stronger creative potential.

Jan van der Noot came from Antwerp and had become a Protestant in 1566. He fled the city a year later when the Spanish troops under the Duke of Alva approached to suppress the rebellion in the Low Countries, and when an attempt by the Antwerp Calvinists to take over the administration of the city had failed. Van der Noot belonged to the aristocracy and had been a member of the city council. If the Calvinist coup had been successful, he would have been appointed Margrave of Antwerp; under the circumstances he became an exile, lived for some years in England where he came into contact with Edmund Spenser, travelled through the Rhineland, visited Paris in 1578 where he claims to have met Ronsard and Dorat, and finally came back full circle to Antwerp and Roman Catholicism. In England Van der Noot published his first volume of poetry, *Het Theatre*, in 1568, and two or three years later his second volume *Het Bosken* (The Grove). The second volume contained his early poetry and its title, derived from Ronsard's *Le Bocage* which had appeared some fifteen years earlier, clearly indicated whom he considered the leader of

JAN VAN DER NOOT

the new poetry. It begins with two poems in the old
Rederijker style, then continues with some odes, sonnets,
epigrams, elegies and closes with religious poetry including
sixteen translations of Marot's psalms. *Het Theatre* has an
entirely different character and was written from a strongly
moralistic point of view. In the dedication, to the Lord
Mayor of London, Van der Noot presents the book as the
fruit of his exile which has made him conscious of the vanity
of all worldly matters. He now wants to put heart into the
Calvinists at home, to make them stand firm by convincing
them too of the worthlessness of the world. He does this in a
series of twenty-one poems, sonnets and epigrams, each
accompanied by an engraving. Only the last four sonnets are
originals, the other sonnets being translations of du Bellay
whereas the epigrams were translations of Petrarch. It is
actually not certain whether one should regard the book
primarily as a volume of poetry since the greater part of it is
taken up by a long treatise in prose which, as the author
says, was there to expand and elucidate the poetry.

One of the ambitions which Van der Noot shared with
most other Renaissance poets was to write a great epic, but,
like most other Renaissance poets—even Ronsard never
finished his *Franciade*—he was not equal to the task. The
history of Van der Noot's epic is particularly curious. It first
appeared in a German version under the title of *Das Buch
Extasis* (The Book Ecstasy), published in Cologne about
1576, and was then followed three years later by a bilingual
edition in Dutch and French, under the double title of *Cort
Begryp der XII Boecken Olympiados, Abrégé des Douze
Livres Olympiades* (Summary of the twelve books of the
Olympiad). The German version is the longest and seems to
have been translated from the French version which must
probably be regarded as the original, although Van der Noot
himself states that he wrote the Dutch version first. The
poem is cast as a dream in which the poet has to overcome
numerous obstacles before he can be united with his beloved
Olympia, the incarnation of virtue and beauty. As the title

indicates, neither the Dutch nor the French version was to be regarded as a finished epic; it seems that Van der Noot had intended to follow up the preliminary publication with a full epic of twelve cantos, which, however, remained unwritten.

From the two earlier volumes and the Olympia epics we come to know Jan van der Noot as the man who took Dutch Renaissance poetry well beyond the stage of experimentation. The forms and prosodic innovations which Lucas de Heere had recommended and tentatively applied were handled by Van der Noot with a remarkable sureness of touch, and although he may not have been the great poet that he himself and some nineteenth-century critics thought he was, and although much of his poetry pales when placed next to the work of Ronsard, he did instil the new forms with so much personal sentiment that he has full claim to a place which is more than just a historical one.

One of the characteristics which makes Van der Noot stand apart from all his predecessors is his tremendously high appreciation of the function of the poet and the hyperbolic terms in which he described his own literary value. Lucas de Heere had made no greater claim for himself than to be a 'good imitator', with a humility that was of the Humanist rather than of the Renaissance writer. Van der Noot was made of different stuff. Sir Philip Sidney may have regarded the poet as 'the monarch of all Sciences' and Edmund Spenser may have believed that heroes and famous poets were born together, they were moderates in comparison with Jan van der Noot. He firmly believed, or at least said he believed, that his poetry had the power to accord immortality. The idea itself was not new. We know it also from Ronsard who in one of his sonnets to Hélène promised her and himself a similar immortality (although there is in Ronsard's poem an elegiac undertone which softens the *superbia*). Van der Noot's assertions were much bolder and much more bare-faced. *Het Bosken* does not give much evidence of this attitude yet, apart from the fact that he included a considerable number of laudatory poems about himself, followed by his own replies. There may have been some justification for this, though, as his book did mean a break with the traditional poetry and he may have felt the necessity of having some poetic authorities acclaiming and supporting the newness of his work, in French, Latin and Spanish. The second volume, *Het Theatre*, was too much an abnegation of the world to allow much room for self-glorification and window-dressing; even so he managed to include some laudatory poems: Was there ever a poet equal to this one? asks Goossenius, and Lucas de Heere proclaims him 'the foremost of our poets'. But then, in a separately published poem *Lofsang van Braband* (Ode to Brabant), Van der Noot declared that he was to Brabant what Homer had been to the Greeks, Virgil to the Romans and Petrarch to the Tuscans, and that, if so desired, he would spread the fame of Brabant over the whole world for many hundreds of years to come. He reached an all-time high in a later poem, *Ode Tegen d'Onwetende Vyanden der Poëteryen* (Ode Against the Ignorant Enemies of Poetry), in which he again mentioned himself in one breath with Homer, Pindar, Virgil and Horace, then stated in passing that he wrote better poetry than any of his Dutch predecessors, and really got into his stride with the promise that he would carve his name in the temple of Fame and would become known over the whole world for all eternity, specifying the world this time as Germany, Denmark, Poland, Sweden, Bohemia, Switzerland, Burgundy, Spain, Scotland, Ireland, England, France, the Netherlands, Italy, Greece, Hungary and India. One may regard this as poetic *hybris* run wild, and it does, of course, look slightly ridiculous in retrospect, particularly when one knows that ten years after his death he was completely forgotten, even in the Low Countries, not to be rediscovered before the middle of the nineteenth century. But a poem such as this *Ode* should perhaps not simply be taken at its face value. The self-glorification of the poet was a common theme in the European poetry of that time, but who knows what personal experience of humiliation or frustration made

Van der Noot overstress it to such an extent and made him
create such a tremendous distance between himself and those
'ignorant enemies of poetry'.

Whatever the interpretation of Van der Noot's assertions,
so much is certain that he was one of the very first poets in
any vernacular language to aim consciously at an international
audience. That is clear from the way he published his Olympia
epics, it is clear from the bilingual French-Dutch publication
of Lofsang van Braband, and from the various efforts he
made to have his work translated: Het Theatre was first
translated into French, then into English—with the help
of young Edmund Spenser who was a teenager at that time,
and with a dedication to Queen Elizabeth—and a few years
later into German. Van der Noot's earnest endeavour was to
win social recognition for the poet in general, and for himself
in particular. His Lofsang van Braband is really nothing else
but an application to the provincial government of Brabant
for the imaginary position of official state poet: since the
state supports so many administrators, magistrates, council-
lors, bailiffs, burgomasters, treasurers, policemen, executioners
and soldiers, what harm would it do if it also supported a
nightingale, nay, a swan who would sing the praise of Brabant
in both Dutch and French? Brabant did not fall in with his
suggestion, and Van der Noot had to turn to private persons
for financial support. Much of his later poetry has a distinctly
mercenary ring, and is of little literary value. The poems often
follow the same pattern: in a few lines the poet describes his
prospective Maecenas and states the reasons for celebrating
his subject, and then in the last lines without any further ado
he declares him or her immortalized. These poems were
published in a kind of adaptable edition, entitled Poeticsche
Wercken (Poetic Works), which was made up for each buyer
individually in accordance with his personal taste, his political
and religious convictions, and, presumably, with what he was
prepared to spend. It is true that much of this later poetry
degenerated into beggary-in-disguise, it is also true that Van
der Noot habitually overplayed his hand, yet he still stands

as the first poet who was seriously concerned with the social function of poetry and the poet's place in society.

Jan van der Noot was a southerner, like Anna Bijns, Matthijs de Castelein and Lucas de Heere. Generally speaking, one can say that up to the middle of the sixteenth century the great majority of the writers came from the South. But this pattern changed. The South, which had always been much more culturally advanced than the North, lost its lead and slipped back into stagnation, whereas the North leapt ahead and took over the hegemony which it was not going to give up again.

It is always difficult to give simple and specific reasons for a cultural rise or decline. Political, intellectual and artistic freedom is probably one of the most important conditions for a flourishing civilization, economic prosperity is another. In the second half of the sixteenth century, and right through the seventeenth, these conditions obtained to a much higher degree in the North than in the South, owing mainly to the different courses which the revolt against Spain took. After the beginning of the revolt in the 1560s, Spanish troops gradually recovered the South, crowning their successes in 1585 with the capture of Antwerp. While the South was being reconquered, it was at the same time converted back to Roman Catholicism and cleaned up of Protestants: at first, under the Duke of Alva, with an iron fist and wholesale executions, later, under the Duke of Parma, with a little more subtlety when the Protestants were given the choice of exile. As a result many thousands of Protestants left the South in the 1580s and settled in the North. The exodus was tremendous: Ghent lost nine thousand families within a few years, Antwerp, which was hit particularly hard when the North closed the Scheldt, lost forty thousand inhabitants out of a population of a hundred thousand. This migration greatly strengthened the North culturally and economically as among the immigrants there were many scholars, scientists, merchants and manufacturers who brought in considerable intellectual and monetary capital. The parents of the

seventeenth-century poets Joost van den Vondel, Constantijn
Huygens and Daniel Heinsius were among them; others were
Simon Stevin, a writer, engineer, mathematician, physicist,
and close collaborator of the Stadtholder Maurits; Petrus
Plancius, the geographer who was the master-mind behind the
epic voyages seeking a northern route to the Indies in the
1590s; Marnix van St. Aldegonde, poet, translator of the Bible
and one of the most eloquent enemies the Roman Catholic
Church ever had; Carel van Mander, poet, painter and the first
Dutch art-historian; Louis de Geer, arms manufacturer, banker and royal money-lender; Lodewijk Elsevier, the publisher
who in 1580 moved his firm from Louvain to Leiden; Willem
Usselincx, one of the most powerful merchants and ship
owners. The departure of each of these men meant a serious
loss to the South, and a great asset to the development of
the North.

Also, after some initial victories, the Spanish troops suffered
serious set-backs in the North when they had to abandon the
sieges of Alkmaar and Leiden in 1573 and 1574. Later on,
the successful campaigns of Maurits in the 1580s and 1590s
resulted in an absolute stalemate along the great rivers. This
stalemate, and the frozen front line which was the result of
it, had far-reaching consequences, for it broke up the national
unity the Burgundians had been at such pains to establish: it
must be regarded as the primary cause of the division of the
Low Countries into the Netherlands and Belgium and of
the differences which now exist between the Dutch-speaking
populations in both countries.

When the South reverted to Spanish rule, it came into an
atmosphere that was not at all conducive to the development
of an independent cultural life. The Reformation had stimu-
lated the use of the vernacular, the Counter-Reformation did
the opposite and discouraged the use of Dutch, the language
of the rebellious and heretical North. Dutch was relegated to a
secondary position in the South and became largely restricted
to domestic use, while Latin and French became the languages
of literature. In the North, where the Reformation had won

the day, the situation was the reverse. The military and political successes intensified the feelings of national pride which expressed themselves in a high appreciation of the vernacular. Several of the foremost writers in the North, notably Hendrick Spiegel and Dirck Coornhert, were at the same time ardent propagandists for their native language. They did more than just gratuitously proclaim Dutch to be equal or superior to any other language, they actively worked to shape it, to purify and enrich it, to regulate it, in much the same way as Thomas Wilson and George Puttenham did in England in the same period. They were also concerned about the varieties of dialect in spoken and written Dutch, and they drew up proposals aimed at building a standard language that could be used in all parts of the country. The most influential book in this respect was Spiegel's *Twespraeck van de Nederduytsche Letterkunst* (Dialogue of Dutch Grammar), published in 1584, in which matters of spelling, pronunciation, declension, conjugation, purification and enrichment of the language were discussed. At the same time the first attempts were made to substitute Dutch for Latin in scientific publications. The great partisan of this cause was Simon Stevin, who after he had left the South settled in Leiden and became Maurits's adviser on fortification. Stevin published books on mathematics, geography, physics and engineering in Dutch, and, determined purist as he was, created a great number of new terms for the subjects he discussed, many of which caught on, so that Dutch is now unique in having its own terminology for arithmetic, algebra, geometry, mathematics etc.

Whether Stevin came to the North for reasons of religion is uncertain; we are not even sure what his religious convictions were. With Marnix van St. Aldegonde we are on firmer ground. Marnix was a fervent Calvinist, who had studied in Geneva under Calvin, had travelled around extensively in the service of William of Orange, was burgomaster of Antwerp for some years, and then settled permanently in the North when in 1585 the city fell to Parma. As a writer he is known for his translations from the psalms and particularly for a prose work, *Biencorf der H. Roomscher Kercke* (Beehive of the Holy Roman Church), of 1569. The book was an assault on the Roman Catholic Church such as there had not been before. In the form of a reply to a pamphlet by a French priest against the Protestants, it attacked the Church left, right and centre, it bombarded it with serious dogmatic arguments and sniped at it with mockery and innuendo, combining the verbal inventiveness of Rabelais with the satirical sharpness of Erasmus. The modern reader who can look at religious questions with a little more tolerance than Marnix was able to muster, will weary every now and then of Marnix's obsessive tenaciousness which leaves no argument unexhausted, but he will be over-awed by his mastery over the language. *Biencorf* is an exercise in prose that does not have its equal in the sixteenth century, and not in many other centuries either. It is hard to say whether his contemporaries were more impressed by the style or by the subject-matter, but we do know that the book became immensely popular and had a great influence on the development of Dutch prose. During Marnix's life it went through six editions, and after his death through about twenty more; in 1578 George Gilpin translated it into English, a year later Johann Fischart made a German adaptation of it.

Marnix is also often regarded as the author of the Dutch national anthem, the *Wilhelmus*, although the evidence for his authorship has never been conclusive. The *Wilhelmus* in its full form is a poem of fifteen stanzas which constitute an acrostic on the name of William of Orange, the Stadtholder of Holland in the early days of the revolt. In the poem William discusses his own background, the sacrifices he has made for the people in their struggle, and prays for their deliverance. The poem was one of a large collection of resistance poems, the so-called *Geuzenliederen*[2] the first of which were published in 1574.

[2] *Geuzen*, from the French *gueux* (beggars), was the name which the leaders of the revolt accepted for themselves.

Another of the emigrant writers, Carel van Mander, gained great fame as an art-historian with his *Schilderboeck* (Book of Painters) in which he gave the biographies of a great number of Dutch, German and Italian painters. The plan of the book was clearly suggested by Vasari's *Lives of the most excellent Painters, Sculptors and Architects* (1550), parts of which Van Mander translated and incorporated in his own work. As a painter Van Mander was a pupil of Lucas de Heere; in his book he mentions De Heere's manuscript on the history of Dutch painting and regrets bitterly that he has never been able to lay hands on it. His own *Schilderboeck,* apart from its value for the history of painting, is a very entertaining prose book, written with a sharp eye for detail and for characteristic biographical data, and enlivened by a great number of anecdotes. As a poet, Van Mander began very much in the *Rederijker* tradition with a volume of religious poetry, *De Gulden Harpe* (The Golden Harp), and then gradually evolved towards the Renaissance style. In the long didactic poem about the principles of painting which introduces the *Schilderboeck*, he made some remarks on prosody which are interesting because they show that unlike most other Dutch poets he received his Renaissance ideas from Italy rather than from France: the connoisseurs, he says, would probably have preferred him to write in the French metre, but that would have made the poem harder for him to write and more difficult for the young to understand; besides, he was not very well at home in the French metre, and therefore chose the Italian octaves, so that the poem, although printed without divisions, in fact consists of a great number of stanzas with the form *abaabbcc,* with each line having a feminine ending.

By the middle of the sixteenth century the traditional *Rederijker* poetry as we know it from the collections of Jan van Stijevoort and Jan van Doesborch, or from the work of Anna Bijns, had become out of date. The Chambers of Rhetoric had become thoroughly impregnated with the ideas of Humanism and Renaissance and the poets began to turn away from tradition. In the North this was a gradual process and one cannot point to any full-blooded Renaissance writer of the type of Van der Noot. Some poets adhered to the old forms while writing in the spirit of the Renaissance, others used the new forms for old ideas, others again evolved by degrees from old to new.

The Humanism of the northern Chambers of Rhetoric found its most complete expression in the work of Dirck Coornhert, engraver, printer, public servant and writer. Born in 1522, he was in his forties when the revolt against Spain began and much of his work reflects the conflicts of that period. In modern terms, Coornhert was very much an engaged writer, without being committed to either the Protestant or the Roman Catholic cause. His main commitment was to the cause of tolerance. He was its great champion in days when tolerance was regarded by many as a dirty word and when life was not made easy for those who had the courage to think along subtler lines than the crude black-and-white schemes presented by the die-hards on either side. Coornhert was not lacking in courage. During the riots of 1566, when the Roman Catholic churches were sacked, and images and paintings destroyed, he reacted against the rioters and hid some church treasures in his own house. The next year, however, he was in prison as a suspected Protestant. He was closer to Protestantism than to Roman Catholicism, but his dislike of dogmatic Calvinism was intense. In 1561 he wrote a treatise against the Calvinist doctrine which Calvin himself honoured with a furious reply in which he denounced his opponent as a 'raving dog' and an 'uncircumcised Goliath'. The Roman Catholics, on the other hand, suspected Coornhert because of his connections with William of Orange whom he met frequently in his capacity of secretary of the Haarlem city council. He spent some time in prison, then went into exile in Germany where he met Jan van der Noot, for whose *Olympia* epic he cut the engravings. After his return to Holland he continued to attack all forms of intolerance whether Roman Catholic or Protestant in writing and in public debates, until he was forced to leave the country again. In 1585 he returned to Haarlem, determined to start an academic study at the University of Leiden (he was then 63 years old). In a letter to the University administration he promised that he would keep quiet in matters of religion and not publish anything against the ministers of the Calvinist Church, with the characteristic addendum: 'unless they force me to it with their own publications'. Leiden seems to have turned him down, however, for Coornhert remained in Haarlem.

Coornhert was one of the most versatile and prolific writers of his time. He was an active translator, mainly of the classics—Seneca, Boethius, Cicero, the *Odyssey* (from the Latin)—but also from Boccaccio. As a dramatist he wrote a number of plays, mainly comedies, in the tradition of the *Rederijker* theatre but with the classical element of choruses after each act. His poetry, collected in the *Liedboek* (Song Book) is also rather traditional. He preferred the *Rederijker* verse to the modern method of syllable counting and was in general opposed to too many prosodic restrictions. On the other hand, he did practise the iambic metre and even wrote some sonnets. But his fame as a writer really rests on his prose, and in particular on his *Zedekunst, dat is Wellevens- kunste* (Ethics, that is the Art of Living Well), written in 1586. It was the first prose ethic in the vernacular and was written at the instance of his younger friend Spiegel. In spite of the many borrowings from classical authors and contemporary Humanists, it is a very original and independent book in which he sets forth his personal philosophy and with great psychological insight discusses man's strengths and weaknesses, not only theoretically, but with practical recommendations for his behaviour as a social being. It is not a polemic book, but Coornhert's attitude towards intolerance and immoderateness, his aversion to dogmas such as original sin and predestination, come through very clearly. His philosophy is not specifically Protestant or Roman Catholic, but has its roots in Erasmian Christianity, with a strong element of stoicism. *Zedekunst* is a monument of sixteenth-century prose, written in a clear and concise style, all the more admirable since this was the first time that Dutch prose was used for material of this kind. It was not, however, Coornhert's first prose. Apart from translations, he had also published several treatises, among them a book on prison reform where he expressed remarkably modern ideas: the prisoner should be educated and given useful work instead of being brutally treated and kept idle. Mention should also be made of his *Kruythofken* (Herb Garden), a book of short prose pieces on topical subjects, containing a famous chapter on the killing of a heretic, in which in less than two pages he demolishes the arguments of the fanatics and at the same time paints an unforgettable picture of the court official and his victim:

'My dearest man, why do you so obstinately stick to these accursed errors of yours, or don't you believe that there is a Hell?' 'I certainly believe that there is a Hell', said the old man, 'but that I am in error, I am not aware'. 'Yes, you are in error', said the court official, 'You are in such horrible error that if you should die in it you will be damned forever'. 'Are you sure of that', said the old man. 'Yes, surer than sure', said the court official, now hoping to gain half the credit of converting the old man; but the latter gave him a completely unexpected reply, saying: 'So then you will be the murderer of my poor soul'. (whereupon the court official had the old man executed as quickly as he could).

In the South, Coornhert had a kindred spirit in Jan Baptist Houwaert, who was also for all practical purposes a Protestant—which cost him a year in jail—but a very liberal and tolerant one, critical of all dogmatic pedantry. Like Coornhert, he was a great translator and in general a very productive writer of plays, didactic poetry and short lyrics in the *Rederijker* manner. He was famous in his time for *Pegasides Pleyn ende den Lusthof der Maeghden* (Pegasus's Plain and the Pleasure Garden of the Maidens), a very elaborate ethic for women, consisting of no less than

58,000 lines and written to the astonishment of his contemporaries within the space of six months. In spite of the tempo of writing, it is a very long-winded poem, and the modern reader has great difficulty in sharing the enthusiasm with which the sixteenth-century writers, including Jan van der Noot, greeted it. Placed next to the work of Van der Noot himself—who was only five years younger—both form and prosody of Houwaert's poem strike one as rather old-fashioned.

In the North, too, the generation that followed Coornhert produced several kindred spirits, of which Hendrick Spiegel, born in 1549, was the most important. Spiegel shared many of Coornhert's views on matters of language and literature, politics and religion, although he himself never left the Roman Catholic Church. Spiegel carried out a plan which Coornhert had cherished for many years but had never been able to complete, namely the writing of a grammar of Dutch, *Twe-spraeck van de Nederduytsche Letterkunst)* (Dialogue of Dutch Grammar), followed by works on dialectics and rhetoric. His way of thinking and his social attitude are neatly characterized by his refusal to accept a public position to which the city of Amsterdam had appointed him: in a letter of appeal to the provincial government he pointed out that his conscience forbade him to accept the appointment because he had once sworn an oath of allegiance to the city administration which was bound by agreement to maintain the Roman Catholic religion; then the administration had changed, had become Protestant, and he had even renounced his citizenship of Amsterdam to avoid being asked for a new oath; he could never accept an appointment which would make him break his former oath; he further considered that he would be more useful to the country as a writer than as a reluctant public servant. Spiegel won this, that is to say, the government regarded him as 'of such strange opinion and disposition that it would not be advisable to use him in a public office', and imposed a fine. Spiegel paid the fine, with the request that the money might be spent on the poor. This

incident characterizes Spiegel as much as it does the
government, and shows that in times of great stress and much
extremism the opinion of a dissenting writer was respected,
even if he was considered a crank. The problem of social
responsibility was a very concrete one in those days and
Spiegel came back to it in his only play, entitled *Numa ofte
Amptsweygheringe* (Numa or the Refusal of Office), which
dramatizes a story by Plutarch about Numa's doubts and
self-searchings before he allowed himself to be crowned king
of Rome.

Spiegel's main work is *Hertspiegel* (Mirror of the Heart), a
philosophical poem in seven cantos in which he describes his
outlook on life. It is clearly reminiscent of Coornhert's *Zedekunst* and must have been strongly influenced by it, although
Spiegel's philosophy differs from Coornhert's in some
respects, for example in his insistence on the indivisible unity
of God, Nature, Reason and Virtue, against Coornhert's
endeavours to define them separately. An important difference between the two works is that Coornhert's book was
written as a didactic book, almost as a textbook of ethical
behaviour, whereas Spiegel stressed that *Hertspiegel* was
written for himself, to help him formulate and elucidate his
own thoughts. That he was sincere in this is supported by the
fact that he made no effort to have it published: it appeared
in 1614, three years after his death. *Hertspiegel* is a more
personal book than *Zedekunst,* more concerned with
Spiegel's personal problems than with those of others or with
generalities, more a demonstration of his own Christian-Stoic
philosophy than a handbook with general prescriptions. It
was written very much in the modern manner, in strictly
counted alexandrines and regularly alternating pairs of
masculine and feminine rhymes. There is a considerable
formal difference between this poem and his earlier work,
and it seems that Spiegel rather suddenly came to appreciate
the Renaissance prosody. In his *Twe-spraeck* of 1584 he
appeared to be unaware of its existence, whereas a year later,
in a theoretical poem *Kort Begrijp des Redekavelings*

(Summary of Dialectics) he recommended and used the new forms.

If one wants to use the term Renaissance for Spiegel—and in view of his prosody, his concern for his native language, his individualism, his knowledge and appreciation of the classics and his philosophical foundations it would be difficult not to—one should be aware that there is nothing in his work of the exuberance or the sensuousness that is usually associated with Renaissance poetry, nor anything of the self-glorification of the poet. Spiegel is consistently level-headed and sober-minded, and also unduly modest about his own achievements as a poet. In the first canto of *Hertspiegel* he states bluntly that he is not a poet, and turns against those who call themselves poets and violate the truth with their exaggerated praise of each other, with their farces and their foreign-inspired love poetry: he would not even like to be a poet if it meant being part of this.

It is probably true that writers like Coornhert and Spiegel and many others did not consider themselves artists and regarded literature as no more than a pastime, diverting and useful, but not all-important. Jan van der Noot, with his exalted ideas on poetry and the place of the poet, stood quite alone. Spiegel's friend and fellow-Amsterdamer Roemer Visscher went even further than Spiegel in his show of modesty, so far in fact that one sometimes suspects that a certain coquetry lurks behind the denigrating terms in which he described his own work. Visscher published his poems—admittedly, many years after they had been written—under various belittling titles: *Brabbeling* (Jabbering), *Rommelsoo* (Mixed Bag), *Tepelwercken* (Trifles). Whether his modesty was sincere or not, it was appropriate, for he was a light-weight poet and most of his work was trifling. He combined a delight in the description of broadly farcical situations with an uncontrollable urge to pun, a combination which only rarely led to anything approaching humour. He was at his best in his satirical poems, in his attacks on the clergy or on social evils, but on the whole his poetry palls quickly because of its lack of sophistication. So far as form is concerned, he belonged to the modernists but his subject-matter and his way of thinking were closely related to the *Rederijker* tradition. Visscher was a *Rederijker,* and an active one: like Spiegel, he was for some time head of the Amsterdam Chamber 'De Eglantier'. Visscher and Spiegel, and later on Hooft, brought the Chamber to great prosperity and raised its standard so much that it became the most influential Chamber in the Low Countries in which in later years Vondel, Hooft and Bredero could feel at home.

While the Amsterdam Chamber of Rhetoric became the centre of the Renaissance poetry in the North, Leiden developed into the centre of Humanist studies. After the city had successfully withstood the siege of 1574, under the most abominable conditions of famine and epidemics, it had been rewarded with the establishment of a university, the first in the North. The new university was able to attract several scholars of great international fame, among them Justus Lipsius, who held a chair at Leiden until 1592 when he went over to the Roman Catholic Church and moved to Louvain, and the equally famous Josephus Scaliger, son of Julius Caesar Scaliger. One of the governors of the university was Jan van der Does, better known under the latinized name of Janus Douza, a nobleman who had distinguished himself as one of the most energetic leaders of the defence during the siege, and who was also a Neo-Latin poet of great repute. Apart from his translation of Janus Secundus's *Basia* which he made together with Jan van Hout, Douza wrote hardly anything in Dutch. On the whole the atmosphere in Leiden seemed biased against the use of Dutch in literature, possibly under the influence of the university, where the official language was Latin. Leiden was to produce the great Neo-Latinists of the seventeenth century, Daniel Heinsius and Hugo Grotius, whereas Amsterdam, which had no university, was the home of Spiegel and Roemer Visscher, propagandists for the native language, and was to produce or adopt three of the four great poets in Dutch of the seventeenth

century: Hooft, Vondel, Bredero. In Leiden the only poet of
any importance writing in Dutch in this period was Jan van
Hout, friend and collaborator of Douza. Van Hout was also
a friend of Spiegel's yet cast in an entirely different mould.
Instead of shunning public offices in the way Spiegel did, he
seemed to collect them: he was town-clerk of Leiden,
secretary of the Board of Governors of the University, public
notary, manager of the city press, and he also made quite a
name for himself as a man of action during the siege. As a
Protestant, his friendship with several avowed Roman
Catholics seems to speak for his tolerance and liberal-
mindedness, an impression which is not enhanced by a well-
known anecdote, which describes him as sitting in church,
listening with mounting indignation to the minister who
preached about the struggle against Spain as a fight for
religion rather than one for freedom, then drawing his pistol
and saying to the burgomaster who was sitting next to him:
'Shall I bring him down?' Whether the story is true or not,
the aggressiveness that speaks from it is matched by his
attack on the old poetry in an address delivered at the
University of Leiden as an introduction to his translation of
George Buchanan's *Franciscanus*. In his opening sentence,
which runs into thirty-eight lines of print without jumping
the rails of syntax, he derided the taste of the masses and
made a plea for individuality and independence in literature:
'I have more regard for the judgment of the least among you
than for all the criticism of those who mistakenly call
themselves Rhetoricians'. In his poetry, too, he ridiculed the
Rederijkers, and with a pun on the popular term of
retrozijnen, called them *retrozwijnen:* retro-swine. His
attacks on the *Rederijkers* suggest the influence of Joachim
du Bellay who had made very similar attacks on the old
school of French poetry, and Van Hout's ideas were
undoubtedly strongly influenced by the poets of the Pléiade.
He was an active translator of Ronsard and Desportes, as
well as of Petrarch, Buchanan and Janus Secundus, but not
many of these translations have been preserved. In general,

most of his work has been lost to us; he published little
during his lifetime and bequeathed all his manuscripts to a
friend who seems to have lost them all when he was forced
to leave the country. All that is left is a collection of about
twenty poems, some prose including the first part of what
was to be a full history of the city of Leiden, and a
humorous play in five acts, *Loterij-spel* (Lottery Play). It is
not enough to enable us to make an accurate assessment of
the literary value of his work, but it does show him as a very
progressive poet who even wrote some blank verse, a daring
venture that was not repeated in Dutch until the eighteenth
century.

Jan van Hout's influence was probably greater than the
extent of his own work would suggest. Time and again he is
mentioned by his contemporaries as the master of the new
poetry. In the introduction to the poem on the principles of
painting, Carel van Mander names only Van Hout when he
writes about the new iambic verse in Dutch. Spiegel, too, in
the fourth canto of *Hertspiegel,* mentions only Van Hout and
Coornhert as the representatives of the new poetry in the
North. It was probably also Jan van Hout who was
responsible for Spiegel's transition from the old to the new
style in his *Kort Begrijp des Redekavelings* which was
dedicated to Van Hout. Even Janus Douza, who took no
great interest in the vernacular literature, praised him as the
poet who wrote a pure Dutch, as against the *Rederijkers* who
in his opinion had wrecked the language. Van Hout may also
have had great value as an intermediary between the Neo-
Latin poets and the poets who wrote in the vernacular. He
was linked to both by feelings of admiration and criticism.
He was Douza's friend and admirer, yet in his attack on the
Rederijkers he criticized in one and the same breath also the
poets who despised the vernacular and wrote in foreign
languages. On the other hand, his criticism of the *Rederijkers*
did not mean that he turned away from them: he took part
in their functions and wrote his play for them. Through his
friendship with Spiegel and Coornhert, and his influence on

Spiegel's development, he also served as an intermediary
between Leiden and Amsterdam. Though the Leiden school
may not have directly contributed as much to Dutch
literature as did Amsterdam, it did have a considerable
influence on the course Dutch literature was taking through
this intermediary function of Jan van Hout and through the
contacts that existed in the seventeenth century between the
Leideners Hugo Grotius and Daniel Heinsius on the one
hand, and Vondel, Hooft and Huygens on the other.

V

THE GOLDEN AGE
SEVENTEENTH CENTURY

The seventeenth century in Dutch history is traditionally known as the Golden Age. It is a romantic and slightly nostalgic term, but not an inappropriate one, for the seventeenth century was undoubtedly a period of unprecedented wealth and prosperity, economically as well as culturally. Yet the term Golden Age needs some qualification. In the first place, it applies only to the period in the northern part of the Low Countries, to what is known as the Netherlands. For the southern provinces the century was anything but golden.

After the diplomacy and the statesmanship of William of Orange had failed to keep the northern and southern provinces together, the break became permanent when the military campaigns of the Stadtholder Maurits, however successful they may have been otherwise, also failed to reunite the North and the South. The military stalemate of the 1590s was a triumph in one respect, but a disaster in another, as it perpetuated the division of the Dutch-speaking people. The South remained under the dominance of Spain and had to give up all hopes of independence. Its cultural development was stunted by the Counter-Reformation which pursued its aims in a most rigorous way by taking control of all education and by establishing a strict censorship. Its economy was severely dislocated by the closing of the Scheldt and the blockading of the coast, and also by the emigration of thousands of its inhabitants to the North. When Philip II in 1598 transferred the sovereignty of the

Low Countries to his son-in-law Albert, Arch-Duke of Austria, this made hardly any difference to the situation, either in the South or in the North. The South was just as dependent as it had been before, and so it was to remain for more than two centuries. The North ignored Albert as it had done Philip. In those years the North gradually developed into an independent republic, the first modern republic in Europe, which was such a novelty that visitors from far and wide came to see how it worked.

Nor should the term Golden Age be taken to imply a period of peace and quiet. On the contrary, the seventeenth century was a period remarkable for its wars and unrest. The war with Spain went on until 1609 when a truce was signed. This truce, a great political triumph for the young republic, lasted for 12 years, but those twelve years were not peaceful years either. During the truce the country seemed to explode from within and at one stage came dangerously close to civil war over issues of internal politics and religion. The trial and execution of Johan van Oldenbarnevelt, one of the ablest Dutch statesmen and architect of the truce, is an indication of the seriousness and the bitterness of the conflict. In 1621 the truce expired and war was resumed. The Treaty of Westphalia of 1648 finally brought this war to a conclusion. It had then lasted for eighty years. After 1648 the Republic came into conflict with several other European countries and the war-list is impressive, particularly for a period that has become known as a Golden Age: between 1652 and 1654 the first of a series of Anglo-Dutch sea-wars was fought; in 1658 the Republic intervened in the conflict between Sweden and Denmark; between 1665 and 1667 the second war with England took place, while on land the Dutch were locked in combat with the Bishop of Munster; from 1672 until 1678 there was almost continuous warfare with France, England and the Bishops of Munster and Cologne, while from 1688 until 1697 the Republic was at war with France again. In other words, for more than half the century the Netherlands was on a war footing with one or more other countries, and one is tempted to ask what was so golden about all this. Yet at the same time it was a period of extraordinary creativity. The wars were mainly fought on the outskirts of the Republic, or at sea, and as there were no incursions of foreign troops before 1672, daily life in the Netherlands was hardly affected. No wholesale destruction took place and artists and writers, architects and builders could work without fear that their creations would be destroyed. And, what is more, on the whole without fear of persecution. In sharp contrast to the South, the cultural climate of the North was one of freedom and tolerance. The Erasmian spirit had taken firm root in the Netherlands, and although there were from time to time powerful factions which managed to suppress those of whom they did not approve, the general atmosphere in the Netherlands was far more liberal than in the surrounding countries. Face to face with this statement one could draw up a lengthy list of those who were molested because of their dissenting views—Vondel would appear on it, and Grotius and Adriaan Koerbagh—but these cases were the exceptions rather than the rule. Had they lived somewhere else, their fate would probably have been a good deal worse.

As early as 1578 William of Orange had published a decree in which he stated that 'in the matter of religion everyone should remain free to answer to God as he shall wish', and even if his principle was not always adhered to, the general attitude of the authorities was characterized by a tolerance that was rare in the Europe of that time. This attitude attracted refugees of all kinds: Jews, French Huguenots, the Pilgrim Fathers, and such famous men as Descartes, Locke, and Bayle. Naturally, the tolerance of the Dutch authorities was not only of benefit to the refugees, but also to the Republic itself. The influx of scholars from many different countries brought an element of internationalism and sophistication to Dutch intellectual life. Also, the comparative freedom of the press made Leiden and Amsterdam the publishing centres of the liberal world:

Galileo was printed in the Netherlands, as were Socinus, Descartes, Spinoza, Richard Simon's Bible criticism and John Locke's *Epistola de Tolerantia*.

To the world at large the most spectacular feature of the Dutch Golden Age is the work of the painters. The names of Rembrandt, Frans Hals, Johannes Vermeer, Adriaan van Ostade, Jan Steen, Adriaan Brouwer and many others are known everywhere and examples of their art can be seen in most countries. Similarly, the achievements of scientists like Anthonie van Leeuwenhoek and Christiaan Huygens, of Hugo Grotius, the founder of international law, and of the philosopher Baruch de Spinoza became common property of the civilized world. But with the writers it was a different matter. The language barrier was a powerful one and prevented most of the writers from becoming more than local celebrities. There were exceptions to this rule, and there were occasions when Dutch literature was able to break through the language barrier and make its mark abroad. In the 1620s, the German poet Martin Opitz translated a number of contemporary Dutch poems into German, thereby introducing the iambic alexandrine into German literature. Opitz became the creator of a new poetic language in Germany, and it was through his contact with the Dutch poets that German literature of those years bears the unmistakable imprint of the Dutch Renaissance. Later in the century, the dramatic work of Joost van den Vondel became influential in Germany through Andreas Gryphius who, like Philipp von Zesen and Paul Fleming, for some time studied in Leiden. Gryphius translated Vondel's *Gebroeders* (Brothers) into German, and his own dramas *Leo Arminius* and *Die Geliebte Dornrose* both owe a large debt to Vondel.

International recognition came more easily to those writers who used Latin as the language of literature. The best-known figures among those were Daniel Heinsius, professor of Greek and History at the University of Leiden, and Hugo Grotius, who was not only a lawyer but also a considerable poet and dramatist. Both achieved European fame in their

lifetime and according to André Jolles, if an educated
European of the 1630s had been asked whom he considered
the greatest Dutchmen of his time, he would have mentioned
Grotius and Heinsius. And the greatest poets? Then he
would have mentioned the same names, but in reverse order.
Jolles was probably right. Heinsius and Grotius were the
great names, and the poets whom we now regard as the
major writers—Vondel, Bredero, Hooft and Huygens—
were graded under the Neo-Latinists for the simple reason
that they wrote in Dutch. Yet the Neo-Latin tide was
turning, and the fact that Heinsius himself also wrote poetry
in Dutch and published it, even if he ranked it well below his
Latin work, is significant. It is equally significant that his
friend Jacob Revius, also a scholar and poet of renown,
wrote both in Dutch and in Latin, but published only his
Dutch poetry and left the Latin poems in manuscript. There
was still uncertainty in the minds of several writers whether
Dutch was as suitable for the kind of poetry they wanted to
write as Latin was, but it was an uncertainty that was
gradually disappearing. In the preface to his *Lofsang van
Bacchus* (1614) Heinsius stated that one of the reasons why
he wrote it was to see whether Dutch was as unfit for this
purpose as some people claimed it to be. Other poets started
off with greater confidence, and neither Vondel nor Hooft
nor Bredero was ever in doubt as to the suitability of Dutch
though they still found it necessary on occasion to defend
their confidence. Of even greater significance was the point
of view of Huygens, who was as much a Neo-Latinist as he
was a Dutch poet. In 1658, in the preface to his Donne
translations he recalled that King Charles I had expressed to
him his disbelief that anyone should be able to translate
Donne satisfactorily: he would not have said that, wrote
Huygens, if he had known the riches of the Dutch language.
    In the early years of the seventeenth century, the
Chambers of Rhetoric were still the centres of literary
activity. But in the course of the century their position
gradually changed. More and more of the important writers

chose to stay outside the *Rederijker* organizations so that the Chambers began to lose much of the authority they had once held. Many Chambers disbanded, particularly in the cities, and after the middle of the century most of them were to be found in the country and were regarded as rather old-fashioned institutions. The situation in Amsterdam provides a good example of the decline of the Chambers.

At the turn of the century there were three Chambers of Rhetoric in Amsterdam of which *De Eglantier* (The Eglantine) was the most prominent. It was also the oldest, dating back to the last years of the fifteenth century, and it became an important force in the literary world through the active membership of poets such as Hendrick Spiegel, Roemer Visscher, Pieter Hooft and Gerbrand Bredero. The other two Chambers, *Het Wit Lavendel* (The White Lavender) and *Het Vijgeboomken* (The Fig Tree) were Brabant Chambers, established by Brabant immigrants in or around 1585. The latter was never of great consequence, but the former could for some years boast the membership of Joost van den Vondel, whose parents had come to Amsterdam from Brabant. *De Eglantier* suffered for a number of years from serious internal strife. Hooft tried to solve this in 1613 by introducing stricter rules and standing orders, but the effect was only temporary. The discord in the Chamber was, personal incompatibilities apart, mainly a matter of new against old. Hooft and his friends were concerned with making *De Eglantier* into a centre of Renaissance poetry and drama, a centre where the new literature would be created, based on the examples of the classical writers. They were thwarted by a group of older members who were more inclined to continue in the non-classical tradition and who adopted as their guide the Spanish dramatist Lope de Vega. The dissension in the Chamber came to a head in 1617 when Samuel Coster, an Amsterdam doctor and playwright, and a friend and partisan of Hooft's, broke with *De Eglantier* and set up a new institution under the name of *Nederduytsche Academie*

(Dutch Academy), which Hooft, Bredero and several other members of the old Chamber joined.

Coster's Academy was something quite new in the Netherlands. It was a combination of several things: theatre, centre for the new literature and institute for higher learning. Teaching was to have an important place in the Academy, and immediately after it had been established, lecturers were appointed in Hebrew, Logic and Mathematics. Amsterdam did not have a university and Coster hoped that the Academy would fill this gap. It was in no way, however, to become a copy of the University of Leiden. On the contrary, Coster intended it to be a counter-balance to the Neo-Latin influence that was exercised by Leiden. The medium of instruction therefore was to be Dutch, not Latin as in Leiden. Also, all teaching was to be entirely independent of religious matters. Coster's ideas were a little too advanced to become very popular. The Academy encountered a great deal of opposition, particularly from the Calvinist ministers in Amsterdam, who succeeded in having the municipal authorities ban all teaching from the Academy only two years after its inception. There was also opposition to Coster's plays, especially to his *Iphigeneia* (1617) which attacked the interference of the ministers in matters of the world and which consequently drew their concentrated fire whenever it was performed. But—and this deserves equal emphasis—it was performed, and not only once, but frequently.

The relationship between Coster's Academy, *De Eglantier* and *Het Wit Lavendel* was complicated, but not entirely hostile. There were several quarrels among the leaders, but there was also a certain amount of co-operation. None of the three seems to have had enough vitality to lead an independent life: in 1630 *Het Wit Lavendel* merged with the Academy, and in 1635 this combination was joined by *De Eglantier*. The institution which resulted from these two mergers was known as *De Amsterdamse Kamer* (The Amsterdam Chamber), but should be regarded more as a dramatic association than as a *Rederijkerskamer* in the old sense of the word. It was very successful: in a few years' time its building became too small for the audiences it was attracting, so that in 1637 a new theatre was built, the first proper theatre in the Netherlands. It was inaugurated in the same year with what was to become Vondel's best-known play, *Gijsbrecht van Amstel*.

Of the four major writers—Vondel, Hooft, Bredero and Huygens—three played a part in the *Rederijker* organizations. Bredero and Hooft were active in *De Eglantier*, Vondel was first a member of *Het Wit Lavendel* and later of *De Eglantier*. They were the last major writers to support the Chambers of Rhetoric. After them, these bodies seemed to have fulfilled their purpose. Some lingered on as theatre groups, others became purely social clubs, but they ceased to be the focal point of literary activity.

These three writers were all born in the 1580s: Hooft in 1581, Bredero in 1585 and Vondel in 1587. This means that they were at least a generation older than most of the major painters. Rembrandt, Van Ostade, Brouwer, Steen, Potter, Bol, Cuyp, Vermeer were all born between 1606 and 1632. If one does not always find the contact and mutual appreciation between painters and writers that one might expect, it should not be forgotten that the difference in ages may have been a contributing factor. Very little is known of Hooft's relationship with the painters of his day, but judging from the group of people that frequently met at his castle at Muiden, he seems to have been more interested in inviting writers, scholars and musicians than painters. Bredero who himself began as a painter, died in 1618, too early to see any work of the painters just mentioned. It is often said that several of Bredero's poems are reminiscent of paintings by Adriaan van Ostade, Adriaan Brouwer and Jan Steen. True, the similarities are often striking, but it is equally true that Bredero cannot have seen a single painting of any of these three, for when Bredero died, Brouwer was thirteen years old, Van Ostade nine, and seven years were to elapse before the birth of Jan Steen. We know that Vondel at times expressed his admiration for Rembrandt—who was nineteen years his junior—but we also know that he never felt any great enthusiasm for his art. He, and many other writers of his generation preferred Rubens, who was twenty-nine years older than Rembrandt. Rembrandt's modernism, his deviation from the accepted rules did not appeal to Vondel, and the approach of Rubens was much closer to his own conception of what art should be. Geerard Brandt, who published a biography of Vondel in 1682, relates how in 1653 Vondel was honoured at a banquet attended by more than a hundred writers and painters, but unfortunately he omits to tell us who were there. We are better informed about Huygens's attitude to the painters, thanks to an autobiographical fragment which he wrote between 1629 and 1631. There he discussed a considerable number of painters, and also gave greatest praise to Rubens whom he called 'one of the wonders of this world' and 'the Apelles of our time'. But Huygens was also one of the first to recognize the genius of Rembrandt, who was only twenty-five years old when Huygens predicted that he would soon surpass all the others. He had only one criticism to make of Rembrandt: he found him too self-sufficient and regretted that he did not want to visit Italy. A few years later Huygens acted as an intermediary when the Stadtholder Frederik Hendrik commissioned Rembrandt to paint a series of Passion paintings. As a token of gratitude Huygens received from Rembrandt his painting *The Blinding of Samson*.

Of the four great writers, Pieter Corneliszoon Hooft was the oldest. He was also the most typical Renaissance poet of that generation, a man who was completely at home in the classics, well versed in French and Italian Renaissance literature, and at the same time fully alive to the importance and value of his own language. His friend Huygens may have reproached Rembrandt for not wanting to go to Italy, such criticism could not be directed against Hooft. He was not yet eighteen years old when he set out on a grand tour which took him through France, Italy and Germany. It should be said that travelling was probably easier for Hooft than it would have been for Rembrandt who was the son of a miller, whereas Hooft's father was a well-to-do merchant and burgomaster of Amsterdam. In May 1601 Hooft was back in Amsterdam, after an absence of almost three years.

When he was in Italy, he sent a kind of poetic circular letter to *De Eglantier,* of which he was a member. It is an informative poem in which he deals with the places he had visited and in which he discusses the writers who had made Italy famous. It is one of the earliest known poems of Hooft and its Renaissance character is unmistakable: it is liberal in its references to classical writers—Virgil, Ovid, Horace, Livy—, it is full of praise for Dante, Petrarch and Ariosto, and its form of alternating pairs of masculine and feminine alexandrines is typical of the Renaissance poem. To Hooft, the Renaissance prosody was not something to be slowly acquired and assimilated, but something that he was born to and that he used from the beginning as a matter of course.

Hooft left another account of his travels in the form of a short prose book which he called *Reis-Heuchenis* (Travel Memoir), probably written from notes after his return. In this book he does not deal with literature at all, but almost exclusively with the cities he had visited. One of the conclusions one can draw from this book is that architecture meant much more to him than painting, and then only classical and 'modern' architecture. As a true representative of the Renaissance he took little interest in the architecture of the Middle Ages. The only aspect of Notre-Dame that impressed him was its size and the amount of money it must have cost; otherwise his terse comment is: 'not beautiful'.

It seems likely that in Italy Hooft came into contact with a genre of literature that was practically unknown in the Netherlands, namely the pastoral play. In 1603 he began to write one himself, *Granida,* which was completed in 1605. In many ways it is an imitation of Guarini's *Il Pastor Fido,* just as John Fletcher a few years later imitated Guarini in his

Faithful Shepherdess (1610). Hooft's *Granida* is not a pure example of the pastoral play. It is a mixture of pastoral and tragi-comedy. Only the first act is pastoral in the strict sense of the word; the other acts, set at the court of Persia, are in subject-matter and situation more typical of Renaissance drama than of the pastoral play. One could even go a step further and argue that *Granida* should be regarded primarily as a lyrical work, eulogizing the triumph of true love, rather than as an example of dramatic art. It is brilliantly written, it has the gracefulness and the lightness of a divertimento, but the situation is too unreal, the characterization too sketchy for the play to be able to make much dramatic impact. Also, against the background of the Holland of that period, a pastoral play has a strong element of artificiality. One of its themes is the contrast between life at court and life in the country, with the inevitable conclusion that country life is vastly preferable, and that shepherds and shepherdesses hold a larger share of the truth than courtiers. In Italy, with its many courts and their entourage of an aristocracy about whose morality there existed grave doubts, the back-to-nature call of the pastoral play could meet with response. In Holland, however, where there was hardly any question of a court and where the aristocracy and the 'courtiers' were worlds apart from their Italian counterparts, the message of the pastoral play fell rather flat.

In spite of the artificiality of this type of play, *Granida* was quite successful and seems to have been performed frequently. Yet it did not inspire many other writers to follow suit. Pastoral plays in Dutch remained few and far between. *Granida's* success was probably not so much due to the genre, but to the elegance and refinement of Hooft's poetry. Hooft himself considered it a trifle and did not publish it until 1615, and then only because the year before two of his earlier plays had been printed without his knowledge and with many corruptions of the original text. Under those circumstances he preferred to publish the play himself. Apart from throwing some light on the pre-copyright

world of publishing, it also shows that Hooft was not a
writer who rushed into print. As a writer—and not only as
a writer—he was akin to Spiegel and Coornhert who regarded
writing as an interesting and absorbing pastime, but as
no more than that. Passion for literary fame, common as
it was among Renaissance writers in general, was rare among
the Dutch writers of that time. In 1610 Hooft began a letter
to Heinsius with the following words: 'I am not a writer,
although I have sometimes written poetry for pleasure, which
to my concern has become known'. The sentiment behind
this statement is partly the studied modesty of the Humanist,
but partly also the conviction of being a writer only in the
second or third place.

As *Granida* suggested, Hooft's strength as a poet was the
lyric and in particular the love lyric. In 1611 he published
his first volume of lyrical poetry under the triple title of
*Emblemata Amatoria, Afbeeldingen van Minne, Emblèmes
d'Amour.* It contains a series of emblems followed by about
fifty lyrical poems, songs and sonnets. They are lyrical poems
not in the romantic sense of outpourings of the heart, but in
the Renaissance sense of well-controlled personal poetry.
Most of them are love poems, tributes to the objects of his
love and laments about the loss of a beloved, some in a philosophical vein, others light and playful. Hooft must have been a
passionate man, but in his poetry his passion is always under
control. Philosophically he was a stoic, and the blows that
love dealt him were cushioned by his stoicism before they
became poetry. Throughout his work there is a carefully
maintained distance between his innermost feelings and their
reflection on paper. Classical and mythological figures sometimes seem to act as shields behind which he could withdraw
when personal feelings were becoming too dominant.
In 1605 he wrote a poem about the end of his love affair
with Brechje Spiegel, a niece of Hendrick Spiegel's:

> Sal nemmermeer gebeuren
> mij dan nae dese stondt

de vrientschap van u oogen
de wellust van u mondt? [1]

After six stanzas in this tone: lofty, tender, elegiac, he
suddenly breaks off, introduces the Lady Venus, and
develops the poem in a new direction of wit and clever
allegory. On the basis of a poem such as this, Hooft has
from time to time been accused of lack of feeling, of being
insensitive to tragedy. There is little truth in this accusation
and a great deal of injustice. To the Renaissance poet,
'feeling' was not the stuff poetry was made of. Wit was, and
sophistication, ingenuity and control of emotion. In Hooft's
circle of friends, control of emotion, in particular of grief,
was a *conditio sine qua non*, in actual life as well as in poetry.
Depth of feeling in literature was not demonstrated
emotionally, but rationally, i.e. in perfection of form, in
ingenious imagery, in elegant diction.

Hooft's best lyrics were written within a rather short space
of time : in the years between 1601 and 1611. He did not
stop writing lyrical poetry after 1611 and some of the later
poems are very good indeed, for example *Klaghte der
Prinsesse van Oranjen* (Lament of the Princess of Orange), to
mention only one. But in the later poems he reached that
level only occasionally, and several of them seem a little
chatty and sometimes more than a little forced. The earlier
poems, on the contrary, stand out through their conciseness
of diction, or rather through their combination of economy
of words and richness of expression. None of these poems is
dull, or slack or too drawn out, and they are unequalled by
any of Hooft's contemporaries. They owe a debt to several
Renaissance poets—Petrarch, Ronsard, Desportes—and to
the classics, but Hooft always maintained a large measure
of independence, and the tone of his poetry is entirely his
own.

As a playwright Hooft wrote several more plays after

[1] Will nevermore occur to me after this hour the friendship of your
eyes, the rapture of your mouth?

Granida. The first of these, *Geeraerdt van Velsen* (1613), may
have been inspired by his surroundings. In 1609 Hooft had
been appointed to the position of *Drost* (Sheriff) at Muiden.
He was only twenty-eight at the time, and one may regard
his appointment as an indication of the prestige he
commanded, particularly since the position had always been
reserved for nobility. The official residence of the Drost was
Muiderslot, the castle at Muiden, a town on the coast of the
Zuiderzee, not far from Amsterdam. The castle which was
then well over three hundred years old, had great historical
fame as the scene of the murder of the controversial Count
Floris V in 1296. The occupant of the castle in those years
had been Gerard van Velzen, one of the main adversaries of
the Count. Hooft dramatized the arrest and death of Floris
V, placing Gerard van Velzen in the centre of the action and
using *Muiderslot* as the setting of the play. To Hooft, Floris
was not the traditional hero and protector of the people,
but a tyrant and a violator, not only of the privileges of the
nobles, but also of the honour of Gerard van Velzen's wife.
Dramatically, the play shows a great improvement over
Granida. The characters are more consistent, not entirely
black and white, and therefore a good deal more credible.
The Count stands condemned right through the play, but he
is allowed a certain dignity, and the remorse that he feels for
his misdeeds is given the mark of sincerity. Gerard van
Velzen is cast as the man who undertakes to defend liberty
against the Count's abuse of power, but the nobility of his
heroism is tainted by the impurity of his motives, driven as
he is by the urge to revenge his wife's honour. If *Geeraerdt
van Velsen* is not entirely successful as a drama, it is mainly
because the characters tend to be personifications of ideas
rather than living people. Hooft used the play to expound his
theories on authority and power, on violence and social
order. In his discussion of the role of the ruler and the
responsibilities of the subjects, he made a strong plea for
unity and tolerance. Written and published during the
Twelve Years' Truce, a period not remarkable for either

quality, the play had a strongly topical aspect and served as a reminder of the consequences of intolerance and discord. In his next play, *Baeto* (1617), Hooft again used the theatre as a platform for his political and constitutional ideas. *Baeto* is also a historical play, dealing, as the subtitle announces, with the origin of the Dutch. The young prince Baeto is persecuted by his stepmother Penta, who engineers a series of attempts on his life. Baeto survives them, but in the last attempt his wife is killed. When he then finds himself attacked by his father, he at first gives battle, but after he has won, he suddenly withdraws and chooses exile in preference to having to rule over a divided kingdom. He leaves the country and settles in an uninhabited area where he becomes the progenitor of the Dutch.

Baeto is the embodiment of Hooft's conception of the ideal ruler. He is an opponent of absolutism and comes very close to the modern constitutional monarch: his main concern is the unity of the country. The play also deals with the relation between Church and State which in the years of the truce was one of the central problems in the Netherlands. Hooft allows an important place to the Church, but as a moral force and not as a seat of political power. Both *Baeto* and *Geeraerdt van Velsen* are typical Renaissance plays. They deal with national subject-matter and they are written in the classical manner, after the example of Seneca. Both consist of five acts, with choruses after the acts, and both observe the unities of time and place. Yet *Geeraerdt van Velsen* also contains some features that are reminiscent of the medieval morality play, such as the two sets of allegorical figures: Discord, Violence and Deceit on the one hand, and Concord, Loyalty and Innocence on the other. At the end of the play, another personification, the river Vecht, prophesies the future prosperity of Amsterdam.

Before *Baeto* was finished and while Hooft was thinking how and when it could be performed, he wrote a comedy, in the hope, as he said in a letter to Grotius, that it might help defray the cost of the *Baeto* production. He spent nine days on it, he added almost apologetically. It was not an original play, but an adaptation of Plautus's *Aulularia*, the play that also provided the material for Molière's *L'Avare*. Hooft's *Warenar* is one of the gems of seventeenth-century comedy and deserves all the praise that Grotius and many others heaped upon it. It is a very lively play, excellent theatre, and so successfully transposed into an Amsterdam atmosphere that it is hard to believe that it was adapted from a Latin play. It also shows—as does Huygens's *Trijntje Cornelis* (1653)—that the aristocrats of the seventeenth century had not cut themselves off from the lower strata of society, but knew exactly what was going on, how people lived and what language they spoke.

In his two major plays Hooft had shown a strong predilection for historical themes. His interest in history was not only that of the playwright who needs material for his work, but more that of a professional historian who is interested in the relation between past and present. It was an interest that had been with him for a long time. Over the years he had made an intensive study of several Latin historians, especially of Tacitus whose work, if we may believe Geerard Brandt, his seventeenth-century biographer, he had read no less than fifty-two times. When Hooft began to write history himself, it was Tacitus whom he adopted as his guide. In order to shape his style, he first translated most of Tacitus's work, then wrote a history of the Medicis and a biography of Henry IV of France, a king whom he admired greatly as being heroic and yet tolerant and peace-loving. In 1628 Hooft began what was to become his *magnum opus: Nederlandsche Historiën* (Dutch History), a history of the revolt against Spain.

Nederlandsche Historiën consists of twenty-seven books, beginning with the year 1555, the year of the abdication of Charles V, and ending in 1587. Unfortunately, completion of the work was precluded by Hooft's death in 1647. The first twenty books appeared in 1642, the other seven were published after his death by his son. It is a work that holds a place in literature as well as in historiography. It is not literature in the sense of romanticized history, or of imagination triumphing over fact, but it is a work of literature by virtue of its style, its vision, its vivid presentation and its masterly organization. As a work of history the book is based on hard fact. Hooft used as many original sources as he could lay his hands on: all kinds of documents, decrees, edicts, letters in Dutch, Latin, French, Italian and Spanish. He also made personal enquiries and interviewed a large number of people who had played a part in the revolt. Like Tacitus, his intention was to write *sine ira et studio,* but, also like Tacitus, Hooft was not an entirely neutral observer. His sympathies were unequivocally on the side of the Dutch, and the revolt against Spain was regarded by him as a legitimate fight against tyranny. Yet, in evaluating events and motives, he tried consistently to be impartial and objective. As in his poetry, he kept his personal feelings in check, and, considering he was writing in the 1630s when memories of the war and all that had happened were still fresh, he was singularly successful in avoiding portraying the Spaniards as black devils and the Dutch as lily-white angels. When heroism and generosity occurred on the Spanish side, he did not refrain from describing it, and when he found cruelty and cowardice among the Dutch, he did not suppress that either. To him, the great hero of the revolt was William of Orange who possessed the very qualities which Hooft valued in a ruler: wisdom, tolerance, resoluteness. Hooft's *History* has had a great influence and has provided many generations with a well-reasoned interpretation of the revolt and the personalities who took part in it. Its concise and elliptical style, strongly influenced by Tacitus's Latin, was too idiosyncratic to find many followers and as a result *Nederlandsche Historiën* is both the most important and the most lonely prose work to have come out of the seventeenth century.

Gerbrand Adriaanszoon Bredero, born in 1585, four years later than Hooft, presents in many respects a contrast with him. Hooft was an aristocrat, the son of an Amsterdam burgomaster, whereas Bredero's father was a shoemaker, well-to-do, to be sure, but much more middle-class than Hooft. Hooft had seen something of the world, had travelled through Europe for almost three years, whereas Bredero hardly ever set foot outside Amsterdam. Hooft had had an excellent education, had studied in Leiden and was fluent in several languages, whereas Bredero on occasion excused himself for his lack of linguistic training and called himself an ordinary Amsterdamer who only knew a little school-French. That was probably an exaggeration, for though he may not have been a scholar like Hooft, his French was certainly adequate and he also seems to have known some English. The contrasts which undoubtedly existed in the lives and in the work of Hooft and Bredero have often been over-emphasized and pushed to extremes: Hooft wealthy and socially successful, Bredero down and out; Hooft reserved, detached and always master of himself, Bredero spontaneous, impetuous and always his own victim; Hooft the poet for the happy few, Bredero a writer for the people.

These characterizations may be true enough for Hooft, they are very inaccurate so far as Bredero is concerned. As our knowledge of Bredero's life is very sketchy, the temptation to infer from what little we know a striking contrast with Hooft has been strong and has not always been resisted. One of the few things we know of Bredero is that he was an ensign in the *schuttery,* a kind of civil militia, and as this was a respected and sought-after appointment, it flatly contradicts the notion of his social failure. It is also known that Bredero was trained as a painter and received lessons from Francesco Badens, a well-known painter at the time but one whose entire *oeuvre* has been lost. The same applies to Bredero: none of his paintings has been preserved. As so little is known of Bredero's life attempts have been made to reconstruct it from his work, but this has proved a perilous undertaking and has led to many misconceptions. A large part of his work consists of love poetry which gives the impression of a young man constantly and always hopelessly in love with a succession of girls. Too literal interpretation of these poems and failure to distinguish between what is 'literature' and what real experience, has led to a portrayal of Bredero as a libertine and profligate, a portrayal that is not borne out by his work as a whole. In fact, it is contradicted by a great deal of his poetry and by the few letters which have been preserved and which suggest a serious, well-mannered and well-educated young man.

Bredero began to write when he was quite young, and, like Hooft, he became a member of the Amsterdam Chamber *De Eglantier*. His early poems were still written in the *Rederijker* manner with liberal borrowings from the French, rich rhymes, complicated rhyming patterns and forced imagery. On the whole there are more traditional elements in his poetry than in Hooft's. In more than one poem one can hear echoes of medieval folksongs and popular poetry, and some of his anecdotal poems, often dealing with farcical love situations, are reminiscent of the work of the medieval *Rederijkers*. After his death in 1618 his poems were published under three headings: *Boertigh, Amoureus en Aendachtigh Groot Lied-boeck* (Comical, Amorous and Religious Great Song Book), a division which recalls the categories of *sotte, amoureuze* and *vroede* used by the *Rederijkers*. In spite of these reminiscences it would be wrong to regard Bredero as a belated *Rederijker*. The form of his poetry, his versification, and often the vision, too, mark his work clearly as part of Renaissance literature. He was undoubtedly influenced by Hooft, whom he knew personally and for whom he had great regard. Whether one prefers Hooft's lyrical poems or Bredero's is, of course, a personal matter. Bredero's poetry lacks Hooft's elegance, refinement and his conciseness of expression. Beside Hooft, Bredero's poetry often seems less tightly organized. It has, on the other hand, a movement and a swing that one does not find in Hooft. Bredero's directness, the impression he makes of giving himself entirely in his poetry—irrespective of whether the poems are truly autobiographical or not—lends his work an air of immediacy which Hooft's work never has, and, one may assume, was never intended to have. The basic difference between the work of these two is that Hooft's poetry is essentially intellectual and musical, and Bredero's visual. Hooft, after all, was a thinker, steeped in philosophy, whereas Bredero was a painter.

The difference in approach between Hooft and Bredero is also apparent from their plays. Bredero was a prolific playwright, but did not write any historical plays, nor did he use his plays as a vehicle for views on statecraft and politics. He was an entertainer rather than an educator and was certainly much closer to the popular taste than Hooft was. When his plays were published in 1617, Samuel Coster stated in his Preface that in the three years in which Bredero's work had been performed by *De Eglantier,* the takings had been greater than in all previous years.

For his first three plays—*Rodderick en Alphonsus, Griane* and *Stommen Ridder* (Mute Knight)—Bredero turned to the sixteenth-century Spanish prose book of *Palmerin de Oliva* which was then very popular in Europe and which he used either in the French or the Dutch translation. These three plays are romantic plays, re-creating medieval subject-matter with the technique of the Renaissance. It was a genre which flourished in Spain and in Elizabethan England, but which never rose to great heights in the Netherlands. Bredero was its best exponent in Dutch, but in spite of his feeling for the theatre and his ability to write excellent dialogue, he did not really succeed in bringing the characters of these plays to life. The most vivid moments are the interpolations, the comical interludes which he added. In those scenes Bredero was at his best. He was then no longer dealing with romantic figures from a distant past, but with contemporaries whom he had observed and whom he knew. That these interludes do not contribute to the unity of the plays, goes without saying.

In the years 1612 and 1613 Bredero wrote three short

comedies: *De Klucht van de Koe* (The Farce of the Cow), *De Klucht van de Molenaar* (The Farce of the Miller), and *De Klucht van Symen sonder Soeticheyt* (The Farce of Simon without Sweetness), of which the first and the second deserve special mention. Both the Farce of the Cow and the Farce of the Miller are based on traditional material. The farmer who sells a cow for a thief without knowing that it is his own, and the miller who thinks that he is entertained by an attractive city woman but unwittingly sleeps with his own wife, were well-known figures in European literature. These traditional figures were transformed by Bredero into purely Dutch characters, and with so much polish that they acquired all the sparkle of completely original creations. At the same time, the composition which left something to be desired in the earlier plays attained a degree of perfection which was beyond the range of any other comedy writer in the seventeenth century. Bredero's ear for dialogue, his eye for detail, his insight into character and his sense of timing, all these qualities which he had always possessed, suddenly coalesced to make these two short plays the highlights of seventeenth-century comedy.

In his next play, Bredero tried a transformation of another kind. *Moortje* (The Moorish Woman) is an adaptation of Terence's *Eunuchus*, set in Amsterdam and placed against a Dutch background in the same manner as Hooft's *Warenar* a year later. Bredero regarded Hooft as his master, but it seems that on this occasion the master followed the pupil. *Moortje*, although good theatre, suffers from similar weaknesses as the first three plays. The best parts, again, are the interpolated scenes for which Bredero could draw upon upon his own observations. But, as in the earlier plays, these interpolations were not always smoothly integrated in the original work and caused some improbabilities in an already complicated plot. With the hindsight of the historian it is easy to see that once Bredero developed those scenes more fully—as he began to do in the short farces—and made his own observations the basis of a play, he would write a masterpiece. Which he did in

1618, the year of his death.

In *Spaanschen Brabander* (Spanish Brabanter) his observations stayed even closer to home than in the farces. The farmer and the miller were certainly people he knew, but not as intimately as the citizens of Amsterdam. And those were the people he put on the stage in his last play. There is a tinsmith and a goldsmith, a painter and a match-maker, there are boys enjoying a slanging match with the dog-whipper, whores gossiping about their trade and old men telling morbid tales of sickness and death. The plot of the play was provided by the Spanish picaresque novel *Lazarillo de Tormes*, which Bredero acknowledged in his introduction, but this time he allowed himself so much freedom, not only in the setting but also in the characterization, that the incongruities which marred some of his earlier work, did not occur. Actually, one can hardly speak of a plot. What there is of it is no more than a framework in which the characters can move. Consequently the play has little dramatic structure. The scenes are contained within five acts, but this division seems rather arbitrary and is more significant as a recognition of the prevailing fashion than as a result of dramatic necessity. Throughout the play the emphasis is on the individual scenes, not on their relation to one another, and it would indeed be best to regard the play as a kind of revue, a series of scenes held together by the two central characters, Jerolimo and his servant Robbeknol.

Jerolimo is a gentleman swindler who makes a living by selling hired goods and who boasts in flowery language of his former grand life in Brabant, continually extolling the virtues of that country, while sounding off at the Hollanders. The play had considerable topicality, for since the 1580s Amsterdam had been the refuge of a fairly large number of Brabanters and other Southerners, and relations between them and the Amsterdamers were often strained. The Brabanters tended to stick together, spoke with a different accent and were regarded by the native Amsterdamers as flamboyant and showy. To make matters worse, it was felt

by both parties that the Brabanters came from an area which
was culturally superior. The result was that the Amsterdamers looked on the Brabant community in their town with
an uncomfortable mixture of admiration and resentment. It
must therefore have been a satisfying experience for them to
see one of those Brabanters thoroughly ridiculed on the
stage. In his introduction to the play Bredero moralizes at
length about bankrupts such as Jerolimo who do not care
about the misery they cause to innocent people, but in the
play itself he adopts a more subtle approach. He does not
attack Jerolimo directly, but he lets him make a fool of
himself in his bombastic speeches so that all his criticism of
Amsterdam and the Amsterdamers boomerangs back on him.
The Amsterdamers could, and did, derive great comfort from
this. But there is more to Jerolimo. He may be a pompous
fool, yet he also has some generous and almost idealistic
traits, he is very resourceful and a man of fortitude in his
own way. He does not complain when things go against him,
he never loses heart and always remains absolutely true to
his own fantasies. He is in fact a latter-day Don Quichote
who in the course of the play wins the grumbling loyalty of
his Sancho, the down-to-earth Amsterdamer Robbeknol. By
tempering his criticism of the Brabanter with an unmistakable
element of affection, Bredero has given this play a subtlety
which none of his other plays possess. It was his last work.
He died in the same year, at the age of thirty-three.

In the years when Bredero was developing a new kind of
comedy, Joost van den Vondel was writing his first dramas.
Vondel, indisputably the greatest dramatist of the seventeenth century, was two years younger than Bredero, and,
from a social point of view, closer to him than to Hooft.
Like Bredero, Vondel belonged to the Amsterdam middle-
class. Yet there was an important distinction between the
two. Bredero came from a very Dutch family which had
lived in Amsterdam for generations whereas Vondel's parents
were not from Amsterdam but from Brabant, which placed
him in a different social context.

Vondel's father, a hat-maker, left Antwerp in 1582 for reasons which have never become entirely clear. The Vondels were Baptists and they may have felt or actually have been threatened in Calvinist Antwerp. They went to Cologne where young Vondel was born in 1587. But in Cologne, which was Roman Catholic, the situation was no less difficult for them than in Antwerp so that they moved again. After some years of wandering through Germany, they finally settled down in Amsterdam in 1596, when Vondel was nine years old. The father opened a shop dealing in silks and stockings in Warmoesstraat, the centre of the Brabant community in Amsterdam. Growing up in this environment, Vondel for a long time felt a Brabanter, a member of a minority group. There is little doubt that spending his early years in a social and religious minority environment was an important factor in the development of his personality and his work.

Vondel's first play, *Het Pascha* (Passover), was a tragi-comedy, a form which was new in Dutch literature. The first tragi-comedies in Dutch were written by Jacob Duym, a poet from Brabant, who in the first years of the seventeenth century lived in Leiden where he was head of the Chamber of Rhetoric. It is likely that Vondel knew his work and that when he wrote his first play as a young man of twenty-three he chose for it that modern form which Duym had recently introduced and which Hooft had also used for two minor plays which preceded *Granida*. *Granida* itself, as much a tragi-comedy as it was a pastoral play, may also have influenced the form of *Het Pascha*. The treatment of the choruses in *Het Pascha* suggests that Vondel was well aware of the function Hooft had given to the choruses in *Granida*. One may therefore say that Vondel's first play linked up with the latest developments in the theatre. Through its subject-matter it was connected with the biblical *Rederijker* play, as written, for example, by Abraham de Koningh, who like Vondel was a member of *Het Wit Lavendel*, the Brabant Chamber of Rhetoric in Amsterdam. A comparison with the

work of De Koningh shows, however, that by reducing the
number of characters and scene changes, and by eliminating
comic allegorical figures Vondel gave the traditional biblical
play a more modern dress. The looseness of *Het Pascha's*
dramatic construction is only partly a relic of the *Rederijker*
play. It is also partly due to Vondel's conception of drama
as a 'speaking picture'. For him the emphasis in dramatic art
was not on action, but on the pictorial aspect. It is a view
that is more clearly discernible in one play than in another,
and more so in the earlier plays than in the later ones, but it
is the principle that underlies all his dramatic work. It
explains the lack of action in his drama, an absence which
many critics have lamented, and also his devotion to detail,
even when the details have no bearing on the action.
Furthermore it helps to explain why Vondel sometimes chose
a subject that was hardly suitable for dramatic treatment,
such as the capture and destruction of Amsterdam in
Gijsbrecht van Aemstel and the fall of the angels in *Lucifer*.
To him they were suitable because of their pictorial
potentialities, static as this may have made the drama.

Het Pascha might best be described as a series of coherent
tableaux, depicting the deliverance of the Jews from Egypt.
The language, too, with its slow but easy flow, its ornateness,
its rich and flowery phrases—strongly influenced by the
exuberant style of du Bartas—stresses almost line by line
the pictorial aspect. The various tableaux had meaning as
illustrations of an episode in biblical history, but they also
referred to the situation in the Netherlands. The play was
written in 1610, the year after the signing of the truce with
Spain. The war had been successful and there was a
widespread feeling that it was all over. The whole of the
North had been freed from enemy troops and the truce had
been concluded on very good terms. To many people there
seemed no reason why the war should ever be started again.
In that first optimistic year of the truce Vondel wrote his
play in which he drew a parallel between the liberation of
the Jews from Egypt and the liberation of the Dutch from

Spain, and in which he celebrated the freedom of the Netherlands and what must have seemed to him the end of the war.

In the years between *Het Pascha* and his next play, *Hieru-salem Verwoest* (Jerusalem Destroyed), Vondel spent much time filling in the gaps in his education. He learnt Latin and English, and improved his knowledge of French by translating parts of du Bartas's *Semaines*. His study of Latin enabled him to read Seneca in the original and for the next ten years Seneca was going to be an important influence in his dramatic work. Seneca at that time was the greatest single influence in the Dutch theatre. Hugo Grotius had started the Seneca fashion in 1601 with his Latin drama *Adamus Exul,* and was followed by Daniel Heinsius in 1602 with *Auriacus* which Jacob Duym translated into Dutch. Through Heinsius the Senecan ideas spread to Hooft, in whose *Geeraerdt van Velsen* they are clearly noticeable. At the house of Roemer Visscher, Vondel met regularly with Hooft and several other poets to read and translate Seneca. Together this group produced a prose translation of *Troades* which Vondel rhymed and published a few years later. Seneca appealed to him for various reasons. He was in full agreement with the way in which Seneca subordinated action to plasticity. He appreciated Seneca's rhetoric and grandiloquence, and also his interest in historical detail. What must also have appealed to him was Seneca's full-blooded treatment of acts of violence, his way of showing horrific examples without any squeamish withholding of gory detail. Vondel followed Seneca's lead with gusto and *Hierusalem Verwoest* contains some very graphic descriptions. It must be said though, that other Baroque dramatists, Andreas Gryphius for one, went a great deal further in this respect.

The year 1618 was the year of the conflict between the Stadtholder Maurits and the Grand Pensionary Johan van Oldenbarnevelt. The following year Oldenbarnevelt was executed, and Grotius and several others were imprisoned. The conflict between Oldenbarnevelt and Maurits, or in a wider context, between Remonstrants and Contra-Remonstrants, had two aspects. In religious matters the Remonstrants were opposed to the Calvinist dogmas of original sin and predestination in their strictly orthodox sense. In politics they supported the sovereignty of the various provinces and resisted the attempts of Maurits to establish a centralized state. Also the fact that Oldenbarnevelt had pushed the truce through against the wishes of Maurits was an important factor in the conflict. Vondel followed the events closely without at first expressing an opinion in public. The political side was not of great interest to him, but his dislike of rigid Calvinist dogma brought him gradually to the side of Oldenbarnevelt and the Remonstrants.

In his biography of Vondel, Geerard Brandt tells us that after the execution of Oldenbarnevelt someone suggested to Vondel that he should write a play about it. Vondel declined, saying that the time had not yet come; but the other persisted and said that he should write it 'with different names'. According to Brandt, Vondel then came across the story of the feud between Ulysses and Palamedes, one of the Greek kings involved in the siege of Troy. Palamedes was in favour of seeking peace with the Trojans, but was accused by Ulysses of high treason and subsequently stoned to death. The evidence produced was a letter which had been forged by Ulysses and a sackful of gold, buried by Ulysses in the tent of Palamedes. It was a story that offered several parallels to the Maurits-Oldenbarnevelt conflict. The idea took some time to germinate and Vondel's *Palamedes* was not completed and published until 1625, the year of Maurits's death. Brandt relates that while Vondel was still working on the play, news came that the Prince was dying. 'Let him die', Vondel replied, 'I am just ringing the death-knell for him'. This anecdote, and the title of the play, *Palamedes of Vermoorde Onnoselheit* (Palamedes or Murdered Innocence), indicate the spirit in which it was written. Palamedes, who stands for Oldenbarnevelt, is the innocent hero, a man too noble to be true, whereas Maurits, represented by Ulysses's friend Agamemnon, is the blackest villain. The characterization of the two leading characters is done entirely in black and white, and Vondel's hero-worship of Oldenbarnevelt in combination with his bitter hatred of Maurits prevented the play from becoming a convincing tragedy. *Palamedes* may not be Vondel's best play, writing and publishing it was certainly an act of courage. The conflict between Remonstrants and Contra-Remonstrants had been a sharp one, the Contra-Remonstrants had won the day, and they were not going to let themselves be accused of murder without hitting back. The first edition of *Palamedes* was seized, and the government in The Hague demanded Vondel's extradition. Fortunately for him the city council of Amsterdam refused and decided to try him in Amsterdam itself. Vondel appeared before the court with a solicitor and two barristers who argued rather disingenuously, but not without success, that *Palamedes* was a Greek tragedy and nothing else. Vondel was reprimanded and fined three hundred guilders, and *Palamedes* went through seven more editions before a year had passed.

Far from intimidating him, the *Palamedes* affair seems to have made Vondel more outspoken, for in the years after 1625 he wrote a great deal of satirical poetry with a political bias. In *Rommelpot van het Hanekot* (Rumbling Pot of the Cock-pit) he attacked the Contra-Remonstrant ministers who had dismissed their colleague Hanecop for having spoken out against the looting of a Remonstrant church; in *Harpoen* (Harpoon) he contrasted the good and the bad ministers; in *Roskam* (Curry-comb) he inveighed against the corruption of modern magistrates. These poems—and he wrote several more of the same kind—are all of them fierce and militant, obviously writtten in anger and ranging in style from the broad Amsterdam dialect of a street-ballad to the lofty tone of his dramatic work. Some are just outbursts and contain more emotion than poetry, but the best ones—*Roskam* for example—are very eloquent expressions of an honest indignation.

Vondel stopped writing these satires as suddenly as he had begun and turned to a new form. He started work on an epic poem about Constantine the Great, the first Christian emperor of Rome. As a protest against the fragmentation of Christianity, he wanted to celebrate Constantine as the great unifying force. But after some years' work, he tore up what he had written. In 1639 he wrote to Grotius who had frequently encouraged him to complete it, that after the death of his wife and two of his children he felt too depressed to continue with it. This may indeed have been the reason, but it is also possible that his intensive study of Constantine's life had brought to light details which were disappointing and which made him regard Constantine as unsuitable for the part of the epic hero who, according to the Renaissance tradition, had to be pure and blameless in all respects.

When he was still hoping to complete the *Constantinade,* he interrupted work on it twice to return to tragedy. First he translated Grotius's Latin drama *Sofompaneas,* then he wrote an original play, *Gijsbrecht van Aemstel,* intended for the opening of the new theatre in Amsterdam in 1637. The occasion demanded an Amsterdam subject which was found in the events following the death of Count Floris V. In a sense therefore, the play continues Hooft's *Geeraerdt van Velsen.* It describes how, eight years after the death of the Count, his partisans laid siege to Amsterdam and burnt it. The form of the play is classical: five acts, choruses after the first four acts, unities of time and place, strict alexandrines. Vondel gave the play an additional classical aspect by closely following the second book of Virgil's *Aeneid,* so that the fall of Amsterdam recalled the fall of Troy and assumed a similar grandeur. As the occasion was a festive one, Amsterdam's rebirth and future greatness were prophesied at at the end of the play by the angel Raphael. This link with the *Aeneid,* together with Vondel's own theory that the pictorial aspect of drama should dominate over the dynamic aspect, gave the play an epic rather than a dramatic quality.

The lack of action in *Gijsbrecht van Aemstel* is notorious. Almost all events are reported instead of being acted out and one might even say that the play consists of a series of monologues. Its main beauty lies in its poetry, in the stately rhythm of the speeches and the lyrical musicality of the choruses. In spite of its static character it was very successful on the stage and went through well over a hundred productions in Vondel's lifetime. It has been suggested that Rembrandt was so impressed by a performance of *Gijsbrecht* that he based his *Night Watch* on its opening scene. The first performance did not take place without difficulty. The play was to open at Christmas, but the Calvinist ministers in Amsterdam suspected it of containing Roman Catholic features, and succeeded in delaying the first performance until 3rd January which till 1968 was its traditional opening date in Amsterdam.

The Calvinist ministers may have been small-minded in holding up the première of *Gijsbrecht*, yet their observations were not entirely wrong. One cannot say that *Gijsbrecht van Aemstel* is a Roman Catholic play, but it is certainly not the work of a man who was hostile to Roman Catholicism. Vondel in those years was becoming more and more dissatisfied with Protestantism and was slowly moving away from it. He moved so far away from it that at one stage he stood in between Roman Catholicism and Protestantism, very much like Grotius, whom he admired greatly. But Vondel went a step further than Grotius and was received into the Roman Catholic Church in 1641. His conversion had a profound influence on his work and in some repects also affected his place in the literary world and in society in general. The Netherlands in those years was governed as a Calvinist state. The Calvinists had identified themselves with the revolt and the war against Spain, and in the 1640s the war, which had been resumed in 1621, was practically won. The Roman Catholics had become identified with the enemy and were the losing party. The Calvinist Church was the Established Church, the Roman Catholic Church was officially forbidden. There were loopholes, though, and bribery often persuaded the authorities not to enforce the law, so often in fact that in some areas of the country these bribes were considered as a kind of tax. In other areas Calvinism and Roman Catholicism co-existed more or less peacefully without bribes or tax. One of those areas was the district of Muiden where Hooft was the civil authority. Hooft, though a Protestant himself, left the Roman Catholics under his jurisdiction a great deal more freedom than the law allowed them. Yet, the treatment of the Roman Catholics in his district led to a conflict with Vondel. With the zeal of the newly converted, Vondel demanded a larger measure of freedom for the Roman Catholics in Hooft's area, adding that if Hooft did not comply he would use his influence in Brussels where Hooft was involved in a lawsuit. Hooft never forgave Vondel for this threat. He no longer invited him to Muiden and in their later contact adopted a tone of cool formality which Vondel resented but never properly understood.

The period immediately preceding Vondel's conversion had been very productive. In 1640 he published three biblical plays: *Gebroeders* (Brothers), translated the same year into German by Andreas Gryphius as *Die Gibeoniter, Joseph in Dothan* and *Joseph in Egypte*. They were followed in 1641 by *Peter en Pauwels* (Peter and Paul), a drama about the death of the two apostles. The first years after his conversion, on the other hand, were rather a lean period. It was five years before he wrote his next play, *Maria Stuart*, which as a drama suffers even more from his worship of the 'innocent hero' than *Palamedes* did. His attack on Queen Elizabeth and his attitude of apologist for Roman Catholicism brought him into court again, even though he had taken the precaution of publishing the play anonymously. He was fined one hundred and eighty guilders, 'which seemed strange to many people', says Brandt, 'considering how much freedom of writing was permitted at that time and considering also that of old the poets were allowed more freedom than others'.

In the same year 1646 another unpleasant incident occurred, also connected with his conversion. Two years before, Vondel had published his collected poems. It was not a complete edition: several poems, notably the satirical ones, were omitted. Now there appeared a second volume of Vondel's collected poems, published anonymously and containing all the poems omitted from the first volume. The book also contained a sneering preface in which the anonymous editor—though praising Vondel as a great poet —recalled that Vondel had now twice changed churches and wondered where he would go next. He also accused Vondel of having acted in bad faith when he published Grotius's *Testament*. After the death of Grotius in 1645 Vondel had translated a selection from his last work and this publication seemed to suggest that Grotius too had become a Roman Catholic. The Remonstrants, who had always regarded Grotius as one of their leaders, were up in arms and accused Vondel of tendentious translation, an accusation which was now repeated by the editor of Vondel's second volume. The book was clearly published in order to avenge Grotius and to embarrass Vondel by showing that he had not always been such a good Roman Catholic. Vondel tried in vain to find out who was responsible. Brandt in his biography talks glibly about a young man of twenty who was later sorry for what he had done. There are good reasons to assume that this young man was Brandt himself.

After these incidents which show that relations between Roman Catholics and Protestants were still very strained, it seems a pleasant sign of tolerance that it was Vondel who wrote the play for the official celebrations of the end of the war. He wrote it in 1647 while negotiations were still going on. *Leeuwendalers* was a kind of pastoral play, written as a glorification of peace. Vondel himself did not call it a pastoral play, but a 'lantspel', a country play, in which the shepherds of the Italian pastoral had given way to Dutch peasants.

Leeuwendalers was an occasional play and as such an interlude in Vondel's work. At the same time it marked the beginning of a new stage in his development as a dramatist. In the introduction to *Leeuwendalers* Vondel for the first time mentioned the Artistotelian notions of 'recognition' and 'reversal of situation', and the adoption of these notions added considerably to the dramatic quality of the plays which followed. In these later plays Vondel broke with the epic tendency of his earlier drama. His hero was no longer an epic hero, no longer an innocent, blameless man destroyed by the evils around him. In the later plays the conflict between good and bad takes place within the hero himself, who is neither wholly good nor wholly bad, but often wavering, and who is finally destroyed by his own deficiencies. In *Salomon* (1648), the protagonist King Solomon is a tragic hero of this kind. He is not entirely bad, but weak, cowardly and a victim of his own sensuality. He arouses pity and fear because of his former splendour and impending fall. He recognizes his guilt and in the end experiences the reversal of his situation.

Lucifer (1654), Vondel's most grandiose play, continues what *Salomon* began. It describes the rebellion of the angels after the creation of man. Lucifer takes charge of the rebellious angels but wavers for a long time between good and bad, between loyalty to God and the evil of an attack on God. Several times he is about to give in to the forces of loyalty and reason, but his army has become too strong for him and he is forced to go ahead. In the clash that follows, Lucifer is defeated and cast out. In order to revenge himself he then causes the fall of Adam and Eve. He is a tragic hero like Solomon, not evil, but over-jealous of his own position, and at the same time hesitant and allowing himself to be pushed in the direction of evil.

Lucifer is Vondel's most Baroque play. Everthing in it is lofty and grandiose. Its intention is to depict the most tragic moment in the history of mankind: the fall of Lucifer and the fall of man. Vondel strove after the highest possible: the characters are angels, the scene is set in heaven. All this is reflected in the style which is more exuberant than in any other of his plays. As poetry, *Lucifer* represents Vondel at his loftiest, as drama it suffers from a lack of action. Right through the play the tension is built up towards the clash between the loyal and the rebellious angels. But the clash itself could not be shown on stage, and when the curtain goes up for the fifth act Lucifer has been defeated and the reversal of the situation has taken place without the audience having been able to watch it. The fault lies not so much in the writing or composition of the play, but in the choice of a subject that was essentially not suitable for dramatic treatment. Milton who hesitated between dramatic and epic form for *Paradise Lost* finally made the wiser choice, irrespective of whether his considerations were aesthetic or pragmatic. The similarities between Milton's poem and Vondel's play are so numerous that it has often been thought that *Lucifer,* which precedes *Paradise Lost* by thirteen years, may have influenced Milton. There are, however, no positive indications for this theory, and the similarities lose much of their conclusive force when one realizes how widespread the theme of the 'celestial cycle' was in European Renaissance literature, and that both Milton and Vondel had read Grotius's Latin drama *Adamus Exul* (1601).

Lucifer was performed only twice in 1654. Brandt tells us that it drew the fire of some Calvinist ministers who did not approve of bringing angels on to the stage. They accused Vondel of sacrilege and also attacked his approach to drama. They succeeded in imposing their will: further performances were forbidden and the publisher's stock was confiscated. The Burgomasters apparently did not pursue the matter any further, for seven new editions were published in the same year. But financially it was a disaster because the complicated set depicting the heavens had cost a fortune. To help the theatre out of its financial difficulties Vondel wrote a new play for which the same set could be used. This play, *Salmoneus,* dealing with a mythological subject, turned out to be a weak play and is also unlikely to have helped financially as three years went by before it was performed. The criticism that was made of *Lucifer* hurt Vondel deeply and from the preface of *Jeptha*, written in 1659, it appears that he set himself the task of writing a model tragedy which would prove all his critics wrong. *Jeptha* is a biblical play and dramatizes an episode from the Book of Judges. Jeptha is waging war and makes the promise that if he wins, he will sacrifice to God the first being to meet him when he returns home. He wins the battle, returns home and is met by his daughter Ifis. Jeptha feels bound to keep his promise, gives his daughter two months respite to prepare herself, and then sacrifices her. It was a well-known subject and Vondel was not the first writer to have been struck by its dramatic potential. Abraham de Koningh had written a *Jeptha* in 1615 and only nine years before Vondel's play Giacomo Carissimi's Latin oratorio *Jepthe* had had its first performance. But the most famous *Jeptha* had been written a hundred years earlier: George Buchanan's Latin drama *Jephthes sive votum*, published in 1554. In the seventeenth century Buchanan's play was still regarded as one of the best Latin dramas, also by Vondel, and Vondel consciously wrote his own play as an *imitatio* of Buchanan's. He had only one criticism to make: Buchanan had not observed the unity of time, i.e. he had incorporated in his play the period of two months' grace whereas the Aristotelian prescription allowed drama a scope of not more than twenty-four hours. Vondel corrected Buchanan by shifting the beginning of the play to the end of the two months. In doing so he sacrificed the drama of the first meeting between Ifis and Jeptha, but complying with the theory was of greater value to Vondel than making a theatrical effect. In the preface Vondel also elaborated on the construction of the play and pointed out that it was in every respect in accordance with the demands of the theorists: the difficulty about the unity of time had been solved, the unities of place and action had been observed, the mood of the characters changed several times, and the tragedy was enacted between close relatives. Though the play ends after the death of Ifis, she does not die on stage, in compliance with a rule laid down by Horace. For the metre Vondel followed the advice of Ronsard and used ten and eleven syllable iambics instead of his customary alexandrines.

Aristotle, Horace, Scaliger, Heinsius, Vossius, Grotius, Ronsard, Buchanan, they are all quoted in the preface as the authorities whose precepts were worth following. Vondel was seventy-two when he wrote *Jeptha* and still eager to learn. Whether because of his preoccupation with theory, or in spite of it, *Jeptha* stands out as one of his most convincing plays. After the Baroque *Lucifer,* its most striking aspect is its simplicity. There is more understatement than overstatement, all extreme dramatic effects have been avoided, and the language, too, is sober, restrained, almost austere, which gives *Jeptha* a terseness that most of his other plays lack.

The period between 1659 and 1667 was an extremely productive time for Vondel. In those eight years he wrote no less than ten tragedies, apart from complete verse translations of *King Oedipus* and *Iphigeneia in Tauris.* From the same period date a long biblical epic, *Joannes de Boetgezant* (John, Preacher of Penitence) and two long didactic poems, *Bespiegelingen van Godt en Godtsdienst* (Contemplations of God and Religion), and *De Heerlijckheit der Kercke* (The Magnificence of the Church). The plays of this last period were predominantly biblical, dealing with King David, David's son Adoniah, Samson, Adam and Noah.

Adam in Ballingschap (Adam in Exile) bears the same title as Grotius's *Adamus Exul* and, like *Jeptha,* must be regarded as an *imitatio* in which the general line of Grotius's play was strictly followed. But Vondel was no longer a Seneca adept as Grotius was when he wrote his play. Vondel's guide was now Sophocles, which means that argumentativeness had made way for lyricism and that strong emphasis was placed on the reversal of the situation. Vondel's last play, *Noah,* is also a biblical play, but well distinguished from the others by the complexity of its

structure. On the face of it the structure seems to be a
switchback to the earlier plays with an epic hero. Noah is
represented in his supreme strength on the day of the Great
Flood. There is no weakness in him, no hesitation, no
wavering between good and bad. He is an epic hero,
reminiscent of John the Baptist in *Joannes*. But on closer
analysis it appears that next to Noah there is another leading
character, the prince Ahiman, who is a tragic hero in the
proper sense of the word, who wavers and who makes the
fatal choice, and in whom the reversal of the situation is
most dramatically shown. *Noah* was Vondel's last play and it
is almost symbolic that he closed his dramatic *oeuvre,* at the
age of eighty, with a combination of the two kinds of drama
into which his work can be divided.

Vondel was a highly talented dramatist, but not a dramatic
genius. Most of his plays suffer from one or more flaws,
whether it is lack of action or longwinded descriptiveness,
shallow psychology or hyperbolic style. He has sometimes
been compared to Shakespeare, but if all comparisons are
invidious, this one is particularly so. For imperfections apart,
there is no play of Vondel which shows the same insight into
human nature or the same awareness of psychological
complexity as the best plays of Shakespeare do. Consequently, Vondel's drama never has the power to jolt a modern
audience in the way Shakespeare still can. One admires the
beauty of its poetry, the nicety of composition and the
probity of the man behind the scenes, but in most cases one
fails to be moved.

It was Vondel's achievement to develop Dutch Renaissance drama into something entirely his own. Strangely, it was
to remain his own, for in spite of the great authority he held,
his plays have found only a few imitators. In the last fifteen
years of his life popular support for his plays waned and
performances became infrequent. *Adam in Ballingschap* was
not performed until 1910! The man who drew full houses
was Jan Vos whose *Aran en Titus* stands out as one of the
most bombastic plays of the century. It was a cheap

showpiece, full of murder, rape and torture, written in hollow grandiloquent verse. But its appeal was enormous, and also the intelligentsia—Hooft, Huygens, Barlaeus, even Vondel himself—praised it highly. 'Seeing before saying' was Vos's motto and with this emphasis on action he placed himself diametrically opposite Vondel's static dramas. The views of Jan Vos won and Vondel lost out. Then towards the end of the century, the plays of Jan Vos and his followers gave way to French classicist drama, and the classicists had their own criticism to make of Vondel's approach to drama. The result of all this was that Vondel was followed by no school and that his influence on the development of drama remained smaller than one might have expected. His epic *Joannes de Boetgezant*, on the other hand, had a great and long-lasting influence. Vondel was the first Dutch poet to write a biblical epic and after him the genre was widely practised until the middle of the eighteenth century.

As a lyricist, too, Vondel's influence was profound. Throughout his long life—he died in 1679 at the age of ninety-one—he wrote lyrical poetry of a tremendous variety: sonnets, odes, nuptial songs, elegies, eulogies, satires, religious poetry, poetic letters and so forth, all written in styles that range from great simplicity to Baroque exuberance. The most striking quality of all these poems is their easy flow and their musicality. It is curious that Vondel who took little interest in music wrote the most musical poetry of the century, much more so than Huygens who was a considerable musician and composer. Vondel's approach to poetry was essentially different from Hooft's and Huygens's. With a little exaggeration one might say that Hooft and Huygens never used two words when one would do whereas Vondel used two or more when they were available. His aim was not conciseness but richness. Not the intellectual, but the sensuous element is dominant in his work. His poetry therefore lacks the measured elegance of Hooft and the terseness of Huygens, but stands out in melodiousness and sonority. In musicality, colour, richness of vocabulary, and also thematically, it often comes close to the poetry of his English contemporary Richard Crashaw, without the conceits, however, of which Crashaw was so fond. Vondel abhorred sophisticated wit and obscurity. We do not know what he thought of Crashaw's poetry—it is unlikely that he knew it —but when he read some translations of John Donne's work he reacted with a sarcastic poem in which he derided Donne's obscurity, calling him 'that dark sun'.

The author of those Donne translations was Constantijn Huygens, the youngest of the four pre-eminent poets of the seventeenth century. He was born in The Hague in 1596 as the son of the Secretary to the State Council. His social background therefore was closer to Hooft's than to Vondel's or Bredero's. His father was a man of erudition who educated his children very much in the Renaissance tradition, with so much success that Huygens at an early age was proficient in Latin, Greek, French, English, German, Spanish and Italian. His earliest poetry, written at the age of eleven, was in Latin, and throughout his life he continued to write poetry in Latin as well as in Dutch, French, Italian and English. For a few years he studied law at Leiden, then left in 1618 to go to England as a diplomatic cadet with a Dutch mission. In 1620 he paid a second visit to England, this time as the secretary of the mission. He made several of these trips to England and they had a profound influence on his work. His Donne translations were written in 1630, but he probably came to know Donne's work in 1621 (in manuscript, for the first edition of Donne did not appear until 1633).

In 1621 also, after he had returned from his second visit to England, he wrote his first major poem: *Batava Tempe, dat is 't Voorhout van 's-Gravenhage* (Batava Temple, that is the Voorhout at the Hague). *Batave Tempe,* the Batavian (Dutch) Tempe valley, is a hymn to the Voorhout, a linden-lined avenue in The Hague. The plan of the poem is simple. In a good hundred stanzas it gives a description of the avenue in the four seasons—with much emphasis on its

summer beauty—and of the people who walk and talk
there. The plan may be simple, the poetry is anything but
simple. From his first work to his last, Huygens was a
cerebral poet who did not express himself in lyrical effusion
but in intellectual wit and subtlety. To him the poet's aim
was to be eloquent, to show his ingenuity and his ability to
give meaning to unusual combinations. His style has many
points of contact with the mannerist styles of poets such as
Marino in Italy, and Lyly, Donne and the Metaphysical
School in England. It is doubtful whether any of these poets
had a direct influence on his work, but it is clear that he
knew their style and that his approach to poetry was
comparable. *Voorhout* abounds in unusual and surprising
expressions. Some seem rather laboured to the modern
reader, some are so far-fetched that they fail to impress, but
some are still very effective. The most striking examples are
to be found in the two stanzas which consist entirely of
circumlocutions for the sun: 'Me you will not chase away,
fierce shiner from up-high, nimble measurer of our days,
compasser of years, roundabout eye, fog dissipater, summer
bringer, day extender, fruit benefactor, animal biter, skin
scorcher, blond wrecker, girl's hate, cloud drover, night
chaser, moon surpriser, star thief, shadow splitter, torch
bearer, thief betrayer, spectacles' help, linen bleacher, hair
curler, all-see-er, never blind, dust disturber, sky roller,
morning raiser, travellers' friend'.

A passage such as this is an extreme case, even for
Huygens, but at the same time it was part of a literary
tradition. One can find similar circumlocutions in Ronsard,
in several Italian Renaissance poets, and in Dutch in Daniel
Heinsius's *Lofsang van Bacchus* (Hymn of Bacchus), while
even Vondel in his *Rijnstroom* (River Rhine) paid a brief
tribute to the fashion. They were usually not meant very
seriously, they were certainly not presented as the *ne plus
ultra* of poetic expression, but rather as an intellectual
entertainment, a 'gaillardise' as Ronsard called it, which
gave the poet the opportunity to show his inventiveness and

originality in a lighthearted way. From this point of view Huygens's circumlocutions for the sun fitted well into his poem, for in spite of its terseness and occasional obscurity, it is essentially a lighthearted poem, playful and cheerful, and full of vitality. It was written as a hymn, but it has nothing in common with the loftiness of the traditional hymn. Huygens may moralize a little here and there, but he does not do it in a heavy-handed way. When he criticizes the silly sentimentality of the lovers in the Voorhout, the extravagant dresses of the girls, or the French phrases of the snob, his criticism is not made with angry seriousness, but in a tone of amusement. Yet the satirical observations are there, and after reading *Voorhout* one is not altogether surprised that in his next long poem Huygens turned to satire proper.

Back in England in 1621 he wrote *Costelick Mal* (Costly Folly), a long satirical poem on fashion. It is a satire more in form than in tone. It does contain some scathing criticism and some sharp attacks on extravagance and hypocrisy, but the general tone of the poem is one of reasoned argument rather than of biting satire. It has been suggested that personal circumstances prompted the writing of *Costelick Mal*. Huygens, who in spite of his father's eminent position, had been brought up in austere Calvinist surroundings, felt a little out of place among the splendid English courtiers. In his letters home he complained of his lack of money which prevented him from dressing as he should. He did not want to compete with the elegance of the English Court, but neither did he want to be conspicuous through lack of elegance. Taking this into account, *Costelick Mal* looks more like a rationalization of his own impecunious situation than like a satire of an evil that needed rooting out. The ending, with its resignation and recognition of fashion as something silly but inevitable, is remarkably mild for a satire. Also, Huygens was too reasonable a man to write a consistently one-sided satirical poem. And even if he had been really angry when he decided to write the poem, much of his anger may have been spent during the preparation of it, for he read a great deal on the subject and made copious notes from various sources, among them John William's *A Sermon of Apparell* of 1620. It is also likely that he read Robert Burton's *The Anatomy of Melancholy* which appeared in 1621, the year in which Huygens began to write *Costelick Mal*. The extensive preparatory studies had the disadvantage of making *Costelick Mal* a much less spontaneous poem than *Voorhout* for which he read little and made few notes.

His volume *Zedeprinten* (Characters) also shows that he was well acquainted with contemporary English literature. The Character poetry had become very popular in England in the first half of the seventeenth century, particularly with the collections of Joseph Hall, John Stephens and Thomas Overbury. Huygens knew the English Character literature and eager as he always was to try his hand at something new, introduced it into Dutch literature. Some of the types described in *Zedeprinten* had also been dealt with by the English writers and were therefore rather derivative; others, such as An Ambassador, The Professor, The Rich Woman were entirely original. They are moralistic portraits, satirical and humorous, and written with a good deal of Huygens's special brand of sophisticated wit.

Real poetry to Huygens had to be intricate, even obscure. Real poetry, he said, needed elucidation. He made this statement in a note to his long poem *Daghwerk* (Daily Business), written between 1627 and 1638, and dealing with his daily life, his work and his attitude to it, his religious views, his views on poetry, and so on. In the same poem he turned the theory into practice by summarizing it stanza by stanza in prose. Not every seventeenth-century writer agreed with his opinion that obscurity was the hall-mark of good poetry. Vondel reacted strongly to his Donne translations, and the poet and playwright Willem van Focquenbroch, a great believer in simplicity in literature, attacked him and Hooft for the demands they made on their readers. 'It seems', Focquenbroch wrote in a poem addressed to Huygens, 'that you and Hooft are constantly trying to be understood by no one else but yourselves. How sad it is, how silly, when a man does not have the talent to say something in poetry without having to explain it again in prose'. One can understand Focquenbroch's annoyance, for *Daghwerk* is a notoriously difficult poem, but his diagnosis was wrong: it was not a matter of being unable to write simply, but a conscious effort to avoid it. When Huygens wanted to write simply, he could do so as well as anyone else, as he showed on several occasions.

His only play *Trijntje Cornelis* (1653), though also notorious for its difficulty, is basically very simple. It describes the adventures of the wife of a barge skipper from Holland who goes on a spree in Antwerp and finds herself the morning after robbed of all her clothes, lying on the rubbish-heap. Situation, plot and action are simple enough, and the difficulties which the modern reader finds on his way are this time not due to Huygens's obscurity, sophistication, mannerism or whatever one would like to call it, but to the dialects which he used: broad Holland and broad Antwerp. The play, which is an excellent piece of theatre, delights in farcical situations and scabrous detail, and shows with great candour the down-to-earth, crude and sometimes vulgar side of Huygens's personality which was just as real as his aristocratic sophistication. *Voorhout* and *Costelick Mal* occasionally give some indication of it, but it found full expression in his play and also in several other poems, particularly in his epigrams, a form to which he seems to have been addicted as he wrote hundreds upon hundreds of them throughout his life.

These two sides of Huygens's personality are puzzling to the modern reader who is often tempted to minimize the vulgar side or to gloss it over indulgently as a slight aberration of an otherwise great man. But a complex personality cannot be reduced to a simple one by ignoring some of its characteristics, and if one wants to understand Huygens properly one must accept the fact that his personality was complex, even if the various traits sometimes seem to be in open conflict with one another.

Huygens was an extremely well-educated man, not to the point of being a great scholar in any particular field, but well-versed in so many subjects that he came closer to the Renaissance ideal of the *uomo universale* than anyone else in the Netherlands. He was an excellent judge of painting, a musician with many compositions to his name, a linguist who had few equals, a diplomat knighted by James II, a writer with many international connections, who counted among his friends and correspondents such people as John Donne, Francis Bacon, Daniel Heinsius, Descartes, Cornelis Drebbel, Ben Jonson and Pierre Corneille. The high level of sophistication suggested by all this was certainly there, but at the same time there was in Huygens a coarseness which was just as much part of his personality as was his refinement. He was on the one hand the most modern Dutch writer of his time, fully alive to the new developments in poetry abroad. It is significant for instance that he even wrote a number of poems in blank verse. On the other hand he was capable of the kind of humour that was not far removed from the crudest medieval farce.

In his emotional life, too, one finds similar contradictions. He was on the whole well-balanced and rational, a Christian Stoic like Hooft. Yet there are also letters and poems of his—*De Uytlandighe Herder* (The Exiled Shepherd) for example—which show that he was very vulnerable and easily depressed, prone to attacks of melancholy. He could be smug and self-satisfied, as in some passages of *Daghwerk,* and at the same time rather uncertain of himself. His personality was a good deal more complex than that of Vondel or Bredero, and the reflection of it on paper certainly looks less harmonious than that of Hooft. He also lacked Hooft's religious tolerance. Huygens was an ardent Calvinist and very anti-Roman Catholic. When Maria Tessel-schade, a close friend of his and Hooft's was converted to Roman Catholicism, Huygens did his utmost to bring her back to Protestantism, whereas there is no evidence at all that

Hooft ever tried to exert any influence in this direction. Also, Huygens was a far more pronounced moralist than either Hooft, Vondel or Bredero; his moralism, in fact, is so prominent that he has often been bracketed with Jacob Cats, the greatest moralist of his time and far and away the most popular writer of the seventeenth century.

Jacob Cats was almost twenty years older than Huygens and was an enthusiastic though slightly paternal admirer of his. *Costelick Mal* had been dedicated to him and he had reciprocated with two laudatory poems in which he praised Huygens as a teacher of morals.But granted their common interest in moralism, it would be difficult to extend the parallel much further. For Cats was primarily a didactic writer whereas Huygens was not. Moralist though Huygens may have been, his main interest in writing was aesthetic. He was always greatly interested in form, in experimenting with form, with metre, rhyme and rhythm, with ways of expression. Everything he wrote gives evidence of his tremendous interest in aesthetic matters, as do his theoretical exchanges with Hooft on syllable quantity and his attempts to convince Corneille of the necessity of regular accentuation in French poetry.

In the work of Cats one finds nothing of the kind. Cats opted for the alexandrine and never moved away from it. Metrical and rhythmical experimentation, even the variations allowed by the alexandrine, were taboo to him. He must have been completely insensitive to rhythm; metre, a strict invariable alternation of accented and unaccented syllables, was all. His lines drone on with the imperturbability of a metronome and have a soporific effect that is matched by no other poet. Yet his comtemporaries were enormously taken by his work, so much so that in many households the only books present were the Bible and a volume of Cats. His editions were incomparably larger than those of any other writer of his time. In 1655 a volume of his poetry was published in 5000 copies, the kind of edition of which Vondel, Hooft and Huygens could only dream—if they had been interested. Since the middle of the nineteenth century Cats's reputation as a poet has gone steadily downhill; it cannot sink much lower, and it seems unlikely ever to rise high again.

The writers discussed so far, were, with the exception of Hooft, predominantly poets and dramatists. Creative prose was a genre not practised by the major writers. Vondel wrote one essay on poetry and the poet, in an excellent style which makes one wish that he had turned to prose more often. Huygens and Bredero stayed away from prose altogether. Yet outside the group of major writers some very interesting prose books were written. There is, for instance, a fairly large collection of travel stories, mainly descriptions of voyages to the East and West Indies, America, China etc., several of which have been translated into English and have been published by the Hakluyt Society. Outstanding among these travel books is the *Journal* of Willem Bontekoe, a very readable account of his ill-fated voyage to the Indies. Among the other prose writers mention should be made of Joan de Brune who in 1657 published a large book of moralistic but often humorous prose pieces under the title of *Bankket-werk van Goede Gedagten* (Banquet of Good Thoughts), and of Adriaan Poirters whose *Het Masker van de Werelt Afghetrocken* (The World's Mask Pulled Away), of 1646, became one of the most widely read books of the century.

Examples of the novel are scarce in the seventeenth century. Perhaps one might include the prose pastoral under the early forms of novel writing. Quite a few were published in the Netherlands in this period, most of them strongly under the influence of Honoré d'Urfé's *Astrée* of 1610. The best known example of this genre in Dutch is Johan van Heemskerk's *Batavische Arcadia* (Batavian Arcady), published in 1637. It is a curious hybrid: a didactic and moralistic work which gives a survey of Dutch history but which is set within the framework of a pleasure trip to the coast made by a group of fashionable ladies and gentlemen who liven up the historical discourse with lighthearted talk about love.

Closer to the modern novel were the picaresque novels, the best of which was written by Nicolaas Heinsius, grandson of Daniel Heinsius and a man who led a picaresque life before he put it down on paper. He became a medical doctor at twenty, was exiled from the Netherlands because of manslaughter, wandered through Europe for many years, was at one time personal physician to Christina of Sweden, at another to the Elector of Brandenburg. Many of his own adventures are recorded in the book which made him famous, *Den Vermakelijken Avanturier* (The Amusing Adventurer), published in 1695. It is not a book that excels in character development or analysis since it consists simply of an entertaining string of adventures, well-told and observed with a shrewd eye for the ridiculous and the phony. The book was a great success, in the Netherlands as well as abroad: it went through many Dutch editions and was translated into French, English, Italian and German.

Occasional successes such as that of Heinsius apart, the work of the poets completely overshadowed that of the prose writers. And again, the work of Vondel, Hooft, Huygens and Bredero overshadowed that of a large number of other poets who would probably have secured a more conspicuous place in the history of literature if they had lived in another period. This is true of Jacob Revius, of Heiman Dullaert, of Jacob Westerbaen perhaps, of Jan Starter, Dirck Camphuysen and Joannes Stalpart van der Wiele. It is also very true of Willem van Focquenbroch.

For a long time Focquenbroch has been denied the recognition that is due to him, because his work does not harmonize easily with the tone of loftiness which dominated seventeenth-century poetry. Focqenbroch took no interest in loftiness except as a subject of parody. His poetry is unembellished, straightforward and simple, far removed from the grand style of Vondel, the refinement of Hooft and the mannerism of Huygens. Focquenbroch was a thoroughly disillusioned man, a medical doctor whose debts and an unhappy love affair seem to have driven him out of the

Netherlands to the West Coast of Africa where he lived out his life. His work reads as a very honest record of his feelings and opinions, and shows him to have been a great pessimist and cynic, who yet all the time rebelled against his fate and who bitterly resented the life he was leading, without ever becoming tearful about it. His work is related to the burlesques of Paul Scarron in France, and in Holland to the earthy comedies of Bredero and Huygens's *Trijntje Cornelis*. Most of his work is lyrical poetry, love poetry and anti-love poetry, anecdotal and occasional poetry, but he is also known for an entertaining comedy, *De Min in het Lazarushuys* (Love in the Madhouse).

As was stated at the beginning of this chapter the South did not share equally with the North in the creativity of the Netherlands in the seventeenth century. The most important southern poet in the early years of the century was Justus de Harduwijn who wrote a volume of typical Renaissance poetry under the title of *De Weerlycke Liefden tot Roosemond* (The Profane Love for Roosemond), full of reminiscences of the Pléiade poets, it is true, but important because of its elegant diction and a mastery of the sonnet form which was unusual in the early years of the century. The volume was completed in 1605— though not published until 1613 —and it shows clearly that in those years a writer like De Harduwijn was still ahead of most of his northern contemporaries. It was also a southerner, Richard Verstegen, who wrote a volume of Characters (in prose) four years before Huygens introduced the genre into northern literature. In the second half of the century the South produced a poet and playwright of some note in Michiel de Swaen whose *De Gecroonde Leersse* (The Crowned Boot) is still occasionally performed. After that, the literature of the South went into hibernation until the middle of the nineteenth century.

VI

CLASSICISTS AND ROMANTICISTS
EIGHTEENTH CENTURY

The eighteenth century has a bad name in Dutch history, and it is unlikely that anyone has ever been tempted to award it the epithet of 'golden'. It was a period, it is often said, which was resting at leisure on the laurels won in the preceding century, an age of stagnation and decline, of false values, corruption and sham, when powdered wigs concealed more than bald heads and bad smells were drowned in perfume. The terms used to describe it are usually of a derogatory nature like inertia, inactivity, complacency, decadence, or worse. True, there is much in the eighteenth century that looks weak in comparison with the energies displayed during the seventeenth century, yet those evaluations are too sweepingly negative and would seem to stem from moral indignation rather than from a dispassionate assessment.

Behind the disparaging qualifications of the eighteenth century lies the fact that during that period the role of the Netherlands as a great power came to an end. Considering the size of the country, its population and the paucity of its natural resources this was not an unnatural course of events. Economically, politically and militarily the Netherlands was overtaken by the much larger surrounding countries which had richer resources and populations many times greater. The decline was not sharp, there was no general collapse, no single mishap that could be held responsible, but a gradual stagnation which eventually resulted in a slower rate of development than that of other European countries. Drastic

152

reforms in the organization of finance, taxation, trade and agriculture, a more careful employment of economic resources, greater frugality and a determined cheese-paring might have slowed down the process, but the outcome was inevitable.

Dutch participation in the wars of the Spanish and Austrian succession is often blamed for the deterioration of the Dutch position in Europe, but since the southern part of the Low Countries was directly involved, staying out of the wars could have been more costly than taking part in them. The main object of Dutch foreign policy in those years was to contain France, which, because of the vulnerability of Paris, sought to extend its borders towards the north by gaining control of the southern provinces. During the Spanish Succession War the Dutch and the English occupied the whole of the South after having defeated the French. At the Peace Conference in 1713, however, the Dutch were outmanoeuvred by the diplomacy of the French and the English, with the result that the threat from France remained as serious as ever. The French ambassador is said to have summed up the situation as follows: 'on traitera de la paix chez vous, pour vous et sans vous'.

Neither was participation in the War of the Austrian Succession (1741-1748) a political adventure. Apart from sending some auxiliary troops to Maria Theresa to whom it was bound by treaty, the Netherlands remained non-combatant until the French invaded Dutch territory. This time the war went badly, and only by military support from England and because of the internal weakness of France was the country saved from disaster.

Between 1780 and 1784 the Netherlands fought its fourth war with England, and this one finally sealed its fate as a European power. At this stage the English fleet outnumbered the Dutch by more than ten to one and the damage done to Dutch shipping, trade and prestige was enormous. After 1784 the Netherlands ceased to exist as a nation which could decisively influence European affairs. Eleven years later, in

1795, the Netherlands followed England into the Franco-Austrian war. A French invasion from the south, meeting with little resistance, and the subsequent pro-French 'velvet revolution' brought the country entirely into the orbit of France.

Decline of military and political power does not necessarily imply a decline of cultural creativity, and it would certainly be wrong to describe Dutch literature of the eighteenth century in terms of what was going on, or not going on, in political and economic life. Although the Netherlands may have been marking time and losing ground in many respects, its literature was developing in several new directions. Admittedly, the eighteenth century did not produce writers of the calibre of Hooft or Vondel, but it did produce some considerable talents who deserve to be judged on their own terms, and not as weak reflections of the radiant lights of the previous era or as the timid pathfinders of the great things to come in the following years. Some writers, of course, did continue in the tradition of the seventeenth century without being able to add much of value to it, but others were fully aware of developments abroad and gave clear evidence that literature at any rate was far from stagnant.

The dominating influence in the first half of the century was that of French classicism. Classicism was imported into the Netherlands where its achievements were to a large extent derivative, but before criticising the lack of originality one should realize that the theories of Dutch scholars such as Daniel Heinsius and Gerardus Vossius had had a profound influence on the formation of classical doctrine in France, and that the importation of classicism can also be regarded as a return to the Netherlands of several notions that had first been developed there. It has been shown by Edith Kern that both Racine and Corneille owed several of their ideas in drama to the theoretical works of both Heinsius and Vossius. Racine owned a copy of Heinsius's *De Tragoedia Constitutione* in the edition of 1643 which he must have studied closely as evidenced by his annotations and his underlining of several passages. Corneille's notion of historical truth always establishing verisimilitude in literature was derived directly from Heinsius, as was his proposition that not the royal descent of the characters but the tragic quality of the action was essential to drama. [1]

The focal point of Dutch classicism was an association established in 1669 under the name of *Nil Volentibus Arduum*. Its founder was Lodewijk Meyer, a doctor, poet and philologist. Meyer had been a trustee of the Amsterdam theatre but had lost his position as a result of his opposition to the bombastic but very popular plays of Jan Vos, and also because of his outspoken preference for French classical drama. Then he established *Nil Volentibus Arduum* which was to be a scholarly and literary association for the study of the arts, the sciences and the literature, and which had the specific aim of introducing classical drama into the Dutch theatre. From the beginning the organizers intended *Nil* to become a body comparable to the *Académie Française* which had been set up in 1635. They wanted *Nil* to do the same things for Dutch language and literature as the *Académie* did for French: they wanted it to become a central authoritative body which would fix and codify the language, and lay down rules and regulations with which the writers would have to comply. They advocated a return to purity of language and simplicity of form which had both been lost, they claimed, during the seventeenth century. Their theoretical bible was Boileau's *Art Poétique* (1674), and *Nil's* own *ars poetica*,

[1] J. W. Johnson, in his book *The Formation of English Neo-Classical Thought*, demonstrates that Heinsius and Vossius also greatly influenced Neo-Classicism in England, and that Dryden's *Essay on Dramatic Poetry*, Johnson's *Lives of the Poets*, and Pope's *Essay on Criticism* were all heavily indebted to Vossius's *Poetics*. Daniel Heinsius, Gerardus and Isaac Vossius, and Johannes Meursius were 'the authorities venerated in England between 1660 and 1800' (p. 142). Johnson even maintains that Vossius's *Poetics* was 'so complete a statement of the later views of Neo-Classicism that it may account for the lack of a similarly complete discourse in English' (p. 149).

Horatius Dichtkunst op onze tijd en zeden gepast (Horace's
Poetics Applied to Our Time and Manners), published in
1677, shows parallels with Boileau's book but is unlikely to
have been influenced by it. Poetry, it was argued, must
be smooth, mellifluous, melodious. It must not have rough
edges, its metre must be even, its vocabulary simple. Clarity
was imperative. The obscurity in which some of the
seventeenth-century poets had delighted, was anathema to
the classicists. The fanciful and the fantastic were despised,
restraint was considered of far greater value than spontaneity. In painting their preference was for Raphael; Rembrandt
was still accused of having placed himself above the rules.
The members of *Nil* often congregated at the house of
Gerard de Lairesse, a very formal painter who in his *Het
Groot Schilderboek* (The Great Book of Painting) of 1707
tried to do for painting what *Nil* was doing for literature.

After the groundwork done by *Nil*, classicism established
itself in the years between 1713 and 1716 in the course of a
series of polemics known as *Poëtenoorlog* (Poets' War), fought
between classicists and anti-classicists, the advocates of the
new and the defenders of the old. The classicists attacked the
loftiness and unnaturalness of their predecessors and in
particular the 'big words' of Vondel. Vondel's plays came in
for a great deal of criticism because of their lack of action
and their biblical subject-matter which, they said, placed them
outside reality. Balthasar Huydecoper, one of the most
influential men of letters of those days, published an
elaborate critique of Vondel's work, setting out his offences
against metre, inflection, conjugation and gender. This kind
of formal criticism was, of course, not peculiar to Dutch
classicism: Voltaire corrected Racine and Corneille in a
comparable way, and Pope spoke of Shakespeare as 'a sad
sinner against art'.

There is no doubt that the classicists went too far in their
desire to codify language and literature, and some of them
never rose above the level of sterile dogmatism. They often
confused craftmanship with art and they were inclined to

attach more importance to 'good taste' than to originality. In their insistence on regularity of metre, they failed to see that deviations from established metre were not necessarily clumsy but could be functional, while their constant reworking of a poem, their polishing and repolishing according to the law of Boileau, often polished the very life out of the poetry.

Yet the classical influence was by no means entirely negative. There was little cause for regret, for instance, when the plays of Jan Vos were swept off the stage by classical drama in the style of Racine and Corneille, nor can it be doubted that the reaction against exaggerated loftiness was a healthy one, even though Vondel's reputation suffered in the process. The criticism which the classicists levelled at the writers who preceded them often seems quibbling and trivial, but this, too, had its positive aspect as the classicists were the first writers to take an interest in the literature of a preceding period. The seventeenth-century writers had been almost entirely ignorant of what had been written by their predecessors and had shown no interest whatsoever in Middle Dutch or sixteenth-century literature. The classicists adopted a different approach and Huydecoper, the Vondel critic, was actually the first writer to make a thorough study of Middle Dutch language and literature. In Middle Dutch he hoped to find the original purity and simplicity which he thought the language should have possessed before the corruption of the seventeenth century set in. Although the motives behind his interest may have been unsound, the results were valuable and his edition of Melis Stoke's *Rijmkroniek* (Rhyme Chronicle) laid the foundations for the serious study of Middle Dutch.

Classicism made its greatest impact on drama, and Huydecoper himself wrote three dramas in the classical style, best known of which is *Achilles* (1719), a well-written and well-constructed, but rather dry and rhetorical play about the haughtiness and arrogance of Achilles. As in all classical dramas, reason plays an important part in it. The hero finds

himself beset by difficulties on all sides because he has left
the path of reason and has allowed himself to become the
plaything of passion. Reason only can resolve the tangle
brought about by unrestrained passion, reason only can save
the hero. These ideas are also to be found in the work of
Lucas Rotgans, an older contemporary of Huydecoper's,
whose *Eneas en Turnus* of 1705 is regarded as the best
example of classical drama in Dutch. But if the plays of
Huydecoper and Rotgans represent Dutch classicism in its
purest form, this does not at all mean that they are the most
valuable works of the period. They are examples of good
workmanship, they show that their authors had a good grip
on technique and—at any rate in the case of Rotgans—on
the psychology of their characters, but there is something
mechanical and lack-lustre about all of them, and their
highly formalized language contributes to the impression that
these plays were written to demonstrate the classical theory
rather than from an emotional necessity.

Comedy, which was hardly touched by classicism,
produced more convincing results than drama. It was
profoundly influenced by the French comedy writers,
especially by Molière, though one must add that it was not
nearly as derivative as drama was. Pieter Langendijk, the
leading writer of comedies and a great admirer of Molière's
warned in the preface to his *Het Wederzijds Huwelijksbedrog* (The Mutual Marital Deceit) against an uncritical
imitation of Molière, and stressed that long before Molière
poets such as Hooft and Bredero had written excellent
comedies which were more consistent and less eccentric than
the plays of the Frenchman. Langendijk was probably referring to the often arbitrary dénouements of Molière and
one must admit that he himself showed great deftness in
untangling and resolving his plots

Langendijk was actually more productive as a poet than as
a playwright, but his poetry has been almost entirely
forgotten whereas three out of his ten plays are still
performed regularly. As a playwright he gradually developed

from the comedy of character to the comedy of manners, but his best results were achieved in his earliest and most unpretentious period. One could even say that he never surpassed his very first play, *Don Quichot op de Bruiloft van Kamacho* (Don Quichote at Kamacho's Wedding), of which the first draft seems to have been written in 1699 when he was sixteen years old. In the play Don Quichote falls among Dutch peasants, which, apart from leading to some very funny scenes, also provided Langendijk with a situation in which he could develop what was to become the main theme of all his plays: the contrast between illusion and reality. One finds this theme in *Het Wederzijds Huwelijksbedrog* where both partners thoroughly mislead each other about their financial standing, in *Krelis Louwen,* in which a stupid farmer is coaxed into believing that he is Alexander the Great, and in *Quincampoix of de Windhandelaars* (Quincampoix or The Speculators), in which he attacked the gross speculations of the early eighteenth century. Langendijk may have made little attempt to explore the psychology of his characters, yet he was an excellent observer and a sharp, though good-humoured critic of society, who had the ability to make his moral points in a light-hearted manner.

Like the comedy writers, the lyrical poets also worked outside the mainstream of classicism. The classical doctrine left little scope for lyricism, and those who were lyricists by nature left the classicist theories to the epic poets, the playwrights and the prose writers.

The most considerable lyrical poet in the early years of the eighteenth century was Jan Luyken. Perhaps one should say: of the late seventeenth century, for although Luyken died in 1712 and published most of his work after 1700, his best volume, *Duytse Lier* (Dutch Lyre), dates from 1671. On the other hand this volume contains some poems that are so far removed from the form and ideas of seventeenth-century poetry that one feels justified in discussing Luyken among the writers of the eighteenth century. His modernity can be seen clearly from the following poem:

AIR

Droom is 't leven, anders niet;
't Glyt voorby gelyk een vliet,
Die langs steyle boorden schiet,
Zonder ooyt te keeren.
d'Arme mensch vergaapt zyn tyt,
Aen het schoon der ydelheyd,
Maar een schaduw die hem vlyt,
Droevig! wie kan 't weeren?
d'Oude gryse blyft een kind,
Altyd slaap'rig, altyd blind;
Dag en uure,
Waart, en duure
word verguygelt in de wind,
Daar me glyt het leven heen,
't Huys van vel, en vlees, en been,
Slaat aan 't kraaken,
d'Oogen waaken,
met de dood in duysterheen. [2]

Neither Vondel, Hooft, Bredero nor Huygens could have written this poem. Apart from laments for deceased relatives or friends, their poetry was hardly concerned with death. And when they did write about death, they looked at it 'sub specie aeternitatis', as a deliverance from life on earth. Luyken's approach is entirely different. Death in this poem is not the beginning of eternal bliss, it is not even peaceful sleep, but a sudden ending of a wasted life. In the last lines the poem expresses a tremendous fear, the fear that death will be experienced consciously as a transition into utter darkness. This realization of the nothingness, of the void which is death, gives this poem a very modern, almost existentialist aspect. There is no sentimentality in it, no

[2] Song. Life is a dream, nothing else. It glides by like a river which shoots past steep banks without ever turning back. Poor man wastes his time gaping at the beauty of vanity, nothing but a shadow that flatters him. Sad! who can avert it? The old greybeard remains a child, always sleepy, always blind; day and hour, valuable and dear, are thrown away. So life glides by, the house of skin, and flesh, and bone begins to creak, the eyes wake with death in darkness.

tearful self-pity such as one often finds in the death poetry of the later romanticists. Luyken simply says: 'sad', with a shrug of the shoulders. The irregular, asymmetrical form is neither that of the Renaissance and Baroque poets, nor that of the classicists. The poem is presented as one unit, but can be broken up into two stanzas of four lines each, rhyming *aaab, cccb,* followed by two stanzas of five lines of which the third and fourth lines may be read as augmented versions of the third lines of the first stanzas. These deviations from the symmetrical pattern are meaningful, stressing as they do the main notion: time, which is valuable and dear, is turned into nothingness.

The poem *Air* is an exception, however, and is not representative of *Duytse Lier* as a whole. It was placed at the end of the volume and expressed regret at what was warmly affirmed throughout the book, namely a life spent in the enjoyment of erotic love and the beauties of nature. In his nature poetry, too, Luyken was a modernist. In seventeenth-century poetry nature was mainly looked at from a utilitarian point of view. Vondel did not describe a landscape for its intrinsic beauty, but used it as a background or setting, as did medieval painting. To him the landscape only acquired meaning when man appeared. Luyken, on the other hand, was struck by nature without immediately thinking of its usefulness, and without moralizing about it. In this respect *Duytse Lier* anticipated the nature poetry of the romantics.

Luyken was twenty-two when he published *Duytse Lier* and in the last poems of the volume he was already dissociating himself from his former life which he regarded as futile, wasteful and as no more than a dream. A few years later he broke radically with it and returned to the pietist ideas in which he had brought up. His later poetry—volumes such as *Jezus en de Ziel* (Jesus and the Soul), *Spiegel van het Menschelijk Bedrijf* (Mirror of Human Affairs)—reflects his change of heart and shows a strong inclination towards mysticism, very much under the influence of the German mystic Jacob Böhme. These volumes of quiet religious lyricism with an undertone of mystic passion are also known for their illustrations. They are emblem volumes for which Luyken, who was a painter and etcher by profession, made the etchings himself, sometimes in collaboration with his son Kasper. As an etcher he earned great fame with his illustrations for Hooft's *Nederlandsche Historiën* in the edition of 1702.

Several poets, of whom Hubert Poot was the most prominent, followed the example of Luyken's nature poetry. Poot, the son of a farmer, was born in a village near Delft in 1689, forty years later than Luyken. The combination of farmer and poet was an unusual one and Poot, the poet behind the plough, became quite an object of interest. In 1723 he left the farm for the city of Delft, where he tried, without success, to become a musician and a painter. A year later, after a period of heavy drinking and after having become thoroughly disillusioned with city life, he returned to the farm and stayed there till his death in 1733.

Poot's poetry is a curious mixture of naturalness and artificiality: it often reads like simplified Hooft, at another time it is full of mannerist elements in the tradition of Huygens. Hooft's echo can be clearly heard in the beginning of his poem *Vliegende Min* (Swift Love):

> Galaté, myn schoone, kom;
> Laat ons minnen, spelen, zoenen . . .[3]

whereas Huygens is present in the first lines of *Zomersche Avont* (Summer Evening):

> De moede zonnewagen
> Staet vrachtloos. D'avontzon
> zinkt in de westerpekelbron.
> Aldus ontglippen ons de wentelende dagen. [4]

Contrasts between artificiality and naturalness are to be

---

[3] Galathea, my beauty, come, let us love, play, kiss,
[4] The tired chariot of the sun stands empty. The evening sun sinks into the western source of brine. Thus the revolving days escape us.

found specifically in his nature poetry. Poot, though a farmer, did not moralize about nature nor did he dwell on what could be gained from it. He was a sensitive observer of the Dutch landscape, but was more interested in the mood created by it, particularly on warm summer evenings and moonlit nights, than in the pictorial details. This probably explains why some of his poems contain elements that are entirely foreign to the landscape as he must have seen it around him. In one poem, for instance, clearly describing a Dutch landscape, he put milking cows in a winding valley, promised the farmer grapes and wine in autumn and observed a swift stream rushing down from steep rocks, though grapes in the Netherlands are only to be found in glass-houses and steep rocks and winding valleys nowhere at all.

The form of the poetry of Poot was on the whole freer than that of Luyken and his classicist contemporaries. Deviations from the established patterns of metre and rhyme occur frequently throughout his work, and although he did now and then use the alexandrine, the favourite form of the classicists, much of his poetry was written in lines and stanzas of irregular length. Poot's innovations were cautious and tentative, and were made intuitively rather than on the basis of a theory. But in the second half of the eighteenth century there was a great deal of theorizing about poetry and poetic form in the course of which concerted attacks were made on the classicist doctrine and its implications for the lyrical poet.

The main theorist of that period was Hieronymus van Alphen, an Utrecht barrister, who as a poet is now chiefly remembered for his children's verse, but whose theoretical works had a profound influence on the development of poetry. In 1778 he published a free adaptation of F.J. Riedel's *Theorie der Schönen Künste und Wissenschaften* which had come out eleven years earlier. In this book Van Alphen turned against the many rules that had been laid down by the classicists. They were detrimental to the development of poetry, he argued, because the rules tended to make the poet a slavish imitator instead of helping him to develop into an original personality. Throughout his work Van Alphen stressed the importance of originality; it became the criterion by which he measured the value of a poet's work. Hooft and Vondel he regarded as really original, but in his own century he found few writers who could lay claim to originality; only Poot was worthy of such praise. In his second book, *Digtkundige Verhandelingen* (Essays on Poetry), he discussed the 'means of improving Dutch poetry'. One of the suggestions he made was the adoption of blank verse, drawing attention to the work of Milton, Young and Thomson. He also came back to his demand for originality and counselled the poets to find a form for their poetry that would be in harmony with their 'imagination' and 'sensitivity' rather than follow the traditional patterns. Van Alphen's book may therefore be regarded as the first theoretical assertion in Dutch of romanticism against classicism.

The theories of Van Alphen caused a great stir and started a controversy that was to last for a considerable time, not the least because he seemed to think so little of the work of his contemporaries. His views on the desirability of blank verse were also strongly criticized. Yet several poets agreed with his ideas and began to put them into practice, among them Jacobus Bellamy.

In Bellamy's first volume, *Gezangen Mijner Jeugd* (Songs of my Youth) which came out in 1782, about half of the poems were written in blank verse. It was a volume of love poetry, written in a style of cultivated simplicity, and in its use of three and four beat iambics reminiscent of Anacreon and German anacreontic poets like Wilhelm Gleim, though Bellamy maintained that at the time of writing he had never read anything by Gleim and knew Anacreon only by name. Immediately after his first volume he began to publish under the pseudonym of Zelandus (he was born in the Zealand town of Flushing) a number of small volumes of political poetry entitled *Vaderlandsche Gezangen* (Patriotic Songs).

When these poems were published, the Netherlands was at war with England. It was a war which provided little food for the patriotic group of poets that suddenly appeared on the scene, and when the Dutch achieved a small success in the naval encounter at Dogger Bank, the poets certainly made the most of it and celebrated the event in a great number of poems and several plays. Bellamy also paid his tribute, and when the English put out peace feelers, he derided any attempt to make peace with these scoundrels before a satisfactory revenge was taken for all the Dutch ships they had captured.

Bellamy died in 1786 when he was only twenty-nine years old, and none of the poetry he left behind can really be called great. His love poems were pleasantly simple, melancholy rather than passionate, while his political poems were rhetorical and loud rather than fiery or angry. His importance lies mainly in his formal innovations which helped to give the later poets considerably greater freedom.

If classicism made little or no impression on the work of the lyricists, it left a far greater mark on that of the epic poets. Epic poetry was a much-practised genre in the eighteenth century, though no single epic of that period can be cited as a masterpiece. Neither Rotgans's *Wilhelm de Derde* (William the Third), nor Feitama's *Telemachus* and *Hendrik de Groote* (Henry the Great) have more than historical value. Much the same can be said of a fairly large number of biblical epics which were written in the first half of the century after the example of Vondel's *Joannes de Boetgezant*, with the rider that their historical interest is rather greater since these biblical epics did not develop in other literatures; only in German literature can some be found, but not before the second half of the eighteenth century. Most of these poems and their authors have now been forgotten, with the exception of Arnold Hoogvliet's *Abraham de Aartsvader* (Abraham the Patriarch), published in 1727, which was by far the best contribution to the genre.

The most characteristic non-biblical epic was written by

Willem van Haren, one of the most curious personalities in
Dutch literature. He was a Frisian nobleman, born in
Leeuwarden in 1710. At an early age he was elected delegate
of the Frisian State Parliament to the Federal Parliament at
The Hague. There he lived a hectic life, involving himself in
several love-affairs and falling heavily into debt. Socially he
faded out completely, and the finishing blow came when he
was accused of embezzling State funds. In 1768 he put an
end to his life by taking poison. He was a kind and
spontaneous man, his friends said, and very talented, but
also a man who lacked the self-discipline to develop his
talents as they should have been.

His main work was the epic poem *Friso*, a poem about
the legendary progenitor of the Frisians who came from
Indian stock and settled in Friesland where he established
the tribe of the Frisians. In his portrait of Friso, Van Haren
showed himself to be a true disciple of eighteenth-century
rationalism and enlightenment. Friso is the prototype of the
modern king, of the enlightened monarch, the genuine
rationalist who accepts only what is recognized by reason,
and who rules his country not by power but by justice. As a
poem, *Friso* is more interesting for its thought, for its
expounding of the theories of enlightenment than for its
poetic content, for Van Haren never really mastered the
language as a poet should. It is not unlikely that his French
education was the cause of this. As was customary for people
of his social standing, his whole education had been in
French, and, moreover, most of his official business and
correspondence was conducted in French. There are good
reasons to believe that this cramped his style when he began
to write in Dutch. His poetry does not flow easily, it is often
stiff and halting, and does not possess much grace or charm.
Yet it was colossally praised and hailed as the great
masterpiece of the new era by the eighteenth-century critics
who had a habit of overstating their case and who without
hesitation placed writers like Feitama and Hoogvliet well
above Milton and Tasso.

Friso was published in 1741 and was followed a year later by a more lyrical poem, *Leonidas,* which tells the story of the Spartan hero who chose a glorious death in preference to a shameful retreat. *Leonidas* is not only more lyrical than *Friso* but also more verbose and rhetorical, and its only remarkable feature is perhaps that, as Van Haren himself claimed, it raised an army of twenty thousand men, which is no mean achievement for any poem. It was written at the time of the Austrian War of Succession, and the Netherlands, though bound by treaty to come to the aid of Maria Theresa, was hesitating whether to intervene or not. Van Haren's attack on the weakness and indolence of the Dutch goverment may indeed have influenced their decision to send auxiliary troops. The success of the twenty thousand men was not spectacular for they immediately settled down in their winter quarters, but that of the poem was. It was praised as highly as *Friso* had been, it was translated into French and drew an enthusiastic laudatory poem from Voltaire who compared Van Haren to Demosthenes and called him 'Pindare au Parnasse'. Later critics liked it less: the nineteenth-century critic Busken Huet regarded it as nothing but 'an eloquent newspaper article' and was probably closer to the truth than Voltaire.

Of all lyrical poems which Willem van Haren wrote, only one has survived the two hundred years of changing literary taste that separate Van Haren from the present time. This poem, *Het Menschelijk Leven* (Man's Life), stands out from his other work through its simple style and the absence of Van Haren's customary rhetorical phrases. Though at first it seems to have been written on an impersonal plane, it is really his most personal poem, and held against the background of his own life it becomes a moving human document, lamenting the transitoriness of life, the vanity of man's undertakings and the vulnerability of his achievements.

Willem van Haren's life was tragic enough in itself but it assumes an extra dimension of doom when one sees that the life of his younger brother Onno Zwier van Haren followed

almost the same pattern. He was also a delegate of Friesland
to the Federal Parliament, and later became president of the
Privy Council. He was a personal friend of Stadtholder
William IV, commanded great respect and was one of the
best-known men in the country, but his fall was perhaps even
greater and more tragic than that of his brother. In 1760 his
two sons-in-law accused him of an attempt at incest with his
daughters. It was agreed that no publicity should be given to
the matter on the condition that Van Haren resign from
Parliament. It has never really become known what the truth
of the accusation was, but there is a strong suggestion that
the sons-in-law were out to break him. Onno van Haren
signed the promise and returned from The Hague to
Friesland. A year later he thought better of it and went back
to The Hague to resume his seat in Parliament. His sons-in-
law then produced the document he had signed. The
resulting scandal ruined Van Haren's political career and
forced him to return to Friesland again. Then he suddenly
began to write, perhaps, as Busken Huet has suggested, in
order to find compensation for the failure of his political
ambitions, to endeavour to achieve something in literature
when political success had been placed out of reach. Huet
might have been right, for Onno van Haren was no more a
born poet than his brother Willem. Moreover, in much of his
work one detects an undertone of self-justification and there
is little doubt that he consciously used poetry to show his
own personality to advantage. His first work, the verse
drama *Agon, Sultan van Bantam,* published in 1769, gives
clear evidence of this.

Agon is set in western Java in the seventeenth century,
and the Sultan Agon is the only Javanese prince who still
resist the authority of the Dutch East India Company and
of the administration in Batavia. He is ageing, however, and
wishes to abdicate in favour of his two sons between whom
he intends to divide the country. But the sons are jealous of
each other, and a feud arises between them. One of the sons
works himself up to such a pitch of hatred of his father and

his brother that he betrays them and turns Bantam over to the Dutch.

The play was based on historical material but Onno van Haren used the material very freely. Events that had happened during the course of several years were compressed within the space of one day, as classical drama demanded, and the characters, as we know them from a historical study written by Van Haren himself, also underwent transformations. In *Agon* the Dutch are unqualified villains, the Javanese are the heroes. It was the first time that colonial subject-matter was brought on to the Dutch stage and it is remarkable that this first play was written entirely from the point of view of the Javanese. Van Haren was undoubtedly moved by the fate of the Javanese prince who lost the independence of his country under such tragic circumstances, but, undoubtedly also, he used the play as a vehicle for the anger he felt towards the Dutch for what had happened in his personal life. In Agon he must have recognized himself: the noble, wise and honest man who was downed by a base conspiracy. *Agon* reads like an idealized self-portrait, just as *Friso* reads like an idealized self-portrait of Willem van Haren. Agon and Friso could have been brothers, just as Onno and Willem were brothers. Like Friso, Agon is the typical enlightened monarch who impresses on his sons that they should rule their subjects according to law and justice, and not according to their own desires. Agon, and some of the other seventeenth-century Javanese look a little out of place with their eighteenth-century ideals of enlightenment and rationalism, but it says a great deal for Onno van Haren's ability as a playwright that in spite of this they come to life. They are not the wooden puppets one might have expected them to be, they are not even types, but individuals whose emotions and ideas never lack conviction. It was probably Van Haren's personal involvement that gave the play its life, for when he again tried his hand at drama—in a play *Willem de Eerste* (William the First) about the assassination of William of Orange—he did not produce

more than an indifferent classical tragedy.
Perhaps Onno van Haren should have concentrated earlier
on comedy, for judging by the only one he wrote, he
possessed undeniable talents for it. Admittedly, his *Pietje en
Agnietje of De Doos van Pandora* (Pietje and Agnietje or
Pandora's Box) was not an original play but a free
adaptation of a French comedy. Yet his adaptation was so
personal and showed such a gift for lighthearted satire that
one might have expected a great deal from him as a comedy
writer had he not died a year after the play was written
(1779).

Pietje en Agnietje was written for the bicentenary of the
Union of Utrecht of 1579 and urged the Dutch to return to
their original virtues, to break with their desire for luxury
and to stop all violence. Pietje and Agnietje, childhood
sweethearts who live in an idyllic village, see their wedding
day and their entire lives endangered by the contents of a
box which Pandora, one of the guests at the wedding, gives
them. The paradisiacal village is invaded by sickness,
jealousy, hatred, corruption, dishonesty, and is taken over by
a dictator who turns it into his private treasure-trove.
Whatever happens around them, Pietje and Agnietje remain
faithful to each other. Finally they decide to leave the village
and are then taken by the gods to a 'low-lying swampy
country, full of water, reeds and rushes', where they become
the founders of the Dutch people.

Like his brother, Onno van Haren also wrote epic poetry,
though of a different kind. In 1769 he published the first
part of a long poem *Aan het Vaderland* (To the Fatherland),
which in its subsequent editions was given the title of *De
Geuzen* (The Beggars). It was written with the intention of
creating a truly national epic poem, celebrating the role
played by the House of Orange in the struggle for freedom
and independence. From the point of view of structure,
however, it is too disjointed to deserve the name of an epic.
In four tableaux it describes the first success of the Dutch in
the revolt against Spain, i.e. the capture of the town of Den

Briel by the Watergeuzen (Sea-Beggars); this was followed by a dream of William of Orange in which he foresees the future prosperity of the Netherlands; the third part gives an account of a delegation sent to England to ask for support from Queen Elizabeth, and the poem concludes with a description of the defeat of the Armada.

After the moderate success that Onno van Haren had achieved with his plays, De Geuzen was badly received by public and critics. Not so much because of its structural weakness, but because of its lack of polish, its irregular metre and impure rhymes. Van Haren took this criticism to heart and reworked the poem assiduously. An important part in the rewriting was played by two other poets, Willem Bilderdijk and Rhijnvis Feith, who assisted in polishing and repolishing De Geuzen until much that was characteristic and personal was polished out of it. Onno van Haren may not have been a great poet and may in several places have expressed himself clumsily, yet some of the irregularities in his poem were definitely functional, and when Bilderdijk and Feith ironed them out they often gave his lines an insipidity which they did not have in the original version. When Van Haren wrote: 'D'ontemb're Lumei is verscheenen' (The indomitable Lumei appeared), one might with Bilderdijk dislike the two elisions, but one has to grant Van Haren that his line, precisely because of the irregularity of metre produced by the combination of iambic and anapaestic, is far more lively and effective than Bilderdijk's polished version of it: 'Lumei, die woestaart, is verschenen' (Lumei, that ruffian, has appeared).

One can argue about the question whether or not the Van Harens and in particular Onno Zwier, ought to be regarded as classicists. Onno van Haren's work was certainly freer from the rules and regulations than the work of most of his contemporaries. Yet he, like his brother Willem, accepted the demands of the classicist doctrine, and his freer form must be considered as a slight deviation from the straight and narrow, and not as an attempt to discover new roads.

In contrast to his brother and to most other classicists, Onno van Haren was also interested in prose writing. He did not write what we now call creative prose, but studies and essays: biographical, historical, political, and also an essay on Dutch poetry. Novels, novellas and stories were not yet regarded as serious contributions to literature. The only writer of the first half of the eighteenth century who ventured into novelistic writing was Justus van Effen.

Van Effen, who was born in Utrecht in 1684, was like the Van Harens gallicized to a high degree, and in the first twenty years of his writing life he wrote exclusively in French. He made his mark as a founder and editor of a number of more or less literary magazines such as *Le Misanthrope, Journal littéraire de la Haye, La Bagatelle, Le Nouveau Spectateur Français* which all ran their courses between 1711 and 1731. These journals were all modelled on *The Spectator* of Addison and Steele whose work Van Effen came to know during the two visits he made to England, the second of which as secretary to the Dutch Ambassador. In England he also came in contact with the work of Jonathan Swift whose *Tale of a Tub* he translated into Dutch in 1721. Van Effen, though a great admirer of Swift's and a convinced moralist himself, entirely lacked Swift's savage satirical frame of mind. He was a critic of society and its morality, but a gentle one; his intention was to reform society, not with cutting sarcasm or the stentorian voice of the preacher of penitence, but by mildly ridiculing the mild vices of his contemporaries. In this he was guided only, as he put it, by the unchangeable principles of reason.

His best work was published in the Dutch journal he set up in 1731: *De Hollandsche Spectator*. At first it appeared weekly, later on every three or four days, with Van Effen as its main, sometimes sole contributor. On the whole the journal dealt with subjects of topical interest which has made it a valuable mirror of life in the first half of the eighteenth century. It attacked and ridiculed the dominating influence of all things French, as well as dandyism, the abundance of titles, speculation in stocks and shares, abuses in university life, and so on. Van Effen often illustrated his critical essays with scenes taken from daily life and with conversations on which he had eavesdropped and which he recorded with great faithfulness. Sometimes these illustrations developed into short stories such as his account of the courting of *Kobus en Agnietje,* which may be regarded as the first novella in Dutch. It is a description of a very innocent love-affair between the daughter of a seamstress and a carpenter: a simple story about ordinary people, written in a simple style, mildly humourous and with a very natural sounding dialogue. It is not without sentimentality, though, and tears flow so freely that Van Effen seems to be anticipating the later romantic sentimentalists. Yet Van Effen's sentimentality was only occasional. In the presentation of his characters, his observations of every day life and his sharp ear for dialogue he was clearly a realist and the precursor of the later realists rather than of the romanticists.

Van Effen's importance as a prose writer can be measured more accurately by the prose he inspired than by what he wrote himself. In spite of his trying to write ordinary language and to avoid anything high-flown, his prose is often stilted and dry. When he died in 1735, *De Hollandsche Spectator* died with him, but it was succeeded by no less than forty other Spectators which continued his work and from which in the course of time the truly literary journals developed. Van Effen also fulfilled an important function by serving as a link between the literatures of France and England. It was he who in his French magazines introduced the ideas of Steele and Addison, and spectatorial literature in general to France. For Dutch literature his importance lies in his establishing a realist prose tradition out of which, about fifty years after his death, the first modern novel in Dutch was to grow.

This novel, *De Historie van Mejuffrouw Sara Burgerhart,* (The History of Miss Sara Burgerhart), was written by two women, Elizabeth Wolff and Aagje Deken. Elizabeth Wolff—

or Bekker, which was her maiden name—was born in 1738 which made her a few years older than Aagje Deken. She began as a poet in the elevated style of the late classicist period. Pope was her great example in those years and an early portrait shows her holding a copy of his *Essay on Man*. Her early poems were rational discussions of a number of general and abstract topics such as mankind, religion, virtue, freedom, tolerance, and were more indicative of a brilliant and erudite mind than of a great gift for poetry. Later on she also wrote lyrical poetry, and then concentrated for a time on satire, often inspired by local incidents which annoyed her. When, for instance, an elder of the church had to resign for having danced at his daughter's wedding, she ridiculed the mentality that had forced the resignation in a famous poem called *De Menuet en de Domineespruik* (The Minuet and the Minister's Wig), and when the Amsterdam theatre burnt down, she laughed at those who regarded the fire as a punishment of God in *Zedezang aan de Menschenliefde* (Moral Song to the Love of Man). Though she was married to a minister of the church when she wrote these poems, she was continually at loggerheads with the orthodoxy. She was a liberal with a very independent mind, as can also be seen from the prose pieces which she contributed to various spectatorial magazines and in which she gave her opinions, often didactic and always moralistic, on education, the relations between men and women, the function of literature, and many other subjects. She became a well-known writer and a controversial figure, with many enemies but also with a strong personal following. From a distance her career was watched with a mixture of admiration and concern by Aagje Deken, a poet who had published a volume of minor religious poetry. In 1776 the two met and became such firm friends that when in the following year Elizabeth Wolff's husband died, Aagje Deken came to live with her. They stayed together till they died in 1804, Aagje eight days after Elizabeth.

After they had set up house together, they at first

published separately, but soon they began to collaborate. The first fruit of their collaboration was not particularly impressive. It was a volume of poems, *Economische Liedjes* (Domestic Songs), intended as educational poetry for the not-so-well-off and containing moralistic poems about virtuous servants and charwomen who loved nothing better than to work hard.

Then, in 1782, they published *De Historie van Mejuffrouw Sara Burgerhart,* one of the lasting novels in Dutch literature. For the Netherlands the book was a new venture, so new that on the title page the authors included the words 'niet vertaald' (not translated). It was written in the form of an epistolary novel, like Richardson's *Pamela* and *Clarissa,* books which were greatly admired by Wolff and Deken. Yet, however much they liked Richardson, they were not slavish imitators. On the contrary, they were able to create something quite original, and, from the point of view of form, to improve considerably upon Richardson's results. If the epistolary novel ideally gives a greater suggestion of authenticity than the straight narrative, Wolff and Deken came closer to the ideal than Richardson did. One of Richardson's weaknesses is the monotony of his style, i.e. the lack of stylistic variation in the letters. Wolff and Deken, on the other hand, made a point of giving each of their correspondents his or her own style. Also, the letters in their book seem to arise quite naturally from the given situation, whereas Richardson now and then had to resort to rather unconvincing situations in order to explain all the letter-writing. Naturalness was an important issue for Wolff and Deken, and in the preface to the book they comment on it: 'In this novel you will not find the misdeeds which even an Englishman can only read with shudders, nor will you find any exaggerated virtues which are unattainable for us weak creatures. There is no duelling in this book. Once, however, a smack is given. There is no abduction nor drinking of poison. Our minds have not invented anything miraculous. Everything is natural'.

There is no doubt that the ideas of Rousseau had also left their mark on Wolff and Deken, but they did not share his great optimism, nor were they in agreement with the emphasis he had placed on spontaneity and the rejection of discipline. 'An excess of liveliness can endanger even the best of girls, or plunge them into the saddest disasters', the preface proclaims. They believed in moderation, and above all in education. Their book was written with the specific aim of educating young girls by pointing out to them the dangers which life held and by showing them the right approach.

The main character of the book is Sara Burgerhart, a young girl of eighteen when the book opens, whose vitality, intelligence, cheerfulness and lightheartedness are reminiscent of Elizabeth Wolff herself when she was young. Sara has been left an orphan at an early age and is brought up by an aunt, a miserly and hypocritical woman who treats her badly. Her guardian, Abraham Blankaart, a gruff and blunt man with a heart of gold, would have been able to help her, but he is in Paris and out of reach. Finally, Sara cannot bear it any longer: one day when her aunt is out, she locks the maid in the cellar and escapes. She goes to live with a widow Spilgoed, an excellent woman who leaves her a great measure of freedom. Too much freedom, in fact, for Sara becomes careless. Danger lurks in every corner. Sara is warned, but she does not listen, and then falls into the clutches of Mr.R., a rake. As had been hinted in the preface, R. does not abduct her: she goes with him of her own free will. She is saved, however, in the nick of time, but in such a state of shock that she becomes seriously ill. The incident with R. and her illness prove to be the turning point. Sara becomes more careful, more serious, and now accepts the hand of the noble Hendrik Edeling whom she had spurned before. After a number of difficulties, created mainly by differences in religion, have been solved, Sara and Hendrik marry and lead the traditional happy life.

The story of Sara was written to set an example, but it is a matter of great credit to the authors that they did not allow the didactic element to run away with their novel. Though in places a little longwinded, it still makes extremely good reading. The characters are well-drawn and are surprisingly subtle for a novel of that period. The fact that Wolff and Deken, in contrast to Richardson, did not believe in the perfection of man and made no attempt to depict any of their characters as the perfect human being, had a great deal to do with the convincingness of their characters. Wolff and Deken were much more realistic than Richardson and less anti-rational. Feeling, sentiment and sentimentality which play such a large part in *Pamela* and *Clarissa* were handled by Wolff and Deken in much smaller quantities. The melancholy which pervades the work of Richardson did not find a place in *Sara Burgerhart*. Instead of it one finds humour, a mild kind of irony, and sometimes satirical passages that don't pull any punches, particularly where bigots and hypocrites are concerned. Wolff and Deken were not anti-religious, far from it, but they reacted sharply against any form of zealotry, and were on the whole more inclined to regard religion as an aspect of society and a function of social life, than as an expression of one's personal relation to God.

Encouraged by the success of *Sara Burgerhart* and by the demands of the reading public for a longer book—though *Sara Burgerhart* consisted of 800 pages of close print—they wrote a second epistolary novel, this time in eight large volumes. The first two volumes of this new book, *Willem Leevend*, are of the same quality as *Sara Burgerhart*, but in the later volumes the novel becomes very argumentative, and time and again the story gives way to long theological and philosophical discussions. In *Willem Leevend* the authors also took issue with the literature of sentiment that was being written in the 1780s. 'A new-fangled disease' is what they called sentimentality. They feared that it might develop into a national disease and for that reason opposed it strongly. They did not deny the value of 'feeling' and sensitivity, but they refused to regard those qualities as autonomous forces beyond any rational control and they rejected the exaltation to which a writer like Rhijnvis Feith worked himself up in his novels. Also, they wholeheartedly rejected the melancholy and gloom which often accompanied the exaltation of the sentimental writers. Wolff and Deken were realists; they did not regard life as being perfect, but neither did they regard it as something unspeakably sad.

Wolff and Deken never revealed what precise form their collaboration took. When asked, they always insisted that both had an equal share in the books. The poet Bellamy who was acquainted with both women and whose fiancée was a close friend of Elizabeth Wolff, said in 1784: 'Wolff is the vinegar, Deken the oil: the two together make a good sauce'. Others were more suspicious and found it hard to believe that Aagje Deken, who was no more than a mediocre writer before she met Elizabeth Wolff, could have contributed as much to the novels as her friend. Busken Huet was one of those. He claimed that all ideas in the books were Wolff's and that the lapses into the first person singular which occur occasionally in the prefaces are an indication of her principal authorship. Huet has not been able to prove his point, nor have other critics who maintained that all bright and cheerful letters were written by Wolff and the serious ones by Deken. It is quite possible, of course, that Wolff and Deken were right, and that Aagje Deken's contribution was as great as that of Elizabeth Wolff. Aagje Deken may have been a mediocre writer before their collaboration, but Elizabeth Wolff may have raised her to her own level, she may have acted as a pacemaker and may have inspired Aagje Deken to write far better than she did when she was writing alone. Other similar cases are known in literature. This still leaves open the question whether they made their contributions to the novels independently, or whether they rewrote one another's work.

The success of *Sara Burgerhart* was great. Within four years the book went through three editions, and it was translated into French and German. The first volumes of

Willem Leevend were also received with enthusiasm, but after that the interest of the readers waned. The book was not reprinted in Wolff and Deken's lifetime, nor was their third epistolary novel, *Cornelia Wildschut,* the least original of the three. The great success of *Sara Burgerhart* perhaps explains why the epistolary novel was written for a longer period of time in the Netherlands than in other countries. The twentieth century even saw a revival of the genre in *De Leemen Torens* (Towers of Loam) by the two Flemish writers Herman Teirlinck and Karel van de Woestijne, and in the novels which Simon Vestdijk wrote in collaboration with Jeanne van Schaik-Willing, Hendrik Marsman and Henriette van Eyk.

It was one of those curious quirks of history when in 1783, barely a year after Elizabeth Wolff and Aagje Deken published their first realist novel in Dutch, Rhijnvis Feith published the most notorious masterpiece of the literature of sentiment, a novel called *Julia,* one of the most tearstained books of all time. Its plot is simple. Eduard has fallen in love with Julia whom he met in a forest where she was praying for a soul-mate. Julia returns his love, but her cruel father refuses consent. Julia does not want to go against his wishes, yet she continues meeting Eduard. Preferably in cemeteries and on tombstones. Their embraces increase in intensity, and one day Julia just manages to stay within the bounds of spiritual love by uttering the word 'immortality'. After this narrow escape they decide to part and Eduard retires to a lonely place. When Julia's father finally relents, Eduard rushes back to Julia, only to meet her funeral procession. Eduard retires into loneliness again. He buys a ruined castle not far from Julia's grave and prepares himself for death, spending most of his remaining days in a hollow tree which he regards as his coffin.

The book is full of the typical details of the literature of sentiment: Julia and Eduard are continually drawn towards cemeteries, they speak almost exclusively of death and eternity, they sigh and weep copiously. It is clear that Feith was not a realist, but a romantic, and a very emotional one at that. Yet the intention of his novel was didactic, just as that of *Sara Burgerhart* was. Like Wolff and Deken, Feith wanted to educate and edify the young. What he wanted to describe was 'true love', which to him was closely related to virtue and religion: hence Julia's virtuous decision to call a halt to the love-making, and Eduard's and Julia's predilection for cemeteries and tombstones. In one of his letters Feith stated that if the young people were to realize the close relation between love, virtue and religion, they would not get married so rashly. He wanted to improve marriage, man, human relationships and society in general, which is precisely what Wolff and Deken were trying to do. When Wolff and Deken are classified as realists this does not mean that they were content to record reality as they saw it: they were intent on improving it. And when Feith is labelled a romantic this does not mean that he turned away from reality. His aims were as practical as those of Wolff and Deken. *Sara Burgerhart* and *Julia* were both written with the purpose of improving certain aspects of society; the difference lies in the approach, in the sugaring of the pill.

Looking back over the development of the Dutch novel in general, *Sara Burgerhart* is a much more modern book than *Julia*. Wolff and Deken were interested in character, in the reactions of their characters to one another, and particularly in the reasons why their characters acted as they did. Moreover, they made some attempt to show development of character, in *Sara Burgerhart* as well as in *Willem Leevend*. In *Julia* one finds nothing of the sort. There is no development in Feith's characters nor is there any psychological justification for their actions. His characters act out of a thick cloud of sentiment which completely obscures their motives.

Feith published his book with some misgivings. Who at such a time, he wondered, would agree with him that love was meaningless without virtue? While he feared that his novel would be ridiculed as too old-fashioned, the attack came from another quarter. Several critics considered that Feith had gone too far, that his descriptions of Eduard and Julia's love-making were too suggestive, and that the book therefore was dangerous. Feith, who was afraid of being dismissed as an out-of-date moralist, found himself considered as a corrupter of morals and a dangerous modernist. To justify himself he wrote a second novel, *Ferdinand en Constantia* (1785) which distinguished itself from *Julia* by a slightly more elaborate plot, a happy ending and the absence of any highly charged passages. For the rest it was as resolutely sentimental as *Julia* was.

Feith's style of writing is usually in perfect harmony with his subject-matter: it is a very unnatural style, overflowing with images and metaphors, often bombastic, and sometimes grotesquely poetic. Yet among all the sentimental rhetoric one is repeatedly struck by passages of truly inspired writing and by images of great originality which show that Feith was a more genuine writer than has often been conceded. These passages occur in both his novels but more frequently in the short prose pieces which he had published earlier and which were re-issued with *Julia*. Otherwise these prose poems, as one would call them nowadays, were not particularly original. Their form was probably suggested to Feith by Salomon Gessner's *Idyllen* of 1756, and in the contents one finds elements from the work of James Macpherson *(Ossian)*, Wieland and Baculard d'Arnaud, just as *Julia* occasionally shows that Feith had carefully read Rousseau's *Julie ou la nouvelle Héloïse* and Goethe's *Werther*. Feith was a voracious reader, his knowledge of contemporary literature of France, England and Germany was extensive, and a great deal of his work was undoubtedly inspired by the work of other writers. This applies to his prose as well as to his poetry.

As a poet Feith was profoundly influenced by Klopstock and Herder, by Percy and Young, and by the French poet F.A. de Paradis de Moncrif whose romances he imitated. The romances as written by Feith and several other poets of that period—Bilderdijk, Bellamy, Staring—were poems which described a touching event in a simple quasi-naive style. They were the first poems to go back to medieval poetry and they were written in a spirit of reaction against the well-polished rational poetry of classicism. Feith's romances, especially *Alrik en Aspasia* and *Colma* are worthy counterparts of his prose poems and novels in so far as they deal with tragic love and the transience of life, and abound in the customary sentimental attributes such as skulls, tombs and howling winds.

These novels and poems were written when Feith was in his late twenties and early thirties. In some of his later work, particularly in his long didactic poem *Het Graf* (The Grave), his always forcefully professed unworldliness acquired a more convincing ring of authenticity. *Het Graf* was written in 1792, a few years after Feith's administrative career as one of the burgomasters of Zwolle had come to an abrupt end because of political upheavals. A little later he went through a period of religious doubts, and *Het Graf* reads as an attempt to reject once and for all the uncertainties of the world in favour of the certainties of death and the hereafter. *Het Graf* is Feith's most personal poem, but at the same time it is part and parcel of the tradition of the English grave poetry as represented by Edward Young's *Night Thoughts,* Robert Blair's *The Grave* and Thomas Gray's *An Elegy Written in a Country Churchyard.*

Feith's sentimental romanticism never became the mainstream of literature, but for a while it was read, praised and imitated by a small group of writers. One of these was Elizabeth Post who gained temporary fame with her novel *Het Land* (The Country). This is also an epistolary novel, in which two friends, Eufrozyne and Emilia, exchange letters about life in the country and life in the city, in the course of which Eufrozyne is converted to country life. In the manner of Feith, the book is full of discussions of religion, virtue and death, and from beginning to end is pervaded by a deep melancholy, though Elizabeth Post never quite plumbed the depths of sentimentality as Feith did. Nature plays a large part in the book, in particular the beautiful disorder of nature. Strangely, in the observations of nature one finds now and again the same foreign bodies as in the poetry of Poot. Emilia, the one who lives in the country, writes about 'my fatherland', but if she really means the Netherlands her observation of winding valleys, high mountain ranges and vines clinging to the front of a house suggests that imagination sees more than eyes do.

Opposition to Feith and his followers was strong from the beginning. The chief opponents were writers like Hieronymus van Alphen and Jacobus Bellamy who, though modernists themselves and not entirely free from sentimentality either, turned against Feith's melancholy and gloom, and against the spinelessness and inertia of his characters which they regarded as demoralizing. As early as 1785 the leading literary magazine *Vaderlandsche Letteroefeningen* which at first had supported romanticism, ridiculed Feith's work in a 'Recipe for the preparation of something sentimental: Take equal amounts of exclamation marks and dashes, euphonious names of women, and pure heavenly, eternal love; sprinkle this with mixed herbs of soul-meltings, sighs, swoons, heart flutters, soul contractions, last farewells, last kisses, hand-pressings, sobs, death, the grave, eternal night, the unfathomable sea of eternity etc. Mix everything well, and pour a sauce of silent, soft, burning hot tears over it: it will be good'. Also, serious and scholarly attacks were made, such as the one by De Perponcher who accused the sentimentalists of not describing authentic feelings and sensations, but feelings that were artificial and had been made to order by the imagination. Feith replied elaborately to this criticism, denying the allegations and pointing out that no-one can judge the sincerity of someone else's feelings. The polemics went on for some time and did great harm to the sentimentalist cause. The greatest damage, however, was done by Johannes Kinker, a young man then who had just taken out his law degree. He was the editor of a critical magazine *De Post van de Helicon* (Helicon Mail) which appeared during the years 1788 and 1789. In the first issue of the magazine he published a devastating parody of Feith's *Alrik en Aspasia* which hit harder than many a serious article.

In his assault on the literature of sentiment Kinker was assisted by Willem Bilderdijk. It was surprising perhaps to find Bilderdijk here as a devoted adversary of sentimentality as he had written some rather sentimental romances himself. Also, his attack on Feith was surprising as some years before they had collaborated closely while rewriting Onno Zwier van Haren's *De Geuzen*. But Bilderdijk was never a man known for consistency. In his life and work, theory and practice were often at cross purposes. He would formulate his views on various subjects—poetry, for instance, or marriage—and when he formulated the theory he was probably sincere and believed in what he was saying, but when it came to a practical application he often did the opposite. His life was full of clashes, conflicts between the two, or more, parts of his personality. His was a very complex personality which makes it impossible to attach a label to him that would cover all facets. He was a sentimentalist and also a critic of sentimentality; one could call him a romanticist, but his work is so full of classicist elements that he is often regarded as the last of the classicists.

Willem Bilderdijk was born in Amsterdam in 1756. When he was six years old he injured his foot so badly that he was unable to move about until he was eighteen. He sat at home and read. He read anything and everything and during those years acquired an extraordinarily extensive knowledge of the most divergent subjects. He claimed in a letter that when he was eighteen months old he knew the main data of biblical history, mythology, the Heidelberg Catechism, and what he called Universal History. At the same time he learned French, and was given the works of Jacob Cats, which he read. He also remembered that at two he had become world weary and had been crying in his cradle longing for death. When he was three, he claimed in the same letter, he wrote love letters to a girl friend praising her soft neck and ivory knees. It has been said that a man could only falsify his youth to such an extent if he had led a very sheltered life and had never been laughed at by his play-mates. This is very true, and the isolation of his first eighteen years helps to explain not only the hyperbolic approach to his own youth but also some of the features of his poetry which often seems to move on stilts designed for giants.

Whether he was three years old or perhaps a little older, he certainly began to write at a very early age. Some poems, written when he was twelve, have been preserved and show that in those early years he was a faithful disciple of Cats. In 1775 he took part in a poetry contest and won first prize with a poem on the influence of poetry on the government of the state. With that poem he entered the literary world, and at the same time the world proper, as he was then well enough to move around. He went to Leiden to study law and when at Leiden published his first volume of poetry, *Mijn Verlustiging* (My Delight), a volume consisting of exuberant and very passionate love poems, original ones and translations from Greek poets such as Anacreon, Theocritus, Bion and Moschus. Passionate as these poems may have been— and they were more passionate than anything that had been written in Dutch before—the underlying principle of them was that the heart should not unconditionally gratify its desires, but that these desires should always remain under the control of reason. This, one might say, was also the main problem of Bilderdijk's personal life. His desires were many, and sometimes so great that his reason, which was not inconsiderable either, lost control. Afterwards, reason began to rationalize and hypocrisy took over from sincerity. The conflicts of his life were often thrashed out in his work for his poetry was largely autobiographical. Even the romances written between 1785 and 1795 were to a certain extent autobiographical poems, the medieval settings of which only served as a disguise.

In 1795 the French revolution was transplanted to the Netherlands, and Bilderdijk, one of the most prominent anti-revolutionists, had to leave the country. He was a barrister at The Hague in those days and was exiled after having refused to sign the pledge of loyalty which the new government required of all civil servants and lawyers. The exile order did not entirely displease him as it provided him with an opportunity to rid himself of his many creditors, and also of his wife whom he had ceased to love. He spent some time in Germany, then settled in London, and later went back to Germany. In London he fell in love with Katherina Schweickhardt to whom he considered himself married after a while. She seems to have been a great inspiration, for during the years of exile he was extremely productive, publishing a total of ten volumes of poetry, among them his best love poems. During his stay in England he also became intimately acquainted with English poetry, particularly with the Ossian poems which he admired so much that he translated almost all of them.

In 1806 the French-inspired 'Batavian Republic' came to an end and was replaced by the no less French-inspired 'Kingdom of Holland', with Louis Bonaparte, Napoleon's brother, as king. Bilderdijk approved of the new monarchical form of government, even though the king was a Frenchman, and when the sentence of exile had become null and void, he returned to the Netherlands. He came into contact with the king and in a short while his situation was radically altered. The king appointed him as his teacher of Dutch and Bilderdijk even wrote an ode *Napoleon* which turned the one-time exile into a poet laureate. In the first year of his return, too, he completed *De Ziekte der Geleerden* (The Illness of the Scholars), a didactic poem in six cantos, dealing with the various physical and mental illnesses and their cures. The most interesting part of the poem is the conclusion where the poet points out that his description of illnesses shows that man's destiny is not to be a scholar or an artist, but to be man, a conclusion reminiscent of Pope's: 'The proper study of mankind is man' and anticipating Multatuli's motto of the 1860s: 'the vocation of man is to be man'. Otherwise, *De Ziekte der Geleerden* is mainly remarkable for its immoderate length. Bilderdijk was an immoderate man, his handling of language and literary form was immoderate. As one of his critics wrote: he threw words about as if they were colossal boulders.

Bilderdijk's predilection for everything that was grand, elevated and colossal then led him to begin writing an epic poem very much in the tradition of Baroque poetry. It was called *De Ondergang der Eerste Wareld* (The Destruction of the First World), and was intended to describe the history of Paradise, a war between humans and titanic Paradisians and finally the destruction of Paradise by the Great Flood. The poem was never finished, however, and was abandoned after three or four months' work. In the preface Bilderdijk already sounded a note of defeatism by stating that neither the times nor the nation were poetic enough to savour an epic poem; this was due, he claimed, to the fashionable French poetry which was in reality anti-poetic, to the current theories which excluded from poetry everything that was poetic, and to the demoralizing effect of modern education. In spite of all this he began to write his epic in 1809, then ground to a halt the next year in the middle of the fifth canto whereas at least twenty were originally planned. The reasons for not finishing it he kept to himself. Only in a letter to Robert Southey did he express some of his feelings about it.

Bilderdijk had come to know Southey when he was exiled in England, and in 1825 he rescued him from a hotel at Leiden where Southey was laid up with an infected foot, not understanding anyone in the hotel nor being able to make himself understood, not even to the point of obtaining medical help. Bilderdijk acted as the friend in need and took him into his house for a few weeks, an event which the grateful Southey later commemorated in his poem *Epistle to Allan Cunningham*, full of praise for Bilderdijk, who, he

said, would be known by everyone 'had not the curse that
came from Babel clipt the wings of poetry', describing him
also as a man 'who had received upon his constant breast the
sharpest arrows of adversity'. Bilderdijk could have written
this himself, and in a letter to Southey, alluding to what
caused him to abandon his epic, he did say very much the
same thing: 'As for my *Ondergang der Eerste Wareld,* if it
had been continued, I believe it would have had some
applause, but in everything it was my lot to be crossed by
the course of events. I dare presume that I might have been
useful in some respects, but this satisfaction was denied to
me'.

Southey and Bilderdijk had more in common than their
views on Bilderdijk's adversities. Southey himself said of
Bilderdijk: 'he is as laborious as I have been; has written upon
as many subjects; is just as much abused by the Liberals in
his country as I am in mine, and does contempt them as
heartily and merrily as I do . . . . . The only child, Lodewijk
Willem, is at home, Mr. Bilderdijk being as little fond of
schools as I am'. Both were poets laureate, both wrote an
inordinate amount, both have gone down a long way in the
estimation of most critics. But there the comparison ends.
Southey built up a great reputation during his lifetime by
assiduity and by joining up with the new romantic poetry of
Wordsworth and Coleridge. Hard work and conformity to
the poetic mode of his time concealed for a while that his
talent was small. Bilderdijk's talent, or genius perhaps, was
highly original and without any conformist tendencies. He
was not a poet who sought to make his mark by adapting
himself to what was fashionable, but one who flew in the
face of fashion. His originality, together with his intellect, his
erudition and his passionate nature ensures that even his bad
poetry still holds a fascination. Part of the fascination is
undoubtedly due to an uncanny mastery of the language in
which he was absolutely unrivalled by any poet of his time.

Like Southey, Bilderdijk practised almost every genre of
literature under the sun: lyrical and epic poetry, drama, and

prose. In drama he expressed qualified admiration for the classicist tragedy of Corneille and Racine, but had only scorn for the 'puerile whims' of Shakespeare and the work of Schiller which he pronounced 'savage' and 'raving'. In his own dramas he followed the classicist tradition, but tried to add more 'dynamics' to it and more 'heart'. The results were unconvincing. His best known play, *Floris V,* was tossed off in three days and bears the mark of this in its verbosity and clumsy stage technique. It deals with the same characters as Hooft's *Geeraerdt van Velsen,* written almost two hundred years earlier, and was clearly written in opposition to it. In Hooft's play Floris was a tyrant who was lawfully deposed by the representatives of the people. Bilderdijk, on the other hand, regarded Floris as the noble prince and sovereign ruler. Written in 1808 when the Netherlands had been a kingdom for only two years, the play was used by Bilderdijk as a vehicle to make propaganda for the monarchical present against the republican past.

The first monarchy was short-lived. In 1810 the Kingdom of Holland was erased from the map and the country was annexed by France. Bilderdijk who had been living on a state pension ran into financial difficulties when his pension was withdrawn, as he found that however much he wrote, living from his pen was impossible. Southey also remarked on this when he was staying with the Bilderdijks: 'the profits of literature here are miserably small. In that respect I am in relation to them [i.e. the Bilderdijks] what Sir Walter Scott is in relation to me'.

In those difficult years between 1810 and 1815 Bilderdijk wrote a short novel which may well be one of his more lasting works. Its full title is *Kort Verhaal van eene Aenmerklijke Luchtreis en Nieuwe Planeetontdekking* (Brief Account of a Remarkable Air Voyage and Discovery of a New Planet), and it is one of the very first science-fiction novels, written as it was in 1811, that is more than fifty years before Jules Verne's *Cinq semaines en ballon.* Bilderdijk published it anonymously, and perhaps to attract more

attention pretended that it had been translated from the
Russian. The story is set in Persia where there are many
rumours about miraculous flying machines made by the
French. The narrator constructs a balloon and makes
hydrogen gas to prove to the incredulous Persians that
air travel is possible. When the balloon rises, his fellow
traveller panics and jumps overboard, throwing all calcula-
tions out of gear. The balloon climbs much higher than it
was intended to, and finally lands on an unknown planet
between the earth and the moon, too small to have been
observed from earth. The narrator explores the planet and
finds some curious animals that prove to be edible. The
water on the planet is bad, brackish and sulphurous, so that
he is constantly plagued by thirst. Also—writers' blood tells
—he laments the absence of paper. After he has been
fiercely attacked by a flock of turkey-like birds, has found a
mysterious skeleton and an inscription in Greek, he manages
to repair the balloon and to produce a fuel that will send
him back into the gravity of earth. He makes a perfect
splashdown into the ocean and is picked up by a Russian
ship.

The *Remarkable Air Voyage* was one of the few
lighthearted and humorous works to come from Bilderdijk's
pen. It caught his readers and critics by surprise and caused
some of them to find hidden meanings, symbolism and
satirical traits, though no-one was quite sure what the
symbolism and satire meant. Otherwise, Bilderdijk's poetry
of those years was sombre and morbid. In several poems he
took leave of the world and the farewells followed one
another in a rapid procession. Titles like *Najaarsbladen*
(Autumn Leaves), *Afscheid* (Farewell) and *Winterbloemen*
(Winter Flowers) speak volumes. He seems to have
contemplated suicide in those days and for a considerable
time took refuge in opium.

Then came 1815, the final defeat of Napoleon and the
restoration of the monarchy in the Netherlands, or rather the
establishment of the first really Dutch monarchy. Bilderdijk

was one of its most enthusiastic supporters and celebrated the new independence in two volumes of poetry entitled *Hollands Verlossing* (Holland's Liberation). He expected a great deal from the new king Willem I, for the country and no doubt also for himself. But disenchantment came quickly. When Bilderdijk expressed enthusiasm for the monarchy he was thinking in terms of an absolute monarchy. It was a rude awakening when he discovered that the new monarchy was a constitutional monarchy which he regarded as a despicable debasement of royal authority: accepting a constitution was identical with sanctioning the French revolution. In his personal aspirations, too, he was bitterly disappointed by the new regime, particularly when he was passed over for a professorship at Amsterdam on which he had set his heart. He went through a period of great bitterness and expressed himself in violently negative terms on any number of subjects: Napoleon, the French, the liberals, the constitution, the revolution, free thinking, the abolition of slavery, and so on and so forth. In a long didactic and at times humorous poem *De Dieren* (The Animals) he opposed the early notions of evolution and professed his belief that animals possessed a soul and were descendants of fallen angels.

Few poets have so consistently and so violently opposed the spirit of their own time as Bilderdijk did. He was an arch-conservative to whom any new development was anathema. Through his forceful personality and great eloquence his ideas became widely influential, in particular during the last years of his life—he died in 1831—when as a kind of private professor he taught a course of Dutch history to a small number of selected students at Leiden. Among the members of that study group were Dirk and Willem van Hogendorp, sons of Gijsbert Karel van Hogendorp, Guillaume Groen van Prinsterer, a historian and founder of the Calvinist Anti-Revolutionary Party, Jacob van Lennep, a novelist and one of the leading men of letters in the middle of the nineteenth century, Isaac da Costa, a poet and Bilderdijks's most devoted disciple who in 1823 followed

in the footsteps of the master when he published his
Bezwaren tegen den Geest der Eeuw (Objections to the Spirit
of the Age). From this group, too, there originated in the first
half of the nineteenth century the movement of the Reveil, a
Calvinist movement which was active in literature and in
politics, and which carried on Bilderdijk's fight against
rationalism, enlightenment and liberalism. It is ironical that
Bilderdijk who was in everything he did first and foremost a
poet, left a greater mark on the development of political
conservatism than on poetry. During his lifetime he was the
giant who dominated the literary scene, but by the middle of
the nineteenth century the more discerning critics began to
write off a large part of his work as rhetorical and hollow. It
takes a determined effort to find some convincing poems
among the masses of verbose and overwritten poetry which
he produced. Yet he was no mediocrity, but a typical case of
'a genius, but...' With his work, curiously hybrid in its
classicist origin and romantic temperament, one may rightly
say that the literature of the eighteenth century came to an
end.

VII

MORALISTS AND ANTI-MORALISTS
NINETEENTH CENTURY

No period in the history of the Low Countries, with the exception of the years between 1940 and 1945, has ever been as miserable as the beginning of the nineteenth century. In the North as well as in the South, national life reached its lowest ebb. The South was ruled by Austria until 1792. Three years earlier, in the year of the French Revolution, there had been a patriotic and vaguely pro-French uprising which had sent the Austrian administrators flying: there had even been a declaration of independence and a theoretical formation of the United States of Belgium. But it had all come to nothing, and after a year of uncertainty and the beginnings of a civil war, Austrian rule had been restored. In 1792 France declared war on Austria; six months later the Austrians were defeated and the southern part of the Low Countries was brought under the rule of France. By 1795 the northern provinces, under the name of the Batavian Republic, were in the same position though with a slightly larger measure of independence.

In retrospect, the French domination of the Low Countries from the 1790s until 1813 was not entirely negative. Far-reaching administrative reforms were introduced which did away with a great deal of antiquated provincial sovereignty. These reforms were on the whole successful, so much so that most of them were retained after the defeat of Napoleon. But at the time, the French rule seemed to offer little for which to be grateful. The economy of the North was hit particularly badly. Forced by France to take part in the

war against England, the northern provinces lost most of
their colonies: the Cape Colony, Ceylon, Malaya, Sumatra
were all taken by the English. Poverty and unemployment
were on the increase, especially after Napoleon's Berlin and
Milan Decrees of 1806 and 1807 which forbade all trade
with England. Trade losses in the North were tremendous
and industry declined at a rapid rate. After the Napoleonic
period seven hundred thousand people, out of a population
of just over two million, were dependent on charity.

Economically the South fared a little better than the North
because of its greater wealth of raw materials and also
because it was more fully integrated into the economic
structure of France. The national debts of the South and the
North after the Napoleonic period clearly show the
difference: the South owed twenty-six million guilders, the
North seven hundred and twenty-six millions, that is
sixty-six times as much, or, per head of population, more
than a hundred times as much. In 1815 when the North and
the South were reunited into a new kingdom under King
Willem I, the discrepancy between these figures proved one
of the stumbling blocks on the road to a complete fusion.

In cultural respects, however, the South was affected more
gravely by French rule than the North since the Dutch
elements in its cultural life were severely repressed. Theatres
were closed to plays in Dutch, Dutch books and magazines
were banned, education became almost exclusively French.
In the North the situation was slightly more favourable, at
least until 1810. Whereas Napoleon regarded the country
only as 'an alluvium of the French rivers', or alternatively as 'a
province of England', his brother Louis who ruled as King of
Holland from 1806 until 1810, tried to preserve some of the
national identity by making concessions to the use of the
Dutch language and by acting on occasion as a patron of the
arts. Louis Napoleon, after all, was a kind of Sunday writer
himself: he had published a short novel before he came to
Holland, and published another one in 1808 under the title
of *Marie, ou les peines d'amour*, later reprinted as *Marie, ou*

les Hollandaises. Though his knowledge of Dutch always remained sketchy, he took a certain interest in Dutch writing— from which Bilderdijk profited—and he was also instrumental in the foundation of the Royal Institute of Sciences, Letters and Art, the forerunner of the Royal Dutch Academy. But his attempt at independent rule ran counter to his brother's plans, and Louis was forced to abdicate in 1910, after which the North was officially incorporated into the French Empire.

The years of French domination were lean years as far as literature was concerned, and apart from Bilderdijk there were few writers who produced anything of value. The repression of national life and the strict censorship imposed by the French administration may to a large extent be blamed for this. Literature rarely flourishes under those conditions. Some of the writers protested against the general atmosphere of malaise and tried to do something about it, mainly by stirring up nationalist feelings and by recalling the days of the glorious past.

In prose it was Adriaan Loosjes who tried to give the Dutch a moral injection with his four-volume novel *Het Leven van Maurits Lijnslager* (The Life of Maurits Lijnslager), the first historical novel in Dutch literature. It was published in 1808, during the reign of Louis Napoleon. In the introduction to the book Loosjes stated that he wrote it ' in order to divert my mind from the calamities that continue to fall upon my afflicted country'. Therefore, he said, he would transport himself to the country's most brilliant period, i.e. the seventeenth century, and specifically the period after the defeat of Spain. This he did, and he brought his hero into the world in the year 1600, two days after the decisive battle of Nieuwpoort. Maurits Lijnslager, a merchant, was born with a silver spoon in his mouth. He sets out on a grand tour of Europe, combining business with education, and wherever he goes he meets celebrities. He travels through Italy in the company of the painter Anthonie van Dyck, in Genoa he is shown around by Rubens, on the way there he squeezes in an interesting conversation with Galilei, in Switzerland he

meets an Englishman who turns out to be none other than
the young Milton with whom he becomes firm friends, he
makes the acquaintance of Vondel, visits Grotius in Paris
and on the way back to Holland finds Admiral Michiel de
Ruyter to be one of his travelling companions, while in his
later years he strikes up a friendship with Admiral Cornelis
Tromp.

The reader's credulity is stretched to the utmost in this
book, but realism was obviously not Loosjes's main concern.
Nor was romanticism, and though *Maurits Lijnslager* must
be called a historical novel, it is certainly not a romantic one
in the ordinary sense of the word. Everything in the book is
presented and interpreted from the point of view of
Enlightenment, and little or no attempt is made to present
the past as it must have been. Loosjes's aim was not to
recreate the past, but to put heart into the Dutch by showing
them that in the past at least there was a great deal to be
proud of. As such the book probably fulfilled its purpose. It
was the first novel that dealt with the seventeenth century
and judging from the literature that followed it, it must have
acted as a great source of inspiration.

Four years later, in 1812, the poet Jan Frederik Helmers
published *De Hollandsche Natie* (The Dutch Nation), a kind
of poetic counterpart of *Maurits Lijnslager*. It is a poem in
six cantos which celebrates the Dutch heritage, also with the
accent on the achievements of the seventeenth century,
spurring the Dutch on to draw strength from the past in
order to overcome the ignominies of the present. As poetry it
was undoubtedly weak, rhetorical and bombastic, but as an
event it was important. The fierce nationalism of the poem
was unacceptable to the censors and it was only published
after it had been thoroughly toned down. Yet even the
emasculated version was received with such enthusiasm that
it, too, aroused the suspicion of the authorities. An order was
issued to have Helmers arrested and sent to Paris to be tried,
but he died before the police arrived. Though one may not
think highly of Helmers as a poet, one must admire his

courage and his attempt to restore the national self-respect. There were also poets who instead of protesting against the sterile apathy of the present, advocated complacency and advised their readers to count their blessings. As there were few to be found in the life of the nation, they concentrated on the family and the joys of domestic life.

Hendrik Tollens, born in Rotterdam in 1780, quickly became the recognized champion of this domestic poetry in which birthdays in the family, the beautiful eyes of a young son and the first tooth of a baby were celebrated with profound feeling. If, as one sometimes suspects, Tollens was trying to approach these subjects from a lighthearted angle, the conclusion must be that this approach failed dismally, since every attempt at humour was immediately drowned by the pompous and banal versification. In the three volumes of *Gedichten* (Poems) which were published between 1808 and 1815, Tollens's domesticity alternated with high-flown patriotic songs, but in either genre he proved himself to be merely an apostle of mediocrity, of self-satisfaction and smugness. It is significant for the general atmosphere in the country at that time that Tollens could become a venerated poet who was covered with honours, especially after 1819 when he carried off first prize in a national poetry competition with his *Tafereel van de Overwintering der Hollanders op Nova Zembla* (Tableau of the Wintering of the Dutch on Novaya Zemlya). It was a long poem, inspired by the fourth canto of Helmers's *De Hollandsche Natie*, but poetically even weaker than its model. Whereas Helmers, in spite of his rhetoric, now and then succeeded in lending an air of heroism to his characters, Tollens reduced them to a level of triviality. Yet Tollens was an even more popular poet than Helmers, and not only in the Netherlands: his *Overwintering* was translated into French and Frisian, twice into German and twice into English, including an American edition which came out in 1884.

The patriotic romanticism of Helmers and Tollens was represented in the South by Jan Frans Willems, who later earned the epithet of 'father of the Flemish movement'. Willems was born in 1793, became an archivist at Antwerp and later devoted much of his time to historical and philological studies. In his younger years he wrote plays and poetry, and made a great impression with his poem *Aan de Belgen* (To the Belgians), published in 1818, three years after the North and the South had been reunited to form the Kingdom of the Netherlands. It is a strongly nationalist poem in which the author urged the Flemings not to forget their language and culture. It may be regarded as the southern analogue of *De Hollandsche Natie,* and, as in the case of Helmers, it was more important as a gesture than as poetry. Also, it was certainly a more positive reaction to the apathetic mood of the Napoleonic and post-Napoleonic years than the complacency of Tollens.

The most original poet of his generation was Anthonie C. W. Staring. His first volume came out in 1786 and consisted of romantic poetry, mainly romances in the style of Rhijnvis Feith, sentimental and sombre, but at times also humorous and satirical. Staring was a friend of Feith's, and an admirer of his work, but never a slavish imitator, nor was he ever a one hundred per cent romanticist. Staring's mentality and temperament were of Enlightenment and Rationalism rather than of Romanticism. From his early poems it was clear that his strength did not lie in romantic mood pieces à la Feith or lyrical effusion à la Bilderdijk, but in anecdotal and narrative poetry. From the beginning his style was precise and clear-cut. If Bilderdijk was the most uneconomical poet of his time, one of the greatest word-spenders ever known, Staring was the very antipode of Bilderdijk. His poetry was concise and terse, at a time when conciseness and terseness were not regarded as anything of high value. Small wonder, then, that his contemporaries, used as they were to the broad flow and the explicitness of Bilderdijk, Helmers, Tollens and many others, complained about Staring's obscurity. Another charge brought against him was the ragged form of some of his poems. Staring was the first poet to break with the dictates of classical metre by which his predecessors and most of his contemporaries—including again Bilderdijk, Helmers and Tollens—were still inescapably bound. He did away with their strict syllable counting and wrote lines of irregular length in which rhythm prevailed over metre. His strong sense of rhythm is one of the most striking technical qualities of Staring's poetry, and not surprising in a man who was deeply interested in music. He drew up plans for the improvement of singing in church, wrote texts for songs and also some cantatas with the specific aim, so he said, of providing work for Dutch composers.

In his choice of subject-matter Staring followed the romantic taste for medieval history and legend, in particular those of Guelderland where he lived all his life as a member of the landed gentry. He wrote about the medieval rulers of Guelderland, on local events during the Eighty Years' War, on the student Jaromir who pretended to be the devil, on the Vampire, on the Nordic god Thor, but also on the first steam-train, the pines on his estate and on love. His poetry reflects little of the political upheavals of his time. The French Revolution, the Napoleonic wars, the establishment of the Kingdom of Holland, the annexation of the Netherlands by France, the liberation of 1813, the restoration of the monarchy in 1815, the reunification of the North and the South, the Belgian Revolution of 1830 and the subsequent separation—all events which rocked the country—are barely mentioned in his work. There is a short poem on the battle of Waterloo and a few poems on the Belgian Revolution, when emotion overwhelmed his customary sobermindedness and he exhorted the young men of the Netherlands to fight against what was regarded as Belgian treachery. Otherwise he cultivated his garden, looked after his estate and wrote agricultural brochures on the manufacturing of resin, on asphalt roads, the planting of American poplars and the destruction of fieldmice.

Staring was not a popular poet as Helmers or Tollens were, and probably never will be. He was an erudite man,

very well-read, and with interests that ranged from poetry
to agriculture, and from archaeology to the study of dialects.
His erudition, in combination with his unusually terse
diction, makes considerable demands on his readers. He
himself expressed this with a touch of irony in one of the
many epigrams which he wrote:

DUISTERHEID

Krijn las, en zei, zoo tusschen waken
en dutten in: 'dat - kon - wel - klaarder - zijn!'
Voor die half slapen, lieve Krijn,
kan 't een, die droomt, slechts duidlijk maken.[1]

Staring's romanticism was really no more than skin-deep
and manifested itself mainly in his choice of subjects. When
he was writing, the first wave of romanticism with Feith as
its chief exponent, had lost much of its original momentum.
In the 1820s, however, romanticism asserted itself again, and
this time its influence was much stronger and far more
widespread. This second phase of romanticism was also
distinctly different from the first phase. The early romanticism
of the 1780s was largely inspired by French and German
literature; during the second phase the English influence
became dominant, particularly through the work of Sir
Walter Scott and Lord Byron.

At the same time, the emphasis which until then had been
placed on 'feeling', began to shift towards 'imagination'. In
1822 Barthold H. Lulofs, a professor at Groningen and a
great friend of Staring's, made a strong plea for a new
romantic literature in the Netherlands, a literature based on
history, folklore and dreams, and one which would give free
rein to the 'romantic play of the imagination'. A few years
later, David J. van Lennep, professor of Classics at
Amsterdam, followed this up in an essay which bore the

[1] Obscurity. Krijn read, and said, in between waking and dozing: 'that -
could - perhaps - be - clearer!' Only one who dreams, dear Krijn, can
make things clear to those who are half asleep.

ponderous but programmatic title of *Verhandeling over het Belangrijke van Hollands Grond en Oudheden voor Gevoel en Verbeelding* (Treatise on the Importance of the Soil and Antiquities of Holland for Feeling and Imagination). In this paper he recommends the native landscape and local history as sources for the poet's imagination and drew attention to the fact that no-one in the Netherlands had yet followed in the footsteps of Sir Walter Scott. A year earlier, in 1826, he himself had given an example in his poem *Hollandsche Duinzang* (Dutch Dune Song), written in classical anapaests, in which he recalled the historic importance of the dunes near Haarlem and lamented the loss of so many monuments of early history. David van Lennep's work made a great impression and its influence can be measured by the fact that almost all themes occurring in the literature between the 1820s and the early 1840s can be traced back to his *Verhandeling*.

Yet there were also sceptics, writers and scholars who had grown up in the tradition of classicism and who found it difficult to become enthusiastic about the new approach to literature. In 1833 *Vaderlandsche Letteroefeningen* carried a review of Victor Hugo's *Le roi s'amuse* by its editor Jacob Yntema, in which the question was asked: What can Europe expect from a nation whose moral sense has become so barbarised that it finds pleasure, nay, delight in such monstrous literature? A year later a similar review of Hugo's *Marie Tudor* appeared in the same paper. Now Yntema was clearly not a sceptic but an uncompromising opponent of French romanticism. The most erudite and eloquent of the former was Jacob Geel. Born in 1789, he studied classics and became Librarian of the University Library at Leiden. He did not write much, and all his literary work is contained within *Onderzoek en Phantasie* (Inquiry and Fantasy, 1838), a single volume of essays and lectures. The quantity is small, but the writing is so clear and unpretentious for its time that Geel must be regarded as a real innovator in Dutch prose style.

In one of his essays, *Gesprek op den Drachenfels* (Discussion on Mount Drachenfels), dating from 1835 and written in the form of a Platonic dialogue, he weighed romanticism against classicism. The discussion is carried on by two friends, one of whom is fiercely in favour of romanticism whereas the other is a scornful opponent. The narrator himself, undoubtedly representing Geel's own point of view, endeavours to keep an open mind but in the course of the debate cannot help revealing his own grave doubts about romanticism and where it would lead. The discussion centres on the limits of reality and the rôle of description in literature. Naturally, nothing was resolved by the dispute, but its intellectual level and imaginative presentation make it stand out as a landmark in the debate on romanticism.

In spite of the reservations of Geel and others, literature was inexorably set on a course towards romanticism, one of whose first adepts was Jacob van Lennep, the son of David. He was born in 1802, studied law at Amsterdam, took a brief interest in theology, then entered the civil service and was appointed solicitor to the Treasury at the early age of twenty-seven. As a writer he took heed of what his father had written in the *Verhandeling* and began by publishing a number of romantic historical poems under the title of *Nederlandsche Legenden* (Dutch Legends), all set in the Middle Ages and written in short lines of three and four-beat iambics. After this publication, although he now and again returned to poetry, he concentrated mainly on prose and quickly developed into a very popular author of historical novels, modelled on Scott, especially the Scott of *Ivanhoe* and *Quentin Durward*.

Van Lennep's first novel, *De Pleegzoon* (The Foster-son), published in 1833, was set in the seventeenth century, the period which during the nineteenth century was long held up as an example to the present. As the title indicates, one of the main themes of the book is the tracking down of a mysterious parentage, which entails a great many adventures and unexpected happenings. Most of

Van Lennep's novels—*De Pleegzoon* as well as *De Roos van Dekama* (The Rose of Dekama), *Ferdinand Huyck* and several lesser known ones—have a strong picaresque element: they are just as much novels of adventure as they are historical novels, if not more so. They abound in mysteries, foster-children, supposititious sons, and parents who disappear and turn up again in the most unpredictable places and situations. Love stories in these books are never simple and straightforward, but of great complexity and apparent insolubility. They are not so because of the complexity of the characters, but because of the intricacies of the plot. Plot is the main thing in Van Lennep's novels, and one must still admire his deftness in constructing highly complicated situations and his elegant way of disentangling them. He was undeniably a narrator of unusual skill, for few writers would be able to hold the attention of their readers with as little character drawing as Van Lennep does. Most of his figures are sketchy, schematic and very flat in comparison to the characters in the novels of Betje Wolff and Aagje Deken, written about fifty years earlier. Van Lennep's characters conscientiously followed the plots that were mapped out for them, so that there is never any sugges- tion of the characters creating the plot.

Van Lennep's novels made him the most popular writer of his time. His sales were large, he went on lecture tours, read from his work to enthusiastic audiences, became the idol of the public and in his later years was generally regarded as the grand old man of Dutch letters. Success of this kind cries out for imitation, and after Van Lennep's books there followed a spate of historical novels. Gradually their character changed, the picaresque element receded into the background and more and more care was given to historical authenticity, something which Van Lennep had not paid a great deal of attention to. With the growing interest in historical detail, the historical novel often became a showcase in which the author devoted all his energies to a display of historical knowledge, making light of plot and characterization.

Other writers, Aarnout Drost for example, made the historical novel into a novel of ideas. Drost's main work, *Hermingard van de Eikenterpen* (Hermingard of the Oak-Hills), published in 1832, presents a picture of Christianity in the fourth century, and although some reminiscences of the novel of adventure can still be found in it, its aim is to show that the only true form of Christianity is evangelical Christianity, as against a Christianity which aspires to attain secular power. This idea, obviously reflecting the author's own conviction, pervades the whole book and makes it into a far more personal novel than the non-committal adventure stories of Jacob van Lennep. Drost died in 1834 at the age of twenty-four, before he had been able to complete his second novel, *De Pestilentie van Katwijk* (The Plague at Katwijk), set in the seventeenth century. Small though his own *oeuvre* may have been, it opened up new possibilities for the development of the historical novel.

The first to adopt the new approach was A. L. Geertruida Toussaint. In her first novel, *De Graaf van Devonshire* (The Earl of Devonshire) of 1838, she immediately showed that the ideas of the historical period—in this case the time of Elizabeth and Mary Tudor—and the bearing of these ideas on the characters, were her main concern. The book still bears the stamp of Scott, but at the same time Geertruida Toussaint made it clear that she had certain reservations about Scott and that she did not want to be regarded as an uncritical imitator. In her preface to the book she stated that the only thing in which she had tried to follow Scott was the 'authenticity of historical characters', adding that this might absolve the author from many an offence against history itself. Her chief interest was in character, and was to remain so throughout her work, even though she sometimes was carried away by her own historical knowledge and heaped historical detail upon historical detail.

Her first work was on the whole well received, except by the leading critic E. J. Potgieter, who in the new literary journal *De Gids* (The Guide) criticized her choice of English subject-matter and advised her to turn her attention to the history of the Netherlands. Her publisher was of the same opinion and asked her specifically to write a novel on the influence of the Reformation on daily life in the Netherlands. After two more novels on English history, she followed their advice and in 1840 published *Het Huis Lauernesse* (The House of Lauernesse), still her best-known book. It is set in the first years of the reign of Charles V when the Reformation was beginning to spread through the Low Countries and the Inquisition was claiming its first victims. The central idea of the book is akin to that of *Hermingard van de Eikenterpen*: pure Christianity will triumph over Christianity which seeks power, while its main theme is the impact made by the Reformation on the characters and the relations between them. As such it was a much more ambitious work than anything by Van Lennep or Drost. *Het Huis Lauernesse,* concerned as it is with the psychological implications of certain events on a set of characters, must be regarded as an early form of the psychological novel. This can also be said of her other books, most significant of which are the *Leicester* novels, a trilogy set in the period when the Earl of Leicester was Governor of the Netherlands. The psychology in all of these books is still static. The characters are seen and described from a given point of view, they react to one another, and the motivations of their actions and reactions are given unfailingly, and usually plausibly, but the characters themselves stay as they are and do not develop.

Only in one of her last novels, *Majoor Frans* (Major Frans) did Geertruida Toussaint—who was then married to the painter Johannes Bosboom—attempt to describe a character in development. Like *Het Huis Lauernesse, Majoor Frans* was written in response to a suggestion, in this case by Potgieter who after the publication of her latest historical novel had remarked that she ought to write a novel in a modern setting. In *Majoor Frans,* then, the psychology is no longer static, but dynamic, since the novel closely follows the development to maturity of a wild and passionate young girl. In the history of the modern psychological novel, it was a decisive step forward. But *Majoor Frans* was published in 1874 and by that time the literary situation in the Netherlands was radically different from the 1830s and 1840s when Jacob van Lennep and Geertruida Toussaint published their first novels.

In the 1830s and 1840s the dominating prose genre was the historical novel, in the North as well as in the South. In the South—which after the separation of 1839 became the Kingdom of Belgium—the genre was energetically represented by Hendrik Conscience, born in 1812, the same year as Geertruida Toussaint. Conscience was also a follower of Scott's though closer in approach to Van Lennep than to Geertruida Toussaint. As a novelist he ranks well below either. His novels—exactly one hundred in all—are often clumsily put together and lack Van Lennep's sureness of touch in handling plot. His characterization is crude and superficial, there is often a complete lack of historical authenticity. But he was the first novelist to emerge from the South in a period which followed a two centuries long suppression of Dutch cultural life. For him there was no tradition of prose writing on which to fall back: if Wolff and Deken and Van Lennep must be regarded as pioneers in the field of the Dutch novel in the North, this qualification applies with double force to Conscience in the South. Also, his aim in writing was not solely literary. He was fiercely committed to the cause of the Flemings, and though he lacked in sophistication and technique, he did not lack in enthusiasm nor in the power to transmit it. His influence, therefore, was immeasurably more profound than the purely literary value of his work would indicate. He wrote with the express purpose of waking up the Flemings, of making them read again, as he said, and in that he certainly was successful. He became one of the most popular Belgian writers of all time, whose best books—*De Leeuw van Vlaanderen* (The Lion of Flanders) and *Jacob van Artevelde* — are still read and whose work has been extensively translated into French, English and German.

While the novel of the 1830s and 1840s developed under the patronage of Scott, the poetry of those years bore the unmistakable imprint of Byron. It was an influence so strong that none of the young poets escaped it. The Byron vogue had started as early as 1822 when the poet Isaac da Costa published a partial translation of *Cain* which had come out in England only the year before. Da Costa belonged to the generation of Jacob van Lennep, and was a disciple and close friend of Bilderdijk who was so taken by Da Costa's translation that both he and his wife also began to translate Byron. It seems incongruous that the Byron vogue was initiated by Da Costa and Bilderdijk, who were both ardent Calvinists and anti-modernists, and to whom the spirit of Byron's poetry must have been entirely alien. Da Costa himself was well aware of this, and his translation of *Cain* was not only selective, but also polemic in the additions which he made to it. Nicolaas Beets, the most enthusiastic of the Byron imitators, was also a Calvinist and even a student of theology when he wrote his first Byronic poems. In 1834, at the age of twenty, he published *José, Een Spaans Verhaal* (José, A Spanish Tale), the next year *Kuser* and in 1837 *Guy de Vlaming* (Guy the Fleming). Passionate, insane, consumptive, incestuous and deeply miserable as his characters may be, they are really no more than pale shadows of Byron's personages. Beet's romanticism, just like Feith's fifty years earlier, seems unreal and artificial. After 1837 Beets shook off his Byronic *mal de siècle,* rejected his earlier poems and in an essay of 1839 spoke ashamedly about his 'black period'. It was unfortunate that the Dutch poets were more impressed by the sombre seriousness of, say, *The Corsair* or *Childe Harold* than by the irony and mockery of *Don Juan,* for when Beets followed the style of the latter poem, as he did in *De Masquerade* of 1835, he was a great deal more successful. *De Masquerade* describes students' festivities at Leiden in a very entertaining style, full of playfully extravagant imagery, Byronic digressions, commentaries and ironic asides which one would not have thought possible of the morbid author of *Guy de Vlaming*.

In 1842 the opponents of Romanticism, and in particular of the Byronic variety, launched a series of cutting attacks in the form of parodies and satires. A group of poets, of whom J. J. L. ten Kate and A. Winkler Prins were the most active, set up a critical magazine *Braga*, entirely written in verse, in which they ridiculed the Byron vogue and unmercifully trounced Beets. Though the imitation of Byron persisted in a slightly subdued form throughout the 1840s—as in Hendrik A. Meijer's *De Boekanier* (The Buccaneer) and *Heemskerk*—*Braga* certainly thinned out the field.

When *Braga* gave up the ghost in 1843 the art of parody did not die with it. On the contrary, thirteen years later it reached an all-time high in the work of Piet Paaltjens who published his first poems in the Leiden Students' Almanac of 1856. Piet Paaltjens was the pen-name of François Haverschmidt, who was born in Leeuwarden in 1835 and came to Leiden in 1852 to study theology. He was known as a cheerful and jolly student, but both in his prose sketches collected in 1876 as *Familie en Kennissen* (Relations and Acquaintances), and especially in his poetry one can discern beneath the conviviality the unconquerable melancholy which in 1894 made him put an end to his life. His output was small, but the single volume of poetry, *Snikken en Grimlachjes* (Sobs and Grimaces), which he did not publish until 1867, assured him of a unique place in Dutch romanticism. There is a strong element of parody in these poems, but it would be wrong to regard them as parodies pure and simple: Haverschmidt was part of romanticism, not an opponent of it. He did parody the romanticism of Beets, Heine, Goethe, Byron and several others, but there is always far more of himself present in these poems than the poets he cocked a snook at. As Nieuwenhuys rightly says, he wrote parodies of Beets because Beets was his favourite poet and he caricatured the suicidal man because he was one himself. Piet Paaltjens provided him with an outlet for his own melancholy, sentimental and macabre feelings, which he tried to render harmless with irony and parody. The poems are in his own words 'a good remedy for the very illness from which they seem to result'. Though they are often very funny because of the exaggerated use of the romantic style, their humour is not gratuitous but of a complicated self-protecting kind which does not really attack the romantics but tries to exorcize their demons, who were tormenting the poet himself. When Piet Paaltjens ran out of steam and stopped writing, the demons could no longer be warded off and destroyed Haverschmidt.

The poetry of Piet Paaltjens proved much more durable than the imitative romantic poetry of Beets which *Braga* and Paaltjens were laughing at. As far as Beets was concerned, their ridicule was unnecessary as he had ceased to write Byronic poetry as early as 1837, devoting himself to religious and domestic poetry until shortly before his death in 1903. When *Braga* appeared, his Byronic period was no more to him than a sin of his youth. Yet Beets is not remembered for his later poetry either, however impressive its quantity may be, but for another youthful sin, his book *Camera Obscura* which he published in 1839 under the pseudonym of Hildebrand.

Camera Obscura is a collection of sketches and stories written when Beets was still a student of theology at the University of Leiden. It is a book that links up with the humorist tradition of Laurence Sterne, Charles Lamb and Washington Irving, while the names of Heinrich Heine and Charles Dickens have also been invoked as literary ancestors. But Beets so thoroughly assimilated these various influences that one could hardly imagine a book more Dutch than *Camera Obscura*. The Beets of this book was very different from the one who wrote the exalted and excited Byron imitations, or, for that matter, from the one who having become a minister of the church and later professor of theology, poured out volume after volume of sweet and sentimental verse. *Camera Obscura*, though mildly romantic and at times not unsentimental, is basically a realistic book mainly concerned with description of character and observation of situation. As such it owes a considerable debt to the work of Wolff and Deken. Its humour is subtle and gently ironic, never offensive, never developing into satire. Beets was a critic of the bourgeois society of the 1830s, but a loyal critic. He never took up a far-out position, he never went to extremes, he ridiculed only what must have been obviously ridiculous to most of his readers: the woodenness of the student Pieter Stastok in *De Familie Stastok* or the bragging of the parvenu Kegge in *De Familie Kegge*. His ridicule is never malicious and always has an undertone of sympathy and understanding. He may laugh at Pieter Stastok, but at moments when it matters he takes his side; he may poke fun at the flashiness of Mr. Kegge, but the story has not been under way for very long before he makes the reader feel sympathetic towards him too. Only obvious villains, such as van der Hoogen in *De Familie Stastok* are dealt with harshly, for *Camera Obscura* is also a highly moral book in which the good are rewarded and the bad come to a sticky end. It was written in an excellent style which avoided all stiffness, stiltedness and grandiloquence. Beets's aim was, as he said, to strip the language of its Sunday suit—as Geel had done a few years earlier—and in doing so he made an important contribution to the development of Dutch prose writing. A failing of the book is the highly favourable role which the author reserved for himself and played with unflinching relish. Hildebrand, the 'I' in the book, can do no wrong. He is always the sensible, calm, noble young man who is master of every situation. He has an excellent sense of humour so long as he is looking at the others, but where he is concerned with himself, he becomes very serious indeed. Consequently, when he keeps himself out of the story, it gains considerably, as in the case of *Een Oude Kennis* (An Old Acquaintance) which describes the estrangement of two old friends. The stories of which the book is made up are really sketches, not novellas or short novels. The characterizations are sharp, but static, the situations are generally loosely connected and without dramatic development. But the observations are uncannily shrewd and have given the book its lasting value. It has become a classic and is one of the two books of the nineteenth century that are most frequently translated, most widely read and most regularly reprinted. It was an immediate success when it came out, both with the general public and the critics. Only Potgieter, the leading critic of *De Gids*, took exception to it. Potgieter expected more from imagination than from realism, and he rejected the book as another example of the 'desire to copy everyday life'.He complimented Beets on his drawing of character and the excellence of his style, but for the rest his praise was so faint as to be damning. The critical arrows which he aimed at his target were sharp enough, but fell wide of the mark. He accused Beets of pessimism, of lack of warmth and of an inhumane approach to his characters. Potgieter always identified himself entirely with the bourgeois society which Beets gently ridiculed, and he may have felt personally slighted by the book. Why else would he have over-reacted by calling *De Familie Stastok* a satire, when it was nothing more serious than a good-natured take-off of some of the stuffier representatives of that society?

Everhardus J. Potgieter was born in 1808 which made him Beets's senior by six years. He spent his early years in Zwolle, until in 1821 an aunt took him to Amsterdam because of financial and domestic difficulties at home. After more financial adversity, Potgieter and his aunt went to Antwerp as representatives of a sugar firm. They arrived there in 1826 when the North and the South still formed an uneasy United Kingdom. Potgieter, who was eighteen years old then, found himself in the midst of a complicated political situation, characterized by grievances of the Belgians against the Dutch administration, and tensions between Flemings and Walloons. The most useful literary contact he made in those years was with Jan Frans Willems, the champion of the Flemish movement. Potgieter's own part in the controversies of those days was that of an observer,

loyal to the Dutch but also sympathetic towards the demands
of the Belgians. Four years later, when the Belgian
Revolution broke out, he left Antwerp and went back to
Amsterdam from where he was sent on a business trip to
Sweden. Back in Amsterdam in 1832, he settled down and
gradually built up a business of his own as a representative
of various commercial firms.

Potgieter published his first poetry during his stay at
Antwerp. It was romantic poetry in which the echoes of
Byron, Lamartine and Victor Hugo can clearly be heard. In
Sweden he wrote the poem *Holland* which no anthologist
ever passes over and which begins with the following stanza:

> Grauw is uw hemel en stormig uw strand,
> Naakt zijn uw duinen en effen uw velden.
> U schiep natuur met een stiefmoeders hand, —
> Toch heb ik innig u lief, o mijn Land! [2]

After his return from Sweden, Potgieter joined up with a
group of young writers who were frustrated by the
conservatism of the literary magazines and were thinking of
setting up a periodical of their own. The most prominent
members of this group were Aarnout Drost, the author of
Hermingard van de Eikenterpen and Reinier Bakhuizen van
den Brink, a theologian, historian and philologist. In 1834
they brought out the first issue of a new magazine which
they called *De Muzen* (The Muses). It was a magazine of
high quality, too high-brow, in fact, to reach a wide
audience: it never achieved more than eighty subscriptions
and consequently lapsed after six months. Potgieter contributed prose and poetry to it, and also criticism. From the
beginning his critiques were sharp and pulled no punches,
though the early ones were written in a curiously self-con-
scious style, half serious and half humorous, obviously the

---

[2] Grey is your sky and stormy your coast, naked your dunes and flat
are your fields. Nature created you with the hand of a stepmother, —
yet I love you intensely, my country!

work of a man who was still trying to find a personal style and approach. Yet it was as a critic that he was to make his name and was to exercise his greatest influence on the course of Dutch literature.

His chance came in 1837, three years after the untimely demise of *De Muzen*, when as a result of a quarrel between two publishers a new periodical was set up. It was given the bold name of *De Gids* (The Guide), and while *De Muzen* was one of the shortest-lived of all Dutch literary magazines, *De Gids* was to beat all records for longevity and it is still going strong today. Potgieter became its chief editor, if not in name then in practice, and in a short while made it into the most influential magazine of its time. He displayed a tremendous energy, published poetry—romances and ballads in the romantic style—, short stories, sketches, and a great deal of criticism. In the prospectus of *De Gids* it had been announced that there was no proper critical review in the Netherlands and that it was a matter of national self-respect to alter this state of affairs. *De Gids* certainly did that. It became so critical, in fact, that because of its blue cover, it earned for itself the name of 'de blauwe beul' (the blue executioner).

In the first volume of *De Gids* Potgieter made his position clear. He advocated—as *De Muzen* had done—a criticism that was unbiassed and not directed at the author himself, but at the work. Yet his criticism was essentially moralistic and far more concerned with the author's approach to life and society than with questions of aesthetics or technique. In his elaborate and very appreciative review of Staring's poetry, for instance, he praised Staring's originality and versatility, his knowledge of seventeenth-century poetry and his 'sensible view of life', but stopped short of a technical analysis: 'we regard it as superfluous to draw attention to the merits of his versification', he stated, and asked: 'what purpose would be served by a cold analysis of the beauties of these original poems?' He also took issue with the Byronic vogue which was still raging in 1837, and when Beets published his *José* he cautiously yet determinedly counselled him to turn in another direction. Potgieter was often a harsh critic, but his aims were constructive. He was assuming the leadership of the new generation of writers and in a paternally authoritarian manner tried to steer them in the direction which he regarded as the most rewarding. What he demanded from the young writers was originality, imagination, an interest in the past, particularly in the seventeenth century and also a belief in the virtues of the liberal bourgeois society in which he himself believed so strongly. When a work fell short of these demands, he reacted against it, however great its literary value might have been. He more or less told Geertruida Toussaint to switch from English to Dutch history, but when *Het Huis Lauernesse* turned out to be an apologetic Christian novel rather than a national historical novel, he declined to review it. He also rejected *Camera Obscura*, surely the most valuable prose book of the first half of the nineteenth century, because he regarded Beets's realism as a lack of imagination, and also because he was irritated by his disdain of the Dutch bourgeoisie.

Potgieter's creative work, too, gave evidence of his interest in national life. In 1841 he published one of his most successful stories: *Jan, Jannetje en Hun Jongste Kind* (Jan, Jannetje and Their Youngest Child), which in allegorical form discusses the decline of the Netherlands after the glory of the seventeenth century. All the sons of Jan—Janmaat the sailor, Jan Contant and Jan Crediet who represent Dutch trade, Jan Compagnie the adventurer who made good in the Colonies, and many others—made the country great through their energy and enterprise, but their achievements are jeopardized by the youngest son Jan Salie, a good-for-nothing who represents everything in Dutch life that is dull and apathetic. Nothing will ever move again in the Netherlands so long as Jan Salie is around. On New Year's Eve, father Jan and his sons decide to make a new start by getting rid of Jan Salie and consigning him to an institution. Potgieter was an optimist who foresaw a great future for the country if only the spirit of Jan Salie could be overcome and be replaced by the vitality of the seventeenth century. Two years later he returned to the same subject in an impressive essay entitled *Het Rijksmuseum te Amsterdam*, in which he used the picture collection of the museum as the basis for a glorification of the seventeenth century, all the time urging the Dutch to revive the Golden Age, from the beginning of the essay with its repeated 'there was a time when...' to the ending with its exhortation to be inspired by the heritage of the past. He also tried to create a new national poetry with his *Liedekens van Bontekoe* (Songs of Bontekoe), published in 1840. It was a small volume of ten poems, written to seventeenth-century tunes and dealing mainly with seventeenth-century subjects. It was an interesting experiment and the poems were pleasant and clever enough, but the attempt itself was too artificial to have any lasting effect.

In his efforts to bring about a national revival, Potgieter had an energetic partisan in Bakhuizen van den Brink who joined the editorial board of *De Gids* in 1838. Bakhuizen was a very talented scholar and writer, but also a man who had great difficulty in organizing his personal life. He ran up some large debts and in 1843 hastily retreated to Belgium to avoid imprisonment. His departure was a heavy blow, not only to Geertruida Toussaint, to whom he was engaged but whom he never married, but also to Potgieter and *De Gids*. Other editors took his place, yet no-one could really replace him, and his absence was one of the reasons why in the late 1840s and the 1850s *De Gids* seemed to go down-hill. In those years Potgieter himself was becoming more and more discouraged and dejected when he realized that the revival for which he had worked so hard was as far away as ever. He became lonely and wrote far less than he did before.

In the late 1850s, however, the tide turned and in the 60s both Potgieter and *De Gids* embarked on a new and productive period which to a large extent may be attributed

to the emergence of the critical talent of Conrad Busken
Huet. When Huet came into contact with Potgieter, he was a
young clergyman with very liberal ideas and a great literary
ambition. He was born in 1826, studied theology at Leiden,
and became a minister at Haarlem in 1850. But, as he wrote
in a letter to a friend, he knew more about French poetry
than about the New Testament. His theology was unorthodox
and strongly influenced by the Bible criticism of David
Strauss, the author of *Das Leben Jesu* (1835). In 1858 Huet
published his own ideas on modern theology in *Brieven over
den Bijbel* (Letters on the Bible), a book that was decried by
the conservatives and the orthodox, and applauded by the
liberals, though even they were critical of Huet's colloquial
style. *Brieven over den Bijbel* was not directly concerned
with literature, but a few years earlier he had published a
small collection of stories and sketches in *Groen en Rijp*
(Green and Ripe), while in the years when he wrote his Bible
criticism he was also publishing, under a pseudonym, a series
of *Brieven van een Klein-Stedeling* (Letters from a Small-
townsman) which show a glimpse of the future satirical critic.
In an attack on smugness and stolid respectability he wrote:

You take refuge in an appeal to Jan Salie? You try to win over our
widows and the spinsters of our almshouses? You speculate on our
national dislike of immodesty? You shake your powdered mane and
throw dust into the eyes of the people? Go ahead, you Dutch scribes
and pharisees! Constant dripping wears the stone, and even if your
shining scalps were not only as smooth as a bare knee but also as
hard as blue-stone, Truth will take revenge for the indignity offered
her by you. With little drops she will drill a hole into that most re-
spectable lid of your most unapproachable brains! Drilling such holes
hurts!

This was hardly language that one expected from a
minister of the Calvinist church in 1858, and it was not long
before Huet's position in Haarlem became difficult. He
hesitated for several years about what to do, until in 1862 he
made up his mind, resigned from the ministry and accepted

appointment as foreign editor of a Haarlem newspaper. Two years earlier he had made his debut as a literary critic with an elaborate article on the poetry of Willem Bilderdijk in which he did irreparable damage to Bilderdijk's reputation. Potgieter immediately recognized Huet as the coming man in Dutch literary criticism and encouraged him to write regularly for De Gids. In 1863 he asked him to become a member of the editorial board, which Huet accepted. Potgieter, who was the life and soul of De Gids, expected much from Huet and treated him exceptionally well, allowing him much higher fees for his articles than any of the other editors and assigning practically all important reviews to him. Huet, ambitious and eager to establish himself as *the* literary critic, worked hard, and there is no doubt that with his editorship a new chapter began in the history of De Gids and literary criticism in the Netherlands.

Though Potgieter and Huet respected and admired each other greatly, their approach to literature and criticism showed marked differences. Huet was strongly influenced by Charles-Augustin Sainte-Beuve whose Causeries du lundi (1851—1862) was one of his favourite books. Consequently, Huet always involved the whole of a writer's personality in his criticism, including all available biographical and psychological data, whereas Potgieter was more concerned with the writer's view of life and society. Potgieter always tried to keep personal matters out of his criticism. Huet did not believe in this and wrote deliberately, fearlessly, but sometimes unfairly, about the personal lives of his subjects. Nor did Huet seem to believe in the original critical program of De Gids as it was published in the prospectus of 1836: 'to replace the sterile criticism of faults by the fruitful and noble criticism of beauty'. Potgieter always adhered to this, and though he did not lack sharpness, he was humane and praised whenever it was at all possible to praise. Huet, on the other hand, with unfailing accuracy discovered the Achilles' heel and then shot his arrow home. Compared with the causticity of Huet, Potgieter's sharpness seems mild. This does not mean that Huet was a negative or destructive critic. He wrote appreciative articles on a great many writers, both Dutch and foreign, but throughout his critical work the accent more often fell on 'fault' than on 'beauty'. He shared Potgieter's interest in the seventeenth century, but with more reservations. He was mainly attracted to Hooft, whereas Vondel, Bredero and Huygens meant less to him than they did to Potgieter. For Cats he had only scorn, and in a famous article he slated him for the first time so thoroughly that Cats's reputation has never been the same since.

In later years, Huet collected his articles in a series of books under the title of *Literarische Fantasieën en Kritieken*, twenty-five volumes in all and a monument of literary criticism. The first half of the title was curious and drew attention to the creative aspect of Huet's criticism. For in Huet the critic, the creative writer was never far behind. In 1864 he tried to fuse criticism with story-writing, which had the unforeseen result of leading to a break with *De Gids*. In the January issue of 1865 he published a dramatized book review: *Een Avond aan het Hof* (An Evening at the Court) in which he had the Queen and four of her companions make fun of a recent anthology. The Queen was not amused and had a sharp letter of protest written to the editorial board. To make matters worse, the same issue carried an attack by Huet on the Liberal Party to which *De Gids* was more or less committed. Both contributions caused a great stir. In Potgieter's view it was all a storm in a tea-cup, but the other editors were not to be pacified and Huet had to resign from *De Gids*. Potgieter then resigned in sympathy.

Huet's editorship of *De Gids* was brief, but forceful and influential, his collaboration with Potgieter fruitful. It is unlikely that Huet would have written as much as he did without Potgieter's constant encouragement and without the opportunities which Potgieter provided for him. Huet, in his turn, rendered Potgieter an important service by editing a volume of his prose, which became unexpectedly popular and gave Potgieter the recognition as a creative writer on which he had no longer counted. Though Potgieter and Huet differed greatly in character and temperament, the bonds between them were firm, and to recover from the emotions of January 1865 they went to Florence together to take part in the large-scale celebrations commemorating the six-hundredth anniversary of Dante's birth. Poetically, the trip bore fruit in Potgieter's long poem *Florence*, published in 1868. It was his most ambitious poem so far. As a homage to Dante it was written in tercets, and in a series of tableaux it evoked Dante's life and work, and the Italian Renaissance in general. At the same time the whole poem was permeated with Potgieter's political idealism and his appreciation of the Italian unity which had been achieved only a few years earlier.

After 1865 the relation between Potgieter and Huet gradually became a little strained. Huet turned away from the liberal doctrine to which Potgieter attached so much value, and their views on national and international politics began to grow apart. Their friendship was severely tested in 1867 when Huet suddenly accepted an appointment as editor-in-chief of the *Java-bode* and sailed for the Indies in May 1868. Later that year it transpired that Huet's passage had been paid by the government and that he had committed himself to advise the government on ways and means to control the liberal press in the Indies. When this became known there was an outcry among the liberals over Huet's betrayal. Potgieter was deeply shocked and at first refused to believe it. Yet he continued to defend Huet whenever necessary: if there ever was a loyal friend, it was Potgieter. Huet himself was very conscious of the impropriety of his actions, and in a letter to his brother-in-law, Dr. J. C. van Deventer, he defended himself by saying: 'You do not find it admirable that I, in order to obtain a free passage, have undertaken to draw up a report, and what is more (doubly precarious for a future journalist) to draw up a report on the press in the Indies. Nor do I. But on the other hand I do not see why I should be bound to perform a continuous series of admirable deeds'. A cynicism perhaps, but in the same letter he made it clear that political liberalism had lost its meaning for him and that he regarded the liberal colonial policy as 'humbug'.

In the same year 1868 there was another Huet-affair, for shortly after he left the Netherlands, his first novel *Lidewyde* came out. He had worked on it, off and on, for several years and had just finished it before his departure. It was eagerly anticipated, for during his years as a literary critic he had made enemies galore, and several of them could hardly wait to pounce on his book and settle some old scores. It was also quickly discovered that the book was immoral, and one of the critics wrote that Huet was like the devil who when he goes away, leaves his stench behind.

Lidewyde was an easy catch for the critics. It was a very full book, full of characters, full of ideas and full of criticism. But what Huet had wanted to depict in the first place was passion. 'Art is passion', he wrote in the introduction, but however much Huet may have professed that passion was the basis of all art, he did not succeed in transmitting much of it to his characters. They lack life and veracity, and more often than not they are just names that make pronouncements. Time and again Huet stops all action and indulges in straightforward essay-writing. His characters carry on long discussions on politics, history and art, in the course of which they have harsh things to say about literature, liberalism and life in general in the Netherlands. It would be unfair to identify Huet with all negative views expressed by the characters in his book, but on the other hand there is little doubt that he used the novel to air his views on a good many things that he detested. As a novel *Lidewyde* may be a failure, as a book it is important for the exposé it gives of Huet's ideas.

In the Indies, Huet developed into an excellent journalist and made the *Java-bode* into a first-rate newspaper. Potgieter assisted him from afar by sending in critical and essayistic material, and long letters full of literary news and gossip. Potgieter's own literary activities in those years centred mainly on the preparation of his collected (or selected) poetry. The *pièce de résistance* of his new volume was a cycle of poems written in 1872 and 1873 under the title of *De Nalatenschap van den Landjonker* (Posthumous Papers of the Country Squire). Potgieter claimed to have been entrusted with these poems by a friend of his, a young country squire from Guelderland. The mystification was so successful that even writers who were as close to him as Geertruida Toussaint and Huet were misled by it.

De Nalatenschap is a very intricate work. The first part is made up of fourteen poems in which the country squire tells of his love for a beautiful woman; these love poems are interspersed by others which describe scenes from country life. The second part bears the title of *Gedroomd Paardrijden* (Dream Ride) and consists of one long poem of nearly four hundred stanzas of six lines each. It represents a dream in which the country squire rides on horseback through the past and witnesses several historical events, until, still within the framework of the dream, his love is fulfilled. *Gedroomd Paardrijden* is a remarkably varied poem, sometimes visionary, sometimes descriptive and narrative, but always very imaginative. It ranges from seriousness in its representation of Potgieter's beloved seventeenth century to humour and playfulness in its whimsical digressions. In no other poem did Potgieter realize his poetic potentialities so fully, probably because the framework of the dream—apart from serving as a unifying element—allowed him to give free rein to the imagination, which to him was always the first requirement of poetry:

> Verbeeldingswereld zijn geen grenzen aangewezen
> Als tijd en ruimte om 't zeerst 't onz' werkelijke doen:
> Wat zij verdwenen wenscht, of wat zij wenscht verrezen,
> Het deinst! het daagt! 't volstaat dat zij de zucht durft voên;
> Des wijsgeers ergernis, die haar de les blijft lezen
> Voor luttel logica in 't wiss'len van visioen. [3]

[3] Translation on page 222.

De Nalatenschap van den Landjonker appeared in Potgieter's
volume *Poëzy II* which was published in 1875. It was his last
work, and he died in the same year.
    A year later Huet returned from the Indies. In 1873 he
had resigned from the *Java-bode* and had started a newspaper of his own, *Algemeen Dagblad voor Nederlandsch-
Indië* (General Daily for the Netherlands-Indies) which he
intended to conduct from Europe. After his return he felt
out of place in the Netherlands and settled in Paris where he
continued to be as productive as ever. He wrote two more
novels: *Josefine* and *Robert Bruce's Leerjaren* (The Years of
Apprenticeship of Robert Bruce) which were to be part of a
large series of novels in the manner of Balzac but which
were never continued. The new novels suffered from the
same faults as *Lidewyde*: argumentativeness of the author
and inability to bring characters to life. Huet was certainly
not a born novelist. He was far more successful with his
studies of the cultural history of the Netherlands. In 1879 he
published *Het Land van Rubens*, followed three years later
by *Het Land van Rembrand*. The latter is a thorough study
of the seventeenth century, placed in perspective by
introductory chapters on the late Middle Ages. Much of the
information given in these books is, of course, antiquated
and several of Huet's interpretations have later been refuted,
but the books still stand as a very readable, intelligent and
sensitive history of seventeenth-century civilization in the
Low Countries. These books also helped considerably to
reconcile public opinion in the Netherlands with Huet. Yet
he lived long enough to offend the country once more. In
1886 he wrote an article in which he ridiculed the King and
insulted the Queen. Another public outcry against Huet was

---

3 To the world of the imagination no limits have been assigned as
time and space vie with each other to limit our real world: whatever
she wishes to disappear, or whatever she wishes to arise, it fades
away! it looms! all that is necessary is that she dares feed the hanker-
ing; the vexation of the philosopher who continues to lecture her on
the lack of logic in the changing of visions.

the result, and his cousin, who was the responsible editor, had to go to prison for it. While the country was still talking about the scandal, Huet died in Paris.

The influence which the activities of Potgieter and Huet had on Dutch literature was profound. For many years they were the dominating force, and they raised the standard of criticism to a level far above that of their predecessors. Reading through Huet's *Literarische Fantasieën en Kritieken* one gets a detailed picture of the literature of his time since all writers of any importance were reviewed by him. All but one, for Multatuli's *Max Havelaar*, which appeared in 1860, was reviewed neither by Potgieter nor by Huet. Their silence was all the more eloquent as *Max Havelaar* was, and still is, the most discussed novel in Dutch literature.

Multatuli was the pseudonym of Eduard Douwes Dekker, born in Amsterdam in 1820. At the age of eighteen he went to the Indies where he made a rapid career in the colonial administration, serving in various places in Sumatra, the Celebes, Amboina and Java. In 1856 he was appointed Assistant-Resident of Lebak in West-Java. It was an un-usual appointment for a man of his age and also a difficult one as Lebak was known to be a poor and troubled district where the population was oppressed by one of its own princes. Dekker was singled out for this position by the Governor-General himself who overruled a recommendation of his Advisory Council because he had been impressed by Dekker's interest in the welfare of the population. When Dekker arrived in Lebak he was therefore under the impression that he had been sent there with the specific purpose of rectifying the situation and removing the oppression. In a romantic-quixotic way he felt the chosen protector of the oppressed and thought that swift action was expected of him. So he carried on from where his predecessor had left off and began an investigation into the abuses of power in the district. After a few weeks in office, he brought a charge against the Indonesian prince who held the position of Regent. The charge was considered hasty and insufficiently documented, and Dekker was advised to withdraw it. He refused, and by-passing his immediate superior, he addressed himself to the Governor-General. In doing so he consciously acted in defiance of the official hierarchy, feeling as he did that he stood in a special relationship to the Governor-General: he knew him personally, he had been appointed by him in a way which ran counter to custom, and he must have thought that he was justified in approaching him in a similarly unconventional way. He also felt that the Governor-General would agree with his point of view and would support him against the weakness and indifference of his chief, the Resident. The outcome, however, was otherwise. After the Council of the Indies had recommended his dismissal for lack of dispassionateness, caution and the necessary sense of subordination, the Governor-General only tried to soften the blow by relieving him of his duties in Lebak and transferring him to another district. Deeply hurt and seething with indignation, Dekker handed in his resignation. A few weeks later he left Lebak and made some attempts to be received by the Governor-General to put his case. The Governor-General, however, was preparing for his return to the Netherlands and refused to see him. Dekker stayed in Java for another year, trying to find a job, making one plan after the other. Finally he went back to Europe, travelling through France and Germany, and at last settled down in Brussels where in 1859 he wrote his novel about what had happened in Lebak.

This novel *Max Havelaar* was not his first excursion into literature. He had been writing from an early age—he even claimed that he had written a play when he was twelve—but he had never published anything. When he came to Brussels he had with him a play called *De Eerloze* (Dishonoured), written in 1844, in which he had dramatized his first clash with the administration. In 1843, when serving as District-Officer in West-Sumatra, he had been accused of embezzling funds. He was found innocent and was fully rehabilitated, but while the case was being investigated he

was suspended from office for about a year, during which
time he had expressed his sense of humiliation in this play.
He had also written a fictional diary, *Losse Bladen uit het
Dagboek van een Oud Man* (Loose Pages from the Diary of
an Old Man), a rather romantic work consisting of childhood
reminiscences, anecdotes, poems and observations on his
own character and prospects. This was the first thing he
wrote, he said in the Diary, and soon he would be
thirty-one years old, adding: 'it is my firm intention to speak
to the people'. Long before he wrote *Max Havelaar*, therefore,
he had been toying with the idea of becoming a writer, and
during his European leave in 1855 he had shown his play to
a publisher who had, however, been non-committal.

In Brussels in 1859 he rewrote *De Eerloze* and
immediately after it was finished wrote the novel in the
incredibly short time of four to five weeks. He sent the
manuscript to Jacob van Lennep who was then a celebrated
novelist and a very influential man in Dutch letters. Van
Lennep was impressed by the book and found a publisher
for it. But Van Lennep, who was active not only in literature
but also in politics, realized that the book contained political
dynamite and had it published in a slightly toned-down
version. To this end he forced Dekker, in an underhand way,
to transfer the copyright to him, and it was only in 1875,
after several court wrangles and the death of Van Lennep
that the copyright reverted to Dekker and the uncensored
version of the book became available.

When the first edition of *Max Havelaar* appeared in May
1860 it was an immediate and enormous success, a success
which has endured to the present day. It has become an
undisputed classic of Dutch literature, and what is more, a
classic which is still alive and kicking, and still capable of
arousing emotions. The centre of the book is an account of
the events in Lebak which led to Dekker's resignation, yet
Max Havelaar is much more than just a case-history of a
civil servant who fell out with his government, more than
just a novel of purpose or a novel of self-justification.

Certainly, Dekker wanted to justify his actions and he never made any bones about it. But what makes the book unique in the history of the novel is the form which he devised to present his case. The novel purports to be written by two people: Droogstoppel (Drystubble), an Amsterdam coffee-broker, and Stern, a young German who works in Droogstoppel's firm to learn the trade. Droogstoppel has been presented with a sheaf of papers by an old schoolfriend of his to whom he refers as Sjaalman (Scarfman, the man who is so poor that he wraps himself in a scarf for lack of an overcoat). From the material contained in these papers, Droogstoppel is going to write a book on coffee-auctions and the dangers that are besetting the market. Realizing that he cannot do it himself, he entrusts the task to young Stern in whose hands the book develops into a justification of Havelaar's actions in Lebak and an indictment of the Dutch colonial administration. Droogstoppel disagrees heartily with the course the book is taking, and now and then writes a chapter himself to redress the balance. These Droogstoppel-chapters are humorous and satirical, they provide comic relief in an otherwise very serious novel, but they also have a function that goes well beyond the simple one of diversification. Droogstoppel, the heartless hypocrite and philistine, is a critic of Havelaar and his comments warn the reader not to criticize Havelaar on pain of becoming another Droogstoppel, which is an unattractive prospect. The possibility of identifying with Droogstoppel is always present because of the subtle characterization: Droogstoppel is indeed an unsavoury character, but he is not all bad; he makes sense; he possesses several traits of a caricature but he is not a caricature all the way. The structure of the book is designed to coax the reader almost imperceptibly into accepting Havelaar and all he stands for. All elements of the book, including Droogstoppel's criticism of Havelaar and the numerous and ostensibly uncontrolled digressions, combine to achieve this effect.

Max Havelaar has often been called an incoherent book, a motley, a rambling novel, because of the constant switching

from seriousness to comedy, the double setting in Lebak and
Amsterdam, the Droogstoppel-digressions, the great variety
of styles, the poems and short stories that are thrown in at
various stages. D. H. Lawrence, in his introduction to the
American edition of 1927, stated bluntly: 'As far as
composition goes, it is the greatest mess possible'.
Lawrence was very wrong, for in spite of its chaotic appearance *Max
Havelaar* is an extraordinarily well-controlled and coherent
novel in which all characters and all situations, however
unrelated they may seem, are closely linked and arranged in
such a way as to put one another in perspective. For
instance, Droogstoppel or the Rev. Wawelaar (Twaddler)
seem at first glance to add little of substance to the book. On
closer examination, however, it appears that both of them, by
debasing and perverting the ideals in which Havelaar
professes to believe, bring the reader a great deal closer to
accepting Havelaar's point of view.

Throughout the book the reader is given two basic views
of Havelaar. The first is the view of Droogstoppel, the
extreme realist, who regards him as an utter failure, and
who through his callous judgments forces the reader to take
Havelaar's side. The other view is given by Stern, a slightly
sentimental, romantic young German 'who enthuses', according to Droogstoppel. This is one of Droogstoppel's observations that show perspicacity: Stern makes Havelaar
his hero and exaggerates a little, not in his presentation of
the facts—which have been checked over and over again
and have been proved amazingly accurate—but in his
larger-than-life portrait of Havelaar. Stern's romanticism,
then, acts as a kind of safety-valve, for whenever the reader
might feel that Multatuli is overdoing things and is
presenting Havelaar in too favourable a light, he must at the
same time realize that he is looking at Havelaar through the
eyes of Stern. Towards the end of the book, when the
novel-aspect is suddenly dropped and reality takes over in
the form of the official correspondence about the events in
Lebak, these two views of Havelaar are both rejected. Both

Droogstoppel and Stern are dismissed from the book, the latter with a few kind words, the former as 'a miserable product of dirty greed and blasphemous hypocrisy'. And then, in the final page, even Havelaar is set aside by Multatuli, 'for I am no fly-rescuing poet, no gentle dreamer like the down-trodden Havelaar'.

The stir caused by *Max Havelaar* was greater than any previous commotion in the history of Dutch literature. The book was discussed in Parliament and one of the speakers remarked with feeling that it had sent a shiver through the country. Its influence on Dutch colonial policy was considerable. One of the objects of Dekker's criticism was the so-called *Kultuurstelsel* (Culture System) whereby the Javanese were compelled to grow certain products prescribed by the government. The Culture System was introduced in 1830 and had been under heavy fire for some time when Dekker published his novel, but its opponents had not yet achieved any concrete results. Dekker's book provided them with a mighty weapon and after 1860 the system began to crumble away. No less important was the influence of *Max Havelaar* on the young generation of colonial civil servants who in the course of time were able to force through a more liberal colonial policy. At the same time one must be careful not to parade Dekker as an anti-colonialist. His quarrel with the government was about matters of policy, not about the principle of colonialism. He repeatedly warned the government that if it adhered to its traditional policy, the colonies would eventually be lost, a prospect which he regarded as disastrous.

In the literary field, the influence of *Max Havelaar* and Dekker's later work was immense, and few of his contemporaries and successors escaped the impact of his pungent style: Busken Huet, Carel Vosmaer, Jacques Perk, Willem Paap, Lodewijk van Deyssel, they all show at some time or other the influence of Dekker's style and ideas. To the writers of the Movement of the Eighties he was one of the few of the preceding generation whom they would accept, and even in the twentieth century his influence can be seen, for instance in the work of Charles Edgar du Perron. Without exaggeration one may say that Dutch prose writing was never the same after the work of Dekker.

Max Havelaar is *the* classic of nineteenth-century literature in Dutch, but it is not a classic that has been laid to rest in a mausoleum where it attracts only an occasional curious visitor. It is a book that is still very much alive, much discussed and much read. Abroad, too, the book made a great impression. It was first translated into English, then into French and German. No less than five different German translations appeared between the two world wars, and new translations in English and French were published in 1967 and 1968 respectively. The German translations and anthologies of Wilhelm Spohr made Multatuli one of the most widely read authors in Germany in the last years of the nineteenth century. *Max Havelaar* holds the record of being the most translated novel in Dutch with editions also in Danish, Swedish, Italian, Russian, Polish, Czech, Slovak, Armenian, Hungarian, Indonesian and Yiddish.

Dekker at first enjoyed the celebrity which the novel brought him: 'When I want to light a cigar, everyone offers a match', he wrote in a letter to his wife. But this state of satisfaction rapidly turned sour. He had written his book with a double purpose: improvement in the position of the Javanese, and rehabilitation for himself. The second objective was never achieved. Not long after his resignation a government committee investigated the charges that he had laid against the Regent and found them justified. Yet Dekker was not rehabilitated and was never offered reappointnent. He resented this bitterly, regarded it as a great injustice and was never able to resign himself to it. He became embittered and turned more and more against the government and the Establishment in general. But he kept on writing.

Max Havelaar was followed in 1861 by *Minnebrieven* (Love Letters), a book which does not fit into any of the conventional literary categories. '*Minnebrieven*', Dekker wrote to his publisher, 'means: my intimate opinions on matters of psychology, Christianity, colonial administration, literature etc. It will be an arabesque of sentiments'. The book was written in the form of a collection of letters exchanged by Max (Havelaar), Tine (his wife), and Fancy, who serves as the symbol of the imagination and who was inspired by Dekker's love for his niece Sietske Abrahamsz. On the one hand the book is an idealization of the relationship between the three of them, on the other it is a sequel to *Max Havelaar,* containing more documents and commentaries on the Lebak case, accusations levelled against the administration and instances of corruption, as well as poetry and stories. It was written with the same virtuosity as *Max Havelaar,* but with more *saeva indignatio* and wider-ranging attacks on the established order of things, especially in the nine *Geschiedenissen van Gezag* (Stories on Authority).

In the course of time Dekker developed into a scathing critic of society, and although he acquired a large following, he always remained a lonely figure who had little contact with the writers of his time. When *Max Havelaar* was published it received a favourable and sixty-page long review in *De Gids,* but the review was not written by Potgieter nor by Huet. Potgieter's aversion to Dekker was predictable: Dekker's iconoclasm was repulsive to him, he found him loud, vulgar and dangerous. In the case of Huet, things were more complicated as he seems to have blown now hot and now cold in his attitude to Dekker. In one of his letters Huet wrote that he could not stand Multatuli, but that can hardly have been the reason for his not reviewing him, for Huet wrote about many people whom he could not stand, and very eloquently at that. Moreover, in another letter he said that he had great admiration for Multatuli's work and called *Max Havelaar* 'brilliant fireworks'. In 1864 Potgieter urged Huet to write against Dekker, stating that 'it was time to seize Multatuli by the collar as this madman makes more young people unhappy than one thinks'. But

Huet did not react, probably because he was torn between his pro and anti-feelings. In the 1860s, when Dekker tried to make contact with Huet, he was put off, diplomatically but firmly. Huet gives the impression of having been frightened by Dekker's rapidly worsening relations with society. Huet, recognizing in Dekker several of his own ideas and characteristics, at that date still expected a great deal of society. In that same year 1864, he wrote to Dekker: 'My attitude to society is less negative than yours, and as a result I am more prosperous. But I do not regard that as having any merit. Each of us must know what he wants'. In later years, when Huet himself was at loggerheads with society, he established closer contact with Dekker. He even gave Dekker who was always in penurious circumstances, a position as foreign correspondent for his Haarlem newspaper. Dekker was living in Germany at the time, and the year 1866 with the war between Austria and Prussia gave him much to write about. His instructions were to write neutral and unbiassed reports, which for a man of Dekker's temperament and pronounced ideas was an impossible task. He therefore invented the *Mainzer Beobachter* which he quoted extensively whenever he wanted to ventilate his personal opinions. It was three years before his mystification was discovered.

Before he went to Germany, Dekker began to write his *Ideën* (Ideas), numbered from 1 to 1282 and eventually collected in seven volumes. These *Ideën* are the most complete expression of a writer's personality to come out of the nineteenth century. No other writer has so freely and independently put on record what he thought of the society in which he was living. Dekker's range of interests was wide, and in the seven volumes one finds his opinions on politics as well as on religion, on the administration of the colonies, on the emancipation of women and the education of children, on literature, on himself. Some of the *Ideën* are short and snappy like a La Rochefoucauld aphorism, others run into many pages. But in every one Dekker is completely present, never hiding behind a mask, never sitting on the fence. He was a moralist, whether he wrote a novel, a play or a political article, whether he analysed a piece of literature or the budget of the Dutch working class. At the centre of all his work lies criticism of one mode of behaviour and defence of another. His main attack was always directed at dogma, whether in religion, politics, education or literature. His ideas may not always have been original— one could easily draw up a list of his sources, which would include Rousseau, Voltaire, Lessing, August Lafontaine, Alphonse Karr and several others—but the force of his personality, his fearless non-conformism, and last but not least his uncluttered and highly original style of writing made him one of the most influential writers in the history of Dutch literature and Dutch society in general.

The *Ideën* also contain a five-act play and, scattered through the seven volumes, a long novel. The play is *Vorstenschool* (School for Princes) in which Dekker expounds his political and social ideas, and argues his preference for an enlightened and paternalistic monarchy. It was seen at the time as a skit on the Dutch Royal Family, but Dekker denied this by saying: 'when our ancestors for the first time saw tea, they cooked it like spinach. I ask you to read, use and judge my play as a play'. The novel is *Woutertje Pieterse*, a novel of childhood and to a certain extent autobiographical. Like Max Havelaar, Woutertje Pieterse is an idealist living in an environment of narrow-mindedness and hypocrisy. Like *Max Havelaar* also, *Woutertje Pieterse* is a curious blend of romanticism and realism. The earlier parts of the book are realistic in their great devotion to detail, in the description of Woutertje's clashes with his surroundings and above all in the sharp observation of the Amsterdam lower middle class in the 1830s. These parts are satirical, humorous, sometimes bitter and always without any illusions about the sweet days of youth. In the second half of the book, Dekker moved away from this realism and concerned himself more with Woutertje's dream world, symbolized by Fancy and represented by Princess Erica. In Dekker's characteristic fashion there are many digressions and there is a great deal of essayistic writing on education, child psychology, language and history. It was the first novel on childhood to appear in the Netherlands, and although it was followed by many others, it has never been surpassed.

While writing the *Ideën*, Dekker also published some shorter books: *Duizend en Enige Hoofdstukken over Specialiteiten* (Some Thousand Chapters on Specialists), an entertaining attack on 'experts', in particular 'colonial experts', and *Millioenen-Studiën* (Studies of Millions), an exposition of an infallible method of winning at roulette, interspersed with portraits of the gamblers and their public. In 1877 the last volume of *Ideën* appeared. It was to be his final work. Dekker died in Germany in 1887.

With the work of Dekker, the criticism of Busken Huet, and the stories and sketches of Beets, prose showed a greater diversity and a higher quality than poetry between 1840 and 1880. Apart from Potgieter, all but one of the poets of those years must be classed as minor poets. The one exception was Guido Gezelle, a Flemish priest from Bruges.

Gezelle was born in 1830 and published his first volume of poetry in 1858 under the title of *Vlaemsche Dichtoefeningen* (Flemish Exercises in Poetry). Unprepossessing though the title may have been, this volume gave a new direction to Dutch poetry: away from traditional romanticism and towards impressionism. It is true, Gezelle was and always remained a romantic at heart, it is also true that his first volume contained several echoes of Willem Bilderdijk's rhetoric, but on the other hand much of the poetry in this volume was characterized by an unusual spontaneity and originality. In his later volumes such as *Gedichten, Gezangen en Gebeden* (Poems, Hymns and Prayers), *Tijdkrans* (Cycle of Time) and *Rijmsnoer* (String of Rhyme), he shed all rhetorical diction and developed into a poet with one of the most personal styles in the Dutch language. He was strongly orientated towards England, in particular the England of the

Cardinals Newman, Manning and Wiseman, and he was influenced to a certain extent by Wordsworth and by Longfellow whose *Hiawatha* he translated. Yet in the case of Gezelle it is more than usually difficult to indicate where similarity ends and influence begins. Influences from outside certainly did not affect his poetry very deeply. The essence of it was entirely his own. What makes his poetry unique is his extraordinary sensitivity to nature. Gezelle showed that to those who can see and feel there is no hierarchy of values in nature. Nothing was too small, too slight, too inferior to be worthy of his attention. In this he was rather like Wordsworth, only more so. Gezelle wrote as if he was part of nature. No other poet has been able to express as he did the movement and rhythm of animals, birds, insects, plants, flowers, clouds, water. All his inspiration was drawn from his own highly developed sensory perception of nature, and often resulted in impressionistic nature poems describing a garden in bloom, the country under an overcast sky, a misty day in winter. In a life punctuated by disappointment, frustration and friction, he often seemed to withdraw from the world of man and to become a second St. Francis talking to the birds or another St. Anthony preaching to the fishes. In trying to capture the rhythms of nature, he developed a very musical style, sometimes strongly onomatopoeic and often approaching *poésie pure*, though never to the extent of sacrificing meaning to sound. His description of nature was never given for its own sake, but its ultimate and often explicitly stated aim was to glorify the creator of nature. However sensuous his poetry may be, in the last analysis it is religious. In *Het Schrijverke* (The Little Writer), an early and famous poem about the water-beetle which is called whirligig in English and a 'little writer' in Dutch, he ended with the lines:

> Wij schrijven, herschrijven en schrijven nog,
> den heiligen Name van God. [4]

[4] We write, re-write and write again, the holy name of God.

and these lines are echoed throughout his work.

Though Gezelle's appreciation of nature never changed, his moods changed with the joys and sorrows of his personal life. In the years when he worked as a teacher at the seminary of Roeselare, and literally lived for his teaching, the tone of his poetry was almost ecstatic. In later years, after he had been removed from his teaching position, the mood was often one of melancholy and sadness. There were also times, between 1862 and 1877 for instance, when he wrote little poetry. In those years he took an active part in politics and became a staunch defender of the Flemish dialect from which he had always liberally borrowed words and phrases for his poetry.

Not everything Gezelle wrote was on the same high level. A considerable part of his poetry is too obviously moralistic and didactic. Also, he wrote a great deal of occasional verse which is often trite. But when he was at his best, his poetry had a sparkle and a movement that was unparalleled in the nineteenth century. During his lifetime he was given little recognition, either in Belgium or in the Netherlands. He died in 1899 and only in the last years of his life did it become clear that the new literary movement which had sprung up in the Netherlands and which was known as *De Beweging van Tachtig* (The Movement of the Eighties), was doing the very thing that Gezelle, singlehanded and without a program or theory, had done more than twenty years earlier: making a clean break with traditional and cliché-ridden romanticism, stressing sensory perception of nature as the poet's source of inspiration, and introducing a new type of imagery that was 'visible' and directly related to the world around. There was an important difference of approach, though, between Gezelle and the poets of the Movement of the Eighties: Gezelle's poetry was intrinsically religious and moralistic, whereas the poets of the Eighties were categorically anti-moralistic and subscribed to the doctrine of 'art for art's sake'. As in the case of Gezelle, the poetic ancestry of the group was to be found in England, not in the work of the

Lake Poets, but in that of Shelley and Keats.
The members of the Movement of the Eighties were not
the first to draw attention to Shelley and Keats. Both poets
had been known in the Netherlands for many years.
Potgieter had written about them, and Busken Huet and
several other writers had frequently shown that they were
aware of their existence. Yet before 1880 one does not find
any traces of their influence on Dutch poetry. Round about
that year the situation suddenly changed. The interest in the
work of the English poets accelerated and developed in the
following years into a Shelley and Keats vogue which was no
less fervent than the Byron vogue of the 1830s. There was,
however, a much greater natural affinity between the poets
of the eighties and Shelley and Keats than there had been
between the poets of the thirties and Byron, with the result
that the poetry of the eighties was far more authentic and
original than the Byronic poetry of the thirties. Shelley and
Keats certainly stood godfather to the Movement—at a
distance of about sixty years—but soon the Movement went
its own course. It was a violent course, and time and again
the members of the group loudly proclaimed themselves to
be revolutionaries who were going to establish an entirely
new literature. With unusual vehemence they turned against
the preceding generation, excepting only Potgieter, Huet and
Multatuli, and by the mouth of Lodewijk van Deyssel
(pen-name of Karel Alberdingk Thijm), the most energetic
and abusive critic of the group, pronounced their predecessors 'buffaloes of mediocrity', 'indecent dwarfs', and
'eunuchs of the mind'. New movements are not generally
noted for generosity towards the older generation, but no
other movement has tried so hard to sweep away at one blow
what was written before them. Their indignation was
understandable. The rank and file of Dutch poets between
1850 and 1880 was undoubtedly mediocre, consisting largely
of well-meaning clergymen whose homely and rhetorical
poetry was primarily intended for the edification of their
audience; it was a provincial poetry which no longer fitted in

the rapidly developing Dutch society of the seventies and eighties. The idea of art for art's sake, so enthusiastically embraced by the Movement of the Eighties, was a healthy and necessary reaction to this kind of poetry.

New movements, however revolutionary, do not fall from the skies, and before 1880 the ground had been prepared by several writers of whom Jacques Perk was the most important. He died in 1881, at the age of twenty-two, too young to have been a member of the group. But the others acknowledged him as their precursor and regarded his poetry as the beginning of the new era. The main body of Perk's work was *Mathilde*, a cycle of 107 sonnets. The use of the sonnet form was a new departure in itself. During the eighteenth and nineteenth centuries the sonnet had become a rare form of expression and the poets of the eighties were the first to rediscover it and to explore its possibilities. Perk's predilection for the sonnet was inspired by the Renaissance and Baroque poets, and also by Goethe, to whose 'Und das Gesetz nur kann uns Freiheit geben' he paid homage in the opening sonnet of *Mathilde*: 'De ware vrijheid luistert naar de wetten' (Real freedom obeys the law). The *Mathilde* sonnets describe his love for a girl whom he met briefly during a summer vacation in the Ardennes, and who became his Muse, his Beatrice, his Laura. In the course of the sonnets, his love for her, always more platonic than erotic, gradually moved away from the actual person of Mathilde and developed into an adoration, later even a deification of Beauty, culminating in the second last sonnet:

Schoonheid, o Gij, Wier naam geheiligd zij,
Uw wil geschiede; kome Uw heerschappij;
Naast U aanbidde de aard geen andren god. [5]

---

[5] Oh Beauty, whose name be hallowed, thy will be done; thy kingdom come; next to you the earth shall worship no other god.

Little of Perk's poetry was published in his lifetime. His worship of Beauty was too radical a break with the moralism of the established poets to become immediately acceptable, and *De Gids*, which was still the leading magazine, rejected his work. His *Mathilde* cycle was published posthumously in 1882 by another young poet, Willem Kloos, who had come to know Perk in the last year of his life, and who had encouraged and advised him when he was working on the *Mathilde* sonnets. After Perk's death, Kloos acquired the manuscripts and published them, not, however, without considerably rewriting several poems.

Like Perk, Kloos was born in 1859, and when the book came out, he was, like Perk again, practically unknown in the literary world. Kloos wrote a lengthy introduction to the book, an essay on the poetry of Perk and poetry in general, and it is this essay which is usually regarded as the manifesto of the Movement of the Eighties. Kloos stressed that imagination was 'the root and the means and the essence of all poetry'; he professed his belief in the inseparability of form and content, and quoted with approval Leigh Hunt's definition of poetry as 'imaginative passion'. He also referred briefly to Shelley's *Defence of Poetry*, too briefly really to do justice to the debt he owed him. He ended by saying that 'poetry is not a soft-eyed maiden . . . . . but a woman, proud and powerful . . . . . poetry is not affection, but passion, not consolation, but intoxication'. Kloos's essay was certainly not a model of literary theory. Its arguments were a little vague and its postulates rather derivative, but it was eloquent and made up in conviction for what it lacked in depth.

In his early poetry Kloos showed himself to be closer to Keats than to Shelley. His *Okeanos* (Ocean), an epic fragment of 1884, was clearly written under the influence of *Hyperion* with its mythological story of an older generation which has to yield to a younger one, its use of blank verse and five-beat iambics. Yet one finds remarkably few echoes of Keats's images and metaphors, and the conclusion must be that by that time Kloos had already developed a poetic language of his own. More of Keats is to be found in the early work of his friend Albert Verwey, born in 1865, whose *Persephone* and *Demeter* stemmed directly from *Hyperion*. The curious coincidence that the early poetry of Kloos and Verwey shows such clear influences of *Hyperion*, and not of, say, *Endymion* or *Lamia*, which were also generally known and admired, can to a certain extent be explained by the fact that the interest in Keats was sparked off by an excellent translation of *Hyperion* which Willem Warner van Lennep, Jacob van Lennep's half-brother, published in 1879 and which made a lasting impression on the young poets.

The awareness of having discovered a new basis for literature sharpened the desire in Kloos, Verwey and some other young writers to possess a journal devoted entirely to their aims and led in 1885 to the foundation of *De Nieuwe Gids* (The New Guide). The name was polemic and plainly showed that the new journal was going to make a stand against *De Gids*. It was set up by Kloos, Verwey, Frederik van Eeden, Willem Paap and Frank van der Goes who together formed the editorial board with Kloos acting as secretary. In the prospectus the editors proclaimed that their conception of literature was totally different from that expressed by the 'authoritative magazines', and that great changes in Dutch literature were urgently required. They added that *De Nieuwe Gids* was not intended to be an exclusively literary magazine, but that contributions on art, science, philosophy and politics were also welcome. Their ambition was to make it the rallying point for all those 'who wish to speak on their subjects in a progressive sense'. For some years they succeeded in this. Apart from poetry and prose by Kloos, Verwey, Van Eeden and several others, the first volume also contained articles on modern chemistry, colonial policy and Roman Law. In the second year the painters Jan Veth and Willem Witsen became regular contributors and stood up for the new impressionist style of painters such as Anton Mauve, the Maris brothers, Hendrik Willem Mesdag. In later years, the composer Alphons

Diepenbrock regularly published articles on modern music. The originally poetic Movement of the Eighties therefore grew into a much wider-ranging *Nieuwe Gids* Movement which sought to bring about changes in social and political life as well as in the arts.

The first years of *De Nieuwe Gids* were a great triumph for the poetic principles of the Movement, particularly in the form they took in the sonnets of Willem Kloos. Kloos was as much a worshipper of Beauty as Perk had been, but less dogmatically so. He did not write the B of Beauty quite as large as Perk had done and was more concerned with the practice of art for art's sake than with the theory. More than with Beauty or Art, though, he was concerned with the Self. All his poetry was first and foremost introspection and self-analysis, from the early love sonnets and the melancholy poems of loneliness and death to the unending stream of turgid *Binnengedachten* (Inner Thoughts) which were published in the later volumes of *De Nieuwe Gids*. Kloos's inspiration was short-lived, and although he kept on writing until his death in 1938, little of the poetry written after his first volume *Verzen* (Poems, 1894) can be considered to be of much value. His best poetry was written between 1885 and 1888, and the sonnets of those years still stand as very successful examples of the individualist and subjective poetry that the Movement of the Eighties demanded. The subjectivity and introspection of these poems, together with the attention given to the musical sound, place them close to the poetry of the symbolist movement in France. One might even say that the early poetry of Kloos and Verwey, though sparked off by the romanticism of Keats and Shelley, represents in fact a Dutch variety of symbolism. Particularly in their views of the poet's place in society, the young Kloos and Verwey showed much more affinity to the symbolists than to the romanticists. Neither of them shared the romantics' hatred of society; like the symbolists, they regarded involvement with society as vulgar and below the dignity of the poet. Their aloofness was a far cry from

Shelley's self-confessed passion for social reform, and Kloos, however Shelleyan he may have been otherwise, always ignored the social side of Shelley's personality. To the Kloos and Verwey of the eighties, art was all, and society was something to be ignored. They made art into a religion, with Beauty and the Self as its twin gods, the ivory tower as its temple, and themselves as its high priests. Although the foundation of *De Nieuwe Gids* in 1885 almost coincided with the publication of Jean Moréas' *Manifeste du Symbolisme* in 1886, and although the analogies between the aims of the symbolists and the Dutch writers of the eighties are unmistakable, Kloos and Verwey seem to have been curiously unaware of them. They never expressed any great enthusiasm for the symbolist movement as such and they were certainly not in sympathy with the attacks made by the symbolists on naturalism. True, Kloos did express some reservations on Zola, reproaching him for his lack of concern with 'inner life' and the subconscious, but Lodewijk van Deyssel, also one of the leading men of the Movement though not an editor of *De Nieuwe Gids*, was one of Zola's most faithful apostles. In one of his articles on naturalism, he pitted Zola against the symbolists, and pronounced him winner on all counts. The best writers of the symbolist group in his opinion were, oddly, André Gide and Camille Mauclair, 'but neither of them is really a symbolist, and both are weak, weak'. Kloos did not discuss symbolism extensively either. He dismissed Jean Moréas and Ernest Raymond as 'just good artists, not masters', and accused Mallarmé of ignoring his own emotions and sensations. He expressed unqualified admiration only for Verlaine and reserved for him the accolade of 'France's greatest poet'. When Verlaine visited the Netherlands in 1892 he was received by the poets, but it is significant for the absence of any close relationship between the Dutch and French writers of those years that the initiative for Verlaine's visit had not been taken by the poets, but by a group of painters. From Verlaine's own account of this visit, *Quinze Jours en Hollande*, it also appears that though he met Kloos, Verwey and Van Eeden, he had more contact with painters such as Philippe Zilcken, Willem Witsen, Isaac Israels and Jan Toorop. The most ambitious poetic achievement of the 1880s was Herman Gorter's *Mei* (May), a long poem in the tradition of Keats and closely related to *Endymion*. Yet *Mei* was much less dependent on Keats than Kloos's *Okeanos* or Verwey's *Persephone*, and Gorter was the only poet of the group who could compete with the English poet on a footing of equality. In its imagery and descriptive passages, *Mei* is often reminiscent of *Endymion*, but it is hard to say whether the similarities are really derivative, or whether similarity of theme and atmosphere led to a similar way of expression. In some respects *Mei* actually has the edge on *Endymion* because of its stricter organization, its strikingly unconventional language, its extremely effective variation in blurring and accentuating rhyme, and its daring use of enjambement.

Gorter began writing *Mei* in 1887, when he was twenty-three—also Keats's age when he wrote *Endymion*—and published the first canto in *De Nieuwe Gids* in 1889. Kloos, Verwey and Van Eeden immediately welcomed it as the most complete expression of the poetic ambitions of the Eighties, and this high appreciation of the poem has endured. *Mei* is a lyrical narrative in which the poet relates a pseudo-mythological story of the month of May, represented as a young girl who cherishes a hopeless love for the blind god Balder. May is rejected by Balder because his absolute loneliness and self-sufficiency make a union impossible. A confusingly great number of interpretations of the poem have been given. Some regard it simply as the account of a tragic love story and relate it to an episode in Gorter's own life. Others regard Balder as a representation of the poet of the Eighties who retired into himself and was blind to the outside world. Others again find in it the realization that the eternal soul (Balder) can never unite with transitory beauty (May), or read it as a poem about poetry which expresses the impossibility of a union between the poet's experience of nature (May) and the essence of nature (Balder). The various interpretations of *Mei* can all be defended up to a point, but in the last analysis none of them is entirely satisfactory. *Mei* is not an allegory, nor even a systematically symbolic poem, and any elaborate interpretation sooner or later breaks down on passages that resist integration into a system of symbols. It seems that Gorter aimed deliberately at symbolic vagueness, for the first draft of the poem was in several respects more explicit than the final version. Moreover, when after publication of the first canto the critics began to give conflicting interpretations of it, Gorter wrote in a letter to an uncle of his: 'I wanted to make something with much light and with a beautiful sound, nothing else. There is a story in it and a little bit of philosophy, but that is so to speak by accident. I knew that the weakness of it is that the story and the philosophy are vague and unsteady, but in the days when I made it I could not do any better. I felt that I could make something with a beautiful sound and full of brightness, and therefore I wanted to do that and nothing else'.

A poet's insistence on what his intention was when he wrote a particular poem should not, of course, take the place of an interpretation, but in the case of *Mei* one must agree with Gorter that the light, the brightness and the musicality of which he speaks in his letter, rather than the philosophical or symbolic content constitute the value of the poem. Like Kloos, Gorter wrote out of a conviction that sensory perception, and particularly visual perception, was the source of poetry. In no other poem of the eighties was the theory more convincingly applied than in *Mei*. The backbone of *Mei* is its imagery, mainly inspired by the Dutch landscape, always 'visible' in accordance with the precept of Kloos, and brilliantly evocative. Its opening lines, with their stress on 'newness' and their visual representation of a memory, set the tone for the whole poem:

Een nieuwe lente en een nieuw geluid:
Ik wil dat dit lied klinkt als het gefluit,
Dat ik vaak hoorde voor een zomernacht,
In een oud stadje, langs de watergracht —
In huis was 't donker, maar de stille straat
vergaarde schemer . . . [6]

After *Mei* Gorter's poetry developed towards extreme individualism. His volume *Verzen* (Poems) of 1890 was characterized by Kloos as 'the most individual expression of the most individual emotion', and this is still the most apt definition of it. In his attempt to formulate the most individual sensations, Gorter often charged the language to breaking point, and in several ways anticipated expressionism. In some of these poems the conventional syntax was discarded and replaced by strings of long and eccentric word-conglomerations, comparable to the compound words of Gerard Manley Hopkins, but more extreme. Kloos, though full of praise for this volume, did not write about it as exuberantly as about *Mei*, but Van Deyssel almost broke the language barrier himself in trying to express his enthusiasm. This, he wrote, was preciesely what he had meant when five years earlier he had tried to define 'sensitivism'.

It was not altogether surprising to find Van Deyssel, the champion of naturalism, on the side of Gorter's sensitivism, for in the eighties Van Deyssel himself was moving towards a hyper-individualist prose. In 1881, at the age of seventeen, when he began writing his novel *Een Liefde* (A Love), he started off in the naturalist tradition, but during the five years that it took him to write the book, he gradually shifted from naturalism to impressionism, i.e. from a detached description of reality to a view of reality as seen through the eyes of his tormented heroine Mathilde. This changing point of view showed that Van Deyssel was a strict

[5] A new spring and a new tone: I want this song to sound like the whistling which I often heard before a summer's night in an old town, along the canal—inside it was dark, but the quiet street gathered twilight....

naturalist for only a short period of time and it also gave the book its peculiar heterogeneous character. In 1891 he officially took leave of naturalism in an article *De Dood van het Naturalisme* (The Death of Naturalism), and after that his prose became, like Gorter's poetry, a record of supremely individualist sensations in which the syntax was often reduced to a stammer.

While Kloos, Gorter and Van Deyssel were carrying literature to the extremes of individualism and subjectivity, other contributors to *De Nieuwe Gids* were moving in the opposite direction. In 1889 radical socialists such as Domela Nieuwenhuis began to publish in the magazine, and Frank van der Goes, one of the original editors, became a convinced socialist himself. So for a while *De Nieuwe Gids* accommodated a group of a-social individualists together with a growing number of socialists. Their co-existence was uneasy, however, and of short duration. Tensions between the two camps developed rapidly and led in 1890 to a series of violent clashes. The polemics started with attacks by Van Eeden and Van Deyssel on Edward Bellamy's *Looking Backward* which Van der Goes had translated into Dutch. Van Deyssel, from the point of view of pure aestheticism, declared socialism to be ugly and dangerous to art. Van der Goes replied that to him a pauperized proletariat was a good deal uglier. Then Van Eeden wrote against both Van der Goes and Van Deyssel without committing himself either way. Kloos weighed in with a sharp article against Van der Goes and Van Eeden in which he supported Van Deyssel's point of view. The result of these polemics was an irreconcilable break between the originally purely aesthetic Movement of the Eighties and the more socially orientated Movement of *De Nieuwe Gids* as it had developed since 1885. Personal antagonisms between the editors, particularly between Kloos, Verwey and Van Eeden, also played a role in the disagreements and hastened the downfall of the magazine. Verwey broke with Kloos for personal reasons and resigned his editorship in 1890. His place was taken by the socialist journalist P. L. Tak, but in 1893 Kloos scrapped all members of the editorial board and from that moment on published *De Nieuwe Gids* under his own name. Because of the irresponsible attitude of Kloos and the sycophants with whom he surrounded himself, the magazine went rapidly downhill. It managed to eke out an inglorious existence until 1943, but only as a caricature of its former self.

The change which the writers of the eighties brought about in the literature of the Netherlands was followed about ten years later in Belgium when a group of young writers under the leadership of August Vermeylen established a literary magazine *Van Nu en Straks* (Now and Later), published between 1893 and 1903. The writers of *Van Nu en Straks* were undoubtedly influenced by the *Nieuwe Gids* writers, but from the beginning they gave their magazine an identity of its own. The excessive individualism of the Eighties in the Netherlands did not appeal to them and they felt it to be slightly antiquated. None of the members of the Belgian group, neither Vermeylen himself, nor Prosper van Langendonck, Cyriel Buysse or Emmanuel de Bom, felt drawn towards the experiments of Gorter or Van Deyssel. Individualist though they were—and Vermeylen even said that most of them had anarchist leanings—they reacted against the artistic isolation of the Dutch writers of the Eighties and opted for an 'art for the community' along the lines of the theories of William Morris. Although *Van Nu en Straks* is often said to have done for Dutch literature in Belgium what *De Nieuwe Gids* did for the Netherlands, the Belgian writers were in actual fact more akin to the group which in the Netherlands supported *De Kroniek* (The Chronicle), a weekly paper which P. L. Tak started in 1895. The main difference between the nineties and the eighties, between *De Kroniek* and *Van Nu en Straks* on the one hand, and *De Nieuwe Gids* on the other, is best expressed in the words of Holbrook Jackson: 'the renaissance of the nineties was far more concerned with art for the sake of life than with art for the sake of art'.

Apart from the ten years that separated the nineties from the eighties, the concept of art for art's sake was a luxury that many Belgian writers felt they could not afford. Their writing in Dutch was not only artistic self-expression, but also an assertion of the linguistic rights of the Dutch-speaking part of the population. As distinct from the Dutch writers in the Netherlands, they felt the need to be part of a community, and the writers of *Van Nu en Straks* were very conscious of their responsibilities in the linguistic battle between French and Dutch in Belgium. In the words of Vermeylen: 'In order to be something, we must be Flemings. We want to be Flemings in order to be Europeans'. Vermeylen's main objective was to free Flemish literature from the provincialism in which it had been caught, excepting the work of Guido Gezelle who received his first proper recognition from the group of *Van Nu en Straks*. The revival of Dutch literature in Belgium during the nineties is in no small way attributable to Vermeylen. Whether he was successful in his endeavour to establish a communal art is a moot point, but he did give a strong impetus and also an intellectual basis to the Flemish movement. This, as well as his books on the history of art and literature—*Geschiedenis der Europese Plastiek en Schilderkunst* (History of European Sculpture and Painting) and *De Vlaamse Letteren van Gezelle tot Heden* (Flemish Literature from Gezelle to the Present Day)—made him one of the most influential Dutch-language writers in Belgium.

Van Nu en Straks showed the same combination of lyrical romantic poetry and naturalist prose as *De Nieuwe Gids*. The main poet of the group, Prosper van Langendonck, wrote sonnets which were reminiscent of Perk, and in their melancholy introspection sometimes also of Kloos. In 1893 Cyriel Buysse published the first Dutch-Belgian naturalist novel, *Het Recht van den Sterkste* (The Law of the Strongest), a sombre and pessimistic book about the Flemish countryside, written in the tradition of Zola and also influenced by the French-Belgian novelist Camille Lemonnier. In this

novel, and in the many that followed, there is nothing left of
the idyllic approach to country life which had been dominant
in Flemish prose before the nineties. His disillusioned view
of society met with considerable resistance in Belgium, but
Buysse's observation is so sharp and honest that one must
agree with Vermeylen that his work is 'the most complete
open-air museum of real Flemish people'.

Disillusionment was also a characteristic element of a
number of novels written in the Netherlands in the nineties,
especially of Marcellus Emants's *Een Nagelaten Bekentenis*
(A Posthumous Confession). Chronologically, Emants belonged to an older generation. He was born in 1848 and had
written enthusiastically about naturalism before Van Deyssel
or Buysse had ever heard of it. He began as a poet and
wrote two long epic poems, *Lilith* and *Godenschemering*
(Twilight of the Gods), an unusual venture in Dutch, but
then turned to prose and wrote a number of plays and
novels. *Een Nagelaten Bekentenis*, his masterpiece, appeared
in 1894. In its pessimism, determinism and emphasis on
heredity, it clearly comes out of the naturalist school, but it
never becomes bogged down in over-attention to detail as
Van Deyssel's work often does. Emants was an excellent
narrator, but his novel really stands out for its razor-sharp
psychological analysis. The main character of the book,
Willem Termeer, has murdered his wife, and the whole book
is an exploration of his reasons and motives. In the nineties,
when the study of psychology and psychiatry began to gain
ground, the novelists, too, began to pay more and more
attention to psychiatric cases. Emants, a poet, playwright,
novelist and journalist, but medically speaking a layman, was
the first to make a psychiatric case the centre of a novel, but
he was closely followed by Frederik van Eeden, who was a
doctor and psychiatrist himself.

In the eighties Van Eeden had made his name with *De
Kleine Johannes* (Little John), a semi-autobiographical,
semi-symbolical novel. The book is rather dated now, but
for many years it made Van Eeden the most popular author

of the Eighties and the darling of the reading public. He
wrote a great deal of poetry and also some plays, but the
book that will probably survive longer than any of his other
works is his novel *Van de Koele Meren des Doods* (The
Cool Lakes of Death) which he wrote between 1897 and
1900. In this book he portrayed the life of an over-sensitive
woman, Hedwig Marga de Fontayne, from her childhood to
her death at the age of thirty-three. The main purpose of
the book was to show to what extent social and environmental
factors determine the development, or in this case the
dissolution, of a personality. Unlike the naturalists, Van
Eeden completely and consciously ignored the influence of
hereditary factors. Emants, in his *Een Nagelaten Bekentenis*,
made it quite clear that to him heredity was the basis of the
personality, and he argued that because of hereditary traits it
was futile to try to change human nature. Van Eeden did not
share his pessimism. He was a kind of world-reformer in the
manner of Thoreau—whose Walden he imitated in the
Netherlands—and he was convinced that the removal of
social evils would lead to a harmonious development of the
personality. In the preface to the second edition of the book
he denied in so many words that the illness of the main
character was inborn and inherited, and laid the blame for
her destruction squarely on society. In the same preface he
also protested against those critics who regarded the book as
a case-history and not as a novel. His protest was justified,
for *Van de Koele Meren des Doods* is undoubtedly fiction,
though Van Eeden may have used case-histories from his
own psychiatric practice just as he used experiences from his
own life. As a novel the book is on the whole convincing
though it is marred by long passages of stilted and often
downright clumsy writing. Van Eeden's anti-naturalism was
not confined to his disregard of hereditary factors but also
extended to a dislike of intimate detail. In 1888 in a letter to
Van Deyssel, which he never dispatched, he attacked Van
Deyssel's explicitness in matters of sexuality and pleaded for
a greater measure of *pudeur*. Yet although *Van de Koele*

Meren des Doods is a chastely written book, in its probing for the causes of mental illnesses and sexual inadequacies it went a good deal further than most novels of that period. The greatest novelist to emerge in the nineties, and the true heir of naturalism in the Netherlands, was Louis Couperus, whose output, both quantitatively and qualitatively, left that of Van Deyssel, Emants and Van Eeden far behind. Couperus was born in 1863 in The Hague, spent six years in Indonesia and returned to the Netherlands in 1877. He made his debut in 1884 as a poet with a volume *Een Lent van Vaerzen* (A Spring-tide of Verse), followed two years later by a second volume *Orchideeën* (Orchids). They were not very impressive volumes, written in an ornate style, full of marble, azure, alabaster, antique vases and jet-black hair. In the eighties, when the accent lay on spontaneity and freshness of imagery, the artificiality of his poetry did not call forth any great enthusiasm. He was rather disheartened by the lukewarm reception his work was given and turned his back on poetry. In 1887 he began to write a novel which in his own words was to be a completely unpretentious story about his own environment, that is the upper middle class and aristocracy of The Hague. The book came out in 1889 under the title of *Eline Vere* and was an immediate success. It describes the last three and a half years in the life of a young woman, hyper-sensitive and romantic like Hedwig in *Van de Koele Meren des Doods*, who feels herself doomed to inactivity and aimlessness, and who in the end unwittingly commits suicide. Most of Couperus's characters live under a doom for which he himself always used the word 'fate' (Noodlot). This fate can be more closely defined as hereditary flaws in the mental make-up of his characters which bring about their downfall. Eline's inertia and her feeling of uselessness were inherited from her father, and also emerge in her cousin Vincent who, like Eline, is incapable of giving his life a positive aim. In his firm belief in the dominance of hereditary characteristics, Couperus was much closer to Emants and the naturalists than to Van

Eeden, though the latter's Hedwig is often reminiscent of Eline. The basis of Couperus's work is certainly naturalistic, but his style is quite different from what one normally associates with naturalism or realism. It is an uneven style, sometimes straightforwardly narrative, but often very mannered and precious. Yet although his mannerisms are at times insufferable, his skill as a narrator and his insight into character are so great that his work has not lost any of its value, whereas other mannerists of that same period—and there were quite a few—are now completely forgotten.

Eline Vere was followed by *Noodlot* (Fate), a gloomy novel about a triangle of two men and a woman who are destroyed by fate, i.e. by the inherited weakness in their characters. The next novel, *Extaze* (Ecstasy), was to be 'a book of happiness', but the almost hysterical platonic relationship in which the main characters express their inadequate feelings for each other seems to belie the promised bliss. In these novels Couperus probably tried to come to terms with his homosexual nature and his desire for heterosexual love, but whatever the books may have meant to him personally, from a point of view of literary value they remained far below the level of *Eline Vere*. The same can be said of the two fictional-historical novels *Majesteit* (Majesty) and *Wereldvrede* (World Peace), published between 1893 and 1895, and written in the atmosphere of utopian expectations which led to the Hague Peace Conference of 1893.

Of much more importance was his *De Stille Kracht* (The Silent Force) of 1900 written and set in Indonesia where he had gone back to live for a year. Like *Eline Vere* it is a novel which describes the complete disintegration of the main character. At the outset of the novel, Van Oudijck, a highly placed and capable administrator in Java, is at the height of his strength and power, but at the end of the novel he is ill, demoralized, beaten by mysterious forces beyond his control. Fate, which played such an important part in the earlier novels, is here transformed into Indonesian *goena*

goena, a magical force in which everyone believes but Van Oudijck. Couperus, who could be as tantalizing as Henry James—with whom he has more traits in common—does not solve the mystery, but leaves the possibility for a rational explanation open. His power to maintain a balance between the ghostly occurrences and their possibly rational origin gives the book its peculiar tension. It is written in a soberer style than *Eline Vere*, and also, it is one of the few books by Couperus which is not too long and ends when it should end.

Couperus was always at his best when he wrote about people and situations in a state of decline. In *Eline Vere*, for instance, he depicted the disintegration of Eline's life so convincingly that everyone is bound to agree when he says at the end of chapter 32: 'Nobody could do anything for her'. When he then turns about, transplants Eline into a new atmosphere and introduces a young man who might be able to save her, the reader remains unbelieving and reacts with the feeling that the book is too long. The downward line of Eline's life has been drawn so convincingly that the upward line lacks all power of persuasion. In *De Stille Kracht* there is no attempt to balance or retard the decline of Van Oudijck by holding out hope, and the book is all the better for it. In the set of novels that follow it, however, one finds a similar structural weakness as in *Eline Vere*. The collective title of these four novels is *De Boeken der Kleine Zielen* (The Books of the Small Souls), and they were published in the years 1901 and 1902. They are also novels of decline and disintegration. The first part, *De Kleine Zielen* (The Small Souls), presents a large family in The Hague in their reactions on the return from abroad of the black sheep Constance. Her arrival works as a catalyst on the seemingly close-knit family and causes it to fall apart. The disintegration takes place in two phases: in the first novel we are shown the breaking up of the family relations, in the second and third novels, *Het Late Leven* (Late Life) and *Zielenschemering* (Twilight of the Souls), the destruction of the characters themselves is described. At the end of the third novel the family has completely disintegrated. Then, in the fourth part, *Het Heilige Weten* (The Sacred Knowledge), a counter-movement begins, an attempt to balance the three books of disintegration with one of integration, when Constance's son Addy, a psychiatrist, tries to save what can be saved. Here Couperus repeated the mistake he had made in *Eline Vere*, only on a larger scale: the inevitability of the decline has been so powerfully suggested, that it is impossible for the reader to believe in an optimistic ending.

The first three volumes of *De Boeken der Kleine Zielen* together form an indisputable masterpiece and a high-water mark in Dutch novel writing. None of Couperus's contemporaries combined narrative power with sharpness of observation and insight into character as he did. He was the chronicler of a small section of Dutch society, i.e. the Hague upper ten, and particularly those who had relations with Indonesia, but he was not an uncritical observer. In *De Boeken der Kleine Zielen* he showed himself to be a severe social critic who saw right through the pretence and phoniness of people like the Van Lowe's, the central characters in the novel. Few of the members of that family escaped his criticism which though always cool and controlled, sometimes had a bite as sharp as that of Multatuli.

His next and last novel about the upper classes of The Hague and their Indonesian background, was *Van Oude Menschen, De Dingen Die Voorbijgaan* (Of Old People, the Things that Pass), published in 1906. Of all Couperus's novels, this one has the most unusual plot. The central characters are an old man of ninety-four and a woman of ninety-seven who sixty years before together murdered the husband of the woman. For sixty years they have lived with their secret which they believe is shared only by the doctor who, in exchange for one night of love, signed the death certificate. The book describes the last eight months in the lives of these three, just as *Eline Vere* described the last years of Eline's life, *De Stille Kracht* the last year of the career of Van Oudijck, and *De Boeken der Kleine Zielen* the last years of a family. It is again a novel about people and situations in their last stages, and its sub-title could have been: the disintegration of a secret. For unbeknown to the three, the secret gradually crumbles away. The main line of tension in the novel is the question: will the three be allowed to die in their belief of having isolated the secret, or will they find in the last months of their lives that their sixty-year long attempt to guard the secret has been futile? The suspense is kept up in such a masterful way that most critics regard it as Couperus's best novel. Yet at the same time one must admit that Couperus, as in *De Boeken der Kleine Zielen* and in *Eline Vere*, failed to recognize the limits to which he was confined by his own power. When the old man dies as the first of the three, the race is over, the tension breaks, but the book goes on. After he has built up the situation to its logical conclusion, Couperus again seems to misjudge the finality of the conclusion and continues beyond it. It is a slight flaw, less distracting than in *Eline Vere* and *De Boeken der Kleine Zielen*, yet an unfortunate one in an otherwise perfectly constructed novel.

In his preoccupation with situations in decline, Couperus was clearly related to the so-called decadent writers such as Baudelaire, Barbey d'Aurevilly, De Gourmont, Gautier, Wilde, Douglas, Swinburne. His 'decadence' was never more clearly demonstrated than in his *De Berg van Licht* (The Mountain of Light) which he began to write in 1904 when *Van Oude Menschen* was not quite finished. It depicts the rise and fall of the child-emperor Heliogabalus, the Androgyne, in whom Jean Lombard, Flaubert and Gautier, and in Germany Karl Wolfskehl, were also very interested. Couperus counted this novel among his best books, but although one cannot deny its grandeur, it suffers seriously from an excess of descriptiveness, an over-abundance of adjectives and adverbs which tend to blunt and dull the senses of the reader. Couperus's writing was always threatened by two dangers: too elaborate description, and repetitiveness. He could ward off these dangers easily in the novels in which the narrative element was strong—*Eline Vere, Van Oude Menschen, De Boeken der Kleine Zielen*—but when the word-painter began to dominate the narrator as in *De Berg van Licht* the damage done to the novel was considerable.

De Berg van Licht was by no means his last work. He wrote a great many more novels, such as *Herakles* (Hercules), *Xerxes, Iskander* (Alexander the Great), *De Komedianten* (The Comedians), *Het Zwevende Schaakbord* (The Floating Chessboard), but none of these really came up to the level of the earlier novels. In his later years he concentrated on journalism, travel stories and essayistic writing which made him one of the most successful Dutch journalists ever. He died in 1923

In Dutch literature, Couperus was a very unusual figure. Decadents were rare in the Netherlands, and so were dandies. Couperus was both, in his life as well as in his work. He powdered his style as he did his face, he manicured his sentences as he did his nails, he dressed up his novels in the same way as he dressed up his body. This dressing up and embellishing is one of his most conspicuous weaknesses, and together with his tendency to longwindedness and his fatal urge to continue a book beyond its logical ending, prevented him from becoming a second Tolstoi, Flaubert or Henry James, in whose class he potentially belonged. Yet if the distinction between major and minor writers is at all meaningful, Couperus was one of the major writers of his time, not only in Dutch literature but in European literature in general. His work has been frequently translated: fourteen of his novels appeared in England, thirteen in the United States, and several in Germany, Italy, Czechoslovakia, Sweden, Denmark, France and Spain.

The only other writer of this period to gain international fame was Herman Heijermans, who made his name not as a novelist—although he did write some novels and a large number of prose sketches—but as a playwright. When he began to write, the Dutch theatre was in a bad way. Many arguments have been advanced to explain why this was so, ranging from the influence of the Calvinist Church to the anti-histrionic disposition of the Dutch. There is no easy answer to the question and most arguments seem to contain some grains of the truth without being entirely satisfactory. In any case, when after the classical era drama ceased to be regarded as the highest form of literary expression and when in the nineteenth century the novel became the leading genre, no new generation of playwrights stepped into the breach. Drama became a sideline for novelists and poets. Several attempts were made during the nineteenth century to revive interest in drama but none can be said to have inaugurated a theatrical golden age, either in the Netherlands or in Belgium.

Marcellus Emants was the most prolific dramatist of the eighties and nineties, and himself maintained that the theatre was his preferred medium. Yet his plays, historical and occasional pieces, and comedies, are all overshadowed by his novels and none of them have been able to hold repertoire. Frederik van Eeden and Albert Verwey were the only founding fathers of the Movement of the Eighties who every now and then wrote for the theatre. In 1885, when Van Eeden captivated his readers with *De Kleine Johannes* he also shocked then with *De Student Thuis* (The Student at Home), a play that was both satirical and realistic. After some vaguely idealist plays such as *Lioba* (1897), he wrote several social satires, but these did not exactly take the theatre by storm. The same can be said of Verwey's historical dramas *Johan van Oldenbarneveldt* (1895) and *Jacoba van Beieren* (1902). All these plays were eclipsed by the work of Herman Heijermans, the only Dutch dramatist after the seventeenth century to have made a contribution to European theatre in general.

Heijermans was born in Rotterdam in 1864 as the son of a well-known journalist. After some abortive business ventures he went into journalism himself and became drama critic and columnist with an Amsterdam newspaper. His first play, *Dora*

Kremer, was a resounding flop when first produced in 1893, but even before its première Heijermans had a second play ready, *Ahasverus,* which he protected with a Russian pseudonym and an elaborate publicity hoax. It was first performed precisely one month after *Dora Kremer* and was so enthusiastically received that André Antoine took it to Paris and produced it there the following month. After this success, his plays came thick and fast, at an average of one a year for the next thirty years. The early plays bear the imprint of Ibsen and some of the later ones show traces of the influence of Hauptmann, but on the whole Heijermans went his own way and worked out for himself how the new drama should be written. His ideas on dramatic structure were radically new and his play *Ghetto* of 1898 was the first example of a new approach.

Ghetto deals with a middle-class Jewish family in Amsterdam and the tensions which exist between the members of the family. For the details Heijermans could draw upon his own orthodox Jewish background and on some personal experiences. In the centre of the play stand a father and a son, Sachel and Rafaël, who bitterly oppose each other. The son has lost his respect for the father because he knows him to be a cheat in business, the father forbids the son to marry a Gentile girl and eventually drives her to suicide. All emphasis is placed on the analysis of the situation, rather than on its development or that of the characters. From this point of view the work may be termed, like several of Chekhov's plays, static rather than dynamic. Heijermans did not want to show an evolving situation but precisely a permanent one. *Ghetto* suggests that father and son will always be separated by their religious convictions and by their outlook on life whatever may happen. Quite independently of one another, Heijermans with *Ghetto* and Chekhov with *Uncle Vanya* (1901) broke in a similar manner and at about the same time with the Ibsonian drama of psychological development.

In 1900 Heijermans wrote *Op Hoop van Zegen* (The Good Hope), which was to be his greatest success. The play is set in

258 MORALISTS AND ANTI-MORALISTS

a North Sea fishing village and attacks shipowners who send
out their crews in unseaworthy ships. Heijermans had lived in
such a village and knew at first hand that the price paid for
the fish was often the loss of human life. As a socialist, he
depicted the plight of the sailors in terms of capitalists versus
the working-class, but not in a crude black-and-white fashion.
Not the shipowner, however callous he may be, but the sea is
the greatest enemy. As in *Ghetto,* the dramatic events do not
alter the basic situation. At the end of the play, the central
character Kniertje, who has lost her husband and three sons
to the sea, carries on as before, and so does the shipowner.
The play does not eschew heavy effect and melodrama, but as
a piece of late nineteenth-century social realism it has few
equals. Its international success was enormous: in Germany
alone it went through more than four hundred performances
in Berlin and Leipzig, and it was also staged in numerous
other cities, including Paris, London, New York, Moscow,
Stockholm, Copenhagen, Riga, Vienna, Jerusalem and
Belgrade.

After *Op Hoop van Zegen,* Heijermans achieved another
great success with *Schakels* (Links, 1904), which was also
widely produced abroad, notably in Berlin by Max Reinhardt.
With this play Heijermans returned to the subject of family
tensions which he had explored earlier in *Ghetto.* This time
the family was not Jewish and the tensions were not caused by
religious intolerance but by greed. The children of a well-to-
do businessman scheme and plot to stop him marrying his
housekeeper and try to get their hands on his money. The
subject of the play has a great deal in common with that of
Hauptmann's *Vor Sonnenuntergang* of 1932, and it is not
impossible that Heijermans's play influenced Hauptmann's to
a certain extent. The main difference between the two plays is
that Hauptmann's protagonist completely breaks down during
the play and in the end commits suicide, whereas Heijer-
man's main character, totally disillusioned though he may be,
carries on, like Kniertje and Sachel, in a situation that is not
essentially different from the one before the catastrophe.

Apart from these static dramas, which also include *De Opgaande Zon* (The Rising Sun, 1908) and *Eva Bonheur* (1916), Heijermans also wrote more conventional dramas of development and change, of which *Glück Auf!* (Good Luck!, 1911), about the exploitation of mineworkers, is the best-known, but in the main they lack the punch and bite of the former. He also tried his hand, with varying degrees of success, at farce, comedy, fantasy and satire. Towards the end of his writing career he scored a hit with *De Wijze Kater* (The Wise Tom-cat, 1917), a very amusing, very well-written and also very angry satirical farce about the hypocrisy and deceitfulness of human society.

As a playwright Heijermans deserves all the praise that has come his way, but this does not mean that his work is above criticism. He can be sentimental and rhetorical; he often spells out emotions instead of suggesting them; his characterisation is not always sharply defined; the intellectual content of his plays is not particularly substantial. Yet there is no doubt that he was a master craftsman who found the form and the words to give his social criticism its optimum impact. His explorations of the dramatic possibilities of the static play place him among the pioneering figures in European drama at the turn of the twentieth century.

VIII

THE MODERN PERIOD
TWENTIETH CENTURY

The Movement of the Eighties is often regarded as the beginning of 'modern' literature in the Netherlands. This is not an unreasonable point of view since the writers of the eighties broke radically with the values and ideas of their predecessors. Yet if one thinks in terms of centuries, the Movement clearly belonged to the nineteenth century, if only because of its links with the French symbolists, the poetry of Shelley and Keats, and the prose of Flaubert and Zola. From this angle twentieth-century literature may be said to begin with the reactions to the Movement of the Eighties, starting in the late nineties and gathering momentum in the early years of the new century.

In 1898 Herman Gorter published a long and elaborate essay entitled *Kritiek op de Litteraire Beweging van 1880 in Holland* (Criticism of the Literary Movement of 1880 in Holland) in which he severely criticized the individualism of the Eighties. He had become a convinced Marxist and regarded literature as a product of economic conditions. The economic situation of society, he argued, was the primary influence on human thought. In the course of his essay he took Albert Verwey to task, accusing him of ignorance in matters of economy and *therefore* of false notions in matters of literature. Beauty to Gorter was no longer a purely aesthetic value outside society and morality, as it had been in the eighties, but it was 'the movement of social development'. He regarded the Movement of the Eighties as the last phase of bourgeois art and he accused Kloos—however much he

260

admired his poetry—of having remained a slave of the
Dutch lower middle class. He did not spare himself either
and stated frankly that the author of *Mei* had also been a
member of the petty bourgeoisie in disguise. He characterized the limitations of the work of Van Deyssel, too, as
limitations of a social nature, since Van Deyssel, unlike Zola,
did not draw his material from a metropolis which in
addition to a bourgeoisie and a lower middle class also
contained a proletariat.

In his attack on the Movement of the Eighties, Gorter did
not reject all individualism, but only what he called
'bourgeois individualism in a state of decline', and in his
creative work he always remained one of the most
individualistic poets of his time. In 1903 he published *Verzen*
(Poems), a new volume of poetry under the same title as the
volume of 1890. It was a volume of socialist poetry, written
as a glorification of socialism and the working class.
Although it is full of socialist propaganda, full of phrases
such as 'socialism is coming', 'socialism lives', 'the stench of
capital', 'the brotherhood of men', and although diction and
imagery are less extreme than they were in the *Verzen* of
1890, the book is basically a collection of individualistic
poetry: it is the self-expression of a man who had found in
socialism his personal happiness and inspiration. Gorter
himself was not blind to the fact that the individualistic
mode of *Verzen* (1903) contradicted his anti-individualistic
theories, and in an attempt to subordinate his inborn
individualism to his anti-individualistic conviction, he then
moved from lyrical poetry to the epic. His first epic poem
was published in 1906 under the title *Een Klein Heldendicht*
(A Short Epic). It deals with socialism in a much more
concrete way than *Verzen* of 1903, and describes a young
man's hesitation to take part in a strike—in 1903 there had
been a railway strike, the first full-scale strike in the
Netherlands—and a young woman's indecision whether to
join a trade union. It also deals with socialist meetings, the
eight-hour working day and Marxist theory in general. In

its subject-matter and 'engagement' it was the complete negation of the precepts of the eighties when social consciousness, let alone political propaganda, was taboo in poetry. Six years later Gorter published a second epic, *Pan*, more abstract and also more symbolical than the former. It is not concerned with two specific people finding their way to socialism, but with the liberation of all mankind by the socialist revolution. In 1916 *Pan* was rewritten and extended to 12,000 lines which, if one disregards some medieval compilations and Cats's *De Proef-steen van den Trou-ring*, makes it the longest poem in Dutch. Its concept was grandiose and ambitious, so ambitious in fact that it overtaxed Gorter's talents as a poet. Twelve thousand inspired lines are rare indeed, and in *Pan* the lack of inspiration shows up again and again. It might best be described as a volume of excellent lyrical poems connected by long passages of versified Marxist theory. As an epic it failed, but one must concede that it was a magnificent failure.

Gorter not only made propaganda for socialism in his poetry, he also played an active part in the socialist movement. In 1897 he became a member of the three-year-old Dutch Socialist Party in which he belonged to the left-wing radicals. After the Railway Strike of 1903 tension developed between radicals and revisionists, and in 1909, following a conflict with the Labour leader, P. J. Troelstra, Gorter resigned from the party. He then became a foundation member of a new left-wing Marxist party, the Social-Democratic Party, which in 1918 changed its name to Communist Party. In those years Gorter also published political essays, the most important of which was *Het Imperialisme, De Wereldoorlog en De Sociaal-Democraten* (Imperialism, the Great War and Social Democrats). It became known internationally and drew the attention of Lenin who particularly appreciated Gorter's attack on Kautsky. In 1920 Gorter went to Moscow to attend the Congress of the Communist Party. There he clashed sharply with Lenin about the value of the parliamentary system.

Gorter believed in a democratic communism and rejected any form of dictatorship. He put principle above power, always adhered to his radical point of view and never made concessions to the practical politicians, whether their name was Troelstra or Lenin. His stand at the Moscow Congress of 1920 caused an unbridgeable rift between him and Lenin, and Lenin's brochure *Radicalism, a Childhood Disease* was mainly directed against Gorter. After his visit to Moscow, Gorter regarded the Communist Party as unprincipled, and resigned his membership in 1921. He died in 1927, leaving behind a lengthy manuscript, posthumously published as *De Grote Dichters* (The Great Poets), in which he discussed Aeschylus, Virgil, Dante, Chaucer, Shakespeare, Milton, Vondel, Goethe and Shelley in their social and economic environments.

Gorter was not the only poet of his time to play an important part in politics. For many years he had an active supporter in Henriëtte Roland Holst (née Van der Schalk), whose political life to a certain extent ran parallel to his. She was born in 1869 and met Gorter in 1893 through Albert Verwey. They studied Marx together and joined the Socialist Party at the same time. The year before, Henriëtte Roland Holst had published her first volume of poetry, *Sonnetten en Verzen in Terzinen Geschreven* (Sonnets and Poems Written in Tercets), with which she immediately distinguished herself from the rather large number of poets who were still following in the wake of the Movement of the Eighties. True, the influence of Verwey is noticeable in this volume, and at a greater distance that of Dante and Spinoza, but the derivative elements shrink into insignificance when compared with the great originality At a time when no sonnet was considered successful unless its rhythm and metre were regular, she used jumpy rhythms and irregular metres which show her disdain for the 'beautiful sound' of the poem as preached by Kloos and the younger Gorter. Her poetry was more cerebral and at the same time more intuitive than that of the poets of the Eighties.

Her first volume was a constant exploration of the Self, and as such egoistic and individualistic, but one also finds in it the same idealism of the brotherhood of men and universal love as in Gorter's later poetry, though not yet connected with socialism. Like Gorter, she was an individualist at heart, and like Gorter again, her individualism was problematic to her. Her next volume, *De Nieuwe Geboort* (The New Birth), published in 1902 and written after she had become a socialist, is characterized by this dilemma of innate individualism and the ideals of a new community. The fear that the two may never be reconciled gives several poems in this volume an accent of tragedy. Gradually her poetry became more positively socialist, and in *Opwaartsche Wegen* (The Upward Roads, 1907) she celebrated the victory of socialism in herself and enthusiastically anticipated it for the whole world.

In the meantime, the conflict between radicals and revisionists had led to Gorter's resignation from the Socialist Party. Henriëtte Roland Holst, though in agreement with Gorter's interpretation of Socialism, did not immediately follow suit, but let loyalty to the party prevail over loyalty to the individual. For two more years she defended orthodox Marxism against revisionism, until in 1911 she also resigned. She did not join Gorter's Social-Democratic Party, but stayed outside politics for some years. Then, in 1915, she founded the Revolutionary Socialist Party which in the following year fused with the Social-Democratic Party.

In her volume *De Vrouw in het Woud* (The Woman in the Forest, 1912) she described her isolation after she had broken with the Socialist Party. Like Dante, she finds herself lost in a forest, but no Virgil or any other guide comes to her rescue: she has to be her own guide. The enthusiasm of *Opwaartsche Wegen* has gone, and its place has been taken by a tone of lament, of disappointment and uncertainty. The conflict in this volume is not so much the clash between inborn individualism and community ideals, but rather between Dream and Action, between the contemplative and active sides of her personality. She is torn between the dream of the socialist state with social equality and justice, and the action, cruel action, without which it cannot be brought about. Reconciliation between the dream and the action seems impossible to her: 'want Droom en Daad kunnen niet samen wonen' (for Dream and Action cannot live together). More and more she became concerned with the idea of revolution and its justification: Would a revolution with all its evils and miseries be justified by the good cause? Sometimes she was inclined to answer the question in the affirmative and in this volume she wrote:

Hoeveel duizend harten ook noodig zijn,
ge moogt ze nemen, en de prijs blijft klein.

De prijs blijft klein voor het mensche-geluk,
al gaan duizendmaal duizend harten stuk. [1]

Gradually she moved away from the idea of revolution and in *Verzonken Grenzen* (Sunken Borders) of 1918 she stated that 'de zachte krachten zullen zeker winnen in 't eind' (the gentle forces will certainly win in the end). In 1923, in her volume *Tusschen Twee Werelden* (Between Two Worlds), she went a step further and rejected the revolution as 'a dreadful disease, a life-and-death crisis in the body of society'. At the 1921 Congress of the Third International in Moscow she was one of the representatives of the Dutch Communist Party, but the Congress shattered her illusions about the revolution and, like Gorter the year before, she returned from the Soviet Union bitterly disappointed. Her ambivalent feelings about the revolution crystallized in the epic poem *Heldensage* (Heroic Saga), published in 1927, which on the one hand is a glorification of the Russian Revolution and on the other an attack on what had become of it. In the same year, also the year of Gorter's death,

---

[1] However many thousands of hearts may be necessary, you may take them, and the price is small. The price is small for the happiness of man though a thousand times a thousand hearts may break.

she resigned from the Communist Party and published a new volume, *Verworvenheden* (Achievements), in which she repudiated Marxism in favour of a religious Socialism. It is a volume full of self-reproach: she deplores ever having advocated violence and is convinced that compulsion will never work. Summing up her life, she realized that little had become of all the plans and ideals of the earlier years. *Verworvenheden* was not her last volume—she wrote and published until shortly before her death in 1952—but it was her final answer to the problems that she had posed in her earlier work. She also wrote some verse dramas, e.g. about Thomas More, and biographies of Rosa Luxemburg, Romain Rolland and Gandhi.

Her importance and influence in the Netherlands was great. For a long time she was the idol of the socialist section of the population and later, after the opposition between socialists and anti-socialists had lost its edge, she was venerated almost as a national figure, also by people who had never read a line of her poetry. Her work reads like a running commentary on her life. All her ideas, her hopes and desires, her disappointments and disillusionments, are reflected in it. Few poets have been so completely present in their work as Henriëtte Roland Holst was. There is no unanimity about the quality of her poetry. Some critics cannot praise it too highly, others regard the liberties that she took in rhythm and metre as chaotic and inadmissible. From a purely poetical and non-political point of view one of the main features of her work is that it represents a clear break with the tradition of the Eighties. Looking back from her work at the poetry of the Eighties, the idea of art for art's sake suddenly seems very remote indeed.

One of the original editors of *De Nieuwe Gids*, Albert Verwey, also turned his back on the ideas of the Eighties. He resigned his editorship in 1890 after a conflict with Kloos and from then on became more and more opposed to the extreme individualism that was cultivated by the Movement. His contributions to *De Nieuwe Gids* became less frequent and after 1893 he sent a considerable amount of poetry to the Flemish journal *Van Nu en Straks* which was far more moderate in its espousal of individualism than *De Nieuwe Gids*. Verwey, however, was by nature a leader rather than a contributor, and in 1894 he set up a new magazine, *Tweemaandelijksch Tijdschrift* (Bi-monthly Magazine), which he needed as he wrote to his publisher, 'in the same way as a clergyman needs a pulpit'. His co-editor was Lodewijk van Deyssel. The combination Verwey-Van Deyssel was a misalliance, as Van Deyssel realized from the beginning. After publication of the first issue he wrote to Verwey: 'I don't feel my relation to this Magazine to be that of an active leader of a certain intellectual movement, but rather that of a director of an institute for publication'. Verwey on the other hand always felt that it was his task to give leadership, and the surer he became of himself, the stronger his leadership grew.

In the German magazine *Blätter für die Kunst*, Verwey, who was keen to give his magazine an international orientation, recognized a congenial spirit in the work of Stefan George. He reviewed George's *Pilgerfahrten* and *Algabal* in 1895. His review led to a meeting with George, and subsequently to several years of friendship and co-operation. They began to translate each other's work and the first fruit of their friendship matured in 1896 when *Blätter für die Kunst* published translations by George from the poetry of Kloos, Verwey and Gorter. The poetry which George and Verwey wrote in the late nineties gives evidence of a firm relationship between the two. George's *Das Jahr der Seele* (1897) shows affinity with Verwey's volume *Aarde* (Earth, 1896), while George's influence, specifically of his *Algabal*, is noticeable in Verwey's *De Nieuwe Tuin* (The New Garden), published in 1898. Through George, Verwey also came into contact with members of the George circle such as Friedrich Gundolf, Karl Wolfskehl, Ludwig Klages and Friedrich Wolters, so that at the beginning of the twentieth century there existed for some years a strong link between German and Dutch literature. What bound George and

Verwey together was their high appreciation of the poet's place in society, their belief in the 'mission' of the poet. Yet there were differences, and against George's cult of the Personality, Verwey placed his own cult of Reality. An early plan to write a book together on German and Dutch art, stranded on this disagreement. Also, Verwey continued for a while to defend naturalism—in which he had grown up, as he said—against George's fierce rejection of it. For several years their basic agreement prevailed over their differences and they continued to co-operate. In 1903 George and Gundolf published a volume of Verwey translations, and Verwey reciprocated with translations of George, Gundolf, Wolfskehl and Hofmannsthal. After that they began to drift apart and the contrast between Verwey, 'the realist', and George, 'the prophet', became more pronounced. Verwey deplored George's development towards a more and more esoteric poetry, especially after publication of Der Siebente Ring (1907) and Der Stern des Bundes (1914). When the First World War broke out, relations between George and Verwey became strained. The attempts made by George and Wolfskehl to justify the German position alienated Verwey, while Verwey's rejection of German nationalism was interpreted by George and Wolfskehl as a betrayal of their friendship. In 1929 Friedrich Wolters gave an account of the relations between George and Verwey in his Stefan George und die Blätter für die Kunst, to which Verwey replied five years later with his book Mijn Verhouding tot Stefan George (My Relation to Stefan George), which must be read as a necessary correction to Wolters's interpretation.

In the meantime Verwey had made the Tweemaandelijksch Tijdschrift into a monthly under the new title of De Twintigste Eeuw (The Twentieth Century). By 1905 the differences between him and Van Deyssel had become too great and in that year Verwey established a new magazine, characteristically entitled De Beweging (The Movement), of which he himself was the sole editor. Though the title of the new magazine referred directly to the Movement of the

Eighties, *De Beweging* was in fact a strong reaction against
part of the heritage of the eighties. It opposed naturalism and
sensitivism, it rejected the 'art of the word' in favour of the
'art of the thought' and it preferred philosophical poetry to
the sensuous poetry of the Eighties. It also opposed
individualism and gradually moved towards a defence of
traditionalism. In 1911 and 1912 two poets belonging to the
group that had formed around *De Beweging*, Geerten
Gossaert and J. C. Bloem, even advocated a return to
rhetoric, i.e. to the traditional imagery which thirty years
before had been decried so loudly, also by Verwey. In an
article written in 1913 and entitled *De Richting van de
Hedendaagsche Poëzie* (The Direction of Contemporary
Poetry), Verwey gave cautious approval to the demand for
tradition and continuity, stating that the individual's belief
that he could create everything out of himself without the
support of a community was 'beautiful but dangerous'. The
attempt to re-introduce an element of rhetoric into poetry—
'inspired rhetoric' as Bloem called it—never grew into a
strong movement and was opposed from the beginning by
other poets who published in *De Beweging* such as Aart van
der Leeuw and P. N. van Eyck; yet it was symptomatic of
early twentieth-century reaction against the individualism
of the Eighties. The socialist anti-individualists, Herman
Gorter, for instance, and Henriëtte Roland Holst, did not
support *De Beweging* either because they regarded it as
insufficiently socialist: they published in *De Nieuwe Tijd*
(The New Era), a socialist journal established in 1898.

In his own poetry Albert Verwey evolved from a youthful
worshipper of Beauty—'a Calvinist visited by the fever of
Beauty', as Kloos maliciously put it—to a philosophical
poet who expanded his relation with Beauty to a relation
with 'the All' and who set himself the task of expressing the
unity of the poet and 'the world'. In the preface to the 1912
edition of his *Verzamelde Gedichten* (Collected Poems), he
formulated the essence of poetry as 'the creative imagination
which is certainly most immediately embodied in poetry, but

which as the primary human instinct is conterminous with life itself'. In all his later volumes—the most important of which are *Het Zichtbaar Geheim* (The Visible Secret), *De Weg van het Licht* (The Way of Light), *De Getilde Last* (The Burden Borne), *De Figuren van de Sarkofaag* (The Figures of the Sarcophagus), all published between 1915 and 1930—he wanted to give expression to what he called the Idea, a concept which he himself defined as 'a forward pushing force which is the essence of all life and becomes visible only in its form', and which in Simon Vestdijk's formulation is 'something related to certain basic pantheistic principles such as the Absolute, the Will, the Unconscious'. Verwey's theoretical occupation with the Idea led to—or was perhaps a rationalization of—a strongly intellectualistic and philosophically introspective poetry, which in its terseness of diction is often reminiscent of Potgieter. This was no coincidence, for Verwey felt a strong affinity to Potgieter and recognized in his work his own ideal of 'Dream and Discipline', of imagination and level-headedness. In 1903 he wrote *Het Leven van Potgieter* (Life of Potgieter), a warmly appreciative study of his life and work showing in its very style the rapport that existed between Potgieter and Verwey.

Though a poet of considerable importance, Verwey, like Potgieter again, exercized his greatest influence as a critic. In his criticism, collected in ten volumes *Proza* (Prose), his ultimate criteria for evaluating a work of literature were intellectual and moral, not aesthetic. The intellectual content, the philosophical background, the moral implications, they were the aspects of the work on which he based his final judgment. As a critic therefore he became the antipode of his erstwhile collaborator Lodewijk van Deyssel who always adhered to the purely aesthetic approach. Verwey was also a student of the history of literature and was the first to rediscover the work of Jan van der Noot after his eclipse of three centuries. Besides his studies of Potgieter and Van der Noot Verwey published books on Hendrick Spiegel, on *Ritme en Metrum* (Rhythm and Metre), and on the poetry of Vondel. In 1924 he was appointed professor of Dutch literature at the University of Leiden. He died in 1937, while working on a new edition of Vondel.

At the time when Albert Verwey, Henriëtte Roland Holst, Herman Gorter and several other writers were in full revolt against the principles of the Eighties, and in theory and practice were trying to steer literature in a new direction, there were also poets who remained true to the individualism and subjectivism of the Eighties. This continuing line of the Eighties is most clearly exemplified by J. H. Leopold and P. C. Boutens in the Netherlands, and by Karel van de Woestijne in Belgium.

Jan Hendrik Leopold was born in 1865, studied classics at Leiden and taught at a grammar school in Rotterdam until his death in 1925. In comparison with the poets of the Eighties, who on the whole began to publish when they were still in their teens, Leopold made his debut rather late. His first poems appeared in *De Nieuwe Gids* in 1893, in the same issue that carried the first poems of Henriëtte Roland Holst. His comparatively late debut is indicative of the reserve and shyness so characteristic of Leopold's personality. He was a lonely man whose inborn tendency towards isolation and aloofness was aggravated by progressive deafness. His life was as outwardly uneventful as that of Mallarmé with whom he has more traits in common. Leopold was probably the purest symbolist poet in Dutch literature and his metaphorical treatment of the poet's creativity and the strongly evocative character of his poetry show a close relationship with the poetry of Mallarmé. Yet if any poet was ever his own man, it was Leopold. It may not be difficult to point out some instances of influence, by Gorter, for example, but it would be impossible to confuse a poem of Leopold's with one of Gorter's or anyone else's. Leopold's poetry is immediately recognizable by its muted tone, its soft humming, as against the trumpet sound of Gorter's verse. When in 1912 the poet Boutens saw Leopold's first volume

Verzen (Poems) through the press—half against Leopold's own wishes—he wrote a short preface to the book in which he characterized the murmuring diction of Leopold as 'audible musing' and 'near silence'. In contrast to the blue and gold that Gorter used so much, Leopold's poems exist in a world of greys, 'half shadow and half twilight glow' as he said in his poem *Voor 5 December* (For the Fifth of December). Even when he wrote about the splendour of a flower-garden, as in *Albumblad II* (Album Leaf II), he seemed to be developing a colour film in an emulsion that was only capable of reproducing shades of grey. Also, whereas much of Gorter's poetry was written out of abundance, out of an almost ecstatic mood, the dominant mood of Leopold's poetry is often that of loss and fear.

Like Gorter, Verwey and several other writers of those years, Leopold was strongly attracted to Spinozist philosophy. The notion of the interrelation of all things, of man being part of universal nature, offered a solution to the problem of the individual and the community. In one of his major poems, *Oinou Hena Stalagmon* (One Drop of Wine), published in 1910, Leopold described in elaborate images how one drop of wine permeates all oceans, and how the fall of an apple influences the balance of the universe; in the same way our thinking affects all seemingly separate lives and is in turn affected by them. At the same time it is a poem about poetry, symbolizing the creative and receptive functions of the poet.

Four years later Leopold resumed these themes in a long poem *Cheops*. It is one of his least accessible poems, and its hermetic character has caused lack of unanimity among the critics. The one aspect of the poem that all critics agree upon is Leopold's objectification of his own solitude in the Pharao Cheops. In image upon image the poem describes the journey through the cosmos which Cheops made after his death. He is shown as part of the procession of those who had 'immaculately arisen', as part of a community in which he, the former absolute monarch, has to conform to others

and suppress his own will. In the second part of the poem
Cheops turns away from the others and returns to the
loneliness of his own pyramid and sarcophagus where he is
'captured by the symbols of the past'. Some critics read the
poem as a eulogy of the poet's creativity, others regard it as
Leopold's final recognition of the isolation of the individual.
The latter interpretation is the more convincing one,
particularly in the context of Leopold's other work which
after *Cheops* became more and more concerned with this
isolation. A good illustration of his development is to be
found in his adaptations of Omar Khayyam's *Rubaiyat*,
which he came to know in 1903 in the translation of E. H.
Whinfield.

The discovery of the *Rubaiyat* meant a great deal to
Leopold. He recognized much of himself in Omar
Khayyam's philosophy of life, his fatalism, his melancholy
enjoyment of life, his occasional bitterness and rebellious-
ness. In Leopold's first series of quatrains, published under
the title of *Oostersch I* (Oriental), the accent lay chiefly on
the transitoriness of human life:

> De wereld gaat en gaat, als lang na dezen
> mijn roem verging, mijn kennis hooggeprezen.
> Wij werden voor ons komen niet gemist,
> na ons vertrek zal het niet anders wezen. [2]

Leopold identified himself with Omar Khayyam and there
was undoubtedly a natural affinity between the two, as there
was between Omar and Edward FitzGerald whose translations were also used by Leopold. On the other hand,
Leopold's quatrains were more than just a faithful rendering
of the *Rubaiyat*. In general one tends to emphasize what
strikes one most, and in his subsequent translations from
Omar Khayyam and other Persian poets—always from the

[2] The world goes on and on, when long after this time
my fame will have gone, my highly lauded knowledge.
We were not missed before we came,
after our departure it will not be different.

English or French editions—Leopold more and more accen-
tuated the bitterness, the futility of life and the aversion to
human contact:

> Omgang met menschen, nabuurschap:
> een sleepend zeer, een chronisch lijden. [3]

Leopold's translations are as much original poems as they
are translations. They are 'original poems on Persian motifs
and in the Persian stanza-form', as Theodoor Weevers rightly
says.

Though translation of the *Rubaiyat* never became quite as
popular in the Netherlands as it did in England after
FitzGerald's edition of 1859, there were several poets who
followed Leopold's example. None of their translations,
however, bears comparison with Leopold's and no other poet
showed the same mastery in handling the quatrain form
aaba or succeeded as Leopold did in giving the poems the
unmistakable stamp of an original creation. The poet who
came closest to Leopold's achievement was Pieter Cornelis
Boutens, who translated FitzGerald's *Rubaiyat*—not Whinfield's as Leopold did—and also a number of quatrains from
a French edition of Persian poetry which had also been used
by Leopold. The *Oud-Perzische Kwatrijnen* (Old Persian
Quatrains) of Boutens and the quatrains which Leopold published under the title of *Soefisch* (Suphic) go back to the same
French source and throw some light on the differences between the two poets who were each other's next of kin in
literature. To Leopold the dominant theme of the Persian
quatrains was the renunciation of the world, whereas Boutens
gave preference to the poems that dealt with mystic contemplation. Their approach to the Persian poems was so different,
in fact, that their selections have only three quatrains in
common.

When Boutens published his *Rubaiyat* in 1913—the

---

[3] Contact with people, proximity: a lingering disease, a chronic
suffering.

Oud-Perzische Kwatrijnen were not published until 1930—
he was already known as the author of several volumes of
poetry such as *Verzen* (Poems, 1889), *Praeludiën* (Preludes,
1902), *Stemmen* (Voices, 1907), *Carmina* (Songs, 1912), and
a modern adaptation of the medieval poem *Beatrijs* (1908)
which became his only really popular work. Born in 1870, he
was five years younger than Leopold and, like him, firmly
rooted in the individualist and subjectivist tradition of the
Eighties. He shared Leopold's admiration for Gorter and in
his early work was considerably influenced by Gorter's
sensitivism. Next to Gorter, it was Leopold for whose work
he felt most, and when in 1912, at the age of 47, Leopold
had not yet published a volume of poetry, Boutens prevailed
on Leopold to let him bring out a collection of the poems
that had so far been published in literary journals. It seems
that Leopold agreed at first, but later, unsuccessfully,
withdrew his permission. Literary ambition, desire for fame
or gain were entirely foreign to Leopold's nature. When later
he was asked why he had washed his hands of this first
publication, he referred with disgust to Boutens: 'That man
spoke of money'. Boutens was different and lacked Leopold's
aristocratic disdain of material things. Yet realistic though he
may have been in his approach to daily life, in his poetry he
was an idealist, steeped in Platonic philosophy and always
concerned with the reality that lies behind the outward
appearance. Boutens gradually developed from lyrical
spontaneity to a more philosophical and cerebral verse, but
always retained his staggering technical virtuosity which
enabled him to write poems of a cool marble-like beauty
even when his 'heart' was not in it.

Both Leopold and Boutens held university degrees in
classics and taught Latin and Greek in secondary schools,
Boutens for a short while only, Leopold for many years. It is
curious to note that whereas before the 1880s the study of
theology seemed almost a pre-requisite for a place in Dutch
literature, the eighties and nineties saw several classical
scholars come to the fore. Beets was a minister of the church

and later a professor of theology, Busken Huet was a minister before he turned to journalism, Bakhuizen van den Brink, Drost, Van Lennep and a score of lesser known writers had all at some time studied theology. After 1880 the theologians receded into the background and their place was taken by the classicists: Kloos, Gorter, Leopold, Boutens. They did away with the moralist poetry of the theologians and devoted themselves to the cult of Beauty. Aestheticism reigned supreme, until poets such as Verwey, Henriëtte Roland Holst and the later Gorter began to challenge it.

The classical training of Kloos, Leopold, Gorter and Boutens was noticeable in a number of formal characteristics that were introduced during the eighties, such as the Homeric similes to be found in Kloos's sonnets and especially in Gorter's *Mei*, or the personifications of dawn, day and moon, so prevalent in the poetry of Boutens, or the crowding of participle constructions which gives Leopold's poetry its curiously open-ended character. This is not to say that the similarity of background led to a uniform poetry. Gorter, Leopold and Boutens were undeniably related, but their differences were just as marked as their similarities, especially in their approach to traditional language and form. Gorter, in his sensitivist period, made a complete break with traditional syntax. Boutens, on the other hand, accepted it, refined it, polished it and worked new miracles with it. Leopold took up a position in the middle: his syntax and his word-formation were more idiosyncratic than Boutens's, but less revolutionary than Gorter's. The same may be said of traditional form: Gorter for several years discarded it, Boutens went back to it and Leopold stood in between, employing some extremely strict forms, poems in which every syllable, every sound and every pause were accounted for, alongside the freer form of *Cheops* with blank verse and lines of unequal length.

Though considerably younger than Leopold and Boutens, the Flemish poet Karel van de Woestijne, born in Ghent in 1878, really belonged to their generation of writers. He did not have their classical background, but studied Germanic languages and was professor of Dutch literature at the University of Ghent from 1921 until his death in 1929. Yet despite his lack of a formal education in the classics, he was almost as steeped in Greek and Latin literature as Leopold and Boutens. His poetry has strong links with both impressionism and symbolism, showing the impressionist's preoccupation with sensory perception, and the symbolist's introspection and devotion to the sound of the poem. At the same time he was a traditionalist who found in Renaissance poetry, particularly in the work of Hooft, the strict verse-form he was looking for. In this respect he was very much like Jean Moréas, the Graeco-French poet who after having been one of the original symbolists and the man who gave symbolism its name, moved away from it at the beginning of the century to advocate a return to the simplicity and the regular poetic forms of the Renaissance. Van de Woestijne held Moréas in high regard—after the latter's death in 1910 he wrote several *in memoriam* poems— and supported his program of a new classicism. In an interview given in 1913, he stated that 'through individualism we come to a neo-classicism, a new classical period, a period of people who are totally conscious and who express themselves with complete sincerity, but who disregard anything that in their particular situation might be too personal, too idiosyncratic'.

Van de Woestijne's combination of impressionism and symbolism, together with his adherence to the new classicism of Jean Moréas, made his work into a unique synthesis of the various streams of European poetry. He owed a debt to many: to the poets of the Eighties (in the first place to Kloos), to *Van Nu en Straks,* to the French-writing poets of *La Jeune Belgique* (in particular Emile Verhaeren and Maurice Maeterlinck), to Baudelaire, Henri de Régnier, Jules Laforgue and Jean Moréas. Yet his poetry was by no means a hotchpotch of influences and reminiscences. The many names with which his work can be linked are not indications of a derivative poetry, but rather of a very complex personality. His poetry, which he himself termed 'a poetic and symbolic biography', is a constant reflection of his attempts to establish harmony between the conflicting elements of his nature. The inability to achieve this harmony gives his work its singularly tragic tone. Locked up in himself, introverted to a very high degree, he sought and glorified solitude, while at the same time he hankered after communication and understanding, and stormed at his very loneliness. His work is pervaded by an intense sensuality to which he often abandoned himself, though never without a feeling of guilt. He longed for a purity which always seemed to elude him, contaminated as it was by his sensuality: 'de reinste dag is zwaar van avond-zwoel begeeren' (the purest day is heavy with sultry-evening desire). His loathing of his own sensuality and lack of purity extended to a revulsion to his entire nature, and gave a good deal of his poetry the character of a painful confession. Both the consciousness and the sincerity of which he spoke in the interview of 1913 are present throughout his work. Introverted though he may have been, on paper he exposed himself and in complete frankness poured forth all his hopes and frustrations, his desires and disappointments, sometimes with a cool but cutting honesty, at other times in lacrymose self-pity.

All this applies in a larger measure to his early volumes such as *Het Vader-Huis* (My Father's House, 1903), *De Boom-Gaard der Vogelen en der Vruchten* (The Orchard of Birds and Fruits, 1905) and *De Gulden Schaduw* (The Golden Shadow, 1910) than to his later volumes *De Modderen Man* (Man of Mud, 1920), *God aan Zee* (God at the Sea-side, 1926) and *Het Berg-Meer* (The Mountain Lake, 1928). The troubled sensuality and morbidity never entirely disappeared from his work, but they were gradually conquered by, or sublimated to, religious sentiments tinged by mysticism. It would be an overstatement to say that Van de Woestijne's tormented mind found its equilibrium in this mysticism, but much of the bitterness of the earlier volumes slowly made way for a tone of serenity and resignation. At the same time the style of his poetry underwent a change. Characteristic of his early poetry was its sonority. Van de Woestijne employed all the tricks of the trade to build up the sound of the poem: assonances, alliterations, internal rhymes were used even more frequently than in the poetry of Perk and Kloos. Though he regarded Hooft as the supreme poet of the Dutch Renaissance, his own style of writing was closer to the baroque loftiness of Vondel. In musical terms, the sound of Van de Woestijne's poetry was not that of a Renaissance harpsichord but that of an organ, and again, not the transparent sound of a Baroque organ but that of a full-bodied Romantic one. The later poems were syntactically simpler and more subdued in sound, though they always retained their character of organ music, only the swell-box was not quite so fully open.

Van de Woestijne's interest in classical literature showed itself in a number of epic poems written between 1910 and 1914, and dealing with Orpheus, Hercules, Penthesilea, Chronos, Hebe and Helena. Quantitatively they constitute a considerable part of his poetic output, qualitatively they do not come up to the level of his lyrical poetry. To Van de Woestijne himself, they were *Interludiën* (Interludes), published in 1912 and 1914, and something which, in his own words, 'happened to him' in between his lyrical poetry. In the same years he wrote a number of prose stories, also often on classical themes (Gyges, Circe, Kandaules, Hercules), and like his poetry, symbolizing his own situation.

In 1915 he began to write an epistolary novel with his friend Herman Teirlinck. The novel was to be called *De Leemen Torens* (Towers of Clay), for, as Van de Woestijne jotted down in his diary, 'We build the tower: it is made of clay, and as we raise it, it crumbles away below'. His pessimistic view was omnipresent, in his novel as well as in his poetry. His interest in plot, action, dramatics was slight, his interest in character was lively, his interest in himself predominant, which made the novel, like all his other work, a searching essay in self-analysis. The book was published chapter by chapter in *De Gids*, but it was never properly finished. Van de Woestijne and Teirlinck intended to describe the impact which the war and the German occupation made on two sets of characters, one in Ghent and one in Brussels, but the atmosphere of the occupation drained them of their enthusiasm. Also, from the beginning there was a certain discrepancy of intention, and Teirlinck who set more store by a well-constructed novel than Van de Woestijne did, was the first to give up. In 1927 Van de Woestijne wrote a final chapter to round off what had already been written, and in 1928 *De Leemen Torens* appeared for the first time in book-form. Though the novel always remained a torso, it is valuable as a double self-portrait of two important writers, and also as a remarkable attempt to revive the epistolary novel which had gone out of fashion after the eighteenth century. *De Leemen Torens* was one of the last published works of Van de Woestijne. He died in the middle of the following year.

Herman Teirlinck was a year younger than Van de Woestijne and belonged originally to the writers of *Van Nu en Straks*. At the time of his collaboration with Van den Woestijne he was already well known as the author of a volume of poetry, some volumes of short stories and several novels, the most important of which were *Mijnheer J. B. Serjanszoon, Orator Didacticus*, published in 1908, and *Het Ivoren Aapje* (The Ivory Monkey, 1909). The former, written in a highly-wrought and very mannered style, portrays the life of an eighteenth-century hedonist. It is a book full of irony and at the same time full of appreciation of the epicurism which Mr. Serjanszoon has made into an art. It is undoubtedly a piece of virtuoso writing, but Mr. Serjanszoon's oratory is the kind of eloquence that hides more than it reveals, and in the last analysis the novel has little to say. At the time of writing it may have seemed to offer a promising alternative to the naturalist novel—a genre which Teirlinck had also practised—but its artificiality, preciousness and ambivalent point of view have caused it to date rather badly. In *Het Ivoren Aapje* Teirlinck moved closer to reality again, depicting the life of the upper middle-class in a semi-realistic Brussels, without, however, sacrificing his mannered style.

In the period between the two wars Teirlinck devoted much of his time and energy to the stage. For many years he was the central figure in the modernization of Flemish theatre, particularly after 1920 when he discovered the potentialities of expressionist drama. Apart from taking an active interest in play production and the training of professional actors, he wrote several plays, among which *De Vertraagde Film* (The Slow-motion Film), a play in which two lovers re-live their life and watch themselves as actors in a film, *Ik Dien* (I Serve), a stage adaptation of the medieval *Beatrijs*, and *De Ekster op de Galg* (The Magpie on the Gallows), a drama about the ravages of old age. His novel-writing took a back-seat during those years, until in 1940 he published *Maria Speermalie*. It is a novel of lust and passion—the association evoked by the name of the main character is no accident—but like the earlier novels it suffers from over-ornateness of style and lacks the power to convince. Most novels of Teirlinck fail to carry conviction because of a certain ambivalence, if not indifference of the author with regard to his characters. This also applies to the book that is usually regarded as his masterpiece, *Het Gevecht met de Engel* (The Battle with the Angel), which was published in 1952 when Teirlinck was seventy-three. It is his most ambitious novel, ranging from the Middle Ages to the present day and describing the struggle between two families of which the one symbolizes 'nature' and the other 'culture'. One cannot deny the book's imaginative force nor its narrative power, but structurally it shows serious defects and it is basically as non-committal as the other novels. A stronger claim for the honorific title of masterpiece can be made for the novel which Teirlinck published in 1956 under the title of *Zelfportret of Het*

Galgemaal (Self-portrait or The Last Meal), a novel in which a seventy-year old banker analyses his own life. He is outwardly successful and respected, but gradually he begins to realize that he is a deceiver, a poseur, a hypocrite, and that the entire façade of his life is phony. It is not a book with a cheerfully heroic ending. The banker in his newly-found self-knowledge does not throw away the mask of insincerity that he has worn so long, for the simple reason that he has worn it so long. The courage and energy needed for a radical break with his past life fail him: 'You have got under way. You step onto the stage'. Teirlinck presents the story without moralizations, he neither condemns nor defends. Whether the title of Self-portrait has to be taken literally, i.e. as referring to the author himself, is a debatable point. In any case, it is not of any great importance to the reader. The main thing is that Teirlinck in this novel was much more involved in the inner life of one of his characters than in any previous book, and that this time he was writing about a man whom he knew inside out. Though Teirlinck remained active and kept writing until shortly before his death in 1967, *Zelfportret* still stands as by far his most convincing book.

Teirlinck was too intellectual a writer to gain widespread popularity, and it was Stijn Streuvels, a nephew of the poet Guido Gezelle, who became the most popular prose-writer of his generation. Streuvels, whose real name was Frank Lateur, was born in 1871. He did not have the erudition of either Teirlinck or Van de Woestijne, or their intellectual background and feel for life in the big city. He grew up in a small town in West Flanders and in the early years earned his living as a baker. His first stories attracted the attention of the writers of *Van Nu en Straks* who asked him through Karel van de Woestijne to contribute to their journal. Once introduced into the literary world, Streuvels developed in a short time into a very prolific and widely-read author.

The work of Streuvels has little in common with that of Teirlinck. For one thing, his world is much smaller. His territory is confined to the countryside of West Flanders. The cities which so fascinated Teirlinck and Van de Woestijne are of no consequence to him. He does not attack or deride city-life, he ignores it. His characters are the peasants whom he saw in the fields and to whom he ascribed uncomplicated, but often violent passions and desires. There is no room in his work for sophisticated psychological nuances, nor is there room for subtle ramifications of plot. His psychology is only concerned with basic emotions and motivations, his plots are simple and straightforward and can usually be summarized in two or three lines. Life is reduced to its essentials: food-production, love, death. In much of his work the focal point is nature rather than man. His human beings live in direct and constant confrontation with nature which is sometimes benevolent, but more often hostile, and which has the power to strike man down with the inescapable force of fate. A man may spend his whole life fighting back, if nature is against him he will end up crushed like Jan Vindeveughel in *Langs de Wegen* (Along the Roads), Streuvels's first full-scale novel which appeared in 1902. In *Langs de Wegen* Streuvels set out to depict, in his own words, 'a man with everything that surrounds him and with the sky that overhangs it all'. The plot develops slowly in circular fashion: Jan works as a groom on a prosperous farm, he gets married, struggles desperately to support his wife and children on a small plot of land, until finally, beaten by nature and forsaken by his children, he returns to the farm where he is now received as a tramp.

In Streuvels's best-known novel, *De Vlaschaard* (The Flax Field, 1907), man is no longer entirely dominated by nature. Fatalism is still present, and the main characters, the flax-growers, are still harshly dealt with by nature, but they are given a modicum of freedom, initiative and success. At the same time, Streuvels gave fuller treatment to the human conflicts that existed between the characters, in particular to the enmity between the farmer Vermeulen and his son which leads to the tragical climax of the book.

Even though *De Vlaschaard* was a great advance on *Langs de Wegen*, plot and development of character were never to become Streuvels's forte. He was at his best in his short stories and novellas in which the characters remained static and in which the slow epic progression of the narrative combined more satisfactorily with the lyrical descriptions of nature than in the novels. The earlier stories, collected in such volumes as *Lenteleven* (Life in Spring), *Zomerland* (Summer Country), and *Zonnetij* (Sun Tide), all published between 1896 and 1898, suffer on the whole from over-descriptiveness. In the later volumes, especially in *Werkmenschen* (Working People) of 1926, he succeeded in striking a much better balance between the lyrical and the epic elements. *Werkmenschen* contains what is without doubt Streuvels's best story, *Het Leven en de Dood in de Ast* (Life and Death in the Oast-House), a masterpiece disputed by few and envied by many. Against the background of a violent rain-storm across the fields, the story focuses on a small group of labourers who work in a chicory drying-house. The work is hard, monotonous and soul-destroying. At intervals they talk about their lives, they reminisce about the past and build up illusory futures. When night falls, the fragments of conversation merge with their dreams; reality and imagination, past, present and future flow together. An old man enters and lies down to sleep. His snoring haunts the others and causes them to draw him into their fantasies. They are only dimly aware that he is dying. When the body is found in the morning, the men return to work, feeling vaguely that the hallucinations of the night were as much reality as their waking hours.

The psychological insight and the hallucinatory atmosphere of this story are an exception in the work of Streuvels. Generally speaking his strength lies in the sharp observation of country-life and in his ability to make the countryside visible. It is sometimes said that Streuvels is to Flanders what Knut Hamsun is to Norway. True, both forced the attention of their readers away from the cities and back to the 'soil', but there the similarity begins and ends. Streuvels is a realist, not a romanticist of the Hamsun-type. Hamsun worships nature and glorifies the simple life of the countryside in a decidedly naive manner. Streuvels may be naive in many ways, but he does not romanticize. He is open to the grandeur of nature, to its exuberance and splendour, but equally to its hostility and threat. He is not an enthusiast, not a preacher like Hamsun, but a fatalist. He observes and records, but he does not try to influence. And, one must add, with all his interest in the land and the soil, he never fell victim to the blood-and-soil mystique in the way Hamsun did.

Streuvels was a prolific author, and when he died in 1969, at the age of 98, his *oeuvre* consisted of well over fifty volumes of original prose, not counting the numerous volumes of translations and adaptations. His own work was also extensively translated, especially into German.

In the Netherlands there was no-one like Streuvels nor did any of his contemporaries try to follow in his footsteps. Only in the generation that came after him does one find some regional novelists who show his influence in their style and choice of subject-matter. The northern writers of his generation were of a different persuasion. On the whole one can say that they were moving away from realism. Some of them—those who are usually grouped together under the heading of neo-romanticism—tried to revive the historical novel which for many years had been eclipsed by the naturalism of the Movement of the Eighties. The naturalist writers took little interest in historical material and dealt mainly with contemporary themes. The neo-romantics, who began to publish in the nineties, returned to the past and often to the Middle Ages. One of the first to do so was Adriaan van Oordt in his novels *Irmenlo* and *Warhold*, published in 1896 and 1906 respectively. These books can only be called neo-romantic because of their medieval setting; the impressionistic, ornate and mannered style makes them very much part and parcel of the aftermath of the Eighties, as does Van Oordt's preoccupation with a very naturalist-looking fatalism. Arij Prins, who had made his debut with a volume of

naturalist prose pieces *Uit het Leven* (From Life), followed
suit in 1897 with *Een Koning* (A King), a collection of stories, some vaguely historical, others purely fantastic, but all
rather reminiscent of the work of Joris-Karl Huysmans who
was a personal friend of his. Prins's best-known work, the
novel *De Heilige Tocht* (The Holy Journey), was published in
1912. Its main subject is a medieval knight who takes part in
a crusade and who, after many adventures, is killed by the
Turks. The fame, or rather the notoriety of the book is not
based on its plot or the presentation of character, but on its
style. Not since the days of Hooft had so many liberties been
taken with the conventional patterns of Dutch prose. Prins
was a painter at heart, and for the visions that he wanted to
describe he developed a style that had little in common with
everyday syntax. Groups of words followed one another according to what the eye took in rather than to the demands of
syntax: what was seen first, took pride of place in the sentence. Words were coupled in extravagant fashion, or unexpectedly split down the middle, the finite verb was often
dropped in order to reduce the action and intensify the pictorial aspect. Unfortunately, Prins did not really have a great
deal to say, with the result that his work now stands in Dutch
literature as a rather forlorn and very dated monument of
eccentricity.

Arij Prins's attempts to turn the language into a painter's
medium were not characteristic of the neo-romanticists in
general. On the contrary, most of them were in full agreement
with Verwey and the poets of *De Beweging* that 'the art of
the word' had had its day and 'the art of the thought' should
take its place. The accent should no longer fall on the individual word, but on the sentence as a whole, not only in poetry,
but also in prose. At the same time, the call for 'the art of the
thought' also meant that problems of a philosophical nature,
which had been excluded from the naturalist novel, would be
admitted again. So Augusta de Wit broached the question of
the relation between eastern and western civilization in her
novel *Orpheus in de Dessa* (Orpheus in the Dessa), published

in 1903. Aart van der Leeuw, a poet and novelist who in 1909 made his debut in *De Beweging*, gave the fatalism of the naturalists a neo-romantic twist in his novel *Ik en mijn Speelman* (I and my Minstrel) of 1928. Though not a historical novel in the strict sense of the word, the book is set in the eighteenth century and broadly speaking follows from a distance the plot of Marivaux's *Le Jeu de l'amour et du hasard*, the message being that man cannot escape his fate, and that this fate may turn out to be rather more pleasant than anticipated.

The most serious attempt to revive the historical novel was made by P. H. van Moerkerken, born in 1877 and for many years Director of the State Academy of Fine Arts in Amsterdam. After having written poetry, drama and a satirical novel *De Ondergang van het Dorp* (The Downfall of the Village), he published in 1914 *De Bevrijders* (The Liberators), his first historical novel. The book was written immediately after the celebrations of 1913 which commemorated the centenary of Napoleon's defeat and the liberation of the Netherlands. It was a very ironic contribution to the general festivities. Van Moerkerken's satirical bent—which apart from his first novel had also expressed itself in his doctoral dissertation on satire in medieval art—made the novel into an entertaining, but nevertheless hard-hitting attack on pseudo-courage and pious falsification of history. A few years later he began to write a series of historical novels under the collective title of *De Gedachte der Tijden* (The Thought of the Times), published between 1918 and 1924. The central theme, which makes these books into a cycle, is man's aspiration to freedom and happiness throughout the ages. The first volume, *Het Nieuwe Jeruzalem* (The New Jerusalem), centres on the Anabaptist movement of the sixteenth century, *De Verwildering* (The Lawlessness) describes the beginning of the Eighty Years' War, and *In de Lusthof Arkadië* (The Pleasure-garden of Arcady) the religious squabbles of the seventeenth century. The fourth volume, *De Vraag zonder Antwoord* (Question without Answer) ranges from the second half of the seventeenth century to the French Revolution. The question that was asked implicitly throughout all the volumes is finally expressed at the end of this book: Why cannot the new world come without bloodshed and misery? It was followed by *Het Demonische Eiland* (The Demonic Island) which dealt with the Paris Commune of 1870. The last volume, *Het Lange Leven van Habhabalgo* (Habhabalgo's Long Life), recapitulated all preceding volumes in a kind of bird's-eye view of history. It was presented in the form of a series of lectures given by an old professor who at the end of the course finds that his audience has dwindled to one yawning student. The irony of the situation is emphasized by Van Moerkerken in the last sentence of the book: 'Perhaps it might have been better if his words had also blown away on the cold wind of the lonely evening'. An ironic conclusion indeed, coming at the end of a series of six novels.

De Gedachte der Tijden is an impressive work and the most ambitious project of neo-romanticism in the Netherlands. The very ambitiousness of the plan was something that was part of the period. *De Beweging* had called upon the writers to think beyond the one poem or the one novel, and to aim at an *oeuvre* that consisted of larger and interrelated units. Verwey himself always thought of his poetry as made up of 'series' rather than of individual poems or volumes. In the field of the novel, Van Moerkerken was the first to put the idea of the cycle into practice. He was likewise one of the first to make the novel again into a forum for intellectual discussion. His work was a considerable achievement and a milestone in the history of the Dutch novel, but whether it was entirely successful artistically is another matter. In his reaction against naturalism, and his endeavour to inject the novel again with intellectual and philosophical content, Van Moerkerken now and then went too far. His characters are continually carrying on decisive discussions, solving religious and social problems, fighting over the solutions. They are always in the thick of things, whether they live in the sixteenth or in the eighteenth century. The ordinary, colourless man, who stays at home and keeps out of strife is nowhere to be seen, however panoramic the books may be otherwise. Everything is intense, highly coloured and highly charged, as if Van Moerkerken was going to show once and for all that people were not as drab as the naturalists—the Dutch naturalists, at any rate—would have us believe. Moreover, Van Moerkerken's world is rather small. His characters keep meeting each other by accident and in unexpected and often unlikely places. It is a world that may be described as a microcosm seen through a magnifying glass. The quality of his writing is generally high. His straightforward, quiet and yet imaginative style has the effect of a breath of fresh air after the accumulation of detail of the later naturalists or the syntactical idiosyncrasies of Arij Prins. Van Moerkerken's work may not be flawless, it deserves attention as one of the more interesting experiments with the novel after the naturalist period, even if it eventually proved to be a dead end.

The honour of having written the very first neo-romantic novel in Dutch is due to Arthur van Schendel who was to develop into one of the major novelists of the Netherlands. He was born in 1874, which made him Van Moerkerken's senior by three years, and he published his first novel *Drogon* in 1896. True, this was the same year in which Adriaan van Oordt's *Irmenlo* appeared, but *Drogon* was written in 1894 or 1895, well before Van Schendel could have read Van Oordt's book. Van Schendel's romanticism was an even more conscious reaction against naturalism, or realism as he called it, than Van Moerkerken's. In a letter to Frederik van Eeden, written in 1897, he stated: 'As a result of materialism, a conception of life holds sway, let us stand by the word realism, which rests on barren soil. Only the poets have had the good fortune to maintain a beautiful balance, but the prose writers of this century have lost this blessing because of their exclusive attention to the perceptible world.' When he wrote this he had already published *Drogon*, a very personal reaction against 'realism', and a book for which he seems to have followed no model or example. Some have suggested that his romanticism was of English origin and have mentioned Horace Walpole, Rossetti and Burne-Jones as his masters; others the work of Ludwig Tieck and Ricarda Huch. It is very unlikely, however, that any of these writers in any way influenced the writing of *Drogon*. It is far more likely that the young Van Schendel, steeped as he was in the poetry of Perk, Kloos and Gorter, harks back to these poets, and that he transformed the lyrical romanticism of their poetry into prose, bypassing the realist novelists of his own day such as Van Deyssel, Emants and Couperus. The reference which he made to the poets in his letter to Van Eeden supports this point of view. Van Schendel's early novels certainly show a greater affinity with the poetry of the Eighties than with the work of any prose writer, either English, Dutch or German.

Drogon, therefore, was the work of a young man of 20 or 21, who was striking out in a new direction, and the book undeniably bears the mark of this. There is an air of laboriousness about it, and it suffers from an unevenness of tone and style, very uncharacteristic of the later Van Schendel. Weak though it may be, it should not be ignored as it already contains much of the thematic material of Van Schendel's later novels. The dominant theme of all his work, that of Fate, makes its appearance in the first pages of the book when Drogon, a medieval knight, is tormented by 'the riddle that was thumping in his heart, the riddle of Ill Fortune, understood by no mortal'. A few pages later, the second major theme is announced. Drogon's brother suggests that they join a crusade, but Drogon declines saying that another 'longing' prevents him from going: he intends to set out on a quest for a ring which contains a drop of Christ's blood. At the same time he is consumed by a desire for his brother's wife. These two desires, the one romantic-idealistic, the other earthy and sensual, are constantly at war in Drogon's mind and determine all his actions, until Fate finally strikes him down.

The themes of *Drogon* were resumed more successfully in *Een Zwerver Verliefd* (A Wanderer in Love, 1904). Tamalone, the main character, is like Drogon a man of loneliness—

his name may be an echo of 'I am alone'—and his life, too, is ruled by two desires, a romantic indeterminate longing, nameless and not directed at anything concrete, and an erotic desire for the wife of his best friend. As in *Drogon*, the erotic desire is 'fatal', i.e. it becomes the instrument through which Fate strikes: Tamalone kills his friend and indirectly causes the death of his wife. Fate, in other words, acts as a moral corrective. In contrast to Drogon, however, Tamalone himself is not destroyed by Fate, and in the sequel to the book, *Een Zwerver Verdwaald* (A Wanderer Lost), Tamalone even finds a certain peace of mind. The strength of these books lies in the evocation of mood and atmosphere, not in the presentation or analysis of character. Tamalone, driven by a longing which he himself cannot define, remains vague, as does Drogon, as does Merona in *Merona, een Edelman* (Merona, a Nobleman), published in 1927. In their dualist longing and in their living under the doom of Fate, the three are closely related. Also, they are all dreamers who prefer musing and pondering to action. When they act, they do so impulsively rather than as a result of a conscious decision. In this respect Van Schendel's neo-romantic novels provide a strong contrast to those of Van Moerkerken, whose gentle dreamers were not averse to action. Van Moerkerken showed that gentle dreaming can lead to cruel action, Van Schendel showed that corruption of the dream invokes the revenge of Fate. Though less ambitious than Van Moerkerken, the novels of Van Schendel are artistically more convincing. Yet even the talents of Van Schendel were not able to do much for neo-romanticism. It always remained an artificial flower, and Van Schendel's claim that realism rested on barren soil could more truthfully be applied to neo-romanticism. Neither Van Moerkerken's novel of ideas nor Van Schendel's novel of atmosphere could ensure its viability, and it was not long before realism asserted itself again.

Around 1930 Van Schendel turned away from neo-romanticism. In that year *Het Fregatschip Johanna Maria* (The Frigate Johanna Maria) appeared, to be followed in subsequent years by a number of novels in which the medieval and southern-European setting of the earlier books was replaced by that of contemporary or near-contemporary Holland. In these novels Van Schendel's style lost its poetic flavour and became more sober and matter-of-fact. The old themes were retained in essence, but they were tightened up, condensed and intensified. The vaguely idealistic longing of the neo-romantic novels became more concrete, and at the same time less idealistic, the erotic desire was relegated to the background or entirely eliminated, Fate grew more important and more destructive. In *Het Fregatschip Johanna Maria* the romantic longing hardened into the very concrete desire of Jacob Brouwer, the sailmaker, to own the ship in which he had sailed for so long. Brouwer's desire is also a good deal more intense than that of Drogon or Tamalone. In fact, desire and longing are no longer the words with which to describe Brouwer's feelings: passion or even fanaticism are closer to the mark. Fate holds off for a long time and only intervenes after Brouwer has realized his dream. When it does strike, its impact is greater than in the earlier novels, for although Brouwer's life had not been entirely irreproachable, he was in a moral sense less guilty than Drogon and Tamalone. Fate by losing its character of being a moral corrective, becomes blinder and more savage.

The theme of the man and his ship is echoed in *De Waterman* (The Waterman, 1933). Maarten Rossaert is wedded to his barge as Brouwer was to his frigate, but whereas to Brouwer possession of the ship was the very aim of his existence, to Rossaert the ship is only a means to an end, the means to become free from his own fears and from the narrow-mindedness around him. He breaks away from his environment, repelled by its hard-line Calvinism and intolerance. He joins a utopian religious community, the New Lights of Zwijndrecht—the book is set in the early nineteenth century—and uses his barge to give financial support to the brethren. But there is no escape from Fate, and the water claims his mother, his sister and his son. In the end, Rossaert himself is also drowned. It is not a cheerful book, but its solid construction, its clear-cut delineation of character and its powerful evocation of the Dutch landscape, the rivers and polders and sombre skies, make it Van Schendel's best.

De Waterman was followed by three novels which are often regarded as his most significant novels of fate: Een Hollands Drama (A Dutch Tragedy), De Rijke Man (The Rich Man) and De Grauwe Vogels (The Grey Birds), published in successive years between 1935 and 1937. All three are tragedies. De Rijke Man is the tragedy of a rich young man who, touched by the story in the Bible, gives away all his possessions and dies in utter loneliness, forsaken and despised by everyone. The other two novels may be called tragedies of responsibility. In the former a grocer ruins his life by paying back a large sum of money which his brother-in-law had stolen, and by undertaking to bring up his brother-in-law's son. In the latter novel, a market-gardener brings about his own downfall by assuming responsibility for his invalid half-brother. The three novels are set in the contemporary Dutch middle class and their characters are all 'grey birds', those ordinary men and women whom the naturalists had placed in the centre of their work and whom the neo-romantics had ignored. It seems that in these books Van Schendel was drawing a little closer to the naturalist tradition from which he had always kept aloof. He devoted more attention to the influence of milieu and upbringing of his characters than before, and, particularly in Een Hollands Drama, he made heredity into a factor of considerable importance. It is, in fact, more meaningful to regard the doom that lies over the main characters of this novel as due to heredity than to fate, unless one wants to equate the two. Similarly, Kompaan in De Rijke Man is the victim of a delusion rather than the victim of fate. Only Kaspar Valk in De Grauwe Vogels is so relentlessly dogged by misfortunes that the word fate seems fully justified.

The five novels from Het Fregatschip to De Grauwe Vogels are undoubtedly Van Schendel's best work. They are ex-

traordinarily well-constructed novels, written with an un-
swerving fixity of purpose. The style is robust and even, unembellished yet evocative, unpoetic yet strongly rhythmic. It is a
style that is fitted to perfection to capture the sombre grandeur of the landscape in *De Waterman* or the dour Calvinism
in *Een Hollands Drama*. After *De Grauwe Vogels* Van
Schendel did not continue in the same direction. He changed
course as he had done in 1934. His next book, *De Wereld
een Dansfeest* (The World, a Dance, 1938), was written in a
more lighthearted vein than the preceding books, though it
was still a tragedy, in spite of the title and the whimsy of the
theme. Whimsical humour became an important element in
Van Schendel's later novels and stories. Yet he was much
more at home in tragedy than in comedy, and although he
kept writing until his death in 1946 he was never able to surpass the five great books of the years from 1930 to 1937.

In the early years of the twentieth century, when Van
Schendel was writing his neo-romantic novels, Verwey's *De
Beweging* was the leading literary journal. It welcomed neo-
romanticism as a healthy reaction to naturalism, and Verwey gave unqualified praise to Van Schendel's 'power of imagination'. Neo-romantic poetry, too, was supported by *De Beweging*, but not to the exclusion of other streams. *De
Beweging* explored all directions which gave promise of leading away from the extreme individualism of the Eighties.
Neo-romanticism was one of these directions, but it turned
out to be a cul-de-sac, in poetry as well as in prose. Neo-
classicism proved to be more creative. Yet, outside neo-romanticism, and neo-classicism, the poet who came closest to
Verwey's ideal of intellectual and philosophical poetry was J.
A. dèr Mouw, a poet who belonged to Verwey's own generation.

Johan Andreas dèr Mouw was born in 1863, two years
before Verwey, but although he had written poetry for many
years, he did not publish any until he was 54. Then, in 1918,
his work suddenly began to appear almost simultaneously in *De
Beweging, De Nieuwe Gids* and the weekly paper *De Amster-*

dammer. Like several other poets of his generation, he was a classicist, and also a philosopher of repute, with an extensive knowledge of mathematics and science. As a philosopher he was strongly opposed to Hegel, and especially to the neo-Hegelians. It was in fact, his dislike of Hegel's system-building which led him, without turning away from European philosophy, to become more and more immersed in the systemless Indian philosophy of the *Upanishads.* There he found the expression of the unity of the Cosmos and the Self which was to become the mainspring of his poetry. Unity is the key-word of his work, and Brahman the symbol of the unity: that which comprises everything without forcing it into a system. He published his poetry, the two volumes *Brahman I* and *Brahman II* (1919 and 1921) under the Sanskrit name of Adwaita, that is 'he who has overcome duality'.

Dèr Mouw was a mystic whose main poetic theme was that of the 'unio mystica'. But as a mystic he was a class apart. His poetry was sometimes ecstatic, but always remained well-reasoned, very precise and nearly always cast in the strict form of the sonnet; it was deeply serious and at the same time humorous; it was philosophical, making considerable demands on its readers, but it was also couched in a most unexpected everyday language. The traditional hierarchy of values, which assumed that elevated thought was best expressed in elevated language, held no meaning for him. One of his best-known sonnets in *Brahman I* begins with the line: 'K ben Brahman. Maar we zitten zonder meid' (I am Brahman. But we are without a maid), and ends:

Dan voel ik éénzelfde adoratie branden
Voor Zon, Bach, Kant, en haar vereelte handen. [4]

In 1919 this was too unconventional to find much response outside the small circle of Verwey, Kloos and Van Eeden. After his death in 1919 he was soon forgotten, and was only

[4] Then I feel the same burning adoration
for Sun, Bach, Kant, and her calloused hands.

rediscovered several years later by the writers of the *Forum* group. The poetry of Dèr Mouw was the crown of the 'poetry of the thought' which was so close to Verwey's heart, but it also marked its conclusion. It was almost symbolical that *De Beweging* ceased publication in 1919, the year of Dèr Mouw's death.

Before Dèr Mouw began publishing, the neo-classicism of Geerten Gossaert (pseudonym of F. C. Gerretson) and J. C. Bloem for some time put its mark on the poetry of the *De Beweging* group. In 1910 Gossaert published a long essay on Swinburne, who had died the year before. In this essay he broke a lance for 'rhetorical poetry', by which he meant poetry with traditional form and imagery. The next year Bloem supported him in a review article on the French neo-classicist poet Henri de Régnier, in which he, too, stood up for 'rhetorical poetry', though he modified Gossaert's phrase to 'inspired rhetoric'. 'In the *Stances* of Jean Moréas', he wrote, 'we have been able to observe how one can write genuine and original poetry with the most often used and the most well-known images, and in the most ordinary form. De Régnier's book is another example of this'. Other poets of *De Beweging*—Aart van der Leeuw, for instance, and P. N. van Eyck—questioned the soundness of the theory of Gossaert and Bloem, and pointed out the dangers that were inherent in a conscious return to rhetoric. Van Eyck, a poet in the mould of Verwey and later his successor as professor of Dutch literature at Leiden, was the most forceful opponent of the new rhetoric. Without rejecting traditionalism, he denied that the term 'rhetorical poetry' had any meaning and he opposed the idea that the poet should use ready-made imagery. As was stated before, Verwey gave qualified approval to the theory and tried to steer a middle course. History has proved the opponents right: rhetoric, inspired or not inspired, did not have much future as a poetic principle. The best example of it is Gossaert's own volume of poetry *Experimenten* (Experiments, 1911). It is an extraordinary volume, linked to the rhetoric of Bilderdijk and Da Costa, with reminiscences of

medieval and seventeenth-century poetry, occasionally influenced by Swinburne and Baudelaire, full of archaic words
and phrases, and, not surprisingly, full of traditional imagery.
Gossaert's own contribution to all this was a tremendous
mastery of poetic technique, a great interest in metrical and
rhythmical variations, passion and sensuousness, erudition
and intellect. *Experimenten* remained a lonely experiment,
and although it had considerable success and went through
twelve editions, it was not the beginning of a new era in
Dutch poetry. Before long it was overshadowed by the poetry
of Bloem which proved of greater value, both intrinsically
and historically.

Born in 1887, Bloem was twenty-four when he made his
plea for traditionalism and coined the phrase of 'inspired rhetoric'. In the same year 1911 he published his first poems, also in *De Beweging*. In their solemn tone, slightly archaic
choice of words and elaborate structure, his early poems were
closely related to those of his contemporaries Gossaert and
Van Eyck. They were firmly rooted in tradition and were perhaps the best examples of the neo-classicism that was assert-
ing itself in those days. At the same time the emotional basis
of these poems was romantic. Just as in the early novels of
Van Schendel, the recurrent theme was 'longing'. In 1915
Bloem wrote a short essay in *De Beweging* under the title of
Het Verlangen (Longing) in which he stated that it was longing which separated 'poetic man' from 'a-poetic man'.
Longing to him was not dissatisfaction, but a 'divine unfulfil-
ledness' which makes one break through the banal confines of
life. Since the longing was nameless and not directed at a specific object, as in the case of Van Schendel's Tamalone, it
could not be fulfilled, and since it was not to be equated with
dissatisfaction, its necessary complement was resignation. In
his first volume, also entitled *Het Verlangen* and published in
1921, the resignation was hoped for and sometimes anticipated, but not attained. The next volume, *Media Vita* (1931),
was characterized by a tone of disillusionment. The longing
could not be fulfilled, but instead of leading to 'life', as

Bloem had intimated in his essay, or to the resignation he had hoped for in his first volume, it forced him more and more towards contemplation of death. The title, derived from the medieval antiphon *Media Vita in Morte Sumus* (In the Middle of Life we are in Death), hints strongly at his preoccupation with death. In *De Nederlaag* (Defeat), his third volume which was published in 1937, the disillusionment was complete and bitterer than in the previous volume. Love, which had held promise of at least temporarily filling the emptiness, failed and became meaningless. All that was left was loneliness and death. The opening poem of *Sintels* (Cinders), a small volume published in 1945, throws doubt even on the meaning of writing poetry which had always been the centre of his existence:

> Is dit genoeg: een stuk of wat gedichten
> Voor de rechtvaardiging van een bestaan . . . [5]

Some twenty years before, in an essay on Baudelaire, Bloem had quoted with approval a poem of Baudelaire's which answered this same question in the affirmative. Now Bloem's disenchantment with life and himself was so great that he even denied himself the satisfaction that was to be derived from poetic achievement.

It has rightly been suggested that when Bloem proclaimed 'inspired rhetoric' as the essential element of the ' tradition française', this French tradition for him was first and foremost represented by Baudelaire. Baudelaire meant a great deal to the generation of Bloem, Gossaert and Van Eyck, and in Bloem's early poetry one can certainly find traces of his influence. Bloem himself, in an autobiographical essay of 1954, mentioned Leopardi, Thomas Hardy and A. E. Housman as the poets who were closest to him. Several parallels between the poetry of Housman and Bloem can be quoted, and Housman's 'they say my verse is sad' is echoed by more than one poem of Bloem's, perhaps even by the title of one of his later

[5] Is this enough: some few poems, to justify an existence . . .

volumes *Quiet Though Sad* (1946). Housman, he says in the essay, is decidedly a minor poet, but when four years later he compared him with Jean Moréas, and noted that neither of them displayed much variety in his poetry, with admirable disdain for the term 'minor poet' he declared both to be very great poets. One could not better characterize Bloem than with a similarly paradoxical phrase as a very great minor poet. His thematic range was limited, but he turned this limitation into a virtue by making even the simplest poem into a perfect work of art. His poetry was essentially modest, its tone was one of understatement, his style of writing, after the first somewhat solemn and grandiloquent poems, was like Housman's, direct and often colloquial.

Bloem's counterpart in Belgium was Jan van Nijlen, born in 1884. His poetry, too, ranged over a limited field, and developed from the solemn diction of *Verzen* (Poems, 1906) to a very simple and direct style in *Het Aangezicht der Aarde* (The Face of the Earth, 1923), *De Vogel Phoenix* (The Bird Phoenix, 1928) and especially in his last volume *Het Oude Kind* (The Old Child, 1938). Much in the same way as Bloem's, his work is concerned with disappointment and an uneasy resignation. Disillusionment is also the dominant mood, but, more often than in the poetry of Bloem, it is occasionally tempered by an ironic turn of phrase, by a shrug of the shoulder. The similarities between the poetry of Bloem and Van Nijlen are striking; the differences are mainly differences of degree. Van Nijlen lamented the loss of his youth, as did Bloem, but the memory of the past was less obsessive to him and less painful. There are several poems in which memory is not presented as pain but as a source of joy. Like Bloem, Van Nijlen recorded the passing of the seasons with feelings of sorrow for the passing of time, but on the whole his poetry was not quite as autumnal as the poetry of Bloem, nor was his view of nature as negative. To Bloem, nature meant little. The opening line of one of his best sonnets, *De Dapperstraat* (Dapper Street), reads: 'Natuur is voor tevredenen of legen' (Nature is for the contented or the empty), and in the course of the poem he expresses his preference for the city, even on a miserable morning, walking in drizzling rain, in a street as depressing as Dapper Street in Amsterdam. Van Nijlen, on the contrary, often wrote appreciatively of nature and landscape, and stated in his poem *De Stad*: 'Ik kan alleen maar houden van de stad / in lente en zomer, in de lauwe nachten' (I can only love the city in spring and summer, in the warm nights).

Both Bloem and Van Nijlen began writing from a common basis of traditional and rather elevated poetry. In the early stages, their styles were influenced respectively by Gossaert and Van Eyck, and by Karel van de Woestijne. Gradually both poets moved away from the formality of their early work, and without breaking away from tradition, evolved a style of writing which stood much closer to everyday language and which paved the way for the colloquial style of later poets such as Martinus Nijhoff. From this point of view Bloem and Van Nijlen were traditional figures, linking the poetry of the mandarins to what Stephen Spender called 'the poetry of the voices in the street'. Poetry in these years was developing towards a *parlando* style, a style that avoided any deliberate poetic idiom and employed as much as possible the vocabulary, syntax and rhythm of everyday speech. It was a development common to Western European literature in general. In France it led to the poetry of Jules Laforgue, in England to the *Prufrock* poems of T. S. Eliot, in the Netherlands to the poetry of Nijhoff. When Bloem and Van Nijlen were writing, the days of the mandarins and high priests were numbered, but not quite over. In the Netherlands, Adriaan Roland Holst (born in 1888) may be regarded as the last of the poets in the grand manner, the last of the prophetic poets. Roland Holst, one may say, related to Yeats as Nijhoff does to the early Eliot.

As in the case of Bloem and Van Nijlen, the basis of Roland Holst's poetry was romantic, but his romanticism was of a different order from theirs. Everything was on a larger scale: his longing, his disillusionment, his alienation from contemporary reality. When Bloem and Van Nijlen spoke of the past, they spoke of their own past, of memories which were sometimes happy, but mostly burdensome. To Roland Holst the past is a mythical period that lies aeons before our time. It is a world not yet affected by the vulgarity and degeneration of the present day, a world in which man was 'lonelier and more beautiful' than he is now. This world often takes the shape of the world of Celtic tradition, re-created by Yeats and peopled by gods and heroes, bards and harpplayers. In a short prose book, *Eigen Achtergronden* (Personal Background, 1946), Roland Holst relates that when he was a student at Oxford between 1908 and 1911, he came across an English translation of *The Voyage of Bran, Son of Febal* which, he said, had the effect of re-awakening old memories. In the same years he came to know the poetry of Yeats which, according to his own testimony again, had a profound and lasting influence on his work. On his return to the Netherlands in 1911, he published his first volume *Verzen* (Poems). It is a collection of elegantly written, but mostly conventional poetry, of which the last poem stands out because of its decisive statement that the only salvation lies in loneliness. In the next volumes, *Belijdenis van de Stilte* (Avowal of Silence) and *Voorbij de Wegen* (Beyond the Roads), the decision to turn away from the world hardened. Personal memories are no longer important; truth and purity are only to be found in what lies beyond these memories, in the lost Elysium of which the voices of the wind and sea are the messengers. These ideas form the nucleus of what gradually became Roland Holst's personal myth, an attempt to relate his own life to the world in which it was placed and to the powers that control it. The poet sees himself as an exile from the lost land. He dreams of his return, but knows that it cannot be, because he himself has lost his purity and has been infected by the evils of the world. Yet he has preserved in himself part of the truth that has long since been lost to man. He is the high priest, one of the initiated, one of the few who know what could have been.

In *De Wilde Kim* (The Wild Horizon, 1925), the high priest changes to a prophet of doom, foreseeing the destruction of the world:

DAY OF RECKONING

Lonely and wild and cold and passionate—
can that still be the sea? What ultimate power,
what final token of that turbulent realm
of blinding, empty and unending light
now claims the waters?—Deserted are the coasts,
forgotten the high dreams of bygone worlds,
and like the brazen cymbal of fate and reckoning
the beating waters toll, in onset came
against the world, and high out of the west
from the steep ramparts of the dead are heard
the passionate, the lonely, the wild and cold
chords of the harps that herald the last day.
The great, raised by the prelude of this storm
out of their mortal trance, now calling come
to man's remaining strongholds, and are seen
on the dark western bastions, stern and gaunt,
and pointing to the fateful mystery
of doom and ruin. The spokesmen of our days
bore names, but these bear no names, being trumpets
condemning all that is to the ancient shadows
of what has been, primeval night, before
on high the four faces out of the spirit
appear: wide eyes and voices jubilant—
cold and impassioned and wild and lonely. [6]

In the years that followed *De Wilde Kim* Roland Holst wrote little, and it was not until 1937 that he published a new volume, *Een Winter aan Zee* (A Winter at the Coast). In this volume, too, the poet is the seer who foretells the cataclysmic end of the civilization in which he lives. His prophecy is sometimes couched in straight and direct terms, at other times symbolized in a bitter farewell to a lost love. The unity of

[6] Roland Holst's own translation of *Einde*, published in *Delta* II, no. 2, 1959.

theme and the strict uniformity of the eight-line stanzas gives this volume the appearance of one long poem. It was the culminating point of Roland Holst's *oeuvre*, and also the swan-song of late romantic poetry in the Netherlands.

In his later volumes, notably in *Tegen de Wereld* (Against the World, 1947), Roland Holst remained a prophet of doom, but, probably as a result of the war, his targets became more specific. In *Eigen Achtergronden* he had made a distinction between Reality and Actuality which, he said, stood in the same relation to each other as a fugue by Bach stood to the noise in the street. He had always shunned Actuality, but now, in his later poems, he occasionally raised his voice against it. Though in his later volumes his poetry shed some of its earlier loftiness and became more colloquial, it never developed into the 'poetry of the voices in the street': it always remained that of a lone aristocratic voice declaiming against the noises of the street.

The prose which Roland Holst wrote was the prose of a poet. It is incantation rather than narration, written in what Du Perron called 'the long rhythms of his poetry'. In *Deirdre en de Zonen van Usnach* (Deirdre and the Sons of Usnach) and *Tusschen Vuur en Maan* (Between Fire and Moon) he symbolized his personal situation in terms of Celtic mythology as he had done in so many poems. In *De Afspraak* (The Agreement), his most powerful prose work, he referred more directly to his myth of the 'foretime' and the lost Elysium.

A large part of the work of Roland Holst, both poetry and prose, is concerned with the formulation and representation of this myth. His stubborn return to the same theme, intensified by recurring key phrases, gives his work a certain monotony: not the monotony of a tale told too often, but rather the spellbinding monotonousness of the wind in the trees or the breaking of the waves. A masterful technique and an almost mesmeric sense of rhythm in the service of a strong personality make his poetry entirely convincing. It was imitated by many, but since his romanticism is of such a personal nature, the imitations rarely led to more than a conventional world-weariness, which is precisely what Roland Holst's poetry does not display.

With the work of Roland Holst the era of late-romantic poetry came to a close. He belonged to the group of traditional poets which also included Gossaert, Van Eyck, Bloem and Van Nijlen. They did not form a homogeneous group, still less a movement but they were linked by their belief that if the poet wants to be understood, he must preserve the poetic tradition. He may refine it, develop it and add to it, but he should not isolate himself from the community by discarding it. The tradition which formed the substratum of the poetry of Roland Holst, Bloem, and Van Nijlen was a Dutch tradition, dating back to the eighties and nineties, to Kloos, Gorter, Leopold and Van de Woestijne. Literary movements abroad left them largely unaffected. When they were influenced by foreign poets, it was also by traditionalists such as Moréas, de Régnier, Yeats. Dadaism, surrealism, expressionism, all movements which sought to bring about a radical break with the past, bypassed them without making any impact. Until 1920, the rallying point of these poets was *De Beweging*, and it was in this journal, too, that Martinus Nijhoff in 1916 published his first work.

Nijhoff, born in 1894, bridged the gap between two generations. He may be seen as a latecomer of the generation of traditionalists who began to publish round about 1910, or as the first of the modernists who in 1916 grouped themselves around the new journal *Het Getij* (The Tide). Whichever point of view one chooses, it is impossible to regard him as a revolutionary poet. His link with tradition always remained strong, from his first publication of ten sonnets in *De Beweging* to his last poem *Het Uur U* (Zero Hour), published in 1942. His interest in the sonnet-form is in itself a clear indication of his loyalty to tradition: his first volume *De Wandelaar* (The Walker) contained 48 poems of which 36 were sonnets.

The title of *De Wandelaar* (1916) was a program. In the title poem the poet presents himself as someone who walks in solitude through the street, past a landscape or inside the walls of a room. He assumes various disguises: that of a Carolingian monk, a Renaissance artist, a Baudelairian poet, and from behind each mask he observes the world around him without taking part in it. He remains a spectator, an outsider to whom life is 'a mosaic without perspective'. This pose of aloofness was an attempt to exorcize the fear caused by the realization that life was meaningless and chaotic. Fear of life, often manifesting itself as longing for death, is characteristic of *De Wandelaar* as well as of Nijhoff's second volume, *Vormen* (Forms), which was published in 1924. The relation between the poet and the world was as problematic to Nijhoff as it was to Bloem and Roland Holst, but Nijhoff's response to it was neither the romantic lament of Bloem nor the prophetic rejection of the world of Roland Holst. Nijhoff's reaction was twofold: sometimes he adopted an attitude of detachment, at other times he tried to come to terms with the world through those whose life was 'unbroken' and meaningful, the representatives of what he called 'the simple life': the mother, the child, the farmer, the soldier. The hesitation between these two attitudes persists throughout his early poetry and is matched by other dualisms: that of the spirit and the flesh, the soul and the body, heaven and earth. They give Nijhoff's poetry its curiously equivocal character and caused the critics to ask questions in the vein of 'Will the real Nijhoff please stand up?' Nijhoff's early poetry is certainly not of a piece as is Roland Holst's; it lacks the unity with which Roland Holst symbolized his relation to the world. *De Wandelaar* and *Vormen* show Nijhoff's personality to be very complex and often divided against itself. Although these dualisms were never completely resolved, they gradually lost their sharp edges.

In *Nieuwe Gedichten* (New Poems, 1934) the fear of life that dominated the earlier volumes disappeared. The poet is more inclined to decide for the earth and against heaven, for the body and against the spirit. The first poem that bears witness to this development is *Het Veer* (The Ferry) in which the martyr St.Sebastian regrets the decision that made him forsake life and die for the spirit. Only after his death does he realize that 'blood is deeper than the heavens are high'. Another poem in this volume, *Het Lied der Dwaze Bijen* (The Song of the Foolish Bees), settles accounts with the mystic urge to transcend the world: the bees rise higher and higher, but their goal remains elusive, and, dying, 'they are whirling down homeward'. Poems such as these make statements about what should not be, they criticize the attitude that rejects the world, but they stop short of suggesting an alternative. Yet there are also poems in *Nieuwe Gedichten* that offer a more positive approach to the world. In the short opening poem, for instance, the poet meditates about loneliness, sterility and mortality, and then suddenly in the last stanza reminds himself that modern society holds the possibility of new life. Written during the years of the Depression, *Nieuwe Gedichten* also contains the poem *De Vogels* (The Birds), the only poem of Nijhoff's which expresses social criticism. The most elaborate, and also the most impressive report of the poet's desire to make contact with the world is to be found in *Awater*, the long poem that closes *Nieuwe Gedichten*.

The theme of *Awater* is expressed in its motto: 'ik zoek een reisgenoot' (I am looking for a travelling companion). The poet has lost his brother, and, wanting to go on a journey, he looks for someone who can take his brother's place. He has seen a man called Awater passing by in the street and he thinks of him as a possible friend. One evening he follows him through the city, from the office where he works, to the barber's, to the café which the poet used to visit with his brother, to a restaurant, to the square outside the station where the Salvation Army is conducting a meeting. At that point their roads part: though Awater seems to recognize the poet, he stays to listen to the speaker, whereas the poet enters the station. He leaves Awater behind and undertakes the journey alone.

Awater is presented as the ordinary man, one out of many. He is not clearly defined. We see him in action, but we do not know his motives or his thoughts. In a lecture on his own

work, Nijhoff commented on Awater and said that he wanted
him to be no more than 'an outline, a clear, translucent surface'. Also, he said, Awater was to be 'an arbitrary human
being with whom I had no personal ties'. The name of Awater strongly hints at this arbitrariness. Since 'A' also means
'water', Awater is twice water, and water in Nijhoff's poetry
is often used as a symbol for multitude or collectivity. In Nijhoff's own words again, Awater was 'no-matter-which individual, a neighbour, a fellow man who was a representative
of the multitude and who had approached me along the slen-
derest thread of contact'. The poem itself makes clear that
Awater is not only a representative of the multitude but also
more specifically of modern society. Through him the poet
hopes to establish a relationship between himself and this society. No real contact is made, however, and in the end the
poet sets out alone. It may be that Awater after all fulfilled
his function and that the distant contact and the fleeting moment of recognition gave the poet the strength to undertake
the journey by himself; or, on the other hand, Awater may
have proved to be a disappointment and the poet may have
realized that there could be no question of involvement in society, that for him there was no alternative to loneliness.
Awater is not a poem that divulges its secrets lightly. Whatever the interpretation, the poem does not end on a tragic
note. The poet has either gained his independence, or he has
resigned himself to his loneliness, but in either case he is cool
and unemotional. In his commentary on *Awater* Nijhoff also
wrote: 'I am not an embittered poet. I am not going around
in a corduroy jacket and long hair fulminating against my
times because my times do not appreciate me and my soul, I
have adjusted myself, I am an ordinary human being'.

Awater may not be an emotional poem, not a cry of
triumph or a *cri de coeur,* yet it is a very personal poem, a
personal drama in which the poet plays himself. The self was
no longer hidden behind the mask of a medieval monk or a
nineteenth-century *poète maudit,* a Pierrot or a clown as in
the earlier poems, but it presented itself as an ordinary hu-

man being without any poetic trappings. In *Awater* Nijhoff
appears as a poet of the type to which also T.S.Eliot belonged: the poet who was no longer a romantic bohemian, nor
a recluse of the ivory tower, but a man among men. It is significant that when Nijhoff first planned the writing of Awater,
he intended to model the main character on Potgieter, who in
the nineteenth century was the prototype of the poet as an ordinary man. Significantly also, Eliot was with Cocteau the only poet whom Nijhoff mentioned as having been of any help
when he wrote *Awater*, and if one wants to place Nijhoff in
his European context, Eliot was his next of kin. Both poets
may be called tradition-bound modernists, both were refor-
mers rather than revolutionaries. Nijhoff acknowledged his
affinity to Eliot by translating several of his poems and *The
Cocktail Party*, but it is no simple matter to assess accurately
to what extent Nijhoff's own poetry was influenced by Eliot.
One can point to some stylistic parallels, or to a common tendency to give ironic treatment to romantic attributes of the
past, but there is little evidence of any direct influence. As for
the most striking parallel between their work, i.e. the remarkably successful use of the vocabulary and the rhythms of
everyday speech, it is more likely that Nijhoff was building
on the foundations laid by such poets as Gorter, Dèr Mouw
and Bloem than that he was following Eliot. Another point of
contact between Nijhoff and Eliot is the fact that both make
considerable demands on their readers. *Awater* may not be
quite as cryptic as *The Waste Land,* but it is a far from easy
poem with its oblique references to the Bible, Joyce's *Ulysses*
and the Parcival legend.

Nijhoff's next long poem, *Het Uur U* (Zero Hour), first
published in 1937, is seemingly a much more accessible work.
Its structure of rhyming couplets is the embodiment of simplicity in comparison to the long assonating stanzas of *Awater*; its imagery is transparent, its references are straightforward and easily located, its language is even closer to everyday
speech than *Awater*'s. Yet it presents as many problems to the
interpreter as *Awater* does.

Both *Awater* and *Het Uur U* are narrative poems, but whereas in the former the poet played an active role as the 'I' who tried to establish contact with Awater, in the latter poem there is no 'I': the scene is observed and recorded without the poet taking part. A man walks through a street on a warm afternoon in summer. He has a strange effect on the street and on the people who live there. Water, gas and electricity under the pavement become audible, the silence begins to vibrate, the atmosphere becomes one of alarm. The doctor who lives in the street sees himself again as a young intern, the judge gives remission of sins and confesses his own guilt, the woman who is known as 'the bitch' finds herself 'naked like Diana' standing in the forest, drinking 'living' water. For one brief moment they experience pure happiness. The children who are playing in the street follow the man until he turns round the corner. Then the spell is broken and life resumes its normal course.

While the man is passing by, the people in the street experience their moment of truth. They see themselves as they were before their lives had gone awry, they are innocent and pure again as they were before their Fall. The man has the power to confront them with their Ideal Selves, to which they react with a mixture of fear and ecstasy. When the spell breaks, they are back in their own reality, face to face with their failings, disenchanted but also relieved. The children who have not yet lost their purity and innocence are unaffected by the passing of the man. The man himself remains anonymous and unknown and because of his mysterious lack of identity the interpretations of the poem have mainly centred on him. He has been likened to the Pied-piper—although he does not entice the children away—, others have seen in him traits of Christ and of Death. These traits are undeniably present in his actions and in the impact that he makes, but his most important aspect is his very lack of identity. Nijhoff said of Awater that he was to be no more than outline; the same is true of the man in this poem, only more so. As soon as one starts filling in the outline, one changes the symbolic poem which *Het Uur U* is, into an allegory which it is not.

When in 1942 *Het Uur U*, considerably rewritten, appeared for the first time in book-form, it was published together with *Een Idylle* (An Idyl), Nijhoff's last long poem before his death in 1953. Though its setting and subject are far removed from those of *Het Uur U*, there is a close relation between the two poems. In *Een Idylle*, Protesilaos, the first Greek to die during the siege of Troy, is allowed to return to the world of the living for one hour in order to visit his wife Laodemia. When the time comes to go back to Hades, Laodemia comes with him as far as the ferry and persuades Hermes to let her cross over with her husband. Hermes also occurred in *Het Uur U*, and apart from this the poems have several images and symbols in common. Like *Het Uur U*, *Een Idylle* deals with a moment of truth. In the former poem the experience was partly horrific and it made the people in the street conscious of their failings; in the latter it is a moment of pure bliss in which love transcends the boundaries of life and death. It has rightly been said that the relation between the two poems is that of a negative and a positive print of a photograph. What *Een Idylle* lacks is the mysteriousness of the other poem. Nijhoff's son maintained that the origin of *Het Uur U* was to be found in a dream which he once had and which he described to his father. This explains to a certain extent the very evocative dreamlike atmosphere of the poem. With a term that is often used for the paintings of A.C.Willink, Pijke Koch and Raoul Hynckes, one might describe Nijhoff's approach to reality as 'magical realism': the forms of everyday realism are there, but they are arranged and coloured in such a way as to suggest a mysterious unreality hiding behind the reality of everyday.

Nijhoff's use of common speech as a language of poetry within the framework of fairly traditional form had a more enduring influence on modern Dutch poetry than the iconoclasm of many a revolutionary poet. As was said before, Nijhoff was not a revolutionary but a reformer. He did not publish manifestos nor did he subscribe to any, and he kept aloof from literary movements. He published regularly in traditionalist magazines such as *De Beweging* and *De Gids*, and only once in *Het Getij*, the journal of the modernists. When in 1919 Ernst Groenevelt, one the editors of *Het Getij*, published an anthology of poetry of the *Getij* group, he stated— rather ruefully, it seems—that Nijhoff had refused to declare himself at one with the group. Yet five poems of Nijhoff appeared in the anthology, and Groenevelt suggested that Nijhoff was well aware that essentially he did belong to the group. Most likely, Groenevelt was wrong, for neither the dualisms of Nijhoff's early poetry nor the coolness of his later work would fit easily into the poetry proclaimed by *Het Getij*. Established in 1916, the journal served for several years as a forum for a group of young writers who were in rebellion against the intellectualism and the lack of spontaneity of the *Beweging* poets. They came out for more passion in poetry, for freer verse-forms and for more individualism. The chief spokesman and most influential poet of the group was Herman van den Bergh, whose name is often linked with the beginning of expressionism in the Netherlands. The term expressionism had been used for the first time in the Netherlands in 1913 by Albert Verwey, but then only in a general sense to indicate poetry that was not impressionist. It is unlikely that Verwey knew the work of such poets as Benn, Werfel, Trakl, Stramm or Heym who had published in or before that year. It is also unlikely that Herman van den Bergh knew them. The Netherlands remained neutral during the First World War, the frontiers were closed and the work of the expressionist poets did not become known in the Netherlands before 1918. Van den Bergh always claimed that when he wrote the poems of his first volume *De Boog* (The Bow), which appeared in 1917, he had never read a single German expressionist poem. Also, in his essays collected in the volume *Nieuwe Tucht* (New Discipline) and written between 1917 and 1922, he did not once mention the word expressionism nor did he refer to any of the German expressionist poets. The striking parallels in word-formation, imagery and use of colour that one finds between his own work and that of the German expressionists are attributable to an independent analogous development rather than to direct influence. In comparison with Nijhoff's *De Wandelaar* which was published a year earlier, *De Boog* seemed to open up a great deal of new ground. Gone was the sonnet-form, gone the measured line and the restrained tone of voice, gone also the vacillation of the poet between the spirit and the flesh. Van den Bergh's poetry was an enthusiastic acceptance of the flesh and the earth, a resounding paean of fertility. Its earthiness was expressed with a vehemence of diction that contrasted sharply with the subdued tones of the *Beweging* poets and the sophisticated elegance of Nijhoff. It was visionary poetry in which image was heaped upon image, not infrequently at the expense of clarity. The critic who said of Nijhoff that he wrote as if he was talking softly to you, could have added that Van den Bergh was the equivalent of a brass band. The newness and loudness of his poetry certainly made an impact. The poet Hendrik Marsman reported later that when *De Boog* appeared, he read it with 'enraptured veneration', and his own early poetry testifies to this admiration. Yet, in proportion to the enthusiasm—and the cries of anarchism—with which Van den Bergh's poetry was welcomed, its influence was limited and short-lived. None of the established writers was converted to expressionism, and among the younger writers of importance it was only Marsman who in his early poetry was affected by it. Expressionism never became a strong force in Dutch poetry. In the Netherlands, that is, in Belgium the picture was rather different.

In the same year 1916, when Nijhoff published *De Wandelaar* and Van den Bergh made his debut in *Het Getij*, the young Flemish poet Paul van Ostaijen (born in 1896) dropped a bombshell with his volume *Music-Hall*. Dutch poetry in Belgium at that time was still dominated by the exuberance, sonority, loftiness and pathos of Karel van de Woestijne, and in all these qualities Van Ostaijen was his opposite. The tone of *Music-Hall* was generally light, the language was as colloquial as Nijhoff's, if not more so, the mood hesitated between a slightly sentimental melancholy and an astringent irony, just as the form of the poems hesitated between traditional form and free verse. The novelty of this volume found its fullest expression in the long title poem which describes a music-hall and everything that goes with it: waiters, dancers, public. The point of view of the poem was the 'unanimist' view of Jules Romains which tried to express the 'one soul', the common spirit of a given community, rather than the psychology of the individual:

> In de Music-Hall is er slechts één hart,
> En één ziel. Eén kloppend hart
> Eén levende ziel. [7]

In his next volume Van Ostaijen progressed from recognition of the 'one soul' to a longing to become part of it, a longing that has been characterized as earthly mysticism. This second volume, *Het Sienjaal* (The Signal, 1918), abounds with poems expressing his belief in the brotherhood of men and in art as all-embracing love. By that time Van Ostaijen must be counted among the true expressionists. Because of the occupation of Belgium by the Germans, the eastern frontier was open and German books were freely available. When he wrote *Het Sienjaal*, Van Ostaijen was probably familiar with the work of Franz Werfel, Else Lasker-Schüler, Theodor Däubler and Kurt Heynicke as the numerous parallels with their work suggest. The names of Apollinaire and Walt Whitman should also be mentioned among those who influenced him in these years. Shortly after the publication of *Het Sienjaal* and a few weeks after the armistice of 1918, Van Ostaijen left Belgium because of the support he had given to the Flemish movement for autonomy, a movement that was also supported by the Germans. He settled in Berlin and there he

---

[7] In the Music-hall there is only one heart, and one soul. One heart that beats, and one living soul.

rapidly lost his humanitarian ideals. He dismissed Werfel, the chief representative of humanitarian expressionism, as a driveller, and rejected *Het Sienjaal* as 'lyrical preening'. Repudiation of his own work was typical of Van Ostaijen. He was by nature an experimentalist who always rejected each former phase of his development in favour of the next. Though his stay in Germany was a continual disappointment, his productivity was great. The poetry which he wrote there was vastly different from his first two volumes. Of his belief in mankind, nothing was left. The poems speak of utter loneliness, of fear, of a feeling of complete alienation from the world and himself. Little was left of traditional form either. In *Feesten van Angst en Pijn* (Feasts of Fear and Pain) all punctuation marks were abandoned and ink of different colours was used to help express the mood. In *Bezette Stad* (Occupied City, 1921) the poems were printed in a dizzying variation of lettertypes. The words were scattered over the page, sometimes haphazardly, sometimes arranged in patterns that corresponded with the content of the poems, rather in the manner of Apollinaire's *Calligrammes* which had appeared three years earlier. The 'rhythmic topography' as he called it, and the jumble of words were a furious expression of Van Ostaijen's disillusionment: all that was left after the loss of his ideals was meaningless chaos: 'lig nou niet te klessen / het leven / alles is zonder zin /nu / kattedrek' (don't talk rubbish / life / everything is meaningless / now / muck).

Bezette Stad was not the end of the line, and in the years that followed he renounced its nihilism. It had been poison, he said, that had been used as an antidote. In the poetry written after *Bezette Stad* he aimed at 'pure lyricism', by which he meant poetry that was entirely disengaged from the poet's own personality. The poem was to be a pure organism without any further connection with its maker. It should not bear a message, it should not communicate emotion. 'The subject of the poem is the poem itself', Van Ostaijen wrote in one of his essays, echoing Baudelaire's 'La poésie-n'a pas d'autre but qu'elle-même'. 'Poetry is not: thought, spirit, well-turned phrases, it is neither doctoral nor dada. It is only a metaphysically anchored play with words'. As a critic and a theorist he applied the same principles. He was fiercely opposed to moral criticism and held that criticism should occupy itself with the poem and not with the poet, anticipating by several years the criticism of *Scrutiny* and the New Critics.

The poems written in these years were meant to be published under the ironic title of *Het Eerste Boek van Schmoll* (The First Book of Schmoll), the title of a piano tutor. Van Ostaijen died, however, in 1928 before he could prepare the book for publication. These last poems are undoubtedly his best work. After *Bezette Stad* they seem strikingly simple and tranquil. Yet they are often enigmatic, in the manner in which a simple nursery rhyme can be enigmatic. They often give the impression of having been written according to the process of free association whereby each word or image calls forth the next without any intervention of reason. Poetry to him was a play of rhythm and words, and he often referred to Guido Gezelle as the man who had understood this best. 'I play with words', he wrote, 'like a juggler with torches. My poems have no contents, only a theme as in music. I only write a largo, an allegretto'. The poetry written in this manner has a mysteriousness and an evocative power that is rivalled only by the later poetry of Nijhoff, though the effects are achieved by entirely different means. Characteristic of many of Van Ostaijen's last poems is the musical element, not in the sense of the poems being sonorous or melodious, but in the sense of being rhythmically arranged sound patterns:

BERCEUSE NR. 2

Slaap als een reus
slaap als een roos
slaap als een reus van een roos
reuzeke
rozeke
zoetekoeksdozeke
doe de deur dicht van de doos
ik slaap.

Van Ostaijen was the first thoroughly modernist writer in the Low Countries, not only as a poet, but also as an essayist and as a writer of whimsical prose pieces which he called grotesques. His field of interest was international, and not confined to literature. It extended to the expressionism of the German poets and the dadaism of Picabia and Schwitters, to the cubism of the French painters and the architecture of 'De Stijl' and 'Bauhaus'. In his essays he co-ordinated the various modernist directions and tried to arrive at a definition of what they had in common. Modernism to him was a natural instinct, something that could not be argued against. The problem of the relation between modernism and traditionalism in literature was an illusory one to him. When he was criticized for being an anti-traditionalist, he replied by saying that being against tradition was as meaningless as being against the air that one breathes: the air exists, tradition exists. At the same time he recognized only one starting point for the poet: from scratch. Du Perron recorded in his *Cahiers van een Lezer* (Journal of a Reader) that when the poet Marsman wrote to Van Ostaijen, saying: 'You want modern poetry all the time, I some of the time', Van Ostaijen was amused: 'Modern poetry to him was a pleonasm; poetry, real poetry, could not be anything else but modern'.

The Marsman who wrote this in or about 1925 obviously had a more ambivalent attitude towards modernism. Born in 1899, three years later than Van Ostaijen, his first poetry was written in the expressionist manner, rather under the influence of Herman van den Bergh. Apart from the free form—much freer than Van den Bergh's—the most striking element of these poems was their cosmic vision. The poet felt himself part of the cosmos, and sometimes its ruler. It is a notion that one finds also in the work of expressionist poets such as Herwarth Walden and Hermann Kasack, but never expressed in such a passionate way as in the early work of Marsman. In 1921 he made a journey through Germany where he met Kasack and Walden, whose poetry he had come to know shortly before that year, either through the famous anthology

Menschheitsdämmerung, published in 1920 by Kurt Pinthus, or through magazines like *Der Sturm* and *Aktion*. As a result of this trip, Marsman wrote a series of poems in which he described various German and Dutch cities he had visited. The poems were originally grouped together under the title of *Seinen* (Signals), and at a first glance they seem to be purely expressionist poetry:

WEIMAR

Doodenhuis
hooge vensters droomen hun vergaan
luikenkruis
vleermuisschaduwen
daaraan. [8]

The outward appearance of a poem such as this is reminiscent of August Stramm, particularly in its use of one-word lines. Yet neither Stramm nor any of the other German expressionists had written this kind of city-portrait. The expressionists were interested in abstraction and wrote about 'the city' or 'cities' in general. They tried to capture the atmosphere of 'the city as such', whereas Marsman was concerned with the momentary impression which each individual city made on him. In poems such as these, the idiom is expressionist, the vision is closer to impressionism.

After the publication of his first volume *Verzen* (Poems) in 1923, Marsman turned his back on expressionism. His admiration of Stramm, Heynicke and Kasack faded away, and in an essay entitled *Tien Jaar na Menschheitsdämmerung* (Ten Years after *Menschheitsdämmerung*), written in 1929, he came to the conclusion that the achievements and 'creative potentiality' of expressionism were slight. Only Trakl and Heym, and 'a few poems by a few others' were excepted from this verdict. 'Poetry', he wrote, 'is not dynamite, but diamond'. Two years later he also dismissed a considerable part

[8] Weimar. House of the dead / high windows dream of their decay / cross of shutters / bats' wings / attached.

THE MODERN PERIOD

of Van Ostaijen's expressionist poetry as 'humanitarian humbug'. By that time Marsman's own poetry had undergone a significant change. His first poems had generally been enthusiastic, passionate, virile, explosive. The poet saw himself as part of the cosmos as in *Verhevene* (The Sublime), or as its dominator as in *Heerscher* (The Ruler). He was lonely, but self-sufficient. Because of their bold and vigorous tone, these poems are often referred to as 'vitalist' poetry. Yet in several poems of the same period there was also a tone of defeat, of failure and death, and it was this tone that gradually grew stronger. The loneliness, which in the early poems had been taken for granted as part of the poet's exalted situation, began to acquire a tragic accent. Consequently, the poetry of the later volumes, *Paradise Regained* (1927) and *Porta Nigra* (1934), was no longer exclusively concerned with the self, but more and more with 'the other'. These poems reflect a desire to overcome the loneliness through love and friendship, they record disappointment and loss, and express the fear of death which was ever present in his later work. At the same time, as in the case of Nijhoff, Marsman's style of writing became greatly simplified. The big words which had given the early poems a touch of grandeur—but which on occasion had sounded a little hollow—were discarded in favour of a more colloquial way of expression.

In 1940 Marsman published a new volume under the title of *Tempel en Kruis* (The Temple and the Cross), which was to be his last work. At first glance it seems a heterogeneous collection of poems, ranging from free verse to strict form and from narrative to lyrical poetry. It is, in fact, a closely-knit volume in which all poems are related to the central theme. Writing in the years just before the Second World War, when Fascism and Nazism were threatening the survival of Western-European civilization, the poet tries to define what to him are the foundations and the value of this civilization. He distinguishes two elements: the heritage of ancient Greece (The Temple) and Christianity (The Cross). Christianity which began as a brave and exciting religion, has degenerated into ritual and dogma, and become unattractive to the poet. Moreover, he rejects as unjust the dogma of original sin. Yet in his search for a community to which he can belong and which can allay his fear of death, he is drawn to the Roman Catholic Church. At the last moment, however, he withdraws and from then on regards his approach to the Church as a betrayal of life. Filled with despair, he travels to the Mediterranean, where in the atmosphere of Antiquity, and far from the memories of his youth, he finds himself again and feels liberated from the oppressive past. The fourth part of the poem, entitled *De Onvoltooide Tempel* (The Unfinished Temple), states that 'twenty centuries breathlessly slipped by' and made way for the peacefulness of Antiquity. The conclusion of the volume is 'to write in the spirit of this sea' and to choose the antique and Dionysian element of modern civilization. In writing these poems and arriving at this conclusion, Marsman was influenced by Nietzsche whose *Also Sprach Zarathustra* he tranlated into Dutch at about the same time.

Since *Tempel en Kruis* was Marsman's last work, it is often regarded as the crown on his poetry. It would be better, though, to regard it as an entirely new departure. Marsman had never before written a cyclic volume, nor had he ever before written such a searching analysis of his own situation. The combination of this intellectual analysis with his great lyrical talents makes *Tempel en Kruis* stand out from his own previous work as well as from that of most of his contemporaries. After 1940 a great deal more could have been expected from Marsman. His development was cut short, however, when in June 1940 the ship in which he was trying to escape from France to England was torpedoed by a German submarine just out of Bordeaux.

Marsman's talents were above all lyrical, and therefore showed to fullest advantage in his poetry. In his prose, his lyricism was often a liability. After writing some prose-poems—modelled perhaps on Trakl's—and also some stories, he embarked on a novel, *Vera*, which can only be regarded as a complete failure. Though he re-wrote it several times, Marsman finally rejected it, and it was not published in book-form until 1962. His second novel, *De Dood van Angèle Degroux* (The Death of Angèle Degroux, 1933), was more convincing in spite of its structural weaknesses. The theme of the book is the inability of the two main characters to break through their own isolation, a theme not uncommon in Marsman's poetry. It is a novel of ideas rather than a novel of character, and the lyrical passages, however well-written and evocative they may be, often seem out of place. Such passages fitted more harmoniously into *Heden Ik, Morgen Gij* (Me Today, You Tomorrow, 1937), an epistolary novel which Marsman wrote together with Simon Vestdijk. The form which they devised for the book allowed Marsman to be his own lyrical self, without this becoming a strain on the narrative framework.

As a critic, too, Marsman was first and foremost a lyricist. His approach, he stated himself, was lyrical and intuitive. It was also aggressively subjective. Objectivity to him was 'a cowardly prejudice, the prejudice of having no prejudices or even preferences'. Criticism was a confrontation between two personalities: the reviewer and the reviewed. As a result, his critiques were very uneven. Sometimes his intuition enabled him to make sharp and valuable observations, particularly on writers to whom he felt an affinity. At other times his extreme subjectivity caused him to dispense with all argumentation and to make totally unsubstantiated, categorical pronouncements. The categorical tone was so dominant in his early critiques that some of them read like literary manifestos, laying down the law for writers, telling them what to write about and what not. Marsman had the temperament of a leader, and in the 1920s and 1930s he was accepted as such by many writers. In 1925 he became editor of *De Vrije Bladen* (The Free Pages), a journal that was set up in 1924 and that after the demise of *Het Getij* in the same year, quickly established itself as the leading journal of the new generation. Marsman's editorship was not an unqualified success. He himself was disappointed because the fiery articles with which he tried to whip up the enthusiasm of fellow writers produced unimpressive, and sometimes undesirable results. The strong personalities went their own way, unaffected by Marsman's 'whiplashes', the weaker ones often contented themselves with becoming Marsman-imitators. This led to tensions within the group of contributors to *De Vrije Bladen*.

In 1931 the growing sense of uneasiness was expressed by Menno ter Braak, the most forceful essayist of the group, in an attack on the epigonism that had developed within the journal. The immediate cause of the attack was *Prisma* (Prism), an anthology of modern poetry edited and introduced by D.A.M.Binnendijk, one of the editors of *De Vrije Bladen*. Ter Braak derided the imitativeness of some of the poets represented in the anthology and put in a strong claim for more originality and character. The ensuing debate quickly moved away from originality and epigonism, and centred on the more theoretical question of which was more important in literature: the beauty of the work itself, or the personality of the man behind it. In a letter to his friend Du Perron, Ter Braak summed up the conflict in the simplest possible terms: 'the only essential thing is that all this beauty means nothing to me if it does not reflect character, whereas he (Binnendijk) carefully wants to peck up even the smallest grain of beauty (in poetry, that is)'. The poet J.C.Bloem summarized the issue with the catching phrase of 'vorm of vent' (form or fellow). Seen in a larger, international context, the opposition of 'form' and 'fellow' was a reflection of the old contrast between an aesthetic and a moralist approach to literature, or, in other words, the contrast between 'art for art's sake' and 'engagement'. Marsman who had resigned his editorship of *De Vrije Bladen* in 1926 and had then become editor again from 1929 to 1931, adopted an ambivalent and slightly aloof attitude during the controversy. He admitted the lack of originality of several poets, but at the same time he dissociated himself from Ter Braak's notion that 'character' in poetry was more essential than 'beauty'.

The results of the 'form or fellow' debate were far-reaching. Ter Braak broke away from *De Vrije Bladen* and with Du Perron and the Flemish novelist Maurice Roelants established a new magazine *Forum* which was to exert a very strong influence on the development of Dutch literature. In the first issue, which appeared in 1932, the editors made a stand against the 'idolization of form at the expense of creative man'. Elaborating on Ter Braak's remarks in the *Prisma* controversy, they declared themselves supporters of the view 'which regards the personality as the first and the last criterion by which the artist is judged'. They gave an indication of their preferences by singling out Multatuli for 'a respectful salute'.

The influence of *Forum* was due in the first instance to the formidable polemic powers of Ter Braak and Du Perron. They emerged victorious from the *Prisma* debate after having defeated Binnendijk and having pushed Marsman into a defensive position. There was continuing opposition from a group of Roman Catholic writers led by the militant Anton van Duinkerken, from a group of humanists led by Anthonie Donker and Dirk Coster, and from the young Protestants led by Roel Houwink and Klaas Heeroma, but there can be no doubt that between 1930 and 1940 the ideas of *Forum* prevailed. During that period most of the important writers were in one way or another connected with *Forum*. Marsman, too, came round. His subjectivity fitted in well with the subjective approach of Ter Braak and Du Perron, and although he remained suspicious of Ter Braak's attitude to poetry, he did become an active contributor to *Forum*. In these later years his criticism lost much of its sweeping character and he showed a greater willingness to enter into the world created by the writer, even when it did not correspond with his own.

Though *Forum* attracted many writers, its main driving force was the team of Ter Braak and Du Perron. When the journal was established, Ter Braak had published one novel, *Hampton Court*(1931), and was writing his second, *Dr.Dumay Verliest* (Dr. Dumay Loses, 1933). They are both very readable books, and of importance because of their autobiographical content, but they are not the books of a great novelist. Ter Braak's real strength lay in the essay. Born in 1902 as the son of a country doctor, he studied history at the University of Amsterdam where he gained his doctorate in 1928 with a thesis on the medieval Emperor Otto III. Then he turned to essay writing and criticism, and in a few years' time proved himself to be a very erudite and intelligent critic. In the first volume of *Forum* he published a long essay under the programmatic title of *Demasqué der Schoonheid* (Beauty Unmasked) which continued the attack on aestheticism begun during the *Prisma* debate. It was Ter Braak's personal settling of accounts with the adoration of Beauty that dated back to the Movement of the Eighties. The greater part of Ter Braak's work can be placed under the heading of 'settling accounts', either with his opponents or with himself. In his next book, *Politicus Zonder Partij* (Politician Without a Party, 1934), he argued—as a true disciple of Nietzsche's—that self-interest was the basis of most of man's actions, even his most idealistic ones. The main theme of the book is the unmasking of 'the spirit' and the 'verbal trickery' that had been perpetrated in its name. In one of the chapters of the book he pitted Nietzsche against Freud, and though full of admiration for Freud's scientific achievements, he finally rejected him as a system-builder and opted for the unsystematic intelligence of Nietzsche. It is a book against 'earnestness', against those 'who maintain that they derive greater pleasure from reading poetry than from eating oysters', against the 'phony proprieties with which we keep up our position vis-à-vis our fellow mammals'. At the same time it is a plea for humour, i.e. for a greater sense of relativity. *Politicus Zonder Partij* makes clear that the invocation of Multatuli in the first issue of *Forum* was no hollow phrase, for there is no other book in Dutch literature that so determinedly continued Multatuli's assault on dogmatism. Ter Braak, as individualistic as Multatuli, rejected all systems, all dogmas and all collectivities, and with them all intellectuals who sought support in a system, a dogma or a collectivity. In *Van Oude en Nieuwe Christenen* (Of Christians, Old and New, 1937) he discussed collective movements such as socialism, fascism, national-socialism and communism in the light of their demand for equality, the origin of which he found in early Christianity. The starting point of his analysis was again provided by a thesis of Nietzsche's which considered the demand for equality to be a product of resentment. Since democracy pursues equality without coercion and leaves the individual more scope than any other system, Ter Braak regarded it as the only acceptable form of government.

Ter Braak's literary criticism, too, was characterized by his urge to expose false values and to track down any trickery with words. True to the ideas expressed during the *Prisma* polemics, he was always more interested in the man behind the work than in the way the work was presented, more in the 'communicative' aspect of poetry than in its 'ornamental' aspect. Dèr Mouw, whom he rediscovered after an eclipse of many years, was often quoted by him as a good example of a 'communicative' poet, while to him Leopold was the representative of what he termed 'ornamental poetry'. Ter Braak's literary criticism, contained in four big volumes, is the most comprehensive collection of criticism since Busken Huet's *Literarische Fantasieën en Kritieken*, and just as readable. The standards which he applied were high, and there is no doubt that they had a salutary effect on the literature of the thirties. On the other hand, there is no doubt either that the critical basis from which he operated was a narrow one. Its narrowness was determined by his own temperament, but also by the period in which he was writing. In the years before the Second World War, when the threat of nazism was becoming stronger every day, questions of aesthetics were more easily overruled by questions of character than they might have been in other times. If the threat of totalitarianism had not been so strong, the personality theory of *Forum* might never have been honed to such a sharp edge. In the last years before the war, Ter Braak became one of the most outspoken opponents of national-socialism. He committed suicide after the German invasion in May 1940. 'He did not wish to survive the triumph of the lie and barbarism', as Thomas Mann wrote in a tribute to him.

His friend and co-founder of *Forum*, Charles Edgar (E.) du Perron, came from an entirely different background. He was born in Java in 1899, and came to Europe when he was twenty-two. Europe to him was the Promised Land, but the Europe he was attracted to was France rather than the Netherlands. He settled in Paris where he lived the life of a bohemian, not from necessity, but because his reading had given him a taste of Montmartre that he wanted to put to the test. He formed friendships with several artists and writers, of whom Pascal Pia and André Malraux were the most important (in 1933 Malraux dedicated his novel *La Condition Humaine* to him). The fruits of Du Perron's Parisian days were poetry and criticism, and also a novel, *Een Voorbereiding* (A Preparation). It was an autobiographical novel, a little naively written and also rather sentimental, but of interest as an account of his first year in Europe. The history of its publication is an eloquent illustration of Du Perron's views on literature which a short time later were to crystallize into the personality theory of *Forum*. The book was first published in 1927 in a small edition of 125 copies, 50 of which Du Perron said he had burned himself. Four years later he partly rewrote it, and then published it again, fully aware that it was still a weak novel, but not wanting to suppress it because it was part of himself. Writing was in the first place a registration of one's own development; suppressing a book because of artistic faults seemed faintly dishonest; the 'fellow' outweighed the 'form'.

Du Perron's criticism was based on the same principles. It was even more personal, more subjective, more 'man to man' than Ter Braak's or Marsman's. It was therefore diametrically opposed to that of Van Ostaijen, who was a close friend of Du Perron's for some years. Du Perron made it quite clear that he did not want to be regarded as a traditional critic by presenting his work under the collective title of *Cahiers van een Lezer* (Journal of a Reader). He never made any claim that his opinions were valid for anyone but himself and a few friends who thought along the same lines. He stated this unequivocally in one of his best-known and, ironically, perhaps most influential essay on Jan Slauerhoff, a poet and novelist of the *Forum* group: 'Mind you, I only maintain that *I*, and if necessary I alone, care a great deal for the poem *Dsjengis* (Slauerhoff) and nothing at all for the poem *Cheops* (Leopold)'. His criticism was essentially directed at finding out whether the man behind the work was 'Friend or Enemy', as indicated in the title of one of his volumes of criticism, *Vriend of Vijand*. He often seemed to use the literary work solely as a yardstick to measure the degree of friendship or enmity to be accorded to the writer. His preferences and aversions were often 'instinctive' as he said, but he went to great lengths to argue them out. In his *Uren met Dirk Coster* (Hours with Dirk Coster), for instance, he painstakingly analysed Coster's work before putting him in the pillory as a phrasemonger and a sloppy thinker. But, as always, the man was worth more than the book, even when it meant going back on an earlier verdict. When in 1939 Dirk Coster proved to be as implacably opposed to nazism as Ter Braak and Du Perron and all other writers of any importance, Du Perron had the remainder of his anti-Coster book destroyed. It is not very difficult to dismiss Du Perron's criticism from an academic point of view as irrelevant and dilettantish. He himself would have been the first to agree. It is far more important to recognize that he was the most lively and the most stimulating critic of the thirties. It is ironical, again, that he who abhorred being regarded as a literary 'adviser', had a greater influence on younger readers and writers than any of his contemporaries. Without exaggeration one may say that a large part of the generation of the thirties and the forties was brought up on his preferences: Stendhal, Gide, Larbaud, Malraux, Wilde, Multatuli, Roland Holst, Slauerhoff, all writers who were what he called 'present' in their work. It has been said that whereas Ter Braak resembled Busken Huet (a comparison against which Ter Braak protested), Du Perron was closest to Multatuli. His affinity to Multatuli was certainly great, and when he was back in Java between 1936 and 1939, he demonstrated this by writing an excellent biography of Multatuli, *De Man van Lebak*, not only a sound documentary, but also an impassioned case for the defence.

Considering his feelings of affinity with Multatuli, it was not surprising that when in 1933 he began writing his second novel, he mentioned Multatuli as the first point of reference. In a letter to Jan Greshoff he wrote: 'The larger part will be taken up by memories of the past in the Indies, but in between there will be short stories, portraits, anecdotes etc. As a whole it will look like the Ideas of Multatuli, but not so far as contents or tone are concerned; in general, it will be more narrative'. The book was entitled *Het Land van Herkomst* (The Country of Origin) and was published in 1935. The *Forum* writers set great store by autobiographical work and Du Perron's novel is also to a large extent autobiographical and self-searching. The main character, Arthur Ducroo, gives a description of his life in Paris in the thirties, relating it all the time to the memories which he retains of his youth in Java. The account of the present and the memories of the past provide the answers to the two questions that underlie the structure of the book: 'Who am I now?' and 'Who was I then?' Malraux formulated the main theme of the book in the following words: 'His constant introspection is not seeking for the key to man; it is endeavouring to fathom its own singularity'. Ducroo tries to define his 'singularity' by linking his present life to his past, by recording his thoughts and opinions, by showing who his friends are and who his enemies. The motivation behind this detailed self-portrait is his wish to present to the woman he loves a picture of himself that is as complete and as honest as possible. This starting-point made the book one of the most unconventional novels in Dutch. It consists of memoirs, diaries, conversations, letters, narration, all put together in a seemingly incoherent fashion. Its heterogeneity recalls Multatuli's *Max Havelaar*, as does the double setting in Paris and Java. It is even further removed from the traditional novel than *Max Havelaar* because it dispenses with any semblance of plot, which Du Perron regarded as artificial. Yet *Het Land van Herkomst*, like *Max Havelaar*, is in fact a novel of great coherence and unity, since the events in the past and in the present are selected in such a way that they constantly put each other in perspective. Though Du Perron rejected the traditional form of the novel and even called his book an anti-novel, in the arrangement and welding together of the various episodes he showed himself to be a craftsman of the first order. The book also gives a clear demonstration of Du Perron's contention that the writer must always be 'present' in his work. It would be a mistake to identify Ducroo with Du Perron on all points, but the book is undoubtedly a thorough and honest attempt at self-analysis. Egoistic though it may be, it never wastes time on irrelevant detail, it never degenerates into exhibitionism, and in addition it gives a valuable picture of the intellectual climate in Paris and the Netherlands in the thirties. Marsman hit the nail on the head when he characterized it as 'the most complete expression of our generation'.

When he wrote *Het Land van Herkomst*, Du Perron was living in Paris where he worked as a journalist. In 1936 he went back to Java, but returned to the Netherlands in 1939, just before the outbreak of the war. Weakened by a heart-attack, he died during the German invasion in 1940, on the same day as Ter Braak.

The impact which *Forum* made on the literature of the thirties manifested itself more convincingly in criticism and in the novel than in poetry. True, most of the writers connected with the journal were poets as well as prose writers, but in all cases except Slauerhoff's, their poetry was overshadowed by their prose. Ter Braak wrote no poetry. Du Perron did, and his volume *Parlando* is still very readable, but it is not the work of a man who expressed himself primarily in poetry. On the whole, the *Forum* poets were minor poets who avoided anything that tended to grandeur or ostentatiousness. They employed the ordinary word and preferred to limit themselves to everyday themes. Though sometimes slightly romantic, their poetry in general was down-to-earth, rational and often anecdotal. In their use of form they were traditionalists. The poet and critic Jan Greshoff may be regarded as the father of the *Forum* poetry. Born in 1888, he belonged to an older generation than Ter Braak and Du Perron, and made his debut more than twenty years before *Forum* was established. During the 1920's he was one of the first to turn towards a deliberately colloquial idiom, and this, together with the personal tone of his work, had a considerable influence on the poetry of the twenties and the thirties. When *Forum* was established, Greshoff became a regular contributor, and when it ceased publication in 1935, he continued to support its case as an editor of *Groot Nederland*, a literary journal that was published between 1903 and 1944.

The only writer of the *Forum* group who was both poet and novelist without the one crowding out the other, was Jan Slauerhoff. He was also the most individualistic member of the group, so much so that one should perhaps not label him as a member of the group at all, or of any group. Apart from some fiery outbursts against writers who had aroused his displeasure, and apart from a short period as a newspaper critic, he was not really active in the literary arena as Ter Braak, Du Perron, Marsman and Greshoff were. He was born in Leeuwarden in 1898 and studied medicine in Amsterdam. After his graduation in 1923 he signed on as a ship's surgeon and made numerous voyages to the East and West Indies, China and Africa, until shortly before his death in 1936. As a poet he made his debut in *Het Getij* in 1921, and published regularly in *De Vrije Bladen* from the moment of its inception. Yet it was from *Forum*, and in the first place from Du Perron, that he received unqualified recognition. When in 1930 Du Perron wrote his influential *Gesprek over Slauerhoff* (Conversation about Slauerhoff), Slauerhoff had published six volumes of poetry: *Archipel* (Archipelago, 1923), *Clair Obs-*

cur (1927), *Oost-Azië* (East Asia, 1928), *Eldorado* (1928), *Saturnus* (1930) and *Serenade* (1930), which taken together had collected a good deal of praise but which had also encountered strong resistance. Marsman had carefully weighed the pros and cons. Slauerhoff's poetry, he wrote, was genuine, it was averse to literary prettiness, it had purity, depth and sometimes greatness; on the other hand, it was careless, nonchalant, suffering from halting rhythms and at times also from a triviality of feeling. Du Perron, with characteristic absolutism, rejected Marsman's approach: 'Perhaps Marsman belongs to those men who, when they love a woman whose nose is a little awry or whose hands are a little heavy, would like to amputate the nose and the hands'. The clash between these two views: qualified and selective approval versus complete acceptance, warts and all, has been a feature of Slauerhoff-criticism ever since.

Slauerhoff certainly was a strange apparition in Dutch poetry in the twenties and thirties. There was something nineteenth-century about him, something of the *poète maudit*, especially of Tristan Corbière, with whom he identified himself in his early years. His themes were love, the sea, the ship, the outsider, the outcast. In many ways his poetry was late-romantic, but it was a romanticism that usually ended on a note of cynicism or bitterness. His directness and his anecdotal style were modern enough, as Marsman well realized. What attracted Du Perron so much was Slauerhoff's being present in all of his work. Not many other poets have so unreservedly expressed their personality in their work as Slauerhoff did. His idealism and his cynicism, his vulnerability and his cruelty, his restlessness and his longing for peace, his recalcitrance, his truculence which sometimes turned against the very poem he was writing, all these contradictory characteristics together give his work its uneven, capricious, but very personal stamp. In everything he wrote, his voice, 'his hoarse, shy tone' as Greshoff called it, was always unmistakably present. It was a tone of melancholy, of disillusionment and often of deep despair that did not care about a smooth-running rhythm, a mellifluous phrase or what the critics were wont to term 'good taste'. That the unevenness of Slauerhoff's poetry should have anything to do with a deficient technique, as has sometimes been suggested, is contradicted by a poem such as *Chineesche Dans* (Chinese Dance) from his first volume *Archipel*, which shows that from the very beginning Slauerhoff had a grasp of poetic technique that was rivalled by few others.

The novels of Slauerhoff are just as idiosyncratic and unconventional as his poetry. They are certainly not impeccable novels. They are neither well-polished nor smooth-running, their composition is sometimes chaotic and the characterization usually minimal. Yet they are by no means insignificant or unsuccessful books, for they hold a fascination that overrules all technical imperfections. *Het Verboden Rijk* (The Forbidden Empire), first published in the first volume of *Forum* in 1932, consists of two interwoven life stories: that of the sixteenth-century Portugese poet Camoens and that of a ship's wireless operator in the twentieth century. Camoens, exiled in Macao, becomes involved with the daughter of the Administrator and is caught up in the intrigues that are rife in the town. He is arrested and taken away. At this point the novel focuses on the Irish wireless operator, who after being shipwrecked feels himself driven by an inexplicable compulsion towards Macao. Gradually his life begins to merge with that of Camoens. He recognizes places where he cannot have been before, he has the sensation that he is about to become someone else, his memories become a mixture of his own experiences and those of Camoens. At the end of the novel he finds himself in a hotel in Macao, liberated from the oppressive weight of his own personality and hoping to be absorbed by the anonymous millions of China. Self-destruction was a pronounced trait of Slauerhoff's character, and the loss of identity experienced by the wireless operator—who is never given a name—is clearly a symbolization of Slauerhoff's personal situation. His next novel, *Het Leven op Aarde* (Life on Earth, 1934), is also set in China and also has as its central figure a wireless operator who this time is given the name of Cameron. Like the former book, *Het Leven op Aarde* is also a novel about the loss of identity: Cameron loses himself, not in the identity of someone else, but in the oblivion of opium. These two novels were to form the first and second part of a trilogy, but the third part was never written. Instead, Slauerhoff wrote a short novel, *De Opstand van Guadalajara* (The Revolt of Guadalajara, 1937), set in Mexico and dealing with a wandering glazier who is persuaded to act as a Saviour to a group of poor and oppressed Indians. In all these books the main characters are outsiders. It is said of the wireless operator that he was 'neither fish nor fowl, neither sailor nor landlubber, neither belonging to the officers nor to the men'. Slauerhoff, who began one of his poems with the lines: 'only in my poems can I live, never did I find shelter anywhere else', was deeply involved in the fate of his outsiders and their attitude to society. His personal involvement and his unique style—sometimes clipped and laconic, at other times lyrical and visionary—give his books a place of their own in the history of the novel.

In the history of the novella one older contemporary was just as much *sui generis* as Slauerhoff. In 1911 J.H.F. Grönloh (1882-1961) published *De Uitvreter* (The Sponger) under the pen-name of Nescio, a pseudonym which he guarded jealously until 1929. The story did not create much of a stir, either on first publication or in 1918 when it appeared in book form together with two more novellas under the title of *Dichtertje, De Uitvreter, Titaantjes* (Little Poet, The Sponger, Little Titans). Yet Nescio's slim volume was to make a great impact, not so much on his own generation but on the writers and readers of the fifties and the sixties. In 1932 Du Perron drew Ter Braak's attention to Nescio's work, and it was Ter Braak who, in the following year, when the book was reprinted, wrote the first full-length and warmly appreciative article on Nescio. He was particularly taken by the subtle way in which Nescio dismissed bourgeois singleness of purpose without uncritically glorifying the bohemian aimlessness of his characters.

Nescio's Little Titans are a group of young men who try to keep society at bay with words rather than with actions:

What we wanted to do never became clear. We would do something. Bekker had a vague idea that he wanted to pull down all offices. Ploeger wanted to make his boss pack all his own clocks and to look on with a cigar stuck in his mouth, cursing the chaps who could never do anything properly. We were agreed that we had to get out. Out of what, and how?

Their ineffectual anarchism leads nowhere. Bekker sells out to society and becomes a well-to-do businessman. Ploeger starts working for the Gas Company in a uniform cap and with a notebook under his arm. Hoyer becomes a trade-union boss. Bavink, the artist, wants to put the sun in a hat box and ends up in a lunatic asylum.

Nescio's novellas are a kind of tragi-comedies: the non-events in his characters' lives are observed humorously but the stories always have a sad ending. The romantic Little Poet goes insane after a comfortable bourgeois life and an uncomfortable love-affair. Japi, the amiable sponger of the first story, who is happiest doing nothing, decides to call it a day after his girl friend has left him for a rich man. He steps from a bridge into the river:

The watchman saw him too late. "Don't get excited, old man", Japi said, and then he stepped from the bridge. You couldn't call it jumping, said the man, he just stepped off.

And like Japi and the poet, the Little Titans are also defeated by their own inefficacy or by society.

The fascination of Nescio's writing lies in his gentle icono-clasm, his humorous irreverence, his melancholy disillusion-ment, his sense of relativity, all of which were unseasonable in the second and third decades of this century. At that time his style of writing seemed, even to Ter Braak, to hark back to the naturalist mannerisms of the Eighties. Now, at a greater distance, it is clear that the similarities with the prose of the Eighties are no more than superficial and that Nescio's colloquial, unemphatic and yet highly sensitive style makes him stand out with Elsschot as far and away the most original prose-writer of his generation. Nescio's only new publications after 1918 were two volumes of short stories, *Mene Tekel* in 1946 and *Boven het Dal* (Above the Valley) in the year of his death. Style, subject matter and approach were very close to those of the first volume. 'Life', said Nescio on the last page of *Mene Tekel*, 'has taught me hardly anything, thank God'. His work constitutes the greatest small oeuvre in Dutch literature.

On the Belgian side, the main novelists of the years between the wars were Willem Elsschot (pseudonym of Alfons de Ridder), Gerard Walschap and Maurice Roelants, who were all connected with *Forum*. Roelants was a founding editor, and Walschap joined in 1934 when a separate editorial board for Belgium was set up. In spite of his early interest in the journal, Roelants was the least typical *Forum* writer of the three. In novels such as *Komen en Gaan* (Coming and Going, 1927), *Het Leven dat Wij Droomden* (The Life We Dreamed, 1931), *Alles Komt Terecht* (Everything Will Come Right, 1937), and *Gebed om een Goed Einde* (Prayer for a Good Ending, 1944), he was above all a psychologist who calmly, thoughtfully and sometimes rather longwindedly analysed the lives of his characters. He is not cynical and down-to-earth like Elsschot nor passionate and rebellious like Walschap, but patient and contented. As a strict Roman Catholic he was never quite at home in the a-religious *Forum* group, and when in 1935 a conflict developed between the Dutch and Belgian editors about a contribution that was unacceptable to the Catholic Flemings, he found himself in direct opposition to the Dutch editors. As a result of this conflict, *Forum* ceased publication.

Willem Elsschot, though never an editor of *Forum*, was much closer to its spirit than Roelants. He also owed a considerable debt to the *Forum* writers, and in particular to Jan Greshoff, for it was their enthusiasm that rescued him from a long period of silence. Born in 1882 in Antwerp, Elsschot was a businessman who ran an advertising agency and wrote only in his spare time. In his early years he wrote some poetry, which remained unknown for over twenty years until *Forum* published it in its first volume. It linked up remarkably well with the poetry written by the much younger *Forum* writers and suddenly met with response. In 1913 he published his first novel, *Villa des Roses*, inspired by a run-down boarding-house in Paris where he had lived some years before. It was written in Elsschot's characteristic spare style, strictly narrative and without any embellishments, cool, dry, cynical and humorous, with a lack of rhetoric that was to appeal greatly to the later *Forum* generation. Elsschot did not go in for character analysis in the way Roelants did. He was first and foremost a narrator who let his figures characterize themselves by what they said and did. At the time of publication, *Villa des Roses* attracted little attention, probably because it did not fit easily into what was then the mainstream of novel-writing: Streuvels and Teirlinck in Belgium, Couperus and Van Schendel in the Netherlands. After two short novels and a longer one, *Lijmen* (Soft Soap,1924), Elsschot was so depressed by the lack of response that he decided to give up writing. Greshoff, who knew him well, wrote of this decision: 'If the indifference towards *Lijmen* discouraged him, it was not out of hurt vanity, but only because he had evidently not succeeded in realizing his artistry so convincingly that it gave meaning to his commercial career while at the same time relegating it to second place'.

Lack of success of an autobiographical book probably hits an author harder than the failure of a work of pure fiction, and there was a great deal of autobiographical material in *Lijmen*. It was a bitter but humorous satire on advertising, that is on Elsschot's own work which he both hated and loved. The main character of the book, Boorman, edits an advertising magazine which has no circulation at all but is sold in thousands of copies to one customer at a time. Boorman, the con-man who successfully trains himself to be hard, was invested with a considerable amount of Elsschot's own business experience—only toned down a little, as he said to Greshoff, otherwise no-one would have believed him—and

so was Frans Laarmans, the timid but willing associate, who
in the later novels more and more developed into a self-portrait of Elsschot. When *Lijmen*, a first-rate and highly original novel, failed to score, Elsschot stopped writing for nine
years. Roused by Greshoff in 1932, he tried again and within
two weeks wrote a short novel *Kaas* (Cheese), which was first
published in *Forum's* second volume of 1933 and which became his most widely-read book. Like *Lijmen*, it is a novel
of business-life and also to a certain extent autobiographical. This time Laarmans is the central character, but the tables are turned: Laarmans finds himself the victim of a hard-
sell and is landed with hundreds of crates of cheese which
he cannot get rid of. A few years later, Elsschot also turned
the tables on Boorman in *Het Been* (The Leg), a short novel
which shows Boorman repairing the damage that one of his
shady deals in *Lijmen* had caused. In later novels such as
Tsjip (Chirp), *De Leeuwentemmer* (The Lion-tamer) and
Het Dwaallicht (Will-o'-the-Wisp), he turned away from
the world of business without abandoning his business-like,
astringent style. *Het Dwaallicht* (1946), a story or novella
rather than a novel, is perhaps his masterpiece. With Laarmans as the narrator, it describes a rainy evening in Antwerp
during which three Afghan sailors make a futile search for a
Flemish girl. There is no plot, hardly any characterization, no
purple passages, and yet the melancholy search of the sailors
and their guide is set down with such evocative power that
the book must be regarded as one of the very best stories in
Dutch. It was to be Elsschot's last work; he died in 1960.

Novels about the business-world were rare both in the
Netherlands and in Belgium. In Belgium most novels written
between the two wars were regional novels which had a rural
setting and dealt with life in the village or on the farm. Popular though this genre was, it did not often produce great literature. A writer like Felix Timmermans, for instance, simply
does not belong in the same class as Elsschot or Roelants,
even though his novel *Pallieter* (1916) was a tremendous national and international success. Stijn Streuvels was an excep-

tion to the rule, and Gerard Walschap, born in 1898, was another. Actually, Walschap can only be termed a regional novelist in a very general sense, for he was really closer to Elsschot and Roelants than to any of the regionalists proper. In the common run of regional novels the characters are often types, whose every thought or action is determined by their being farmer, land-owner, priest, loyal hard-working son or profligate son who has an eye on the city. Walschap's novels are totally devoid of these stereotypes. They are also entirely free of the sentimentality that is often associated with the regional novel, neither is there any trace of the blood-and-soil mystique. Walschap is as matter-of-fact as Elsschot, though more of a moralist. Elsschot did not leave much doubt about what he thought of Boorman, but he did not write against him. Indeed, one could easily imagine him having an amiable conversation with Boorman. Walschap is angrier. One of the main themes of his earlier novels— *Adelaide, Eric, Carla, Trouwen* (Marriage), *Celibaat* (Celibacy), *Sybille,* all published between 1929 and 1939—is the interaction of sexual and religious problems. Walschap was a Roman Catholic when he wrote these books, but his attitude was critical and he blamed the Church for much of the mental illnesses that he had come across. His characters are often pathological cases, tormented by fear and guilt-ridden, on the brink of insanity like Adelaide, physically and psychologically maimed like André d'Hertenfeldt in *Celibaat,* or haunted by religious doubts like Sybille. With the exception of *Trouwen,* they are deeply pessimistic books, dealing, like the work of Couperus and Van Oudshoorn, with people and situations in a state of decay. Elsschot was a pessimist, too, but his pessimism was always tempered by humour, something which is absent in most of Walschap's novels. Equally absent is Elsschot's cynicism, his acceptance of the world as a place of corruption. Instead of cynicism, the basis of Walschap's work is moralism. This does not imply that his novels are tedious moralizations; it only means that in contrast to Elsschot he is concerned with the clash between good and evil in his characters, and with the good and evil influences that work on them. The Flemish poet and critic Karel Jonckheere rightly called him a 'conscience-builder'.

In 1939, with the publication of *Houtekiet*, Walschap made a change of front. The book might be called a regional novel, but then a regional novel with a difference, for Jan Houtekiet is so many times larger than life that one could almost read the book as a parody of the regional novel. Houtekiet is a force of nature, a man completely outside the conventions of society who resists every rule that restrains his freedom and who takes whatever he needs: food, land, women. He is nature's protest against civilization and sophistication. Involuntarily he becomes the founder of a small prospering community and the progenitor of a tribe of which each family includes at least one little Houtekiet. Gradually he begins to realize that every community, however free, places limitations on the freedom of its members. For a long time he ignores these limitations, but in the end he gives in and allows himself to be domesticated to a certain extent. *Houtekiet* is Walschap's most cheerful novel, though in spite of its lightheartedness, it has some harsh things to say of the Roman Catholic Church. In the following year Walschap took the consequences of his criticism and broke openly with the Church. In *Vaarwel Dan* (Farewell Then, 1940), he stated his reasons and also gave a bitter account of the agitation that the Church had carried on against him. In his later novels such as *Ons Geluk* (Our Happiness, 1946), *Zwart en Wit* (Black and White. 1948), *Zuster Virgilia* (Sister Virgilia, 1951), *De Ongelooflijke Avonturen van Tilman Armenaas*, (The Incredible Adventures of Tilman Armenaas, 1960), and many others, the religious problem was relegated to the background or entirely eliminated. With it, unfortunately, went the passion and the personal tone of the earlier books, and however well the later novels are written, none of them carries the conviction of the early work.

In the years between the two wars, when Willem Elsschot, Maurice Roelants and Gerard Walschap were the prominent novelists in Belgium, the 'big three' in the Netherlands were Arthur van Schendel, Ferdinand Bordewijk and Simon Vestdijk. One should not pass over J. Van Oudshoorn (pseudonym of J.K.Feylbrief), though, who during his lifetime was never given the same acclaim as the other three, but whose work nevertheless is of considerable importance. As a writer Van Oudshoorn had the misfortune of sitting uneasily between two generations. He was born in 1876 which made him technically a contemporary of Van Schendel and Van Moerkerken, but when in 1914 he finally began to publish, his work had nothing in common with that of his contemporaries. On the one hand he continued the naturalism of Emants, which was then regarded as rather old-fashioned, on the other hand his books were so modern that almost forty years were to pass before they were given proper recognition. His first novel was *Willem Mertens' Levensspiegel* (Mirror of Willem Merten's Life, 1914), an intensely sombre book that records the self-analysis of a man whose life is warped by loneliness, frustration and feelings of guilt, mainly of a sexual kind. Willem Mertens is an anti-hero of the type of Willem Termeer in Emants's *Een Nagelaten Bekentenis,* a man who feels himself an outcast of society, who dreams of love and purity, but only succeeds in aggravating the sordidness in which he lives. All his life he suffers from the memories of his first sexual experiences, and from the self-disgust in which they resulted. Like Van Eeden in *Van de Koele Meren des Doods,* Van Oudshoorn drew attention to sexual frustration as a cause of mental disorders, but his book was more personal, less theoretical, better written and therefore more impressive than Van Eeden's. His later books—*Louteringen* (Purifications, 1916), *Tobias en de Dood* (Tobias and Death, 1925), and his many stories—were all deeply pessimistic and often concerned with psychopathic characters. Though he sometimes lays it on rather thick, Van Oudshoorn was basically a realist writer. His work constitutes a link between the naturalism and realism of the eighties and nineties, and the new realism of the post-war novelists such as Willem Hermans. Van Oudshoorn's touches of surrealism, especially in his occasional dream-like imagery, also seem to anticipate certain surrealist aspects of the work of Hermans. Bordewijk, whose early work also shows some surrealist traits, was perhaps thinking of this element of Van Oudshoorn's work when he mentioned him as one of his early influences, for otherwise there is little common ground between the two.

What one calls Bordewijk's 'early work'—the three volumes *Fantastische Vertellingen* (Fantastic Tales), the novels *Blokken* (Blocks), *Knorrende Beesten* (Grunting Animals), *Bint* and *Rood Paleis* (Red Palace)—was not really so early, for like Van Oudshoorn, Bordewijk began to publish comparatively late. Born in 1884, he was 35 when his first volume of short stories appeared, and 50 when *Bint* was published in 1934, the novel with which he made his name. These early books of Bordewijk's are the best representatives in Dutch literature of the 'Neue Sachlichkeit' as practised by the architects and painters of the German 'Bauhaus' and the Dutch group of 'De Stijl'. Bordewijk's style of writing in these short novels is terse, fast, functional, the sentence structure is simple, the descriptions are reduced to a minimum. *Bint* is the story of a headmaster who demands an iron discipline from his pupils. He scorns the effeminacy of modern education and derides the notion that the teacher must try to understand the pupil. In Bint's view the teacher must never descend to the level of the child, but the child must reach for the level of the teacher. After the suicide of a 'weakling', the school revolts against Bint, but the uprising is put down with the energetic help of a class nicknamed 'the hell' and consisting of monstrous creatures who are generally described in terms of animals. 'Bint's most perfect creation', one of the teachers says of 'the hell'. Bint's system seems to work, but Bint himself is weaker than his system and shortly after the revolt he resigns. Then it is clear that the system will collapse for want of executors. The book is not a glorification of inhuman discipline, nor is it a satire on modern education. It is essentially a realistic picture, but so much enlarged that it is sometimes hard to recognize it as such. Though Bordewijk at times comes close to surrealism—for instance in his descriptions of 'the hell', or of the freaks that occur in *Rood Paleis* and some of his short stories—he never entirely severs his contact with reality. He achieves his effects by enlarging certain aspects of reality, without distorting the enlargements to caricatures. Some of the characters are very much larger than life, they are more awesome, more menacing, more brutal than their life-size equivalents could have been. Yet if they had become caricatures, i.e. if one or more details had been emphasized at the expense of others, one would not have been forced to take them seriously, one could have laughed them away. It is Bordewijk's achievement that one cannot. Bint, then, is not an amusing caricature, but the enlarged portrait of a strict headmaster whose theories and actions one either applauds or abhors, but whom one cannot dismiss as a preposterous invention. Bint and his pupils are not demons from another world; when allowances are made for the blown-up dimensions, they are easily recognizable as inhabitants of our own planet. In the course of his later work, Bordewijk scaled down his enlargements. In *Karakter* (Character, 1938), his best-known novel, he described a relation between father and son. The father tries to build up his son's character by obstructing him as much as he can. It is a relation not unlike the relation between Bint and his pupils, but the characters are not enlarged to quite the same proportions, and on the whole *Karakter* is closer to everyday reality than *Bint*. After this novel, Bordewijk drew closer and closer to reality. The freaks, the monsters and the enlarged characters disappeared from the later novels such as *Eiken van Dodona* (Oaks of Dodona, 1946), *Noorderlicht* (Aurora Borealis, 1948), *De Doopvont* (The Baptismal Font, 1952), *Tijding van Ver* (Tidings from Afar, 1961). They are good, competent psychological novels, but they lack the strange fascination of the earlier books.

Without doing injustice to anyone, one may say that all writers of the first half of the twentieth century, in the Neth-

erlands as well as in Belgium, have been overshadowed by
the genius of Simon Vestdijk, who was born in 1898 and died
in 1971. He was a unique phenomenon in Dutch literature,
and it is unlikely that there are many other literatures that can
boast a writer of his calibre and versatility. His production was
staggering; nothing in literature went out of date quite so
quickly as his bibliography. This inspired Adriaan Roland
Holst to a quatrain in which he addressed Vestdijk as the man
'who writes faster than God can read'. Prolificness and high
quality rarely go together for very long, but in the work of
Vestdijk they went hand in hand for many years. One of the
most astonishing aspects of Vestdijk's work is the range of his
interest and knowledge. Not only has he published about fifty
novels, seven volumes of short stories, twenty-two volumes of
poetry, eighteen collections of essays and criticism, and many
translations, he has also ventured outside the field of literature
with books on the theory of music, on religion, on psychology, on the relation between astrology and science, and on
the philosophy of time. What is more, in none of these books
is he a mere dabbler or amateur; on the contrary, in everything he undertakes he proves himself a serious scholar who
combines original ideas with sound knowledge. Menno ter
Braak gave his book on Vestdijk the title of *De Duivelskun-
stenaar*, the man who has made a pact with the devil and who
has received from him supernatural powers.

   Like Slauerhoff, with whom he went to school in Leeuwarden, Vestdijk studied medicine in Amsterdam and made some
voyages as a ship's doctor. Since 1929 he devoted himself
entirely to writing. In 1932 he made his debut with a volume
of poetry, *Verzen* (Poems). In this as in all his later volumes
he shows himself to be an intellectual poet akin to the group
of Verwey, Dèr Mouw, Van Eyck and to a certain extent also
to Nijhoff. As to form, he is a traditionalist, never a modernist like Van Ostaijen or the early Marsman. His poetry is cerebral, cool and reserved. In his early years he wrote in the
parlando style favoured by *Forum*, often with irony in the
manner of Du Perron. Later he became more lyrical, though

his lyricism is never of an effusive kind; it is always cool and intellectual, basically descriptive. To Vestdijk, poetry is 'a trinity of sound-image-thought, the image being the middle slice, which is the tastiest part of the fish'. This certainly holds for his own poetry, the main element of which is always the imagery. Though a firm friend of Ter Braak's and Du Perron's and an editor of *Forum* in 1934 and 1935, the reservedness of his poetry and his reluctance to lay himself open, made him a slightly uneasy member of the *Forum* group. As a critic he was even more of an outsider. In 1934 he wrote to Marsman: 'I have one-sidedly and for good and all opted for talent, if need be even with a completely inferior personality'. A heresy, so far as *Forum* was concerned. Vestdijk, on his part, later pronounced the whole problem of 'form or fellow', of talent or personality, to be a pseudo-problem: 'talent without personality is not worth talking about, and neither is personality without talent'. In his own criticism he was always concerned in the first place with the work itself, and not with the man behind it. By temperament he was less polemic than Ter Braak and Du Perron, and a great deal more objective. His critiques, especially his long essays on Rilke, Valéry, Kafka, Joyce and Emily Dickinson, are not in the first place professions of friendship or declarations of war, but scholarly introductions to the work under review. He was more sceptical than Ter Braak and Du Perron, and saw more readily the relativity of the various points of view.

Notwithstanding the high value of his poetry and criticism, Vestdijk is known in the first place as a novelist. When an author has written as many novels as Vestdijk has, there is always a strong temptation to divide them into neat categories, either chronologically in an early, middle and late period, or according to subject matter or setting. Vestdijk's novels could be divided into autobiographical novels, historical novels and novels of fantasy, while the remaining ones could be classed, a trifle lamely, as psychological novels. Having gone so far, one might then refine the system and divide the first category into strictly autibiographical novels, such as the series of eight

Anton Wachter novels, and novels that are only partially autobiographical such as *De Koperen Tuin* (The Garden Where the Brass Band Played) or *Het Glinsterend Pantser* (The Glittering Armour). According to their setting, the historical novels could be divided further into Irish novels such as *Ierse Nachten* (Irish Nights) and *De Vijf Roeiers* (The Five Oarsmen), and novels with a Greek or Roman setting such as *Aktaion onder de Sterren* (Actaeon among the Stars), *De Verminkte Apollo* (The Mutilated Apollo), *De Nadagen van Pilatus* (The Latter Days of Pilate). A classification of this kind facilitates the discussion, but one cannot demand much more from it, especially in the case of Vestdijk. In all his novels, whether autobiographical, historical or otherwise, his approach to his characters always remains the same. His main interest is to find an answer to the questions: Who are they? What are they? Why are they what they are? This applies as much to his own *alter ego* Anton Wachter as to Pontius Pilate and Mary Magdalen in *De Nadagen van Pilatus*, to El Greco in *Het Vijfde Zegel* (The Fifth Seal) and to the female pirate Anne Bonney in *Rumeiland* (Rum Island). The autobiographical novels centre just as much on these questions as the historical novels. It is typical of Vestdijk that he mostly chose historical figures of whom important aspects are unknown. El Greco has always been a puzzle, and it has often been wondered what lay behind his style of painting: symbolism, a religious theory, astigmatism? He is a mysterious and problematical figure like Pilate, of whom little is known after his encounter with Christ: Was it just an incident in the life of a Roman official, or did it leave a mark? Anne Bonney, the pirate from Jamaica, is also a riddle. It is known that she existed, there are references to her in historical sources, but what kind of girl she was or what made her take up piracy are questions to which there are no ready answers. Vestdijk's historical novels, then, are not so much concerned with re-creating the past, but rather with discovering the driving-forces behind these mysterious characters. His historical novels are really psychological novels in a historical setting. Though his approach to the characters never varied, he allowed himself a great deal of variation in his approach to the setting. In *Het Vijfde Zegel*, for instance, the reader is given an elaborate picture of seventeenth-century Spain, down to the last detail of dress, food, class distinctions and the philosophical hairsplitting that was the order of the day. In fact, there was so much historical detail that a critic like Ter Braak complained about it and considered it overdone. In *De Nadagen van Pilatus*, published in 1938, that is one year after *Het Vijfde Zegel*, the historical details are reduced to the bare minimum. One has the impression that there is a certain playfulness in Vestdijk's attitude to historical detail: it seems that he wants to show that he can write a historical novel with or without it. After abandoning the abundance of historical detail in the novel about Pilate, he came back to it with a vengeance in *Puriteinen en Piraten* (Puritans and Pirates, 1947), which apart from being a gripping adventure story and a convincing psychological novel, also comes close to being a handbook on sailing vessels in the eighteenth century.

In his very first novel, *Meneer Visser's Hellevaart* (Mr. Visser's Journey to Hell, 1936), Vestdijk probed for the inner life of an insignificant little man, using the technique of 'interior monologue' that Joyce had so spectacularly employed in *Ulysses*. Mr. Visser is an ordinary man, but he lives a secret life in which he is a great and cruel tyrant who models himself on Robespierre. Why is Mr. Visser what he is? Why does he only think in terms of revenge and punishment? Why is he deliberately ruining the life of his wife? Vestdijk follows Visser for twenty-four hours and records all his actions, thoughts and dreams, including half-finished sentences and embryonic notions. Visser is, as it were, baring his subconscious to an imaginary psychiatrist.

Meneer Visser's Hellevaart was the first novel Vestdijk wrote, but not the one that he published first. When it was finished he was asked by his publisher to submit another novel first, as the innermost thoughts of Mr. Visser were often nasty and bound to shock a good many readers. Vestdijk then went back to a large manuscript which he had written in 1933 under the title of *Kind Tussen Vier Vrouwen* (Child Between Four Women), but which had been rejected because of its bulk: it consisted of 940 closely written pages. He rewrote part of it and published this in 1934 as *Terug Tot Ina Damman* (Back To Ina Damman). Though published first, the book was to be the third volume of the series of eight autobiographical novels known as the Anton Wachter novels. It is generally considered the best of the series and more than one critic regards it as Vestdijk's best novel. The book describes the love of Anton Wachter, who is then in his second year in high school, for Ina Damman, who is in first form. One could hardly call it a love story, for Ina Damman has little idea of what is going on inside Anton. The main subject of the book is an analysis of Anton's feeling for the girl, and one would be hard-pressed to find another novel in which a relationship between schoolchildren is given such a razor-sharp analysis. It is a relationship in which little is said and less done, but at the same time it is so powerful that Anton will never be able to rid himself of it. The image of Ina Damman is going to pursue him throughout his life, every new girl he meets is measured against the memories that he retains of Ina, and although she is absent from the later books, they too are dominated by the indelible impression she has made on Anton. In *De Rimpels van Esther Ornstein* (The Wrinkles of Esther Ornstein, 1959), the seventh volume of the series, Vestdijk says of Anton: 'He was not afraid of Nel Blanken, but of Ina Damman he was. Very much so; if one should cut him up, dissect his heart, burn what was left, dissolve the ashes, vaporize the solution, then the residue would be fear of Ina Damman,—or love—and that was the quintessence of Anton Wachter'. Any writer can make a statement of this kind, but Vestdijk is one of the few who can make it ring true. After reading *Terug Tot Ina Damman* one is convinced that this was Anton's one and only great love, that it was an experience never to be repeated during his lifetime and certainly never to be surpassed. Vestdijk achieves this effect

firstly by taking the 'affair' as seriously as it is taken by children of that age. Then, with an extraordinary memory for
mood and atmosphere he succeeds in giving it complete verisimilitude. Furthermore, he places the relationship absolutely
central in the book. Everything Anton does or thinks is related
to it and every detail has a function in the building up of
the situation. The other characters exist only in so far as they
are connected with Anton. Nol Gregoor in his book on the autobiographical background of the Anton Wachter novels, remarks that we have no idea of what the other characters do,
say or think when Anton is not there to see or hear them. He
also makes the observation, and it is a very true one, that
when on one occasion we listen in to a conversation between
Ina and a friend of hers without Anton being present, we re-
gister this as a flaw in the presentation: 'as if', Gregoor says, 'a
member of a choir suddenly begins to sing a solo'.

Although the Anton Wachter novels are Vestdijk's most
strictly autobiographical novels, they are all written from the
same objective point of view that is so characteristic of Vestdijk's work, whether it is poetry, criticism or a novel. Anton
is seen as through a telelens: the details are sharp, but the
distance is long enough to prevent the author from becoming
emotionally involved with his subject. The need of distance is
an essential trait in Vestdijk, so essential and personal that
one also finds it as a trait in Anton. A good example of this
is to be found in Sint Sebastiaan (St. Sebastian), the first volume of the Anton Wachter novels. Anton is going to play
with a little girl of whom he has dreamt for a long time. The
afternoon is a failure, however, 'because she was much too
close'. Love can only exist at a distance, nearness destroys
the illusion. This theme of the distant unattainable woman
occurs in a great many of Vestdijk's novels, from the early
Anton Wachter novels to the novels written in the last decade.
In the last novel of the series, De Laatste kans (The Last
Chance, 1960), it seemed for a moment that Vestdijk was
going to objectify his own writing: Anton Wachter who has
almost finished his medical course, decides to write a book

about his own life, and even quotes by anticipation the opening sentence of *Sint Sebastiaan*. Vestdijk must have thought better of it, though, for no further sequels have appeared. Yet a few books earlier, in *Het Glinsterend Pantser*(1956) he had done something similar by introducing one of the main characters as S. who lives in D.—Vestdijk lived in Doorn for many years—and who is a writer. This novel, with its two sequels *Open Boek* (Open Book, 1957) and *De Arme Heinrich* (Poor Heinrich, 1958), marks the culminating point of Vestdijk's post-war production. Together these three books describe the life of Victor Slingeland, a conductor, who because of a skin disease is constantly frustrated in his relations with others, especially women. Through his friendship with S., it gradually becomes clear that it is his art as much as his skin that creates a distance between him and the others. The initials of Victor Slingeland and S. almost inevitably force the reader to an identification of the musician and the writer with Simon Vestdijk, but Vestdijk does not take the last step and keeps the reader guessing as to the autobiographical basis of the books. These three novels, now known under the collective title of *Symphonie van Victor Slingeland* (Victor Slingeland Symphony) can be regarded as the synthesis of Vestdijk's main themes and motives. As he did in so many other novels, Vestdijk continually probes for the mystery surrounding the life of Slingeland. Why does he sometimes act in such a strange way? Why his sudden, almost hysterical outbursts? Why his apparent cruelty to women? When towards the end of the first volume the disease is revealed, the reader still feels that he has been given only part of the truth. There is rarely one single key to Vestdijk's mysteries, and the following two books show Slingeland to be even more complex than one had been led to believe in the first volume. The theme of the unattainable woman also plays an important part, as do two other favourite themes of Vestdijk: the isolation of the artist, and friendship. The Slingeland novels again show that Vestdijk is at his best when he combines intense personal involvement with cool observation. In the novels that followed he seems less directly involved in the situations and the characters he is exploring. Yet even if these books do not show the same inner necessity, and suffer from a certain gratuitousness, Vestdijk must still be regarded as the greatest craftsman of the modern Dutch novel.

The continuity of Dutch literature was interrupted by the war years. Ter Braak, Du Perron and Marsman died in 1940, while Slauerhoff had died four years earlier. Consequently, when the war was over, two of the most prominent poets and two of the most influential critics had gone. During the German occupation from 1940 until 1945, the Nazis attempted to take control of literature and to steer it on a national-socialist course by setting up in 1942 a 'Kultuurkamer' (Chamber of Culture) of which all writers who wanted to publish were required to be members. The result was that nothing of importance was published between 1942 and 1946. When freedom of publication was restored, it became clear that the generation of post-war novelists distinguished itself in several respects from the pre-war generation. The pre-war writers, especially those who were connected with the *Forum* group, were basically moralists. Their moralism did not always correspond with the norms prescribed by the society in which they lived, but they were concerned with these norms: they accepted or rejected them, they formulated new ones or redefined the old, but in all their work they were constantly preoccupied with their relation to society. They may have appeared at the time to be pessimistic or destructive—in the thirties Ter Braak and Du Perron were not infrequently decried as negativists and immoralists—yet their so-called negative qualities were effectively contradicted by their impassioned defence of the values they cared for. The post-war writers are different. Their starting-point is a realization that life is hopeless and absurd. Moralizing to them has become pointless. They are not interested in psychological analysis but only in representation.

The first post-war writer to demonstrate this was Gerard Kornelis van het Reve, (born in 1923), who in 1947 published his novel *De Avonden* (The Evenings). The book caused a great stir when it was first published because of the frankness with which it depicted the post-war gloom and the despairing attitude to life of the main character. It is a novel entirely without plot. In ten chapters it describes ten evenings in the life of Frits van Egters, a young man who vaguely works in an office but who regards only his evenings as 'life'. Yet life in the evenings is hardly less disconsolate than life at the office. He visits his friends, tries to make conversation by telling sick jokes and gruesome newspaper stories, or he stays at home and is irritated by his parents. He has no real contact with anyone, he takes no interest in anything, but drifts along aimlessly from day to day in a mood of dissatisfaction and frustration. The dreariness of the subject matter recalls the work of the nineteenth-century naturalists of whom Van het Reve may be regarded as a descendant. Yet there is an important difference between him and the naturalists, and that is the directness of his presentation, the lack of elaboration on the development of his character. A naturalist like Emants devoted quite a few pages of *Een Nagelaten Bekentenis* to the youth of Willem Termeer, to the hereditary factors that were responsible for his personality, and to the circumstances under which he grew up. There is nothing of the kind in *De Avonden*. Van het Reve offers no explanations, no comments, no psychological key. He presents Frits van Egters in what he does and what he says, and in the reactions to him of other people. The only information we are given about his 'past' is that he did not finish high school; for the rest, Frits van Egters *is*. Another quality which sets Van het Reve apart from the naturalist writers is his sense of humour. *De Avonden* is a harrowing book, but at times it is terribly funny. Frits van Egters marks the distance that separates him from those around him by using an oddly high-flown style of speaking which also serves as a cover for his own vulnerabilities. The solemnity of his speech provides a wry, ironical, and often very humorous contrast to the ordinariness of his surroundings and the sober functionalism of Van het Reve's descriptive style. After a masterly autobiographical novella *Werther Nieland* (1949), and two volumes of stories, *Tien Vrolijke Verhalen* (Ten Cheerful Stories, 1961) and *Vier Wintervertellingen* (Four Winter Tales, first published in English as *The Acrobat and Other Stories* in 1956), Van het Reve concentrated on a curious form of his own invention, an intermediate form between story and letter. He has published two such volumes, *Op Weg naar het Einde* (On the Way to the End, 1963) and *Nader tot U* (Nearer to Thee, 1966), brilliantly written and highly entertaining literature, undoubtedly, but having much less to say than *De Avonden* or *Werther Nieland*.

Then in 1972 Van het Reve changed course again with the publication of *De Taal der Liefde* (The Language of Love), a book that signalled his return to the novel, though it still combined straight fiction with letter-writing. The book consists of three parts: the first and third sections present the main novel in which a narrator describes his homosexual experiences, often with sadistic overtones, while the central part is made up of a large number of letters addressed to a friend, a contemporary Dutch writer. The function of these letters is to provide a commentary on the novel proper, to explain how it came into being and to throw light on the circumstances under which it was written. The book was a phenomenal success, partly because of its form, its new and effective blending of fact and fiction and its stylistic brilliance, partly also because of its unusually frank treatment of homosexual love. Its success must have spurred on Van het Reve to give more of the same, for within three years he wrote another four novels in the same vein, all dealing with homosexuality and sadism and with what he calls 'Revism': the keenest pleasure is derived vicariously from someone else's enjoyment. Of these four—*Lieve Jongens* (Dear Boys, 1973), *Het Lieve Leven* (Sweet Life, 1974), *Ih Had Hem Lief* (I Loved Him, 1975) and *Een Circusjongen* (A Circus Boy, 1975)—the first is the best, perhaps even better than *De Taal der Liefde,* whereas the others do little more than repeat what had been said in the earlier books. *Lieve Jongens* stands out because of its firm structure and its skilful way of preserving a precarious balance between reality and the fairy-tale elements which Van het Reve—his name now simplified to Gerard Reve—introduced in his later novels. The narrator of *Lieve Jongens* is a latterday male Scheherezade who by telling a tensely drawn-out story tries to arous his friend's sexual emotions because of his own desperate fear of loneliness and lack of love, which in various guises have always been Van het Reve's main themes. *Lieve Jongens* is one of Van het Reve's most melancholy books and has not been equalled by its successors.

Two years after *De Avonden*, Willem Frederik Hermans (born in 1921) published a novel *De Tranen der Acacia's* (The Tears of the Acacias) which met with the same mixture of horror and enthusiasm as *De Avonden*. Needless to say, the horror subsided and before long Hermans was rightly recognized as the most important post-war novelist. The outlook on life of Arthur Muttah, the main character of *De Tranen der Acacia's*, is strikingly similar to that of Frits van Egters. Muttah is just as lost and just as isolated. 'Why doesn't anybody want to have anything to do with me?' he wonders, though without the slightest trace of self-pity. The book is set in Amsterdam during the last months of the war, and Muttah is so much an outsider that he is never sure which side his best friends are on: are they working for the Resistance or for the Germans? Yet although the mentality of Muttah and Egters is very similar, there are basic differences between the two books. In the first place Hermans's novel is much more dynamic than Van het Reve's. In *De Avonden* there is no development, no causal progression of events. All episodes are more or less independent and the chapters could be shuffled around considerably without upsetting the structure of the book. *De Tranen der Acacia's*, on the contrary, is full of intrigues and complications that are dependent on one another. The same difference can be seen in the representation of the characters. Whereas Frits van Egters remains what he is throughout the book, Muttah undergoes changes and is much closer to total defeat at the end of the novel than at the beginning. Another difference between the two novels is to be found in the information which the authors give about their main characters. Van het Reve gives hardly any, whereas Hermans provides several clues: Muttah is an illegitimate child who has never known his mother, is neglected by his father, is brought up by a malicious grandmother etc. Hermans, in other words, is closer to the traditional novel than Van het Reve. He not only gave Muttah more background than Van het Reve gave to Egters, but also more depth. The only positive ambition Frits van Egters had was not to waste the present day as completely as he had done the previous one. Muttah tries hard to establish a certain order in the chaos of his existence, to find a solution to the absurdity. He thinks that the solution may lie in Brussels where his father lives: reunion with his father may give meaning to his life. His urge to go to Brussels and to find shelter in his father's house is not just an incident in the book, but a characteristic theme in the work of Hermans. He often uses a house as a symbol of meaningfulness, as something that might neutralize the chaos. Yet Hermans's houses never provide shelter for very long; they are either pulled down, blown up or being rebuilt, and they always betray those that seek shelter in them. The stories Het Behouden Huis (The House of Refuge) and Paranoia, two of the best stories in modern Dutch and both published in Hermans's collection of stories Paranoia (1953), illustrate this clearly. In the work of Hermans chaos always wins, there is never a lasting solution to the absurdity of life.

Hermans once declared in an interview that he belonged to the category of authors who always write the same book. It is certainly true that his novels and stories often focus on the absurdity of life as their central theme. In 1958 he elaborated this theme in a long and very successful novel, De Donkere Kamer van Damocles (The Dark Room of Damocles). Set in war time again, it deals with a rather insignificant man, Henri Osewoudt, who becomes involved in Resistance work through a mysterious figure named Dorbeck, a man who is Ose-

woudt's very image, only more virile. Osewoudt is arrested
and beaten up by the Germans, he is freed by Resistance
workers, and arrested again. He manages to escape and to
make his way to the liberated southern provinces where he is
immediately arrested by the Dutch who regard him as one of
the most dangerous German agents. The only man able to
vouch for him would be Dorbeck, but Dorbeck is nowhere to
be found. Osewoudt pins his hopes on a roll of film which
should contain photographs of Dorbeck, but when the film is
developed, it only shows Germans. In a daze Osewoudt walks
out of the prison camp and is shot dead by the guards. Reality
and hallucination are interwoven in this novel in a way that
recalls Kafka. Hermans himself made light of the connection
with Kafka and instead pointed out a resemblance between
Osewoudt and Kleist's *Michael Kohlhaas*. The plot of the novel was suggested by the so-called 'Englandspiel', a series of
espionage and counter-espionage events during the war in
which it was also difficult to determine the dividing line between hallucination and reality. All Osewoudt's actions seem
perfectly meaningful to himself, but in a larger context they
prove to be utterly meaningless. Everything he does is given a
different interpretation by the people he comes in contact
with—the Germans, the Dutch, the English—until in the
end he cannot extricate himself. Compared to Arthur Muttah,
Osewoudt makes a more forceful effort to give meaning to his
life: 'He was going to take hold of everything that might still
happen with *this* passion, as if life were an enormous woman
whose sweaty smell caused nothing but an invincible ecstasy
in a really virile man. Not just once, but always, without taking rest. Never sleep again'. These last three words, *Nooit
Meer Slapen*, became the title of a new novel, published in
1966 and dealing with an even more determined character
than Osewoudt. In this novel, Hermans—who until 1973 was a
Reader in Physical Geography in the University of Groningen—
describes a geologist on an expedition to Finmarken where he
hopes to find evidence for a hypothesis that certain craters were
caused by meteorites. But in the world of Hermans the impor-

tant things can never be found: Osewoudt cannot find
Dorbeck, Muttah cannot find shelter in his father's house, and
the geologist Alfred Issendorf does not succeed in finding the
proof he is looking for. Having come to the end of the search,
there is nothing but chaos. 'Mankind thinks in terms of an
order which does not really exist, and is blind to the original
chaos. There is only one real word: chaos'. Hermans wrote this
in 1953 in the *Preambule* (Preamble) to *Paranoia*, and he has
consistently made this notion the focal point of his work. No
other writer in the Netherlands or Belgium has given expression to his view of life with so much persistence, intelligence
and skill as Hermans has. There is no doubt that on the basis
of these books he is the major novelist of the post-war years.

Hermans and Van het Reve have sometimes been likened
to the 'angry young men' of the post-war English novel, but
it is a comparison that is quite false. No-one could deny
that they were young and angry when they wrote their first
books, but that is about the only similarity between their
work and that of, say, Kingsley Amis or John Wain. Hermans
and Van het Reve present themselves and their views on society in a much more direct manner than Amis and Wain do,
and never hide behind the mask of a comic hero. The picaresque element is absent from their work, as are the gratuitous
happy endings. Though they do not lack humour, it is not of
the whimsical kind of the English writers, but sardonic, grim
and often black. Their anger is considerable, expecially Hermans's, and especially in his novel *Ik Heb Altijd Gelijk* (I
Am Always Right, 1951), and in his collection of polemic criticism *Mandarijnen op Zwavelzuur* (Mandarins in Sulphuric
Acid, 1964). In the equally corrosive *Boze Brieven van
Bijkaart* (Bijkaart's Angry Letters, 1977) Hermans made
scathing attacks on a large assortment of writers, politicians
and academics. His polemics recall those of Multatuli and
Du Perron: they display the same virtuosity and the same
doggedness in the pursuit of his victims.

The polemical element also entered his novels, first *De
God Denkbaar Denkbaar de God* (The God Denkbaar

Denkbaar the God, 1956), a hallucinatory surrealist book, and later its sequel *Het Evangelie van O. Dapper Dapper* (The Gospel according to O. Dapper Dapper, 1973). In these novels the polemics are incidental and fairly light-hearted; they poke fun at their targets without trying to demolish them. But in his latest two novels, *Herinneringen van een Engelbewaarder* (Memoirs of a Guardian Angel, 1971) and *Onder Professoren* (Among Professors, 1975), the approach is quite different, especially when compared with that of the novels he wrote in the forties, fifties and sixties. In his early books Hermans had portrayed life as an absurdity and his central characters as victims: Arthur Muttah, Henri Osewoudt and Alfred Issendorf put up a fight against the chaos in which they found themselves, but however hard they tried to win, ended as losers. Hermans did not laugh at them or attack them—if anything, he showed compassion for their plight. All these characters gained the reader's sympathy. In the two last-mentioned novels, however, it is difficult to feel such sympathy for any of the protagonists: they are scheming, self-righteous, dishonest, mediocre, pompous, stuffy or phoney. The tragic qualities of the earlier novels has been reduced to irony. The geologist Alfred Issendorf lost his compass, broke his pencils, searched for elusive aerial photographs which turned out to be useless when they were eventually located, but emerged from the debâcle with the dignity of despair, accepting, as he said, that life has to be lived 'blind', without landmarks. There are echoes of this in the latest novels, but they are no more than echoes. In *Herinneringen van een Engelbewaarder* the pompous publisher ceremoniously closes the gates of his firm: 'Until Hitler has been hanged from the highest tree, Erik Losekaat will not publish another book. Damn, the lock doesn't work'. The irony of the situation makes Losekaat into a figure of fun, but it does not give him the stature of a tragic hero. There is more humour in these books, but their dramatic impact is weaker.

A third post-war writer, Harry Mulisch (born in 1927),

started off more good-humouredly than Hermans and Van het
Reve. His first novel, *Archibald Strohalm* (1952), playfully and
rather baroquely describes an ineffectual artist in his struggle
with his art and with the world around him. The book contains
a good deal of social criticism, but at the same time it shows a
much more optimistic view of life than the novels of Van het
Reve and Hermans do. After two more novels, *De Diamant*
The Diamond, 1954) and *Het Zwarte Licht* (the Black Light,
1956), and some volumes of short stories, Mulisch published
Het Stenen Bruidsbed (The Stone Bridal Bed, 1959) which so
far is his most ambitious novel. It is the story of an American
dentist, Norman Corinth, who attends a congress in Desden,
the city that he bombed when he was a pilot during the war. He
has a brief love-affair with a German girl, Hella, who has lived
through the bombing and now, as a member of the organizing
committee of the congress, shows Corinth around the town.
Their relationship is doomed from the beginning, love and
friendship are killed by the memories of the war. Corinth
tries to find a meaning in the bombing of the town, but he
cannot find any. He tries to regard it as part of history—the
meaningful past—, but it remains what Mulisch calls 'anti-
history', a meaningless episode in the past that has no
connection with the present. The optimism of Hella, who is
dedicated to rebuilding the city and reforming society, is
pointless to Corinth, but Mulisch gives as much weight to her
belief in the future as he does to Corinth's feeling of futility.

In later years Mulisch gave an account of his childhood in
Voer voor Psychologen (Fodder for Psychologists, 1961),
wrote a reportage of the Eichmann trial in *De Zaak 40/61*
(The Affair 40/61, 1962), gave an analysis of the Dutch Provo
Movement and the disturbances in Amsterdam during 1965
and 1966 in *Bericht aan de Rattenkoning* (Report to the King
Rat, 1966), collected a number of autobiographical, political
and satirical pieces in *Wenken voor de Jongste Dag* (Hints for
Doomsday, 1967) and gave his sympathetic view of the Cu-
ban revolution in *Het Woord bij de Daad* (The Word to the
Deed, 1968). Having begun as a good-natured and playful

critic of society, Mulisch became much angrier in these later
books and developed into one of the most vocal opponents of
the Establishment.

The sixties were lean years for Mulisch as a novelist and it
was not until 1970 when his next novel, *De Verteller* (The
Narrator), was published. It was a novel with a vengeance,
and it soon became known as one of the most cryptic ever
written in Dutch. Basically it is the story of a man who at the
age of forty-three looks back at his youth, but the narrative is
constantly interrupted by seemingly unconnected fragments of
text, such as a long cut-up letter, parodies of a Dutch
children's book, of Karl May, Ian Fleming and science
fiction, while it is complicated further by frequent name-
changes and time-shifts, not to mention a surfeit of
mysterious allusions, puns and other word-games. Confusion
among readers and critics was profound and Mulisch felt
compelled to write an explanatory book, *De Verteller Verteld*
(The Narrator Explained, 1971), in which he put his cards on
the table, disclosed his sources and elaborated on what he had
been trying to achieve. In the same year he stated in an
interview: 'If you ask me why the book has this fragmented
form, then the answer is because the world is fragmented. *De
Verteller* reflects this. The chronological form of (Hermans's)
De Engelbewaarder is not acceptable to me: in my own life I
see no evidence of this either'.

Yet Mulisch did not continue in this manner: the structure
of his next novel, *Twee Vrouwen* (Two Women, 1975), was so
orderly and clear-cut that it provided a striking contrast with
that of the previous novel. It is one of the few fictional
treatments in Dutch of a lesbian relationship. Mulisch presents
it as a tender love story which at first seems to hold great
promise for the partners until it founders on the desire of the
older woman to have a child, primarily in order to become
independent of her mother: 'When you have always felt a
daughter, there is only one way of freeing yourself of your
mother, and that is by becoming one yourself'. This is a
variation on the oedipal theme of mother, son and father

which recurs throughout the work of Mulisch, from his early books to the title story of *Oude Lucht* (Old Air), published in 1977.

Though much of the work of Jan Wolkers, born in 1925, is concerned with opposing the dominant father, it lacks the oedipal overtones which are present in Mulisch. Wolkers's opposition was mainly directed at his Calvinist upbringing, at the repression of sexuality, and in general at the established values of the older generation. One finds this fiercely expressed in his first stories, *Serpentina's Petticoat* (1960), in his first novel, *Kort Amerikaans* (Crew Cut, 1961), which also reflects his training as a sculptor, in a further volume of short stories, *Gesponnen Suiker* (Candy Floss, 1963), and at its best in *Terug naar Oegstgeest* (Oegstgeest Revisited, 1965), in which a man of forty revisits his parental home. The book is written as a search for the self: the narrator is uneasy about his blurred sense of indentity and tries to give it sharper definition by confronting the memories of his youth with his present-day appreciation of the situation at home. The tension of the book, and the conviction it carries, are in the first place due to its composition, which in a very skilful way alternates chapters on the past with those on the present, but also to a spare style which avoids the shock-tactics of the earlier books and the boisterous tone of the later ones. Four years after this Wolkers scored a spectacular popular success with *Turks Fruit* (Turkish Delight, 1969), a full-blooded account of a tragic love story, the writing of which was marred by exhibitionism and sentimentality. In his later novels, *De Walgvogel* (The Dodo, 1974) and *De Kus* (The Kiss, 1977), Wolkers went further along the road of melodrama and gave free rein to his ever-present inclination to overstate and overwrite.

The first important post-war novelist to emerge on the Belgian side was Louis Paul Boon who, born in 1912, is considerably older than the Van het Reve-Hermans-Mulisch generation. He published his first books during the war—*De Voorstad Groeit* (The Suburb Grows, 1943) and *Abel Gholearts* (1944)—, but his three main works were published in the fifties: *De Kapellekensbaan* (Little Chapel Road, 1953), its sequel *Zomer te Ter-Muren* (Summer at Ter-Muren, 1956), and *Wapenbroeders* (Brothers in Arms, 1955). Together these three books constitute the most successful attempt in the Low Countries to find a new form for the novel. In the first two novels, Boon experimented with a simultaneous representation of various layers of time. The main story, that of Ondine, Oscar and Valeer, runs from the end of the nineteenth century to the outbreak of the Second World War, and is constantly evaluated and commented upon from the situation of the time of writing, while a continuous counterpoint is provided by the medieval tale of Reynard the Fox. At the same time, Boon filled out the story of Ondine with a large slice of the history of socialism in Flanders. Both novels are teeming with characters and chock-full of events. Boon is not a cool observer, but a deeply involved commentator who exposes the evils of society without pulling his punches. He can be bitter and angry and cynical, but also compassionate, gentle and enthusiastic. At heart he is an idealist, 'searching', as he says at the beginning of *De Kapellekensbaan* 'for the values that really count'. In *Wapenbroeders* he developed the counterpoint story of Reynard the Fox into a novel in its own right, mixing past and present, deliberately obscuring the boundaries between the world of the animals and the world of man, and cleverly weaving in his own comments. His next novel, *De Bende van Jan de Lichte* (The Gang of Jan de Lichte, 1957), was presented in a more orthodox and objective form. In a way it is a historical novel, centering on a Flemish robber-chief who in the middle of the eighteenth century tried to organize an uprising of paupers. In the course of the novel, the emphasis shifts slightly away from the exploits of Jan de Lichte and it becomes clear that Boon wanted to do more than just write an entertaining picaresque novel. The book develops into a subtly allegorical representation of revolution in general, from its idealistic beginnings to its corruption by human greed. It is Boon's achievement that he managed to bring this off without depriving the book of its narrative power. Although Boon rejects most aspects of contemporary society and has consequently been condemned as a nihilist, he is in the last analysis a moralist, an unconventional one, to be sure, yet a man who stands up for what he believes to be right and who attacks what he detests. This was also apparent from his *Pieter Daens* (1971), one of the few successful examples of what Truman Capote in 1966 termed the 'non-fiction novel'. It relates the life of a Flemish journalist who at the end of the nineteenth century played an important part in the organised labour movement in Belgium. In this book, Boon's social consciousness, his anger at the inequalities of society and his compassion for the underdog combined in a most felicitous way with his gifts as a storyteller to produce the most impressive non-fiction novel to date. He is undoubtedly one of the greatest narrative talents the Low Countries have yet produced.

Moralism and narration are more conventionally combined in the work of Marnix Gijsen (pseudonym of J.A.Goris). He was born in Antwerp in 1899, which makes him a contemporary of Vestdijk and Walschap, of Marsman and Van Ostaijen, rather than of Boon or Hermans or Mulisch. In 1925 Gijsen published a volume of expressionist poetry, *Het Huis* (The House), then wrote literary criticism and travel books, and after the war suddenly developed into a prolific novelist. His first novel, *Joachim van Babylon* (1947), struck a new note in Dutch literature, yet was close enough to tradition to become an immediate success. It is an ironic account of the story of the chaste Susanna, who is accused of adultery by two old men but saved in the nick of time by Daniel. The story is told by her husband Joachim who has suffered a great deal from her beauty, chastity and virtue: 'For thirty years I was married to Virtue.—It was not funny at all'. The book may not be an autobiographical novel in the strict sense of the word, yet there is no doubt that the opinions and judgments of Joachim frequently coincide with Gijsen's own. Quotations from contemporary writers, thinly disguised under distorted names, provide a link with the present and are as it were an invitation to look for the author behind the portrait of Joachim. Through Joachim, Gijsen settles accounts with a good many things: beauty, philosophy, religion, and society in general. He does so almost as devastatingly as Boon does, but in a deceptively mild and ironical tone of voice, and without any apparent anger. Gijsen is a moralist, but, like Boon, a moralist without any dogma. In each new novel he gropes for moral certainties, for norms that might take the place of the religious values that he discarded when he broke with Roman Catholicism. In *Goed en Kwaad* (Good and Evil, 1950) he went furthest in his rejection of the traditional moral code: the main character murders his friend and justifies the act to himself as a necessary act of self-liberation. The book is set in New York where Gijsen lived for many years as Director of the Belgian Government Information Center. It was the first of a series of novels which are set in America and which are perhaps his best work. The most entertaining one of the series is *De Vleespotten van Egypte* (The Flesh Pots of Egypt, 1952). Here, too, the main character is a Flemish immigrant whose view of America is nostalgically coloured by his memories of Europe. He is an emigrant of the type that is 'very happy aber nicht glücklich', until he comes to terms with the country through his marriage to an American girl. Whereas Gijsen's American novels often deal with the ambivalent feelings of the European towards the New World, his Flemish novels often centre on childhood experiences, as in *Telemachus in het Dorp* (Telemachus in the Village, 1948). Basically there is no difference between the two categories of novels: they are all concerned with the search for essential moral values and at the same time show the hand of a master narrator.

Apart from Louis Paul Boon, it was Hugo Claus who steered the post-war Flemish novel in a new direction. Born in Bruges in 1929 he is much younger than Boon, and is closest in age, though not in literary approach, to Harry Mulisch. His first novel, *De Metsiers* (1950), was a derivative work with Faulkner written all over it, from the choice of characters to the mode of narration, each character in turn telling his side of the story. Claus was not yet twenty when he wrote this book and he soon shook off Faulkner's influence. In later novels such as *De Hondsdagen* (The Dog Days, 1952), *De Koele Minnaar* (The Cool Lover, 1956), *De Verwondering* (Wonderment, 1962) and *Omtrent Deedee* (About Deedee, 1963), he established himself, in fact, as one of the most original novelists in the Low Countries. His novels are as far removed from the traditional psychological novel as Van het Reve's *De Avonden* or Boon's *De Kapellekensbaan*. Yet Claus does not dispense with plot as Van het Reve and Boon do. On the contrary, his novels are highly organized structures with subtle, often cryptic, and sometimes over-elaborate ramifications of plot and intrigue. The break with the traditional novel manifests itself primarily in the point of view of the author. In *Omtrent Deedee*, for instance, he employed a narrative technique similar to that in his first novel by presenting the tensions that are developing at a family reunion as seen through the eyes of the various members of the family. It is a technique that aims at a greater measure of objectivity in the presentation of the situation than the conventional narrative does, and objectivity, dispassionateness and coolness are the best words to characterize the novels of Claus, even if his prose is often more poetic than that of his contemporaries. Claus is in fact, as much a poet as a novelist. Coolness is also one of the main characteristics of his personages, who are often 'indifferents', adolescents who look at the world of the adults as something absurd and corrupt. His coolness precludes any expression of the anger to be found in Hermans and Boon. It only shows through in the situations which he presents, in his 'world', which is no less chaotic and absurd than that of Hermans. Claus does not argue against the chaos, he only observes, registers, represents: his characters make no attempt to find a solution.

Some of Claus's novels, especially the later ones, show evidence of a tendency, found generally in the modern novel, to give greater emphasis to the exploration of a situation than to analysis of character. What Claus places before his readers is the complexity of events rather than that of the human mind, somewhat in the manner of the practitioners of the 'nouveau roman' in France. In *Omtrent Deedee* he had already considerably moved in this direction, and in *Schaamte* (Shame, 1972) and *Jessica!* (1977) he went further. *Schaamte* is the more important of the two and describes a Belgian television unit which is filming a passion play on a tropical island. The members of the group are shallow, if not empty-headed people, who have no understanding at all of the surroundings they are working in. Claus deliberately refrained from making them into what E. M. Forster used to call 'round characters': he pared down characterization to the bare minimum and made analysis of the situation the focal point of the novel.

Claus is certainly the most versatile writer of his generation. He is not only a poet, a novelist and a short-story writer, but also a painter, a writer of film scenarios—*Het Mes* (The Knife) and *De Vijanden* (The Enemies)— and a very success-ful playwright. It is noteworthy and gratifying that after a long barren period prominent writers in Belgium and the Netherlands are showing a renewed interest in writing for the theatre. True, in the pre-war years Ter Braak had written a play, as had Slauerhoff, Walschap and Bordewijk, while Nijhoff had produced a series of three religious verse dramas, published together under the title of *Het Heilige Hout* (The Sacred Wood, 1950). But these were exceptions and none of these works can be regarded as a major contribution to the theatre. Neither in Belgium, nor in the Netherlands can one speak of a significant dramatic tradition after the death of Herman Heijermans. The post-war writers made a more per-sistent effort. Van het Reve has as yet only one play to his name, *Commissaris Fennedy,* but Hermans has published *Drie Drama's* (Three Dramas), a screenplay, *De Woeste Wandeling* (The Wild Hike), and two television plays, *King Kong* and *Periander,* while Mulisch has written *De Knop* (The Button), *Tanchelijn* and *Oidipous, Oidipous.* Claus is the most prolific playwright of this group with an *oeuvre* of many plays of which *Een Bruid in de Morgen* (A Bride in the Morning), *Suiker* (Sugar), *De Dans van de Reiger* (The Dance of the Heron), *Vrijdag* (Friday), *De Spaanse Hoer* (The Spanish Whore) and *Pas de deux* are the most important.

The novel of situation, pioneered by Claus in Belgium, was also practised in the Netherlands, though with a difference. In some novels by Gerrit Krol (born in 1934), characterization is explicitly presented as problematic. In *Het Gemillimeterde Hoofd* (The Closely Cropped Head, 1967), he wrote: 'Time: 19.30. Question: would I be able to describe Marie, her face, in such a way that the reader would recognize her in the street?', and in *De Chauffeur Verveelt Zich* (The Driver is Bored, 1973) the narrator comments: 'Everything about Peggy is exterior, just as in my own case'. This recalls Hugo von Hofmannsthal's thesis: 'Die Tiefe musz man verstecken. Wo? An die Oberfläche', a quotation which recurs frequently in modern criticism and which might have been the starting-point of *Een Avond in Amsterdam* (An Evening in Amsterdam, 1971) by K. Schippers (pseudonym of G. Stigter, born in 1936). The book consists of ten conversations between the author and a friend who works in an Amsterdam office. It is a book that cannot be categorized easily: it is not a novel in the accepted sense, nor a volume of short stories, nor a collection of conventional interviews. It is a particularly obstinate attempt to reconstruct a small segment of reality: the reality of a man who leaves his office at ten to six and then walks home, performing a large number of habitual and automatic actions about which he is remorselessly questioned by his interviewer. It is an extreme, but at the same time very successful example of 'profundity hidden on the surface', as the book manages to give as full a portrait of the protagonist as a traditional psychological novel could have hoped to do.

In the work of Gerrit Krol and several others of his generation one also finds evidence of essayistic and documentary elements penetrating the novel. As in other literatures there is a notable shift from fiction to non-fiction for which

the term defictionalization has been used. The process is not
entirely new and non-fiction elements have been present in the
novel for quite some time. In the middle of the nineteenth
century Multatuli blended fact and fiction in *Minnebrieven*
and *Ideën* as well as in *Max Havelaar,* and more recently it
can be seen in the novels of the neo-realist writers of the
thirties such as Jef Last (*Zuiderzee,* 1934) and M. Revis
(*8.100.000 m³ Zand,* 1931), and during the last decades in the
work of Norman Mailer, Michel Butor, John Berger and many
others abroad and in the Low Countries.

Krol used non-fiction elements—mainly mathematical
formulae and proofs—not in order to defictionalize the novel,
but, on the contrary, to place fiction in a new perspective.
Others have lost their belief in the possibility or desirability of
writing within the traditional forms. Jacques Firmin Vogelaar
regards traditional language and literature as an obstacle to
social reform and therefore set out to dismantle both in
Kaleidiafragmenten (1970), a collage of narrative fragments,
quotations, illegible typescript and unconnected sentences,
served by an index that is symbolically useless as the pages of
the book are not numbered. Not all experimenters attacked
the novel in such a hostile manner, even though they may
greatly distrust the validity of traditional form. Bert
Schierbeek, in *De Derde Persoon* (The Third Person, 1955),
tried to blur the distinction between prose and poetry; Jef
Geeraerts used the form of a diary for his fierce outbursts
about his years in the Congo (Zaïre) in *Gangreen 1* (Gangrene
1, 1968) and *Gangreen 2* (1972), and the epistolary form in
Tien Brieven Rondom Liefde en Dood (Ten Letters About
Love and Death, 1971); Ivo Michiels 'depersonalized' the
novel and substituted types and 'masks' for traditional
character in *Het Boek Alfa* (The Book Alpha, 1963), while
Daniel Robberechts went even further in eliminating character
in *Tegen het Personage* (Against Character, 1968) and
Aankomen in Avignon (Arriving in Avignon, 1970).

Such radical experimenters are, however, a minority
and most writers still stay away from defictionalization, de-

personalization and the destruction of tradtion, witness the
work of A. Alberts, J. M. A. Biesheuvel, Willem Brakman,
Andreas Burnier, Maarten 't Hart, F.B. Hotz, Frans Kellen-
donk, Mensje van Keulen, Hannes Meinkema, Henk Romijn
Meijer, Doeschka Meijsing, A. Koolhaas, Ward Ruyslinck,
Jan Siebelink, Jos Vandeloo, to mention only a few very
diverse contemporary writers.

In poetry, the war arrested the development of the literature
of the thirties as dramatically as it broke the continuity of
prose. After the death of Slauerhoff and Marsman, and as a
result of the near-silence of Nijhoff and Bloem, Adriaan
Roland Holst provided one of the few links with pre-war
poetry. Another link was formed by the poets beloning to the
group of *Criterium* (Criterion), a journal that was established
in 1940, only a few months before the German invasion.
Criterium did not represent any particular view of life or
literature as, for instance, *De Beweging* and *Forum* did,
but served as a meeting place for poets of diverse creeds.
With the advent of the 'Kultuurkamer' in 1942, *Criterium*
ceased publication. When it was resurrected in 1945, most
of its original contributors—Eduard Hoornik, M. Vasalis,
Adriaan Morriën, Bertus Aafjes—returned to it, thus
providing a certain continuity with what Hoornik called
their 'romantic-rationalist poetry'. In the early years after
the war it became clear, though, that the greatest talent of the
group and one of the greatest talents of modern Dutch poetry
in general, was Gerrit Achterberg.

Few poets have devoted themselves so exclusively to poetry
as Achterberg did. He never wrote any prose, no novels,
stories or criticism, he did not belong to any movement and
never took part in the politics of literature. Born in 1905, he
published his first volume, *Afvaart* (Departure) in 1931, and
from that date until his death in 1962, he gave all his creative
energy to one of the most extraordinary experiments in poetry: the creation of a world in which the death of the beloved
would be negated. In poem upon poem and volume upon volume he expressed his hopes and fears, his belief that his po-

etry might bring her back to him, and also his disbelief and his disappointment in the power of 'the word'. In his second volume, *Eiland der Ziel* (Island of the Soul, 1939), the tone is positive and optimistic, and a great number of poems give evidence of his conviction that the power of his poetry will make a reunion possible. In the next volume, *Dead End* (1940), the optimism breaks, and gives way to a feeling of inadequacy. In the course of Achterberg's poetry, collected in four volumes under the general title of *Cryptogamen* (Cryptogamia, 1946—1961), the notion of 'the beloved' gradually expanded, and the 'you' and 'thou' to whom the poems were addressed with such great frequency, were no longer related only to the beloved who had died, but also to love, to death or to God, or even to the poem itself. Achterberg's poetry, in fact, is addressed to a complex notion of which the beloved, love, death, God, poetry, Beauty and the Absolute are all aspects. Sometimes it is a romantically tinted, absolute, unattainable ideal, at other times it takes on an aspect of mysticism through the poet's aspiration to identify himself with it. Only a great poet can pursue the one theme for thirty years and throughout twenty-five volumes without becoming a bore, and Achterberg must be counted among the great. In creating his private world he called upon all natural—and according to some: unnatural—resources of the language. His attempt to define the complexity of 'the beloved' made heavy demands upon the language and led to unusual syntactical constructions and many neologisms, some of which do not even fit into the normal categories of parts of speech, such as 'gingend', a present participle derived from a past tense. Equally heavy demands were made upon imagery, and one field after another was systematically explored in the search for images with which to approach 'the beloved'. In the first volume the imagery was chiefly taken from nature, but after that various fields of science and scholarship were mined to provide new images: mathematics, chemistry, physics, biology, technology, photography, archaeology, philology, philosophy, religion, economics, and the list is not complete. Some critics

have protested against Achterberg's use of scientific terms and
have condemned them as non-poetic, much in the same way
as some nineteenth-century critics complained of the non-
poetic imagery of Wordsworth, Coleridge and Shelley. It
would be more to the point to state that Achterberg has
proved once and for all that there is no such thing as a non-
poetic image. If one of the tasks of the poet is 'to hold the
language to ransom', as Adriaan Roland Holst said, then
Achterberg certainly exacted the highest price. Though his
poetry is not entirely isolated from the pre-war tradition—
one can point to influences from Leopold, Roland Holst and
Marsman—it was new enough to be regarded as the beginning of a new period, especially in its use of imagery and in
its emphasis on the act and function of poetry. In the early
fifties when a number of young poets grouped themselves under the banner of Experimentalism and turned against the
poetry of their predecessors, they singled out Achterberg as
the only one of the previous generation whose work had
opened up new perspectives.

In between Achterberg and the Experimentalists, by age
and by work, stands Leo Vroman, born in 1915. In the heat
of the Experimentalist revolution he seems at first to have
been rather overlooked. In Simon Vinkenoog's anthology *Ato-
naal* (Atonal), which appeared in 1951 and may be regarded
as the first manifestation of the Experimentalists as a group,
Vroman's name was absent, whereas Gerrit Achterberg, Paul
van Ostaijen, Pierre Kemp and Herman Gorter were all given
a mention as poets who had left the beaten track. Yet Vroman is as experimental as the best of them and one of the
most original phenomena in modern poetry. What distinguishes him immediately from all his contemporaries is the curiously personal tone of his work: he uses 'I' as frequently as
Achterberg uses 'you'. He creates a very intimate relationship
between himself and the reader, whom he invites into his private life, and tells about his wife Tineke and his two daughters, about what he thinks of America where he works as a
biologist, and what of the Netherlands which he left at the

outbreak of the war. Vroman often gives the impression of stripping himself bare in front of his readers, but he never gives away the last secret and does not reveal to what extent the 'I' of the poem is identical with the Leo Vroman who wrote it.

There are several sides to Vroman's poetry. It can be cheerful, humorous and funny, but also macabre, cynical or full of fear. Vroman appears to keep open house in his poetry, radiating sweetness and light, showering the reader with love and compassion, sometimes to the point of sentimentality. Yet on other occasions he will slam the door in your face and look at you with the eyes of a very unsentimental biologist who sees man as a pathetic being, ineffectual and oddly put together. Linguistically, Vroman is the most inventive of the post-war poets, at times devising his own syntax and coining neologisms that are even more difficult to decode than Achterberg's. Yet the basis of his poetry is, like Achterberg's, rational, and that is what sets him apart from the Experimentalists proper who began to publish in the early fifties.

The poetry of the Experimentalists is characterized in the first place by the dominant place taken by imagery. What the poets of this group had in common was impatience with the poetry of the thirties and forties, especially the rational poetry of *Forum* and after. Against the poetry of reason they placed a poetry of spontaneity and intuition, a poetry that would circumvent logic and reason with the force of imagery. Their poetry does not argue or explain, it does not narrate or describe, but it progresses by leaps and bounds from image to image. A poem, one of their spokesmen has said, should be a gathering of images. The Experimentalists were no longer interested in the 'confessional' poetry of the older generation in which the poet confided to the reader his private opinions, his joys and his miseries. Neither did they want to be thinkers or teachers or moralists. Their aim was to represent 'the reality of this time', distorted as little as possible by the interpretation of the poet. They went back to a certain extent to the intuitive writing of the Dadaists, and when they started off they invoked quite a number of names in support of their ideas: Ezra Pound, Hans Arp, Paul Eluard, René Char, Henri Michaux, Antonin Artaud. They had the feeling that Dutch poetry was lagging behind and they wanted to bring it in line with developments abroad. Yet the group preserved a typically Dutch character and in their technical achievements, especially their exploration of the function and the potentialities of imagery, they owed a larger debt to Achterberg and Vroman, and at a further remove to Van Ostaijen and Gezelle, than to any of their foreign godfathers.

When the group made its first appearance, it gave the impression of forming a solid front, just as the poets of the Eighties had done. The newness of their work obscured the individual differences. In the years that have since passed, however, the group proved to be no more homogeneous than most other literary groups. As a group, said one sceptical critic, they were just a number of poets who had given up capital letters, full stops and commas. It subsequently became clear that Lucebert (pseudonym of L. J. Swaanswijk, born in 1924), a painter as well as a poet, was far and away the greatest talent of the group and one of the most versatile poets of the last decade. He can be a cool observer of the world around him, as well as a tender lyricist or a devastating satirist; he can be passionately involved with society or sublimely detached; he can be mocking, or angry, or humorous. In his poems the images flash past or accumulate slowly. More than in any other poet of the Experimentalist group, the images are the essence of his poetry, and have become entirely autonomous. The one calls forth the other, and they are bound together by subtle sound-effects and by the repetition of rhythmical patterns. The tone of his poetry ranges from a shout to a whisper. Much of his poetry, as he has said himself, should be read aloud in order to achieve an effect. His torrents of words sometimes recall Dylan Thomas, but he has also written poems that are as economical as a Japanese haiku. He is a man of extremes, a poet of grand gestures. The demands that he makes upon the associative faculties of his readers are great, particularly in his early volumes *Triangel in de Jungle* (Triangle in the Jungle, 1951) and *Apocrief* (Apocryphal, 1952). In later volumes such as *Van de Afgrond en de Lucht-mens* (About the Abyss and the Air Man, 1953) and *Amulet* (1957) his diction became simpler and his imagery more transparent. On the whole, the poems became quieter, even more traditional, without, however, losing their satirical bite, their irony and their humour.

After the first united assault on tradition, every one of the Experimentalists—Simon Vinkenoog. Jan Elburg, Jan Han-lo, Hans Andreus, Remco Campert, Bert Schierbeek, Sybren Polet,Gerrit Kouwenaar, Hugo Claus, Paul Snoek—has gone his own way. Some, like Jan Elburg, have remained true to the original ideas; others, like Hans Andreus, have returned to a more traditional form, others again. like Gerrit Kouwenaar, developed a more intellectual poetry.

Besides the imagist and associative poetry of the Experi-mentalists, the fifties also saw the emergence of a strongly realist movement in poetry, represented in the first instance by the journals *Gard-Sivik* (Civic Guard) in Belgium and *Barbarber* in the Netherlands. The poets connected with these journals opted for a poetry that was, in the words of Armando (born in 1929) 'the result of a personal selection from reality'. They regarded isolating a section of reality as a means of intensifying it and thereby making it into poetry. Armando gave a good illustration of this approach in his volume *September in de Trein* (September in the Train, 1963) in which he reproduced a number of conversations overheard in a train, without any comment or interpretation. The theory underlying this kind of poetry is that selecting has the same value as making. Poetry, in this view, no longer has anything to do with self-expression, but should only draw attention to the reality around us. In its pure form this poetry of 'ready-mades' has a tendency to wear out rather quickly, and there-fore the poets soon began to add another dimension to their samples of isolated reality. Armando's cycle *September in de*

Trein ends with the lines:

- wat slingert dit rijtuig, hè.
- nou.
- je kan merken dat het het laatste is.
- ja.
- ja, d'r zit niks meer achter, hè. [9]

It is a very simple dialogue, humorous perhaps because of its very banality, but it assumes an extra dimension of meaning because of its end position in the volume and its built-in exhortation not to look for anything behind it. Poets such as C. Buddingh' (born in 1918) and J. Bernlef (pseudonym of H. J. Marsman, born in 1937) have achieved impressive results with this technique of giving ready-made elements a specific function within the poem.

In their attitude to reality, the poets of *Gard-Sivik* and *Barbarber* were rebelling against the imagist bias of the experimentalist poetry of the fifties. In their own work there was a marked return to narration and description, to logic and reason. *Barbarber* resisted the Expermentalists from its inception in 1958, while *Gard-Sivik* in 1964 demonstrated its farewell to the Movement of the Fifties by depicting on its cover a traffic sign with the number 50 cancelled by a bold stroke.

The poets of these journals were not the only ones to oppose the Experimentalists, for in 1957 the new periodical *Tirade* had attracted another group of poets who, without aggressive manifestos, quietly pursued a line of direct and unembellished poetry, not as radically realist as that of *Gard-Sivik* and *Barbarber*, more rational and at the same time more lyrical than that of the Experimentalists. The *Tirade* poets—of whom Jan Emmens (1924-1971), Hanny Michaelis (born in 1922),

[9] - isn't this carriage swaying about!
- I'll say.
- you can tell it's the last one.
- yes.
- yes, there is nothing behind it, is there?

Judith Herzberg (born in 1934) and Rutger Kopland (pseudonym of R. H. van den Hoofdakker, born in 1934) are the most prominent—rarely use ready-mades, but they do observe everyday reality closely and avoid all grandiloquence or poetic intoxication. In a sense they can be regarded as heirs to the legacy of *Forum*, after the journal *Libertinage*, which had been its trustee since 1948, ceased publication in 1953.

In the sixties the Forum tradition was vigorously opposed by a new journal, *Merlyn*, which between 1962 and 1966 sought to replace the personalist attitude to criticism by an ergocentric approach in the manner of Paul van Ostaijen, the American New Critics and the Russian Formalists. It scored a considerable success: after four years the editors—Kees Fens, H. U. Jessurun d'Oliveira and J. J. Oversteegen—considered their task as finished and called it a day. One of its regular contributors, the poet H. C. ten Berge, in 1967 established *Raster* (Grid) which ran until 1973 and then started a new series in 1977. In the first issue Ten Berge (born in 1938) set out his views on the direction poetry ought to take. He turned against all 'emotional poetry' and advocated 'logopoeia' which he defined as 'poetry of which the intellect is a permanent and impelling force, and in which it is given a clear-cut task, as in Pound's *Cantos*'. He did not reject the poetry of the Movement of the Fifties, but suggested that its achievements and the possibilities which it had created were to be underpinned by Pound's credo that the new poetry should be 'harder and saner', that it should be 'as much like granite as it can be', and that 'its force will lie in its truth, its interpretative power'.

In his own poetry Ten Berge practised what he preached. He stripped his poetry of all direct personal emotion and gave the intellect pride of place. In the five volumes published to date—*Poolsneeuw* (Polar Snow, 1964), *Swartkrans* (1965), *Personages* (1967), *de witte sjamaan* (The White Shaman, 1973) and *Va-banque* (1977)—he borrowed extensively from other cultures and literatures, from the Aztecs and Eskimos, from Japanese Noh plays, legends from North American

Indians and sacred hymns from Central Mexico. These borrowings, in addition to the many allusions to western poetry, are used for their contrastive effect and for their ability to translate personal emotion to a more general level. Needless to say, this technique makes his poetry cryptic, if not hermetic, and the reader needs considerable erudition and a well-developed skill in decoding before he can make his way to the inner sanctum of Ten Berge's poetry.

In the seventies several different approaches to poetry exist side by side. There is the intellectualist stream, there is the personal lyricism of *Tirade*, there are still echoes of the realism of *Barbarber* and *Gard-Sivik*, there is even a neo-neo-romanticism harking back to the nineteenth century. New groups are being formed and new theories are being put forward, and where the present tense asserts itself, History bows out.

376

SELECT BIBLIOGRAPHY
OF WORKS ON DUTCH LITERATURE
IN ENGLISH, FRENCH AND GERMAN

Bachrach, A.G.H., *Sir Constantine Huygens and Britain: 1596-1687. A pattern of cultural exchange.* Volume 1. 1596-1619. Leiden and London 1962.

Backer, F. de, *Contemporary Flemish Literature.* Brussels 1939.

Barnouw, A.J., *Coming After. An Anthology of poetry from the Low Countries.* New Brunswick 1949.

Barnouw, A.J., *Vondel.* New York 1925.

Bauwens, J., *La tragédie française et le théatre hollandais au XVIIe siècle.* Paris 1921.

Baxter, B.M., *Albert Verwey's Translations from Shelley's Poetical Works. A study of their style and rhythm and a consideration of their value as translations.* Leiden 1963.

Beekman, E.M., *Homeopathy of the Absurd: The Grotesque in Paul van Ostaijen's Creative Prose.* The Hague 1970.

Brachin, Pierre, *Etudes de littérature néerlandaise.* Groningue 1954.

Brachin, Pierre, *La littérature néerlandaise.* Paris 1962.

Brachin, Pierre, *Faits et valeurs: douze chapitres sur la littérature néerlandaise et ses alentours.* La Haye 1975.

Breugelmans, R., *Jacques Perk.* Boston 1974.

Brulez, R. *Ecrivains flamands d'aujourd'hui.* Bruxelles 1938.

Bulhof, F. (ed), *Nijhoff, Van Ostaijen, "De Stijl". Modernism in the Netherlands and Belgium in the First Quarter of the 20th Century.* The Hague 1976.

Closset, F., *Aspects et figures de la littérature flamande.* Bruxelles, 2e ed. 1944.

Closset, F., *Aspects et figures de la littérature néerlandaise depuis 1880.* Bruxelles 1957.

Closset F., *Joyaux de la littérature flamande du Moyen Age; présentés et traduits par F. Closset.* Bruxelles, 2e ed. 1956.

Closset, F., *La littérature flamande au Moyen Age.* Bruxelles 1946.

Colie, Rosalie L., *Some Thankfulnesse to Constantine. A study of English influence upon the early works of Constantijn Huygens.* The Hague 1956.

Davies, D.W., *Dutch Influences on English Culture, 1555-1625.* Ithaca 1964.

Dorsten, J.A. van, *Poets, Patrons and Professors. Sir Philip Sidney, Daniel Rogers, and the Leiden Humanists.* Leiden and London 1962.

Dorsten, J.A. van (ed.), *Ten Studies in Anglo-Dutch Relations.* Leiden, London 1974.

Dubois, Pierre H., *Dutch Art Today. Literature.* Amsterdam 1956. *Dutch Studies.* Vols. 1, 2, 3. The Hague 1974-1977.

Eringa, S., *La Renaissance et les rhétoriqueurs néerlandais.* Amsterdam 1920.

Fens, K., *Twenty Years of Dutch Literature. Some Trends and Central Figures.* Rijswijk 1973.

Fessard, Louis J.E., *Jan Slauerhoff (1898-1936). L'homme et l'oeuvre.* Paris 1964.

Flaxman, Seymour L., *Herman Heijermans and his Dramas.* The Hague 1954.

Flinn, J., *Le Roman de Renard dans la littérature française et dans les littératures étrangères au Moyen Age.* Toronto 1963.

Forster, Leonard, *Janus Gruter's English Years. Studies in the continuity of Dutch literature in exile in Elizabethan England.* Leiden and London 1967.

Forster, L., *Die Niederlande und die Anfänge der Barocklyrik in Deutschland.* Groningen 1967.

Graaf, J. de, *La révolution littéraire en Hollande et le naturalisme française (1880-1900).* Amsterdam 1938.

Goris, J.A., *Belgian Letters.* New York, 2nd ed. 1948.

Greshoff, Jan, *Harvest of the Lowlands. An anthology in English translation of creative writing in the Dutch language with a historical survey of the literary development.* New York 1945.

Guest, Tanis M., *Some Aspects of Hadewijch's Poetic Form in the 'Strofische Gedichten'.* The Hague 1975.

Guiette, Robert, *La légende de la sacristine. Etude de littérature comparée.* Paris 1927. (discusses the Dutch *Beatrijs).*

Harmsel, Henrietta ten, *Jacob Revius, Dutch Metaphysical Poet.* Detroit 1968.

Hechtle, M., *Die flämische Dichtung von 1830 bis zur Gegenwart.* Jena 1942.

Hyma, Albert, *The 'Devotio Moderna' or Christian Renaissance (1380-1520).* Grand Rapids 1924.

Johannessen, K.L., *Zwischen Himmel und Erde. Eine Studie über Joost van den Vondels Biblische Tragödie in Gattungsgeschichtlicher Perspektive,* Oslo 1963.

Johnson, J.W., *The Formation of English Neo-Classical Thought.* Princeton 1967. (in particular Chapter VII: 'Holland').

Kern, Edith G., *The Influence of Heinsius and Vossius upon French Dramatic Theory.* Baltimore 1949.

King, P.K., *Dawn Poetry in the Netherlands.* Amsterdam 1971.

King, P.K., *Multatuli.* New York 1972.

King, P.K. and P.F. Vincent (ed.), *European Context. Studies in the History and Literature of the Netherlands presented to Theodoor Weevers.* Cambridge 1971.

Kirkconnell, Watson, *The Celestial Cycle. The theme of Paradise Lost in world literature with translations of the major analogues.* Toronto 1952. (Contains a discussion and translations of Hugo Grotius's Adamus Exul, and Vondel's Lucifer and Adam in Ballingschap).

Kirkconnell, Watson, *That Invincible Samson. The theme of Samson Agonistes in world literature with translations of the major analogues.* Toronto 1964. (Contains a discussion of Samson-plays by Vondel, Abraham de Koningh and Claude de Grieck, as well as a translation of Vondel's Samson of Heilige Wraeck).

Lilar, Suz, *The Belgian Theatre since 1890.* New York 1950.

Lissens, R.F., *Rien que l'homme. Aspects du roman flamand contemporain.* Bruxelles 1944.

Lissens, R.F., *Flämische Literaturgeschichte des 19. und 20. Jahrhunderts,* Köln 1970. *Lyrical Holland.* Amsterdam 1954.

Mallinson, Vernon, *Modern Belgian Literature 1830-1960.* London 1966.

Meijer, R.P., *Max Havelaar 1860-1960.* Melbourne 1960.

Meijer, R.P., *Dutch and Flemish: Two Literatures or One?* London 1973.

Minis, Cola, *Textkritische Studien über den Roman d'Eneas und die Eneide von H. von Veldeke.* Groningen 1959.

Noot, Jan van der, *The Olympia Epics. A facsimile edition of 'Das Buch Extasis', 'Een Cort Begryp der XII Boecken Olympiados' and 'Abrégé des douze livres Olympiades'.* Edited by C.A. Zaalberg. Assen 1956.

Pannwitz, R., *Albert Verwey und Stefan George: Zu Verwey's hundertstem Geburtstag.* Heidelberg, Darmstadt 1965.

Pienaar, W.J.B., *Influences in Dutch Literature and Justus van Effen as 'Intermediary'. An aspect of 18th century achievement.* London 1929.

Post, R.R., *The Modern Devotion. Confrontation with Reformation and Humanism.* Leiden 1968.

Ridder, André de, *La littérature flamande contemporaine (1890-1923).* Anvers 1925.

Riet, F.G. van der, *Le théâtre profane sérieux en langue flamande au Moyen Age.* La Haye 1936.

Romein-Verschoor, A., *Silt and Sky. Men and movements in modern Dutch literature.* Amsterdam 1950.

Russell, James Anderson, *Dutch Poetry and English.* Amsterdam 1939.

Russell, James Anderson, *Romance and Realism. Trends in Belgo-Dutch prose literature.* Amsterdam 1959.

Schönle, Gustav, *Deutsch-Niederländische Beziehungen in der Literatur des 17. Jahrhunderts.* Leiden 1968.

Schoonhoven, E., *Paul van Ostaijen. Introduction à sa poétique.* Anvers 1951.

Sellin, Paul R., *Daniel Heinsius and Stuart England.* Leiden and Oxford 1968.

Smit, W.A.P., et P. Brachin, *Vondel. Contribution à l'histoire de la tragédie au XVIIe siècle.* Paris 1964.

Stillman, Clark and Frances, *Lyra Belgica. Guide Gezelle and Karel van de Woestijne in English translation.* New York 1950.

Stuiveling, Garmt, *A Sampling of Dutch Literature. Thirteen excursions into the works of Dutch authors.* Translated and adapted by James Brockway. Hilversum (n.d.).

Tielrooy, J., *Panorama de la littérature hollandaise contemporaine.* Paris 1938.

Voorde, U. van de, *Panorama d'un siècle de la littérature néerlandaise en Belgique.* Bruxelles 1931.

Vries, T. de, *Holland's Influence on English Language and Literature.* Chicago 1916.

Warnke, Frank J., *European Metaphysical Poetry.* New Haven and London 1961. (contains translations from Revius, Vondel, Huygens, Dullaert, Luyken).

Weevers, Theodoor, *Poetry of the Netherlands in its European Context, 1170-1930. Illustrated with poems in original and translation.* London 1960.

Weisgerber, Jean, *Formes et domaines du roman flamand 1927-1960.* Bruxelles 1963.

The most useful histories of Dutch literature are:

Winkel, J. te, *De Ontwikkelingsgang der Nederlandsche Letterkunde.* Haarlem, 2nd ed. 1912-1925, 7 vols.

Baur, F. ed., *Geschiedenis van de Letterkunde der Nederlanden.* 's-Hertogenbosch en Brussel 1939- . Appeared so far vols. I-VI, VII and IX.

Knuvelder, G., *Handboek tot de Geschiedenis der Nederlandse Letterkunde.* 's-Hertogenbosch, 6th ed. 1976-1977, 4 vols.

Bibliographies of Translations:

Hermanowski, Georg, en Hugo Tomme, *Zuidnederlandse Literatuur in Vertaling.* Hasselt 1961.

Huffel, A. J. van, *Nederlandsche Schrijvers in Vertaling (Van Marcellus Emants tot Jan Eekhout). Proeve van eene Bibliographie.* Leiden 1939. Supplement, Leiden 1946.

Morel, P. M. *Translations of Dutch Literature 1900-1957.* In: *Bibliographia Neerlandica.* The Hague 1962.

Raan, E. Van, *Het Nederlandse Boek in Vertaling. Bibliografie van Vertalingen van Noord- en Zuidnederlandse Werken.* Vol. 1, 1958-1967; vol. 2, 1968-1972; vol. 3, 1973; vol. 4, 1974; vol. 5 1975. 's-Gravenhage 1974-1977.

An important series of translations in English was published between 1963 and 1967 by Sythoff and Heinemann under the title of *Bibliotheca Neerlandica, a Library of Classics of Dutch and Flemish Literature.* The series consists of ten volumes, containing translations of medieval religious and secular literature, including Reynard the Fox, and work by Ruusbroec, Hadewijch, Multatuli, Couperus, Coenen, Van Oudshoorn, Van Schendel, Walschap, Vestdijk, Elsschot and Teirlinck.

Twayne Publishers (Boston) publish a *Library of Netherlandic Literature* in which nine volumes have appeared to date, containing work by Anna Blaman, Hubert Lampo, Frederik van Eeden, Marnix Gijsen, Marcellus Emants, Stijn Steuvels, Bert Schierbeek and Louis Paul Boon, as well as a volume of short stories.

A comparable series of translations in French is being published by Editions Universitaires in Paris under the title of Pays-Bas/Flandre. The series includes work by Ruusbroec, Multatuli, Emants, Gijsen, Walschap, Van Schendel and Teirlinck.

The Foundation for the Promotion of Translation of Dutch Literature in Amsterdam publishes a quarterly bulletin under the title of *Writing in Holland and Flanders* which reviews recent literature and gives information on new translations.

INDEX

Graal Queeste 13.
Graf, Het (Feith) 182.
Granida (Hooft) 113-115, 117, 127.
Grauwe Vogels, De (Van Schendel) 293, 294.
Grave, The (Blair) 182.
Gray, Thomas 182.
Greco, El 344.
Gregoor, Nol 347.
Greshoff, Jan 327, 329, 330, 335, 336.
Griane (Bredero) 123.
Groen en Rijp (Busken Huet) 216.
Groenevelt, Ernst 311.
Groen van Prinsterer, Guillaume 191.
Grönloh, J. H. F. *see also* Nescio 332.
Groote, Geert 29, 30-32, 67.
Groot Nederland 329.
Grote Dichters, De (Gorter) 263.
Grotius, Hugo 100, 103, 106, 107, 108, 119, 129, 132, 133, 135, 137, 139, 196.
Gryphius, Andreas 107, 129, 134.
Guarini, Giamattista 113.
Guiette, Robert 21.
Gulden Harpe, De (Van Mander) 93.
Gulden Schaduw, De (Van de Woestijne) 278.
Gundolf, Friedrich 267, 268.
Guy de Vlaming (Beets) 207, 208.

Hadewych 17-20, 29, 32, 33, 69.
Hall, Joseph 145.
Halle, Adam de la 40.
Hals, Frans 107.
Hampton Court (Ter Braak) 322.
Hamsun, Knut 284, 285.
Hanlo, Jan 372.
Harduwijn, Justus de 151.
Hardy, Thomas 298.
Haren, Onno Zwier van 167-172, 184.

Haren, Willem van 166-167, 168, 169, 171.
Harpoen (Vondel) 131.
Hart, Maarten 't 367.
Hauptmann, Gerhart 257, 258.
Haverschmidt, François, *see also* Paaljens, Piet 208-209.
Hecastus (Macropedius) 56, 77.
Heden Ik, Morgen Gij (Marsman and Vestdijk) 320.
Heemskerk (H. A. Meijer) 208.
Heemskerk, Johan van 149.
Heere, Lucas de 82-84, 86, 87, 89, 93.
Heer Halewijn, Ballade van 35.
Heerlyckheit der Kercke, De (Vondel) 139.
Heeroma, Klaas 322.
Hegel, Georg Friedrich Wilhelm 295.
Heijermans, Herman 255-259, 364.
Heilige Tocht, De (Prins) 286.
Heilig Weten, Het (Couperus) 253.
Heine, Heinrich 207.
Heinric en Margriete van Limborch, Roman van 36.
Heinsius, Daniel 78, 90, 100, 103, 107, 108, 115, 129, 139, 143, 147, 150, 154, 155.
Heinsius, Nicholaas 150.
Heldensage (H. Roland Holst) 265.
Heliand 20.
Helmers, Jan Frederik 196-197, 198, 199.
Hemelechede der Hemelycheit (Maerlant) 15.
Hendrik de Groote (Feitama) 165.
Herakles (Couperus) 255.
Herder, Johann Gottfried 181.
Herinneringen van een Engelbewaarder (Hermans) 356, 358.
Hermans, Willem Frederik 339, 352-356, 357, 358, 359, 363, 364.
Hermingard van de Eikenterpen (Drost) 205, 212.
Hertspiegel (Spiegel) 98, 99, 102.

394INDEX